THE MOUNTAINS
as confronted by David Roberts in
"The Mountain of My Fear"

THE RIVERS
as pictured by John James Audubon in his
"Missouri River Journals"

THE DESERTS
as celebrated by Mary Austin in her
"Land of Little Rain"

THE CANYONS
as seen by John Wesley Powell in his
"Exploration of the Colorado River"

THE SHORES
as brought to life by Rachel Carson in
"The Edge of the Sea"

*All are part of the vast panorama that
moves across the pages of—*

THE WILDERNESS READER

FRANK BERGON, the editor of *Looking Far West*
(available in a Mentor edition) and *The Western Writings
of Stephen Crane* (available in a Signet Classic edition),
is professor of English at Vassar College.

THE
WILDERNESS
READER

EDITED BY
FRANK BERGON

A MENTOR BOOK

NEW AMERICAN LIBRARY

NEW YORK AND SCARBOROUGH, ONTARIO

Acknowledgment is made to the following publishers
and holders of copyright for permission to reprint
material under copyright:

ABBEY, EDWARD: DESERT SOLITAIRE. Copyright ©
1968 by Edward Abbey. Reprinted by permission of the
Harold Matson Company, Inc.

BYRD, WILLIAM: THE PROSE WORKS OF WILLIAM
BYRD OF WESTOVER. Reprinted by permission of the
publishers from THE PROSE WORKS OF WILLIAM
BYRD OF WESTOVER, edited by Louis B. Wright, Cam-
bridge, Mass.: The Belknap Press of Harvard University
Press, Copyright © 1966 by the President and Fellows of
Harvard College.

CARSON, RACHEL: THE EDGE OF THE SEA. From
THE EDGE OF THE SEA by Rachal Carson, published by
Houghton Mifflin Company. Copyright © 1955 by Rachel L.
Carson. Reprinted by permission.

LEOPOLD, ALDO: A SAND COUNTY ALMANAC. From
A SAND COUNTY ALMANAC WITH OTHER ESSAYS
ON CONSERVATION FROM ROUND RIVER by Aldo
Leopold. Copyright © 1949, 1935, 1966; renewed 1977 by
Oxford University Press, Inc. Reprinted by permission.

MC PHEE, JOHN: COMING INTO THE COUNTRY. Reprinted with the permission of Farrar Strauss & Giroux, Inc.
from COMING INTO THE COUNTRY by John McPhee.
Copyright © 1976, 1977 by John McPhee.

PLENTY-COUPS: PLENTY COUPS: CHIEF OF THE
CROWS. Pp. 58-67 from PLENTY-COUPS: CHIEF OF
THE CROWS by Frank B. Linderman (John Day Company). Copyright © 1930 by Frank B. Linderman. Copyright
renewed 1957 by Norma Linderman Waller, Verne Linderman and Wilda Linderman. Reprinted by permission of
Harper & Row, Publishers, Inc.

(The following page constitutes an extension of this
Copyright page.)

MENTOR TRADEMARK REG. U.S. PAT. OFF. AND FOREIGN COUNTRIES
REGISTERED TRADEMARK—MARCA REGISTRADA
HECHO EN WINNIPEG, CANADA

SIGNET, SIGNET CLASSIC, MENTOR, ONYX, PLUME, MERIDIAN AND NAL
BOOKS are published *in the United States* by NAL PENGUIN INC.,
1633 Broadway, New York, New York 10019,
in Canada by The New American Library of Canada Limited,
81 Mack Avenue, Scarborough, Ontario M1L 1M8

First Mentor Printing, October, 1980

4   5   6   7   8   9   10   11   12

PRINTED IN CANADA

Acknowledgements

I would like to thank Elizabeth Burroughs Kelley, Zeese Papanikolas, and Dan Peck for their help with portions of the book's introductory material, David Roberts and Michael Wall for their suggestions concerning the book's contents, and Jim Stapleton, Director of Studies at the John Burroughs Sanctuary, for his advice and assistance with the general introduction. My deepest debt is to Holly St. John Bergon for her collaboration during every stage of the book's preparation.

To the staff and students
of the Skidmore College
Adirondack Institute

A waste and howling wilderness
Where none inhabited
But hellish fiends, and brutish men
That Devils worshipped.
—*Michael Wigglesworth (1664)*

When I think of these times [the early 1800s along the Ohio River], and call back to my mind the grandeur and beauty of those almost uninhabited shores; when I picture to myself the dense and lofty summits of the forest, that everywhere spread along the hills, and overhung the margins of the stream, unmolested by the axe of the settler; when I know how dearly purchased the safe navigation of that river has been by the blood of many worthy Virginians; when I see that no Aborigines are to be found there, and that the vast herds of elks, deer and buffaloes which once pastured on these hills and in these valleys, making for themselves great roads to the several salt-springs, have ceased to exist; when I reflect that all this grand portion of our Union, instead of being in a state of nature, is now more or less covered with villages, farms, and towns, where the din of hammers and machinery is constantly heard; that the woods are fast disappearing under the axe by day, and the fire by night; that hundreds of steamboats are gliding to and fro, over the whole length of the majestic river, forcing commerce to take root and to prosper at every spot; when I see the surplus population of Europe coming to assist in the destruction of the forest, and transplanting civilization into its darkest recesses;—when I remember that these extraordinary changes have all taken place in the short period of twenty years, I pause, wonder, and, although I know all to be fact, can scarcely believe its reality.

—*John James Audubon (1831)*

What would the world be, once bereft
Of wet and of wildness? Let them be left,
O let them be left, wildness and wet;
Long live the weeds and the wilderness yet.
—*Gerard Manley Hopkins (1881)*

Contents

Introduction: Literature of the American Wilderness

Americans are insensible to the wonders of inanimate nature, observed Tocqueville during his visit to the United States, and by "inanimate nature" he meant forests, meadows, grasses, and wild flowers, as well as mountains, glaciers, rivers, lakes, deserts, canyons, and swamps; everything, in short, that with the addition of "animate" wildlife—mammals, fishes, amphibians, reptiles, and birds—makes up what we traditionally call the American wilderness. "Americans," continues Tocqueville, "do not see the marvelous forests surrounding them until they begin to fall beneath the ax. . . . The American people see themselves marching through wilderness, drying up marshes, diverting rivers, peopling the wilds, and subduing nature." Now that nature has been largely subdued, the wilds peopled, the Colorado River dammed, Glen Canyon and Yosemite's Hetch Hetchy Valley flooded, and only vestiges of wilderness are left in the land, our sense of loss seems to have reached a zenith. It is an old story that man comes to love what he has lost, and American appreciation of wilderness has grown as its actuality has diminished. Predictably, what little wilderness remains now seems threatened by masses of visitors trampling into extinction what they clamor to preserve. Wilderness might still be defined, as it was over a hundred years ago during Tocqueville's visit, as an untamed, uncultivated region marked by the presence of wild animals and the absence of man. Once seen negatively as the antagonist to progress or civilization or technology, it is now seen by many as the last alternative to the sterile products and defunct values of our civilized society. Despite this apparent appreciation of wilderness and wilderness values, we might still question what part the wonders of inanimate nature bear to our daily lives, and how our experience is affected by the decimation of the bison or the extinction of the auk. Can we honestly deny the broad truth of Tocqueville's observation that wilderness appreciation is of peripheral interest to a people, like ourselves, who no longer live by nature but by technology?

No one denies the importance of the wilderness to our national past. Historians debate the degree, but not the fact, of our wilderness origins. Our early sense of identity is evident in a national mythology in which men in the wilderness from Boone to Carson achieved the stature of heroes. An attraction to wilderness persistently accompanied its conquest, and these ambivalent feelings have been documented by Hans Huth in *Nature and the American: Three Centuries of Changing Attitudes* and by Roderick Nash in *Wilderness and the American Mind.* Even during the destruction of wilderness witnessed by Tocqueville, American magazines were self-consciously developing the image of the country as Nature's Nation; Thomas Cole, Asher Durand, and other painters of the Hudson River School were finding in wildness the distinctive characteristic of America's grandeur; and urban dwellers were buying oversized picture books and going on tours to glimpse the sublime and picturesque vistas of wild nature while it still existed. The relationship of wilderness to civilization has been a major preoccupation of poets from Bryant to Whitman and of novelists from Cooper to Faulkner, and we cannot ignore that our cultural heritage developed out of a great deal of philosophizing, romanticizing, and fantasizing about the wilderness. But Tocqueville's observation still stands. All the enthusiasm for wilderness that accompanied its conquest does not necessarily indicate an appreciation for the actual phenomena of wilderness itself—its trees, bogs, snakes, rocks, wolves, and dirt.

There is a small but distinctive body of American literature that does concern itself primarily with the wilderness as physical fact. These prose works of nonfiction are often by botanists, ornithologists, foresters, geologists, explorers, and mountaineers whose intimate acquaintance with the wilderness allows them to speak with authority about nature in its wild state. The classics of this genre successfully avoid the mere objective classifications and descriptions of scientific reports just as they avoid the extreme subjective responses and reflections of those who write about the wilderness as spirit or scenery or symbol without sufficient attention to the physical presence of the wilderness itself. The result is a literature of the American wilderness that blends feeling with informed observation. Although scientific considerations may be central to such works, their purpose is literary, for they successfully convey the *experience* of participating firsthand in the life of the wilderness.

Two of the fullest and liveliest personal accounts of wilderness experience to appear in the eighteenth century are classics of early American literature, William Byrd's *History of the Dividing Line* and William Bartram's *Travels*. It is not surprising that Byrd, a colonial gentleman and wealthy member of the aristocratic landed class, was the writer whose freedom from economic dependence on the wilderness allowed him to introduce a note of pleasure to his experience in the southern Appalachian wilds. Americans struggling for survival in the wilderness understandably shared Cotton Mather's seventeenth-century judgment about nature that "what is not useful is vicious." Byrd, alert to changing attitudes in Europe and England, took care to note that even the dirty and useless Dismal Swamp offered "one beauty" since "its moisture of the soil preserves a continual verdure and makes every plant an evergreen." Byrd's primary interest in the wilderness was practical, but he was responsive to the intrinsic value of scientific curiosities and unexplainable wonders, and once, in making the choice to sleep in the fields rather than in available lodging, he found he had "magnificent dreams" and concluded that "mankind are the great losers by the luxury of feather beds and warm apartments."

Even more exuberantly than Byrd, the American botanist and ornithologist William Bartram experienced what was "inexpressibly beautiful and pleasing" as he tramped through the wilderness of the Carolinas and Florida collecting specimens for his English patron. Bartram was instrumental in making the second of what Howard Mumford Jones has said were the two discoveries of the New World—one beginning with Columbus, the other beginning, so to speak, with the discovery that God spoke in the waterfalls, mountain ranges, and endless sweep of the wilderness. It was the notion of the "sublime" that helped Bartram give value to what was terrible, violent, and humanly incomprehensible in the wilderness, for then one might experience the pleasurable counterpart to fear "amidst sublimely high forests, awful shades." What distinguished Bartram from others who shared his sense of the sublime, like the naturalist Thomas Jefferson, who discovered on his own property the sublimity of the Natural Bridge of Virginia, was his role as a participant in the wilderness. No

doubt he excited the imaginations of Romantic poets and
novelists in England and Europe not so much for what he
said about the wilderness but for his concrete dramatization
of himself as a man located firmly and naturally in the wilderness, along with the Indian and alligator and curlew and
everglade.

Wonder, astonishment, and a sense of adventure pervade
the literature of the American wilderness throughout the
nineteenth century, but the wilderness itself, especially the
vast and extremely frightening and strange forms it took west
of the Mississippi, began to evade more and more any sense
or order imposed by man-made notions such as the beautiful
and sublime. The journals kept by Lewis and Clark, who fulfilled Jefferson's dream of exploring a stretch of the continent
from the Missouri to the mouth of the Columbia on the
Pacific, documents the triumph of the wilderness as it over-
whelms human expectations and preconceptions. Language itself had to be altered to give expression to this new country;
words were coined and twisted and adapted to distinctive
needs so that, according to the lexicon compiled by Elijah
Criswell, Lewis and Clark were responsible for the first usage
of 1,859 words in the American language. Meriwether Lewis
gradually abandoned his attempts to present his experience
through conventional romantic notions and allowed the wilderness to speak for itself through plain facts and events.
What emerges from this understated catalog of trials by
mosquitoes, floods, hunger, storms, and grizzlies is a record
of the wilderness as a place of incredible hardship. The response to such experience is simple acceptance and endurance, as Lewis unaffectedly but memorably records in this
incident:

> I directed a pint of corn to be given each Indian who
> was engaged in transporting our baggage and about the
> same quantity to each of the men which they parched
> pounded and made into supe. one of the women who
> had been assisting in the transportation of the baggage
> halted at a little run about a mile behind us, and sent on
> the two pack horses which she had been conducting by
> one of her female friends. I enquired of Cameahwait the
> cause of her detention, and was informed by him in an
> unconcerned manner that she had halted to bring fourth
> a child and would soon overtake us; in about an hour

the woman arrived with her newborn babe and passed us on her way to camp apparently as well as she ever was.

While many Americans, removed from wilderness hardships, were busy transforming imaginary Indians into Noble Savages or advocating a salvific return to wild nature, those immersed in the wilderness were responding differently. Rather than sentimentalizing the Indians' demise, wilderness wanderers like John James Audubon, Clarence King, Francis Parkman, and John Muir presented occasionally harsh portraits of Indian peoples in their deteriorating and demoralized condition. Others like William Byrd, who urged intermarriage between Indians and whites, and still others like William Bartram, Lewis and Clark, George Catlin, and John Wesley Powell, who were compiling a valuable ethnographic record of Indian life, granted Indian peoples the dignity of their humanity by refusing to elevate them into wilderness demigods.

It is true that wilderness writers after Lewis and Clark tended to romanticize their own adventures; the edge of danger glistens romantically in the *Reports* of John C. Frémont, and after threats from Indians and wild beasts had disappeared, self-conscious adventurers like geologist Clarence King and surveyor Verplanck Colvin sharpened the risks of their mountain-climbing exploits; but even in the heightened writings of these men, the mountains themselves and their real dangers helped keep these romantic leanings within the bounds of actual experience. Those who maintained a worshipful distance from the wilderness might see reflected there a benevolent God and a peaceable millennium, but Francis Parkman, looking into an actual wilderness pond, concluded that "from minnows to men, life is incessant war." Terror overwhelmed those in the wilderness more often than delight. In the woods we return to reason and faith, Emerson had said, but above the timberline on Mt. Katahdin, Henry David Thoreau found nothing rational, and his discovery of only spiritless rock on the summit terrified him. Few who wrote about their wilderness experience ever advocated a primitivist return to wild nature, and several have shared Meriwether Lewis's view of a mountain range as "that icy barrier which separates me from my friends and Country, from all which makes life esteemable."

What many did find akin to paradise in the nineteenth-century wilderness was its incredible abundance of wildlife, the ay alive with soaring hawks, eagles, and geese; rivers thick with salmon, beaver, and trout; mountains filled with howls of wolves and the clattering of bighorn; and the plains, as Catlin reports, often blanketed with buffalo as far as the eye could see. From our perspective, Meriwether Lewis does seem like a new man in a new Eden walking peacefully among animals that do not scare and giving names to some, like the pronghorn, never before recorded by white men:

> ... the whole face of the country was covered with herds of Buffalo, Elk & Antelopes; deer are also abundant, but keep themselves more concealed in the woodland. the buffaloe Elk and Antelope are so gentle that we pass near them while feeding, without appearing to excite any alarm among them; and when we attract their attention, they frequently approach us more nearly to discover what we are, and in some instances pursue us a considerable distance apparently with that view. . . .

Such a peaceable kingdom was not constant, and Lewis's complacent notions about certain animals, especially grizzly bears, were dramatically altered. In the space of one day, while hunting buffalo, he was chased into a river by a bear, attacked by a "tyger cat," and charged by three buffalo bulls; "it now seemed to me," he wrote, "that all the beasts of the neighborhood had made a league to distroy me."

Hunting animals and birds, not only for specimens and food, but for sport, was a basic part of wilderness experience for many explorers and naturalists. Although a hunter himself, Audubon separated himself from others by expressing compassion for the suffering of individual animals, a concern later shared by Thoreau, Muir, and Burroughs, who, to varying degrees, disapproved of both specimen and game hunting. Burroughs, distinguishing among kinds of hunters, defended Theodore Roosevelt as one who loved certain animals more than Burroughs himself did "because his love is founded upon knowledge, and because they had been part of his life." John Muir also appreciated Roosevelt's opposition to the wanton slaughter of animals by hide hunters, but he urged the president to adopt a more enlightened attitude toward all wildlife and "to get beyond the boyishness of killing things."

A similar growing appreciation of what the older naturalists called "inanimate nature" might be traced through Bar-

tram's concern for individual plants, Thoreau's interest in the
succession of forest trees, and Muir's discovery of the person-
alities of various trees, all countering the utilitarian view of
forests as merely woodlots and so many potential board feet.
Even mountains and canyons and arid plateaus became animate in the writings of geologists like John Wesley Powell,
Clarence King, and Clarence Dutton, who, sharing a recognition of panoramic beauty with explorers like Frémont and
travelers like Isabella Bird, discerned as well the continuing
drama of geologic change in apparently static landscapes.
Knowledge of canyon country as a process created by powerful forces of water, wind, and fire informed Dutton's aesthetic response to what had been seen as desolate and
changeless. Less dramatic desert landscapes became a series
of shifting forms and colors in the writings of John C. Van
Dyke, while Mary Austin portrayed the arid soil of the desert
itself as a living thing.

With this emphasis at the turn of the last century on what
Muir, as one of its chief appreciators, called the "Majesty of
the Inanimate," the literature of the American wilderness, as
we have been examining it, comes to an end, for the American wilderness it evokes also had come to an end. Most subsequent writing in the twentieth century has been by necessity
a rearguard defense of wilderness preserves, usually in the
form of national parks, as seen in the wilderness writings of
Edwin Way Teale, Wallace Stegner, and Edward Abbey. But
wild America as it once existed will never return, and only
through the writings of these explorers, artists, travelers,
scientists, and naturalists can we vicariously experience, as
they were, the deserts of Austin and Van Dyke, the Badlands
of Roosevelt, the southern and southeastern wilds of Byrd and
Bartram, the Katahdin summit of Thoreau, the Rocky Mountains of Bird, the Adirondacks of Colvin, the canyon country
of Powell and Dutton, the Upper Missouri of Catlin and Audubon, the Great Basin and Cascades of Frémont, the Great
Plains of Parkman, the Sierra Nevada of King and Muir, and
the Bitterroot, Salmon, Snake, and Columbia rivers of Lewis
and Clark.

Although the wilderness condition of an earlier America
has vanished, much of the landscape remains, and it is possible, among certain peaks, lakes, and rivers, to experience at
least a diminished sense of what earlier Americans knew.
During the summers, while conducting American literature

courses for the Adirondack Institute of Skidmore College, I
lead groups on ten-day backpacking trips into a wilderness
area in the San Juan Mountains of Colorado. Responses to
the wilderness vary, and I remember one particular day when
our group, composed of ten students and two instructors,
were ascending through rock and snow above the timberline
toward a high saddle between two peaks. The slope grew
fairly steep, especially near the top, and the snow was hard
and slick so that ice axes were needed to chop steps and occasional handholds as the group inched its way up. At the
bottom of the long snow slide below us a frozen lake was
cloudy green, looking as foreign in its strange colors as a lake
on Venus. When we reached the saddle, there were whoops
of relief, and while we snacked on crackers and cheese, one
person, clearly moved, asked that there be a moment of
silence. We sat there looking out over the peaks and sky to
the plains seemingly stretching all the way to Kansas. When
we had reached the top, one young woman had begun to cry,
saying she had never been so scared; she had wanted to cry
all the way up but was afraid that if she did, she wouldn't be
able to see and would fall.

Later that night, camped comfortably in a valley by a lake
and talking about the day's climb, one person said he had
learned something about mountains—that people who make a
successful climb and are standing on a peak must simply be
more happy at that moment than at other times in their lives.
Another said she physically felt a power from the group
keeping her going, and when she saw a butterfly alone up on
the snow, she knew then she was going to make it. Another
(not the woman who had cried) said that she didn't want to
do anything like it again; as she climbed she felt the mountain wanted her to fall and she kept imagining hands popping
out of the ice to push her off. Her husband said it wasn't the
mountain's hostility he felt but its unwelcome, letting him feel
he didn't belong where it was unnatural for humans to be.
Another said he hadn't felt any of those things; he just saw
the climb as a challenge and he never doubted that he would
succeed, but now he was scared, because he knew what he
had kept himself from feeling was the fact that he didn't belong on the mountain—rocks did, and that thought scared
him because for a moment he didn't know where he belonged. Finally someone said that what affected him most
was the view of the country itself, empty of people, but it

made him sad to know that his grandchildren, and maybe even his children, would never have the chance to see what he had seen.

That sense of loss, or impending loss, runs commonly through even early writings about the wilderness, and our own complicity in furthering that loss by our presence in the wilderness troubled our discussions. It is easier to oppose powerful oil, timber, mineral, and real-estate interests, whose ravages are obvious, than to oppose ourselves, whose effect on the wilderness seems so minor. But Americans have always been shortsighted about the vulnerability of the wilderness. Even when vast herds of bison still covered the plains, John James Audubon foretold their disappearance, and his regretful description of the transformations that had occurred along the Ohio River in the short space of twenty years stays in our minds as we read John McPhee's present-day account of seeing so many thousands of salmon swimming in Alaska that there seemed to be more salmon than water in the Kobuk River. Even on wild stretches of Alaskan tundra, McPhee notes, snow machines have already left the ground scarred with brown trails.

The need to protect the wilderness and ways of doing it form a complicated history in the nineteenth century, running from George Catlin's call for a national park in the 1830s through the conservation and reclamation years of Powell and Roosevelt to the battles between conservationists and preservationists at the end of the century. Americans gradually recognized that without wilderness protection there would be no valuable watersheds, no timber, no wild game. Subsequent economic, recreational, scientific, aesthetic, and spiritual reasons for protecting wilderness eventually led to the larger truths most ably articulated in this century by Aldo Leopold and Rachel Carson. Because of these writers, many learned that conservation is not just the struggle to establish wilderness playgrounds for the recreational and aesthetic delights of a few (though such purposes are important). Wilderness protection is linked to protection of the whole environment, and attitudes toward one affect the other. Leopold showed how forests, soil, water, and wildlife are mutually interdependent, and if one part of this living web is unnaturally destroyed, all parts are weakened. Thoreau's observation, "In Wildness is the preservation of the World," can no longer be seen as mere poetic sentiment. If the world becomes a place where no wilderness can survive, neither can man.

Traces of this way of thinking might be found in American wilderness literature even before the term "ecology" was coined in the 1860s by the German evolutionist Ernst Haeckel. William Bartram's sense of the "Unifying Principle" animating the intertwined relationships of plants, animals, and man points to Leopold's perception of the land as a "fountain of energy flowing through a circuit of soil, plants, and animals." Growing interest in phenology, ethology, and other studies of nature's interrelationships have brought increased attention to Thoreau's scientific pursuits, including those journal observations that were once dismissed as dry, meaningless factual details about grasses, snowfalls, tree rings, lichens, seeds, and other natural phenomena. Tree ring research has today opened into a means of studying world climate and its relation to the production of food. "Let us not underrate the value of a fact," Thoreau wrote, "it will one day flower in a truth." Commonly criticized as either too mystical or too coldly factual, Thoreau's seemingly contradictory pursuits as a naturalist are being seen, and will increasingly be seen, as sensible aspects of the whole enterprise of a man who rightly saw himself as "a transcendentalist, a mystic, and a natural philosopher to boot." John Muir has also been misunderstood as loving only wilderness in general rather than specific natural things, but Muir embraced the whole Sierra Nevada, the Range of Light, as he called it, and its trees, mountains, birds, and animals as a living community. "As soon as we take one thing by itself," he wrote, "we find it hitched to everything in the universe." John Burroughs, too, as Jim Stapleton has shown, anticipated findings by later scientists through his incisive observation of birds in their interlocking relationship to each other and their natural surroundings. Aldo Leopold reminds us that we are still barely beginning to learn about the complex workings that make a healthy natural community, and without the norms of health offered by unviolated wilderness areas, we will be stymied in our pursuits, for no laboratory can create a wilderness.

Man's role in this world community must be that of a responsible participant, for as Burroughs said. "Hedge or qualify as we will, man is a part of nature." Sharing Thoreau's recognition of his kinship with the fish in Walden pond. Burroughs wrote about animals with the intention of making us "feel their kinship, that we may see their lives embossed in the same iron necessity as our own, that we see in their minds a humbler manifestation of the same psychic power and intelligence that culminates and is conscious of itself in man." Such attitudes would not be unfamiliar to even older ways of responding to the natural world and the wilderness in particular. Plenty Coups, tribal chief of the Mountain Crow people, presents in his autobiography a view of man's kinship with animals and even his spiritual dependence upon them. To become wise, Plenty Coups maintains, man must regain the ability to learn from nature:

> Our Wise Ones learned much from the animals and birds who heal themselves from wounds. But our faith in them perished after the white man came, and now too late, we know that with all his wonderful powers, the white man is not wise. He is smart, but not wise, and fools only himself.

What has helped man continue to fool himself into thinking he is superior to nature and not part of it, to close his eyes to what he has been doing to his physical home, including the wilderness, and to behave as if he himself is subject to no ecological laws is the now discredited twofold belief that the world is simply too vast to be significantly harmed by his actions and that if anything does go wrong, science and technology will fix it up. As early as 1864, George Perkins Marsh predicted in *Man and Nature* that man's continued abuse of land, water, and air would lead to "the deprivation, barbarism, and perhaps even extinction of the species." Marsh saw that the "ravages committed by man subvert the relations and destroy the balance which nature had established . . . and she avenges herself upon the intruder by letting loose her destructive energies." A few years later, John Burroughs, mulling over the fact that a hundred years of modern life exhausts more natural resources than a millennium of life in antiquity, looked ahead to when coal and oil would be used up, mineral wealth depleted, the fertility of the soil washed to sea, wild game extinct, and primitive forests gone, and then, Burroughs reflected, "what a sucked orange the earth will be." Such a vision is perhaps now commonplace, but even in the 1960s, when Rachel Carson warned that the addition of pesticides to water anywhere threatened the purity of water everywhere, *Time* magazine called this idea "nonsense." Experts scoffed at the idea that their chemicals, accumulating in the tissues of plants and animals, could alter the very material of heredity. Meanwhile, DDT has wiped out the eastern race of the peregrine falcon and has left the continued existence of the western peregrine in doubt; it has spread through the rivers and oceans to polar icecaps, and has recently been found in the rain falling on New York.

Rachel Carson did not oppose science and technology in themselves—nor can we, unless we pretend to deny our own historical reality as technological creatures—but she did object to attitudes that allowed the now obviously indiscriminate use of materials by experts who were largely or wholly ignorant of their harmful effects. "The 'control of nature' is a phrase conceived in arrogance, born of the Neanderthal age of biology and philosophy, when it was supposed that nature exists for the convenience of man. The concepts and practices of applied entomology, for the most part, date from that Stone Age of science." Man continues his technological assaults on the earth while making claims out of arrogance and in ignorance. We have seen chemicals destroy what the experts claimed they would protect. We have seen PCB, endrin, methyl mercury, and plutonium succeed DDT as major toxic threats. We have seen the soil sterilized by huge dams and irrigation projects that surprised the experts by waterlogging, eroding, and salting the land these projects were supposed to fertilize. Perhaps we can still hear the experts at MIT saying a few years ago that there was only a one-in-a-million-year chance of a serious nuclear-reactor accident. As if to demonstrate that even man's seemingly most enlightened schemes are not necessarily those of nature, when Pelican Island was declared the nation's first wildlife refuge in 1903, the pelicans flew away and stayed away for the next thirty years. What is now clear is that we are destroying the earth because we don't understand it. Technology continues to create more problems than technological thinking can solve, and we are faced with accepting the biblical injunction that, without vision, the people perish.

From the point of view of wilderness, perhaps it would be best if the people did perish. Man's short history as a species certainly forms an ignoble record. Although other species have slowly and naturally come and gone, no other predator, it seems, has exterminated whole species the way man has done. But no species has ever extended its dominance indefinitely, and there is no evidence to think man must be an exception. Even if it is true that man cannot thrive without wilderness, it does not follow that wilderness could not flourish without man. Thinking ourselves central to the grand scheme of wild nature may be our own arrogant illusion. Just as mutations in other species have led to short-term improvement and long-term extinction, it has been argued that the developments of man's brain and the evolution of consciousness have exceeded their biological purposes and now lead away from survival. But we need not believe such speculation to see that we have taken evolution into our own hands and don't know what we're doing with it. One consequence may indeed be the destruction of our environment and ourselves, but our own destruction does not necessarily mean the demise of the world. What could remain is a nonhuman world where peregrine falcons once again tower over peaks and mountain valleys.

Glimpses of such a nonhuman world may be one of the most valuable experiences that wilderness areas still offer most of us—not the sense of comfortable kinship with nature, but the experience Thoreau knew on Mt. Katahdin when he felt himself repulsed by dark stone. It is then that we might recognize that the world moves by orders other than those of man alone, and it is then that "we may measure," as Wallace Stegner suggests, "the world in its natural balance against the world in its man-made imbalance." Out of such a perspective may come a respect for the intrinsic value of wilderness apart from man, a humility that lets us recognize that no part of the wilderness is insignificant simply because it is small or because we are ignorant of its effects or origin, a deeper love and appreciation of wild things for their own sake that, in the end, as Edwin Way Teale shows, form the only enduring component of any conservation movement.

It is then that we may best know what has been lost with every gain of civilized life. Edward Abbey demonstrates that we may see our constructions of concrete, Formica, and neon as triumphs of order over chaos, but by cutting ourselves off from a greater world and encapsulating ourselves in boxes of artificial light and tyrannical noise, we have "exchanged a great and unbounded world for a small, comparatively meager one." Climbing a mountain, on the other hand, does not necessarily guarantee insight or salvation. "We found no answers to life," mountaineer David Roberts says about his ascent to the summit of Alaska's Mt. Huntington, but "perhaps only the room in which to look for them." But that room may be answer enough. A world reduced to the inner walls of man-made shells provides little perspective for the questions forced upon Thoreau by the inanimate stone of Mt. Katahdin, questions that the experts, the technicians, and all of us may no longer ask but must learn to ask again: "rocks, trees, wind on our cheeks! the *solid* earth! the *actual* world! the *common sense! Contact! Contact! Who* are we? *where* are we? . . ."

Frank Bergon
Vassar College

William Byrd

History of the Dividing Line

William Byrd II of Westover (1674–1744), a third-generation Virginian and son of one of Virginia's wealthiest landowners, was an urbane, aristocratic gentleman whose experience in the colonial wilderness produced an early classic of American wilderness literature. Educated in England, Byrd wrote satiric and occasional verse, became an acquaintance of such London literary figures as Congreve and Wycherly, dabbled in science, and got himself elected to the Royal Academy. Inheriting his father's 26,000-acre Virginia estate, he expanded his holdings to 179,440 acres over the next forty years and founded the city of Richmond on his property. Next to Cotton Mather of Boston, Byrd owned the most extensive library in the colonies, a collection of over 3,600 titles. Active in politics as a representative in Virginia's House of Burgesses and as colonial agent in London, Byrd was named chief Virginia commissioner for the survey of the disputed boundary—"the dividing line"— between North Carolina and Virginia in 1728. His duties took him into a raw wilderness when buffalo and elk still thrived east of the Mississippi, and his narrative forms a useful record of early flora and fauna. Byrd was responsive to the practical military, farming, trade, and mining uses of the wilderness, and he even planned ways to drain the Dismal Swamp, but unlike the early chronicles of other men in the wilderness, Byrd's History of the Dividing Line, which remained unpublished until 1841, also marks an early appreciation of the wilderness as a place of intrinsic interest and delight.

[Oct. 25, 1728]   The air clearing up this morning, we were again agreeably surprised with a full prospect of the mountains. They discovered themselves both to the north and south of us on either side, not distant above ten miles, according to our best computation. We could now see those to the north rise in four distinct ledges one above another, but those to the south formed only a single ledge and that broken and interrupted in many places, or rather they were only single mountains detached from each other. One of the southern mountains was so vastly high it seemed to hide its head in the clouds, and the west end of it terminated in a horrible precipice that we called the Despairing Lover's Leap. The next to it, toward the east, was lower except at one end, where it heaved itself up in the form of a vast stack of chimneys. The course of the northern mountains seemed to tend west-southwest and those to the southward very near west. We could descry other mountains ahead of us, exactly in the course of the line though at a much greater distance. In this point of view, the ledges on the right and left both seemed to close and form a natural amphitheater. Thus 'twas our fortune to be wedged in betwixt these two ranges of mountains, insomuch that if our line had run ten miles on either side it had butted before this day either upon one or the other, both of them now stretching away plainly to the eastward of us.

It had rained a little in the night, which dispersed the smoke and opened this romantic scene to us all at once, though it was again hid from our eyes as we moved forward by the rough woods we had the misfortune to be engaged with. The bushes were so thick for near four miles together that they tore the deerskins to pieces that guarded the bread bags. Though, as rough as the woods were, the soil was extremely good all the way, being washed down from the neighboring hills into the plain country. Notwithstanding all these difficulties, the surveyors drove on the line 4 miles and 205 poles.

In the meantime we were so unlucky as to meet with no sort of game the whole day, so that the men were obliged to make a frugal distribution of what little they left in the morning. We encamped upon a small rill, where the horses came off as temperately as their masters. They were by this time

From William Byrd, *The History of the Dividing Line Betwixt Virginia and North Carolina, Run in the Year of Our Lord 1728,* in *The Prose Works of William Byrd of Westover: Narratives of a Colonial Virginian,* edited by Louis B. Wright (Cambridge, Mass.: Harvard University Press, 1966).

grown so thin by hard travel and spare feeding that hence forth, in pure compassion, we chose to perform the greater part of the journey on foot. And as our baggage was by this time grown much lighter, we divided it after the best manner so that every horse's load might be proportioned to the strength he had left. Though after all the prudent measures we could take, we perceived the hills began to rise upon us so fast in our front that it would be impossible for us to proceed much farther.

We saw very few squirrels in the upper parts, because the wildcats devour them unmercifully. Of these there are four kinds: the fox squirrel, the gray, the flying, and the ground squirrel. These last resemble a rat in everything but the tail and the black and russet streaks that run down the length of their little bodies.

[Oct. 26] We found our way grow still more mountainous, after extending the line three hundred poles farther. We came then to a rivulet that ran with a swift current toward the south. This we fancied to be another branch of the Irvin, though some of these men, who had been Indian traders, judged it rather to be the head of Deep River, that discharges its stream into that of Pee Dee, but this seemed a wild conjecture. The hills beyond that river were exceedingly lofty and not to be attempted by our jaded palfreys, which could now hardly drag their legs after them upon level ground. Besides, the bread began to grow scanty and the winter season to advance apace upon us. We had likewise reason to apprehend the consequences of being intercepted by deep snows and the swelling of the many waters between us and home. The first of these misfortunes would starve all our horses and the other ourselves, by cutting off our retreat and obliging us to winter in those desolate woods. These considerations determined us to stop short here and push our adventures no farther. The last tree we marked was a red oak growing on the bank of the river; and to make the place more remarkable, we blazed all the trees around it.

We found the whole distance from Currituck Inlet to the rivulet where we left off to be, in a straight line, 240 miles and 230 poles. And from the place where the Carolina commissioners deserted us, 72 miles and 302 poles. This last part of the journey was generally very hilly, or else grown up with troublesome thickets and underwoods, all which our Carolina friends had the discretion to avoid. We encamped in a dirty valley near the rivulet above-mentioned for the advantage of the canes, and so sacrificed our own convenience to that of our horses. There was a small mountain half a mile to the northward of us, which we had the curiosity to climb up in the afternoon in order to enlarge our prospect. From thence we were able to discover where the two ledges of mountains closed, as near as we could guess about thirty miles to the west of us, and lamented that our present circumstances would not permit us to advance the line to that place, which the hand of Nature had made so very remarkable.

Not far from our quarters one of the men picked up a pair of elk's horns, not very large, and discovered the track of the elk that had shed them. It was rare to find any tokens of those animals so far to the south, because they keep commonly to the northward of thirty-seven degrees, as the buffaloes, for the most part, confine themselves to the southward of that latitude. The elk is full as big as a horse and of the deer kind. The stags only have horns and those exceedingly large and spreading. Their color is something lighter than that of the red deer and their flesh tougher. Their swiftest speed is a large trot, and in that motion they turn their horns back upon their necks and cock their noses aloft in the air. Nature has taught them this attitude to save their antlers from being entangled in the thickets, which they always retire to. They are very shy and have the sense of smelling so exquisite that they wind a man at a great distance. For this reason they are seldom seen but when the air is moist, in which case their smell is not so nice. They commonly herd together, and the Indians say if one of the drove happen by some wound to be disabled from making his escape, the rest will forsake their fears to defend their friend, which they will do with great obstinacy till they are killed upon the spot. Though, otherwise, they are so alarmed at the sight of a man that to avoid him they will sometimes throw themselves down very high precipices into the river.

A misadventure happened here which gave us no small perplexity. One of the commissioners was so unlucky as to bruise his foot against a stump, which brought on a formal fit of the gout. It must be owned there could not be a more unseasonable time, nor a more improper situation for anyone to be attacked by that cruel distemper. The joint was so inflamed that he could neither draw shoe or boot upon it, and to ride without either would have exposed him to so many rude knocks and bruises in those rough woods as to be intolerable even to a stoic. It was happy indeed that we were to rest here the next day, being Sunday, that there might be leisure for trying some speedy remedy. Accordingly, he was persuaded to bathe his foot in cold water in order to repel the humor and assuage the inflammation. This made it less painful and gave us hopes, too, of reducing the swelling in a short time.

Our men had the fortune to kill a brace of bears, a fat buck, and a wild turkey, all which paid them with interest for yesterday's abstinence. This constant and seasonable supply of our daily wants made us reflect thankfully on the bounty of Providence. And that we might not be unmindful of being all along fed by Heaven in this great and solitary wilderness, we agreed to wear in our hats the maosti, which is in Indian the beard of a wild turkey cock, and on our breasts the figure of that fowl with its wings extended and holding in its claws a scroll with this motto, *Vice coturnicum*, meaning that we had been supported by them in the wilderness in the room of quails.

[*Oct. 27*] This being Sunday, we were not wanting in our thanks to Heaven for the constant support and protection we had been favored with. Nor did our chaplain fail to put us in mind of our duty by a sermon proper for the occasion. We ordered a strict inquiry to be made into the quantity of bread we had left and found no more than would subsist us a fortnight at short allowance. We made a fair distribution of our whole stock and at the same time recommended to the men to manage this, their last stake, to the best advantage, not knowing how long they would be obliged to live upon it. We likewise directed them to keep a watchful eye upon their horses, that none of them might be missing the next morning to hinder our return.

There fell some rain before noon, which made our camp more a bog than it was before. This moist situation began to infect some of the men with fevers and some with fluxes, which however we soon removed with Peruvian bark and ipecacuanha.

In the afternoon we marched up again to the top of the hill to entertain our eyes a second time with the view of the mountains, but a perverse fog arose that hid them from our sight. In the evening we deliberated which way it might be most proper to return. We had at first intended to cross over at the foot of the mountains to the head of James River, that we might be able to describe that natural boundary so far. But, on second thoughts, we found many good reasons against that laudable design, such as the weakness of our horses, the scantiness of our bread, and the near approach of winter. We had cause to believe the way might be full of hills, and the farther we went toward the north, the more danger there would be of snow. Such considerations as these determined us at last to make the best of our way back upon the line, which was the straightest and consequently the shortest way to the inhabitants. We knew the worst of that course and were sure of a beaten path all the way, while we were totally ignorant what difficulties and dangers the other course might be attended with. So prudence got the better for once of curiosity, and the itch for new discoveries gave place to self-preservation.

Our inclination was the stronger to cross over according to the course of the mountains, that we might find out whether James River and Appomattox River head there or run quite through them. 'Tis certain that Potomac passes in a large stream through the main ledge and then divides itself into two considerable rivers. That which stretches away to the northward is called Cohungaroota and that which flows to the southwest hath the name of Sharantow. The course of this last stream is near parallel to the Blue Ridge of mountains, at the distance only of about three or four miles. Though how far it may continue that course has not yet been sufficiently discovered, but some woodsmen pretend to say it runs as far as the source of Roanoke; nay, they are so very particular as to tell us that Roanoke, Sharantow, and another wide branch of Mississippi all head in one and the same mountain. What dependence there may be upon this conjectural geography I won't pretend to say, though 'tis certain that Sharantow keeps close to the mountains, as far as we are acquainted with its tendency. We are likewise assured that the south branch of James River, within less than twenty miles east of the main ledge, makes an elbow and runs due southwest, which is parallel with the mountains on this side. But how far it stretches that way before it returns is not yet certainly known, no more than where it takes its rise.

In the meantime, it is strange that our woodsmen have not had curiosity enough to inform themselves more exactly of these particulars, and it is stranger still that the government has never thought it worth the expense of making an accurate survey of the mountains, that we might be masters of that natural fortification before the French, who in some places have settlements not very distant from it. It therefore concerns His Majesty's service very nearly and the safety of his subjects in this part of the world to take possession of so important a barrier in time, lest our good friends, the French, and the Indians through their means, prove a perpetual annoyance to these colonies. Another reason to invite us to secure this great ledge of mountains is the probability that very valuable mines may be discovered there. Nor would it be at all extravagant to hope for silver mines among the rest, because part of these mountains lie exactly in the same parallel, as well as upon the same continent, with New Mexico and the mines of St. Barb.[1]

[Oct. 28]   We had given orders for the horses to be brought up early, but the likelihood of more rain prevented our being overhasty in decamping. Nor were we out in our conjectures, for about ten o'clock it began to fall very plentifully. Our commissioner's pain began now to abate as the swelling increased. He made an excellent figure for a mountaineer, with one boot of leather and the other of flannel. Thus accoutered he intended to mount, if the rain had not happened opportunely to prevent him. Though, in truth, it was hardly possible for him to ride with so slender a defense without exposing his foot to be bruised and tormented by the saplings that stood thick on either side of the path. It was therefore a most seasonable rain for him, as it gave more time for his distemper to abate.

Though it may be very difficult to find a certain cure for the gout, yet it is not improbable but some things may ease the pain and shorten the fits of it. And those medicines are most likely to do this that supple the parts and clear the passage through the narrow vessels that are the seat of this cruel disease. Nothing will do this more suddenly than rattlesnake's oil, which will even penetrate the pores of glass when warmed in the sun. It was unfortunate, therefore, that we had not taken out the fat of those snakes we had killed some time before, for the benefit of so useful an experiment as well as for the relief of our fellow traveler. But lately the Seneca rat-

[1]Santa Barbara, Chihuahua, Mexico.

tlesnake root has been discovered in this country, which, being infused in wine and drank morning and evening, has in several instances had a very happy effect upon the gout, and enabled cripples to throw away their crutches and walk several miles, and, what is stranger still, it takes away the pain in half an hour.

Nor was the gout the only disease amongst us that was hard to cure. We had a man in our company who had too voracious a stomach for a woodsman. He ate as much as any other two, but all he swallowed stuck by him till it was carried off by a strong purge. Without this assistance, often repeated, his belly and bowels would swell to so enormous a bulk that he could hardly breathe, especially when he lay down, just as if he had had an asthma; though, notwithstanding this oddness of constitution, he was a very strong, lively fellow and used abundance of violent exercise, by which 'twas wonderful the peristaltic motion was not more vigorously promoted. We gave this poor man several purges, which only eased him for the present, and the next day he would grow as burly as ever. At last we gave him a moderate dose of ipecacuanha in broth made very salt, which turned all its operation downwards. This had so happy an effect that from that day forward to the end of our journey all his complaints ceased and the passages continued unobstructed.

The rain continued most of the day and some part of the night, which incommoded us much in our dirty camp and made the men think of nothing but eating, even at a time when nobody could stir out to make provision for it.

[Oct. 29]   Though we were flattered in the morning with the usual tokens of a fair day, yet they all blew over, and it rained hard before we could make ready for our departure. This was still in favor of our podagrous friend, whose lameness was now grown better and the inflammation fallen. Nor did it seem to need above one day more to reduce it to its natural proportion and make it fit for the boot; and effectually the rain procured this benefit for him and gave him particular reason to believe his stars propitious.

Notwithstanding the falling weather, our hunters sallied out in the afternoon and drove the woods in a ring, which was thus performed: from the circumference of a large circle they all marched inward and drove the game toward the center. By this means they shot a brace of fat bears, which came very seasonably, because we had made clean work in the morning and were in danger of dining with St. Anthony, or His Grace Duke Humphrey.[2] But in this expedition the unhappy man who had lost himself once before straggled again so far in pursuit of a deer that he was hurried a second time quite out of his knowledge; and, night coming on before he could recover the camp, he was obliged to lie down without any of the comforts of fire, food, or covering; nor would his fears suffer him to sleep very sound, because, to his great disturbance, the wolves howled all that night and panthers screamed most frightfully.

In the evening a brisk northwester swept all the clouds from the sky and exposed the mountains as well as the stars to our prospect. That which was the most lofty to the southward and which we called the Lover's Leap, some of our Indian traders fondly fancied was the Kiawan Mountain, which they had formerly seen from the country of the Cherokees. They were the more positive by reason of the prodigious precipice that remarkably distinguished the west end of it. We seemed however not to be far enough south for that, though 'tis not improbable but a few miles farther the course of our line might carry us to the most northerly towns of the Cherokees. What makes this the more credible is the northwest course that our traders take from the Catawbas for some hundred miles together, when they carry goods that roundabout way to the Cherokees.

It was a great pity that the want of bread and the weakness of our horses hindered us from making the discovery. Though the great service such an excursion might have been to the country would certainly have made the attempt not only pardonable but much to be commended. Our traders are now at the vast charge and fatigue of traveling above five hundred miles for the benefit of that traffic which hardly quits cost. Would it not then be worth the Assembly's while to be at some charge to find a shorter cut to carry on so profitable a trade, with more advantage and less hazard and trouble than they do at present? For I am persuaded it will not then be half the distance that our traders make it now nor half so far as Georgia lies from the northern clans of that nation. Such a

discovery would certainly prove an unspeakable advantage to
this colony by facilitating a trade with so considerable a nation of Indians, which have sixty-two towns and more than
four thousand fighting men. Our traders at that rate would be
able to undersell those sent from the other colonies so much
that the Indians must have reason to deal with them prefera-
bly to all others. Of late the new colony of Georgia has made
an act obliging us to go four hundred miles to take out a li-
cense to traffic with these Cherokees, though many of their
towns lie out of their bounds and we had carried on this
trade eighty years before that colony was thought of.

[*Oct. 30*]   In the morning early the man who had gone
astray the day before found his way to the camp by the
sound of the bells that were upon the horses' necks.

At nine o'clock we began our march back toward the rising sun, for though we had finished the line yet we had not
yet near finished our fatigue. We had, after all, two hundred
good miles at least to our several habitations, and the horses
were brought so low that we were obliged to travel on foot
great part of the way, and that in our boots, too, to save our
legs from being torn to pieces by the bushes and briers. Had
we not done this, we must have left all our horses behind,
which could now hardly drag their legs after them; and with
all the favor we could show the poor animals we were forced
to set seven of them free not far from the foot of the mountains.

Four men were dispatched early to clear the road, that our
lame commissioner's leg might be in less danger of being
bruised and that the baggage horses might travel with less difficulty and more expedition. As we passed along, by favor of
a serene sky we had still from every eminence a perfect view
of the mountains, as well to the north as to the south. We
could not forbear now and then facing about to survey them,
as if unwilling to part with a prospect which at the same
time, like some rakes, was very wild and very agreeable. We
encouraged the horses to exert the little strength they had
and, being light, they made a shift to jog on about eleven
miles...

We encamped on Crooked Creek near a thicket of canes.
In the front of our camp rose a very beautiful hill that bounded our view at about a mile's distance, and all the intermediate space was covered with green canes. Though to our

sorrow, firewood was scarce, which was now the harder upon us because a northwester blew very cold from the mountains.

The Indian killed a stately, fat buck, and we picked his bones as clean as a score of turkey buzzards could have done. By the advantage of a clear night, we made trial once more of the variation and found it much the same as formerly. This being His Majesty's birthday, we drank all the loyal healths in excellent water, not for the sake of the drink (like many of our fellow subjects), but purely for the sake of the toast. And because all public mirth should be a little noisy, we fired several volleys of canes, instead of guns, which gave a loud report. We threw them into the fire, where the air enclosed betwixt the joints of the canes, being expanded by the violent heat, burst its narrow bounds with a considerable explosion.

In the evening one of the men knocked down an opossum, which is a harmless little beast that will seldom go out of your way, and if you take hold of it will only grin and hardly ever bite. The flesh was well tasted and tender, approaching nearest to pig, which it also resembled in bigness. The color of its fur was a goose gray, with a swine's snout and a tail like a rat, but at least a foot long. By twisting this tail about the arm of a tree, it will hang with all its weight and swing to anything it wants to take hold of. It has five claws on the forefeet of equal length, but the hinder feet have only four claws and a sort of thumb standing off at a proper distance. Their feet, being thus formed, qualify them for climbing up trees to catch little birds, which they are very fond of. But the greatest particularity of this creature, and which distinguishes it from most others that we are acquainted with, is the false belly of the female, into which her young retreat in time of danger. She can draw the slit, which is the inlet into this pouch, so close that you must look narrowly to find it, especially if she happen to be a virgin. Within the false belly may be seen seven or eight teats, on which the young ones grow from their first formation till they are big enough to fall off like ripe fruit from a tree. This is so odd a method of generation that I should not have believed it without the testimony of mine own eyes. Besides, a knowing and credible person has assured me he has more than once observed the embryo opossums growing to the teat before they were completely shaped, and afterwards watched their daily growth till they were big enough for birth.[3] And all this he could the more easily pry into because the dam was so perfectly gentle and harmless that he could handle her just as he pleased.

I could hardly persuade myself to publish a thing so contrary to the course that nature takes in the production of other animals unless it were a matter commonly believed in all countries where that creature is produced and has been often observed by persons of undoubted credit and understanding. They say that the leather-winged bats produce their young in the same uncommon manner; and that young sharks at sea and young vipers ashore run down the throats of their dams when they are closely pursued.

[*Oct. 31*]   The frequent crossing of Crooked Creek and mounting the steep banks of it gave the finishing stroke to the foundering of our horses, and no less than two of them made a full stop here and would not advance a foot farther, either by fair means or foul. We had a dreamer of dreams amongst us who warned me in the morning to take care of myself or I should infallibly fall into the creek; I thanked him kindly and used what caution I could but was not able, it seems, to avoid my destiny, for my horse made a false step and laid me down at my full length in the water. This was enough to bring dreaming into credit, and I think it much for the honor of our expedition that it was graced not only with a priest but also with a prophet. We were so perplexed with this serpentine creek, as well as in passing the branches of the Irvin, which were swelled since we saw them before, that we could reach but five miles this whole day.

In the evening we pitched our tent near Miry Creek, though an uncomfortable place to lodge in, purely for the advantage of the canes. Our hunters killed a large doe and two bears, which made all other misfortunes easy. Certainly no Tartar ever loved horseflesh or Hottentot guts and garbage better than woodsmen do bear. The truth of it is, it may be proper food perhaps for such as work or ride it off, but, with our chaplain's leave, who loved it much, I think it not a very proper diet for saints, because 'tis apt to make them a little too rampant. And, now, for the good of mankind and for the better peopling an infant colony, which has no want but that of inhabitants, I will venture to publish a secret of impor-

---

[3]Byrd seems to think that the embryos were formed in the pouch, whereas in fact the mother places the immature embryos there after natural birth.

tance which our Indian disclosed to me. I asked him the reason why few or none of his countrywomen were barren. To which curious question he answered, with a broad grin upon his face, they had an infallible secret for that. Upon my being importunate to know what the secret might be, he informed me that if any Indian woman did not prove with child at a decent time after marriage, the husband, to save his reputation with the women, forthwith entered into a bear diet for six weeks, which in that time makes him so vigorous that he grows exceedingly impertinent to his poor wife, and 'tis great odds but he makes her a mother in nine months. And thus much I am able to say besides for the reputation of the bear diet, that all the married men of our company were joyful fathers within forty weeks after they got home, and most of the single men had children sworn to them within the same time, our chaplain always excepted, who, with much ado, made a shift to cast out that importunate kind of devil by dint of fasting and prayer.

William Bartram

Travels in Florida

*William Bartram (1739–1823), an accomplished naturalist
and artist, wrote a work of natural history that became the
earliest book by an American to achieve widespread literary
recognition in England and Europe. Bartram was trained in
the observation and appreciation of nature by the country's
foremost botanist, his father, John Bartram, who had planted
North America's first botanical garden on his property near
Philadelphia. William joined his father in 1765 on a botanical trip up the St. Johns River, and he later extended these
explorations of the wilderness on his own when he began four
years of travel through Florida, Georgia, the Carolinas, and
the Indian territories to the west. Bartram's volume of Travels was not published until 1791 in Philadelphia, but it was
quickly followed by editions in London and Dublin and by
translations in Berlin, Vienna, Haarlem, and Paris. Bartram's
interest extended beyond scientific description of plants and
wildlife to include an expression of reverence for the wilderness and the creative principle animating all its parts, even
the seemingly terrible or insignificant. Coleridge used the sen-
suous landscapes of Bartram's Travels in his poem "Kubla
Khan," as did Wordsworth in "Ruth" and Chateaubriand in
his exotic novels Atala and René. Carlyle later praised Bartram's book as the kind that all American libraries ought to
keep "as a future biblical article." Because of Bartram's skill
as a naturalist, Thomas Jefferson invited him to join an up-
coming expedition into the unknown wilderness west of the
Missouri, but Bartram declined because of his age. In his
Travels, Bartram's exuberant rendition of a sublime wilderness is based on careful observation of individual plants,
birds, and animals, and even the following controversial
dramatization of belligerent and bellowing alligators has been
supported by later naturalists as rooted in fact.*

The Indian not returning this morning, I set sail alone. The coasts on each side had much the same appearance as already described. The Palm trees here seem to be of a different species from the Cabbage tree; their strait trunks are sixty, eighty or ninety feet high, with a beautiful taper of a bright ash colour, until within six or seven feet of the top, where it is a fine green colour, crowned with an orb of rich green plumed leaves: I have measured the stem of these plumes fifteen feet in length, besides the plume, which is nearly of the same length.

The little lake, which is an expansion of the river, now appeared in view; on the East side are extensive marshes, and on the other high forests and Orange groves, and then a bay, lined with vast Cypress swamps, both coasts gradually approaching each other, to the opening of the river again, which is in this place about three hundred yards wide; evening now drawing on, I was anxious to reach some high bank of the river, where I intended to lodge, and agreeably to my wishes, I soon after discovered on the West shore, a little promontory, at the turning of the river, contracting it here to about one hundred and fifty yards in width. This promontory is a peninsula, containing about three acres of high ground, and is one entire Orange grove, with a few Live Oaks, Magnolias and Palms. Upon doubling the point, I arrived at the landing, which is a circular harbour, at the foot of the bluff, the top of which is about twelve feet high; and back of it is a large Cypress swamp, that spreads each way, the right wing forming the West coast of the little lake, and the left stretching up the river many miles, and encompassing a vast space of low grassy marshes. From this promontory, looking Eastward across the river, we behold a landscape of low country, unparalleled as I think; on the left is the East coast of the little lake, which I had just passed, and from the Orange bluff at the lower end, the high forests begin, and in-

From William Bartram, *Travels Through North and South Carolina, Georgia, East and West Florida, the Cherokee Country, the Extensive Territories of the Muscogulges, or Creek Confederacy, and the Country of the Chactaws, Containing an Account of the Soil and Natural Productions of those Regions, Together with Observations on the Manners of the Indians* (Philadelphia: James and Johnson, 1791). Reprinted in Naturalist's Edition, edited by Francis Harper (New Haven: Yale University Press, 1958).

crease in breadth from the shore of the lake, making a circular sweep to the right, and contain many hundred thousand acres of meadow, and this grand sweep of high forests encircles, as I apprehend, at least twenty miles of these green fields, interspersed with hommocks or islets of evergreen trees, where the sovereign Magnolia and lordly Palm stand conspicuous. The islets are high shelly knolls, on the sides of creeks or branches of the river, which wind about and drain off the super-abundant waters that cover these meadows, during the winter season.

The evening was temperately cool and calm. The crocodiles began to roar and appear in uncommon numbers along the shores and in the river. I fixed my camp in an open plain, near the utmost projection of the promontory, under the shelter of a large Live Oak, which stood on the highest part of the ground and but a few yards from my boat. From this open, high situation, I had a free prospect of the river, which was a matter of no trivial consideration to me, having good reason to dread the subtle attacks of the alligators, who were crowding about my harbour. Having collected a good quantity of wood for the purpose of keeping up a light and smoke during the night, I began to think of preparing my supper, when, upon examining my stores, I found but a scanty provision, I thereupon determined, as the most expeditious way of supplying my necessities, to take my bob and try for some trout. About one hundred yards above my harbour, began a cove or bay of the river, out of which opened a large lagoon. The mouth or entrance from the river to it was narrow, but the waters soon after spread and formed a little lake, extending into the marshes, its entrance and shores within I observed to be verged with floating lawns of the Pistia and Nymphea and other aquatic plants; these I knew were excellent haunts for trout.

The verges and islets of the lagoon were elegantly embellished with flowering plants and shrubs; the laughing coots with wings half spread were tripping over the little coves and hiding themselves in the tufts of grass; young broods of the painted summer teal, skimming the still surface of the waters, and following the watchful parent unconscious of danger, were frequently surprised by the voracious trout, and he in turn, as often by the subtle, greedy alligator. Behold him rushing forth from the flags and reeds. His enormous body

swells. His plaited tail brandished high, floats upon the lake.
The waters like a cataract descend from his opening jaws.
Clouds of smoke issue from his dilated nostrils. The earth
trembles with his thunder. When immediately from the opposite coast of the lagoon, emerges from the deep his rival
champion. They suddenly dart upon each other. The boiling
surface of the lake marks their rapid course, and a terrific
conflict commences. They now sink to the bottom folded together in horrid wreaths. The water becomes thick and dis-
coloured. Again they rise, their jaws clap together, re-echoing
through the deep surrounding forests. Again they sink, when
the contest ends at the muddy bottom of the lake, and the
vanquished makes a hazardous escape, hiding himself in the
muddy turbulent waters and sedge on a distant shore. The
proud victor exulting returns to the place of action. The
shores and forests resound his dreadful roar, together with
the triumphing shouts of the plaited tribes around, witnesses
of the horrid combat.

My apprehensions were highly alarmed after being a spectator of so dreadful a battle; it was obvious that every delay
would but tend to encrease my dangers and difficulties, as the
sun was near setting, and the alligators gathered around my
harbour from all quarters; from these considerations I concluded to be expeditious in my trip to the lagoon, in order to
take some fish. Not thinking it prudent to take my fusee with
me, lest I might lose it overboard in case of a battle, which I
had every reason to dread before my return, I therefore furnished myself with a club for my defence, went on board,
and penetrating the first line of those which surrounded my
harbour, they gave way; but being pursued by several very
large ones, I kept strictly on the watch, and paddled with all
my might towards the entrance of the lagoon, hoping to be
sheltered there from the multitude of my assailants; but ere I
had half-way reached the place, I was attacked on all sides,
several endeavouring to overset the canoe. My situation now
became precarious to the last degree: two very large ones attacked me closely, at the same instant, rushing up with their
heads and part of their bodies above the water, roaring terribly and belching floods of water over me. They struck their
jaws together so close to my ears, as almost to stun me, and I
expected every moment to be dragged out of the boat and instantly devoured, but I applied my weapons so effectually
about me, though at random, that I was so successful as to

beat them off a little; when, finding that they designed to renew the battle, I made for the shore, as the only means left me for my preservation, for, by keeping close to it, I should have my enemies on one side of me only, whereas I was before surrounded by them, and there was a probability, if pushed to the last extremity, of saving myself, by jumping out of the canoe on shore, as it is easy to outwalk them on land, although comparatively as swift as lightning in the water. I found this last expedient alone could fully answer my expectations, for as soon as I gained the shore they drew off and kept aloof. This was a happy relief, as my confidence was, in some degree recovered by it. On recollecting myself, I discovered that I had almost reached the entrance of the lagoon, and determined to venture in, if possible to take a few fish and then return to my harbour, while day-light continued; for I could now, with caution and resolution, make my way with safety along shore, and indeed there was no other way to regain my camp, without leaving my boat and making my retreat through the marshes and reeds, which, if I could even effect, would have been in a manner throwing myself away, for then there would have been no hopes of ever recovering my bark, and returning in safety to any settlements of men. I accordingly proceeded and made good my entrance into the lagoon, though not without opposition from the alligators, who formed a line across the entrance, but did not pursue me into it, nor was I molested by any there, though there were some very large ones in a cove at the upper end. I soon caught more trout than I had present occasion for, and the air was too hot and sultry to admit of their being kept for many hours, even though salted or barbecued. I now prepared for my return to camp, which I succeeded in with but little trouble, by keeping close to the shore, yet I was opposed upon re-entering the river out of the lagoon, and pursued near to my landing (though not closely attacked) particularly by an old daring one, about twelve feet in length, who kept close after me, and when I stepped on shore and turned about, in order to draw up my canoe, he rushed up near my feet and lay there for some time, looking me in the face, his head and shoulders out of water; I resolved he should pay for his temerity, and having a heavy load in my fusee, I ran to my camp, and returning with my piece, found him with his foot on the gunwale of the boat, in search of fish, on my coming up he withdrew sullenly and slowly into the water, but soon returned and placed himself in his former position, looking at me and seeming neither fearful or any way disturbed. I soon dispatched him by lodging the contents of my gun in his head, and then proceeded to cleanse and prepare my fish for supper, and accordingly took them out of the boat, laid them down on the sand close to the water, and began to scale them, when, raising my head, I saw before me, through the clear water, the head and shoulders of a very large alligator, moving slowly towards me; I instantly stepped back, when, with a sweep of his tail, he brushed off several of my fish. It was certainly most providential that I looked up at that instant, as the monster would probably, in less than a minute, have seized and dragged me into the river. This incredible boldness of the animal disturbed me greatly, supposing there could now be no reasonable safety for me during the night, but by keeping continually on the watch; I therefore, as soon as I had prepared the fish, proceeded to secure myself and effects in the best manner I could: in the first place, I hauled my bark upon the shore, almost clear out of the water, to prevent their oversetting or sinking her, after this every moveable was taken out and carried to my camp, which was but a few yards off; then ranging some dry wood in such order as was the most convenient, cleared the ground round about it, that there might be no impediment in my way, in case of an attack in the night, either from the water or the land; for I discovered by this time, that this small isthmus, from its remote situation and fruitfulness, was resorted to by bears and wolves. Having prepared myself in the best manner I could, I charged my gun and proceeded to reconnoitre my camp and the adjacent grounds; when I discovered that the peninsula and grove, at the distance of about two hundred yards from my encampment, on the land side, were invested by a Cypress swamp, covered with water, which below was joined to the shore of the little lake, and above to the marshes surrounding the lagoon, so that I was confined to an islet exceedingly circumscribed, and I found there was no other retreat for me, in case of an attack, but by either ascending one of the large Oaks, or pushing off with my boat.

It was by this time dusk, and the alligators had nearly ceased their roar, when I was again alarmed by a tumultuous noise that seemed to be in my harbour, and therefore engaged my immediate attention. Returning to my camp I found it undisturbed, and then continued on to the extreme point of the promontory, where I saw a scene, new and surprising, which at first threw my senses into such a tumult, that it was some time before I could comprehend what was the matter; however, I soon accounted for the prodigious assemblage of crocodiles at this place, which exceeded every thing of the kind I had ever heard of.

How shall I express myself so as to convey an adequate idea of it to the reader, and at the same time avoid raising suspicions of my want of veracity. Should I say, that the river (in this place) from shore to shore, and perhaps near half a mile above and below me, appeared to be one solid bank of fish, of various kinds, pushing through this narrow pass of St. Juans into the little lake, on their return down the river, and that the alligators were in such incredible numbers, and so close together from shore to shore, that it would have been easy to have walked across on their heads, had the animals been harmless. What expressions can sufficiently declare the shocking scene that for some minutes continued, whilst this mighty army of fish were forcing the pass? During this attempt, thousands, I may say hundreds of thousands of them were caught and swallowed by the devouring alligators. I have seen an alligator take up out of the water several great fish at a time, and just squeeze them betwixt his jaws, while the tails of the great trout flapped about his eyes and lips, ere he had swallowed them. The horrid noise of their closing jaws, their plunging amidst the broken banks of fish, and rising with their prey some feet upright above the water, the floods of water and blood rushing out of their mouths, and the clouds of vapour issuing from their wide nostrils, were truly frightful. This scene continued at intervals during the night, as the fish came to the pass. After this sight, shocking and tremendous as it was, I found myself somewhat easier and more reconciled to my situation, being convinced that their extraordinary assemblage here, was owing to this annual feast of fish, and that they were so well employed in their own element, that I had little occasion to fear their paying me a visit.

It being now almost night, I returned to my camp, where I had left my fish broiling, and my kettle of rice stewing, and having with me, oil, pepper and salt, and excellent oranges hanging in abundance over my head (a valuable substitute for vinegar) I sat down and regaled myself chearfully; having finished my repast, I re-kindled my fire for light, and whilst I was revising the notes of my past day's journey, I was suddenly roused with a noise behind me toward the main land; I sprang up on my feet, and listening, I distinctly heard some creature wading in the water of the isthmus; I seized my gun and went cautiously from my camp, directing my steps towards the noise; when I advanced about thirty yards, I halted behind a coppice of Orange trees, and soon perceived two very large bears, which had made their way through the water, and had landed in the grove, about one hundred yards distance from me, and were advancing towards me. I waited until they were within thirty yards of me, they there began to snuff and look towards my camp, I snapped my piece, but it flashed, on which they both turned about and galloped off, plunging through the water and swamp, never halting as I suppose, until they reached fast land, as I could hear them leaping and plunging a long time; they did not presume to return again, nor was I molested by any other creature, except being occasionally awakened by the whooping of owls, screaming of bitterns, or the wood-rats running amongst the leaves.

The wood-rat is a very curious animal, they are not half the size of the domestic rat; of a dark brown or black colour; their tail slender and shorter in proportion, and covered thinly with short hair; they are singular with respect to their ingenuity and great labour in the construction of their habitations, which are conical pyramids about three or four feet high, constructed with dry branches, which they collect with great labour and perseverance, and pile up without any apparent order, yet they are so interwoven with one another, that it would take a bear or wild-cat some time to pull one of these castles to pieces, and allow the animals sufficient time to secure a retreat with their young.

The noise of the crocodiles kept me awake the greater part of the night, but when I arose in the morning, contrary to my expectations, there was perfect peace; very few of them to be seen, and those were asleep on the shore, yet I was not able to suppress my fears and apprehensions of being attacked by them in future; and indeed yesterday's combat with them, notwithstanding I came off in a manner victorious, or at least made a safe retreat, had left sufficient impression on my mind to damp my courage, and it seemed too much for one of my strength, being alone in a very small boat to encounter such collected danger. To pursue my voyage up the river, and be obliged every evening to pass such dangerous defiles, appeared to me as perilous as running the gauntlet betwixt two rows of Indians armed with knives and fire brands; I however resolved to continue my voyage one day longer, if I possibly could with safety, and then return down the river, should I find the like difficulties to oppose. Accordingly I got every thing on board, charged my gun, and set sail cautiously along shore; as I passed by Battle lagoon, I began to tremble and keep a good look out, when suddenly a huge alligator rushed out of the reeds, and with a tremendous roar, came up, and darted as swift as an arrow under my boat, emerging upright on my lea quarter, with open jaws, and belching water and smoke that fell upon me like rain in a hurricane; I laid soundly about his head with my club and beat him off, and after plunging and darting about my boat, he went off on a strait line through the water, seemingly with the rapidity of lightning, and entered the cape of the lagoon; I now employed my time to the very best advantage in paddling close along shore, but could not forbear looking now and then behind me, and presently perceived one of them coming up again; the water of the river hereabouts, was shoal and very clear; the monster came up with the usual roar and menaces, and passed close by the side of my boat, when I could distinctly see a young brood of alligators to the number of one hundred or more, following after her in a long train, they kept close together in a column without straggling off to the one side or the other, the young appeared to be of an equal size, about fifteen inches in length, almost black, with pale yellow transverse waved clouds or blotches, much like rattle snakes in colour. I now lost sight of my enemy again.

Still keeping close along shore, on turning a point or projection of the river bank, at once I beheld a great number of hillocks or small pyramids, resembling hay cocks, ranged like an encampment along the banks, they stood fifteen or twenty yards distant from the water, on a high marsh, about four feet perpendicular above the water; I knew them to be the nests of the crocodile, having had a description of them before, and now expected a furious and general attack, as I saw several large crocodiles swimming abreast of these buildings. These nests being so great a curiosity to me, I was determined at all events immediately to land and examine them. Accordingly I ran my bark on shore at one of their landing places, which was a sort of nick or little dock, from which ascended a sloping path or road up to the edge of the meadow, where their nests were, most of them were deserted, and the great thick whitish egg-shells lay broken and scattered upon the ground round about them.

The nests or hillocks are of the form of an obtuse cone, four feet high and four or five feet in diameter at their bases; they are constructed with mud, grass and herbage: at first they lay a floor of this kind of tempered mortar on the ground, upon which they deposit a layer of eggs, and upon this a stratum of mortar seven or eight inches in thickness, and then another layer of eggs, and in this manner one stratum upon another, nearly to the top: I believe they commonly lay from one to two hundred eggs in a nest: these are hatched I suppose by the heat of the sun, and perhaps the vegetable substances mixed with the earth, being acted upon by the sun, may cause a small degree of fermentation, and so increase the heat in those hillocks. The ground for several acres about these nests shewed evident marks of a continual resort of alligators; the grass was every where beaten down, hardly a blade or straw was left standing; whereas, all about, at a distance, it was five or six feet high, and as thick as it could grow together. The female, as I imagine, carefully watches her own nest of eggs until they are all hatched, or perhaps while she is attending her own brood, she takes under her care and protection, as many as she can get at one time, either from her own particular nest or others: but certain it is, that the young are not left to shift for themselves, having had frequent opportunities of seeing the female alligator, leading about the shores her train of young ones, just like a hen does her brood of chickens, and she is equally assiduous and courageous in defending the young, which are under their care, and providing for their subsistence; and when she is basking upon the warm banks, with her brood around her, you may hear the young ones continually whining and barking, like young puppies. I believe but few of a brood live to the years of full growth and magnitude, as the old feed on the young as long as they can make prey of them.

The alligator when full grown is a very large and terrible creature, and of prodigious strength, activity and swiftness in the water. I have seen them twenty feet in length, and some are supposed to be twenty-two or twenty-three feet; their body is as large as that of a horse; their shape exactly resembles that of a lizard, except their tail, which is flat or cuniform, being compressed on each side, and gradually diminishing from the abdomen to the extremity, which, with the whole body is covered with horny plates or squamae, impenetrable when on the body of the live animal, even to a rifle ball, except about their head and just behind their forelegs or arms, where it is said they are only vulnerable. The head of a full grown one is about three feet, and the mouth opens nearly the same length, the eyes are small in proportion and seem sunk deep in the head, by means of the prominency of the brows; the nostrils are large, inflated and prominent on the top, so that the head in the water, resembles, at a distance, a great chunk of wood floating about. Only the upper jaw moves, which they raise almost perpendicular, so as to form a right angle with the lower one. In the fore part of the upper jaw, on each side, just under the nostrils, are two very large, thick, strong teeth or tusks, not very sharp, but rather the shape of a cone, these are as white as the finest polished ivory, and are not covered by any skin or lips, and always in sight, which gives the creature a frightful appearance; in the lower jaw are holes opposite to these teeth, to receive them; when they clap their jaws together it causes a surprising noise, like that which is made by forcing a heavy plank with violence upon the ground, and may be heard at a great distance.

But what is yet more surprising to a stranger, is the incredible loud and terrifying roar, which they are capable of making, especially in the spring season, their breeding time; it most resembles very heavy distant thunder, not only shaking the air and waters, but causing the earth to tremble; and when hundreds and thousands are roaring at the same time, you can scarcely be persuaded, but that the whole globe is violently and dangerously agitated.

An old champion, who is perhaps absolute sovereign of a little lake or lagoon (when fifty less than himself are obliged to content themselves with swelling and roaring in little coves round about) darts forth from the reedy coverts all at once, on the surface of the waters, in a right line; at first seemingly as rapid as lightning, but gradually more slowly until he arrives at the center of the lake, when he stops; he now swells himself by drawing in wind and water through his mouth, which causes a loud sonorous rattling in the throat for near a minute, but it is immediately forced out again through his mouth and nostrils, with a loud noise, brandishing his tail in

the air, and the vapour ascending from his nostrils like
smoke. At other times, when swollen to an extent ready to
burst, his head and tail lifted up, he spins or twirls round on
the surface of the water. He acts his part like an Indian chief
when rehearsing his feats of war, and then retiring, the exhibition is continued by others who dare to step forth, and
strive to excel each other, to gain the attention of the favourite female.

Having gratified my curiosity at this general breeding place
and nursery of crocodiles, I continued my voyage up the
river without being greatly disturbed by them: in my way I
observed islets or floating fields of the bright green Pistia,
decorated with other amphibious plants, as Senecio Jacobea,
Persicaria amphibia, Coreopsis bidens, Hydrocotile fluitans,
and many others of less note.

The swamps on the banks and islands of the river, are generally three or four feet above the surface of the water, and
very level; the timber large and growing thinly, more so than
what is observed to be in the swamps below Lake George; the
black, rich earth is covered with moderately tall, and very
succulent tender grass, which when chewed is sweet and
agreeable to the taste, somewhat like young sugar-cane: it is
a jointed decumbent grass, sending out radiculae at the joints
into the earth, and so spreads itself, by creeping over its surface.

The large timber trees, which possess the low lands, are
Acer rubrum, Ac. nigundo, Ac. glaucum, Ulmus sylvatica,
Fraxinus excelsior, Frax. aquatica, Ulmus suberifer, Gleditsia
monosperma, Gledit. triacanthus, Diospyros Virginica, Nyssa
aquatica, Nyssa sylvatica, Juglans cinerea, Quercus dentata,
Quercus phillos, Hopea tinctoria, Corypha palma, Morus
rubra, and many more. The Palm grows on the edges of the
banks, where they are raised higher than the adjacent level
ground, by the accumulation of sand, river-shells, &c. I
passed along several miles by those rich swamps, the channels
of the river which encircle the several fertile islands, I had
passed, now uniting, formed one deep channel near three
hundred yards over. The banks of the river on each side, began to rise and present shelly bluffs, adorned by beautiful
Orange groves, Laurels and Live Oaks. And now appeared in
sight, a tree that claimed my whole attention: it was the Car-
ica papaya, both male and female, which were in flower; and
the latter both in flower and fruit, some of which were ripe,

as large, and of the form of a pear, and of a most charming
appearance.

This admirable tree is certainly the most beautiful of any
vegetable production I know of; the towering Laurel Magnolia, and exalted Palm, indeed exceed it in grandeur and mag-
nificence, but not in elegance, delicacy and gracefulness; it
rises erect, with a perfectly strait tapering stem, to the height
of fifteen or twenty feet, which is smooth and polished, of a
bright ash colour, resembling leaf silver, curiously inscribed
with the footsteps of the fallen leaves, and these vestiges, are
placed in a very regular uniform imbricated order, which has
a fine effect, as if the little column were elegantly carved all
over. Its perfectly spherical top, is formed of very large lobe-
sinuate leaves, supported on very long footstalks; the lower
leaves are the largest as well as their petioles the longest, and
make a graceful sweep or flourish, like the long ſ or the
branches of a sconce candlestick. The ripe and green fruit are
placed round about the stem or trunk, from the lowermost
leaves, where the ripe fruit are, and upwards almost to the
top; the heart or inmost pithy part of the trunk is in a manner hollow, or at best consists of very thin porous medullae
or membranes; the tree very seldom branches or divides into
limbs, I believe never unless the top is by accident broken off
when very young: I saw one which had two tops or heads,
the stem of which divided near the earth. It is always green,
ornamented at the same time with flowers and fruit, which
like figs come out singly from the trunk or stem.

After resting and refreshing myself in these delightful
shades, I left them with reluctance, embarking again after the
fervid heats of the meridian sun were abated, for some time I
passed by broken ridges of shelly high land, covered with
groves of Live Oak, Palm, Olea Americana, and Orange
trees; frequently observing floating islets and green fields of
the Pistia near the shores of the river and lagoons.

There is in this river and in the waters all over Florida, a
very curious and handsome bird, the people call them Snake
Birds, I think I have seen paintings of them on the Chinese
screens and other India pictures: they seem to be a species of
cormorant or loon (Colymbus cauda elongata) but far more
beautiful and delicately formed than any other species that I
have ever seen. The head and neck of this bird are extremely
small and slender, the latter very long indeed, almost out of
all proportion, the bill long, strait and slender, tapering from

its base to a sharp point, all the upper side, the abdomen and thighs, are as black and glossy as a raven's, covered with feathers so firm and elastic, that they in some degree resemble fish-scales, the breast and upper part of the belly are covered with feathers of a cream colour, the tail is very long, of a deep black, and tipped with a silvery white, and when spread, represents an unfurled fan. They delight to sit in little peaceable communities, on the dry limbs of trees, hanging over the still waters, with their wings and tails expanded, I suppose to cool and air themselves, when at the same time they behold their images in the watery mirror: at such times, when we approach them, they drop off the limbs into the water as if dead, and for a minute or two are not to be seen; when on a sudden at a vast distance, their long slender head and neck only appear, and have very much the appearance of a snake, and no other part of them is to be seen when swimming in the water, except sometimes the tip end of their tail. In the heat of the day they are seen in great numbers, sailing very high in the air, over lakes and rivers.

I doubt not but if this bird had been an inhabitant of the Tiber in Ovid's days, it would have furnished him with a subject, for some beautiful and entertaining metamorphoses. I believe they feed intirely on fish, for their flesh smells and tastes intolerably strong of it, it is scarcely to be eaten unless constrained by insufferable hunger.

I had now swamps and marshes on both sides of me, and evening coming on apace, I began to look out for high land to encamp on, but the extensive marshes seemed to have no bounds; and it was almost dark when I found a tolerable suitable place, and at last was constrained to take up on a narrow strip of high shelly bank, on the West side. Great numbers of crocodiles were in sight on both shores; I ran my bark on shore at a perpendicular bank four or five feet above the water, just by the roots and under the spreading limbs of a great Live Oak: this appeared to have been an ancient camping place by Indians and strolling adventurers, from ash heaps and old rotten fire brands, and chunks, scattered about on the surface of the ground; but was now evidently the harbour and landing place of some sovereign alligator: there led up from it a deep beaten path or road, and was a convenient ascent.

I did not approve of my intended habitation from these circumstances; and no sooner had I landed and moored my

canoe to the roots of the tree, than I saw a huge crocodile
rising up from the bottom close by me, who, when he perceived that I saw him, plunged down again under my vessel;
this determined me to be on my guard, and in time to
provide against a troublesome night: I took out of my boat
every moveable, which I carried upon the bank, then chose
my lodging close to my canoe, under the spreading Oak; as
hereabouts only, the ground was open and clear of high grass
and bushes, and consequently I had some room to stir and
look round about. I then proceeded to collect firewood which
I found difficult to procure. Here were standing a few Orange
trees. As for provisions, I had saved one or two barbecued
trout; the remains of my last evenings collection in tolerable
good order, though the sultry heats of the day had injured
them; yet by stewing them up afresh with the lively juice of
Oranges, they served well enough for my supper: having by
this time but little relish or appetite for my victuals; for constant watching at night against the attacks of alligators, sting-
ing of musquitoes and sultry heats of the day; together, with
the fatigues of working my bark, had almost deprived me of
every desire but that of ending my troubles as speedy as possible. I had the good fortune to collect together a sufficiency
of dry sticks, to keep up a light and smoke, which I laid by
me, and then spread my skins and blankets upon the ground,
kindled up a little fire and supped before it was quite dark.
The evening was however, extremely pleasant, a brisk cool
breeze sprang up, and the skies were perfectly serene, the
stars twinkling with uncommon brilliancy. I stretched myself
along before my fire; having the river, my little harbour and
the stern of my vessel in view, and now through fatigue and
weariness I fell asleep, but this happy temporary release from
cares and troubles I enjoyed but a few moments, when I was
awakened and greatly surprised, by the terrifying screams of
Owls in the deep swamps around me. and what encreased my
extreme misery was the difficulty of getting quite awake, and
yet hearing at the same time such screaming and shouting,
which increased and spread every way for miles around, in
dreadful peals vibrating through the dark extensive forests,
meadows and lakes, I could not after this surprise recover the
former peaceable state and tranquility of mind and repose,
during the long night, and I believe it was happy for me that
I was awakened, for at that moment the crocodile was dashing my canoe against the roots of the tree, endeavouring to

get into her for the fish, which I however prevented. Another time in the night I believe I narrowly escaped being dragged into the river by him, for when again through excessive fatigue I had fallen asleep, but was again awakened by the screaming owl, I found the monster on the top of the bank, his head towards me not above two yards distant, when starting up and seizing my fuzee well loaded, which I always kept under my head in the night time, he drew back and plunged into the water. After this I roused up my fire, and kept a light during the remaining part of the night, being determined not to be caught napping so again, indeed the musquitoes alone would have been abundantly sufficient to keep any creature awake that possessed their perfect senses, but I was overcome, and stupified with incessant watching and labour: as soon as I discovered the first signs of day-light, I arose, got all my effects and implements on board and set sail, proceeding upwards, hoping to give the musquitoes the slip, who were now, by the cool morning dews and breezes, driven to their shelter and hiding places; I was mistaken however in these conjectures, for great numbers of them, which had concealed themselves in my boat, as soon as the sun arose, began to revive, and sting me on my legs, which obliged me to land in order to get bushes to beat them out of their quarters.

Meriwether Lewis

Across the Continent

Meriwether Lewis (1774–1809) chose fellow soldier William Clark (1770–1838) to serve as co-commander of what became the most skillfully managed expedition in the history of North American exploration, an expedition that lasted twenty-eight months and covered eight thousand miles between the mouth of the Missouri and the Pacific outlet of the Columbia River. As a soldier for six years, Lewis had served on the frontier and had risen to the rank of captain in the First U.S. Infantry. In 1801 he was appointed President Jefferson's private secretary, and over the following two years, Lewis's further preparation for his role as official commander of the Corps of Discovery included some training in astronomy, botany, and zoology by scientists in Philadelphia. Despite the political, economic, and scientific importance of the 1804–1806 expedition across the continent, the journals of these two leaders were available only in a truncated and rephrased version until the twentieth century, when in 1904–1905 Reuben Thwaites published the Original Journals of the Lewis and Clark Expedition, *composed of seven volumes and an atlas, and in 1953 Bernard DeVoto published an abridged edition of the original journals. No excerpt can do justice to the epic quality of the complete journals, for their effect is cumulative. What follows is a sample from the writings of Lewis as the expedition breaks winter camp near the Mandan villages north of present Bismarck, North Dakota, and travels toward the headwaters of the Missouri in the Rockies. The expedition at that time was composed of thirty-three people and included York, Clark's black slave; Sacajawea, a Shoshone woman; and Pompey, her seven-week-old baby. Lewis's struggles with language, as reproduced from the original journals, help enhance the Adamic quality and overwhelming experience of this "Voyage of Discovery" into a wilderness never before seen by white man.*

[*Fort Mandan April 7th, 1805*]   Our vessels consisted of six small canoes, and two large perogues. This little fleet altho' not quite so rispectable as those of Columbus or Capt. Cook, were still viewed by us with as much pleasure as those deservedly famed adventurers ever beheld theirs; and I dare say with quite as much anxiety for their safety and preservation. we were now about to penetrate a country at least two thousand miles in width, on which the foot of civilized man had never trodden; the good or evil it had in store for us was for experiment yet to determine, and these little vessells contained every article by which we were to expect to subsist or defend ourselves. however, as the state of mind in which we are, generally gives the colouring to events, when the immagination is suffered to wander into futurity, the picture which now presented itself to me was a most pleasing one. enterta[in]ing as I do, the most confident hope of succeeding in a voyage which had formed a da[r]ling project of mine for the last ten years, I could but esteem this moment of my departure as among the most happy of my life. The party are in excellent health and sperits, zealously attached to the enterprise, and anxious to proceed; not a whisper of murmur or discontent to be heard among them, but all act in unison, and with the most perfict harmony. Capt. Clark myself the two Interpretters and the woman and child sleep in a tent of dressed skins. this tent is in the Indian stile, formed of a number of dressed Buffaloe skins sewed together with sinues. it is cut in such manner that when foalded double it forms the quarter of a circle, and is left open at one side here it may be attatched or loosened at pleasure by strings which are sewed to its sides for the purpose. . . .

[*Tuesday April 9th*]   when we halted for dinner the squaw busied herself in serching for the wild artichokes which the mice collect and deposit in large hoards. this operation she performed by penetrating the earth with a sharp stick about some small collections of drift wood. her labour soon proved successful, and she procured a good quantity of these roots. the flavor of this root resembles that of the Jerusalem Artichoke, and the stalk of the weed which produces it is also similar, . . .

From Meriwether Lewis, in *Original Journals of the Lewis and Clark Expedition, 1804–1806,* 8 vols., edited by Reuben Gold Thwaites (New York: Dodd, Mead, 1904–1905).

[*Saturday April 13th*]   The wind was in our favour
after 9 A.M. and continued favourable untill three 3. P.M.
we therefore hoisted both the sails in the White Perogue, consisting of a small squar sail, and spritsail, which carried her
at a pretty good gate, untill about 2 in the afternoon when a
sudden squall of wind struck us and turned the perogue so
much on the side as to allarm Sharbono who was steering at
the time, in this state of alarm he threw the perogue with her
side to the wind, when the spritsail gibing was as near overseting the perogue as it was possible to have missed. the wind
however abating for an instant I ordered Drewyer to the
helm and the sails to be taken in, which was instant executed
and the perogue being steered before the wind was agin
plased in a state of security. this accedent was very near cost-
ing us dearly. beleiving this vessell to be the most steady and
safe, we had embarked on board of it our instruments, Papers, medicine and the most valuable part of the merchandize
which we had still in reserve as presents for the Indians. we
had also embarked on board ourselves, with three men who
could not swim and the squaw with the young child, all of
whom, had the perogue overset, would most probably have
perished, as the waves were high, and the perogue upwards of
200 yards from the nearest shore; just above the entrance of
the little Missouri the great Missouri is upwards of a mile in
width, tho' immediately at the entrance of the former it is not
more than 200 yards wide and so shallow that the canoes
passed it with seting poles.

we found a number of carcases of the Buffaloe lying along
shore, which had been drowned by falling through the ice in
winter and lodged on shore by the high water when the river
broke up about the first of this month. we saw also many
tracks of the white bear of enormous size, along the river
shore and about the carcases of the Buffaloe, on which I
presume they feed. we have not as yet seen one of these ana-
mals, tho' their tracks are so abundant and recent. the men as
well as ourselves are anxious to meet with some of these
bear. the Indians give a very formidable account of the
strength and ferocity of this anamal, which they never dare
to attack but in parties of six eight or ten persons; and are
even then frequently defeated with the loss of one or more of
their party. the savages attack this anamal with their bows
and arrows and the indifferent guns with which the traders

furnish them, with these they shoot with such uncertainty and
at so short a distance, that (*unless shot thro' head or heart
wound not mortal*) they frequently mis their aim & fall a
sacrefice to the bear. this anamall is said more frequently to
attack a man on meeting with him, than to flee from him.
When the Indians are about to go in quest of the white bear,
previous to their departure, they paint themselves and perform all those supersticious rights commonly observed when
they are about to make war uppon a neighbouring nation.
Oserved more bald eagles on this part of the Missouri than
we have previously seen. saw the small hawk, frequently
called the sparrow hawk, which is common to most parts of
the U. States. great quantities of gees are seen feeding in the
praries. saw a large flock of white brant or gees with black
wings pass up the river; there were a number of gray brant
with them. . . .

[*Thursday April 25th 1805.*]   the water friezed on
the oars this morning as the men rowed. about 10 oclock
A.M. the wind began to blow so violently that we were
obliged to lye too. my dog had been absent during the last
night, and I was fearfull we had lost him altogether, however,
much to my satisfaction he joined us at 8 oclock this morning. Knowing that the river was crooked. from the report of
the hunters who were out yesterday. and beleiving that we
were at no very great distance from the Yellow stone River; I
determined, in order as mush as possible to avoid detention,
to proceed by land with a few men to the entrance of that
river and make the necessary observations to determine its
position; accordingly I set out at 11 OCk. on the Lard. side,
accompanyed by four men. when we had proceeded about
four miles, I ascended the hills from whence I had a most
pleasing view of the country, particularly of the wide and fertile vallies formed by the missouri and the yellowstone rivers,
which occasionally unmasked by the wood on their borders
disclose their meanderings for many miles in their passage
through these delightfull tracts of country. I determined to
encamp on the bank of the Yellow stone river which made
it's appearance about 2 miles South of me. the whol face of
the country was covered with herds of Buffaloe, Elk & Antelopes; deer are also abundant, but keep themselves more
concealed in the woodland. the buffaloe Elk and Antelope are

so gentle that we pass near them while feeding, without appearing to excite any alarm among them; and when we attract their attention, they frequently approach us more nearly to discover what we are, and in some instances pursue us a considerable distance apparently with that view. we encamped on the bank of the yellow stone river, 2 miles South of it's confluence with the Missouri. ...

[*Friday April 26th 1805*]   about 12 O[cl]ock I heard the discharge of several guns at the junction of the rivers, which announced to me the arrival of the pa[r]ty with Capt Clark; I afterwards learnt that they had fired on some buffaloe which they met with at that place, and of which they killed a cow and several Calves; the latter are now fine veal. after I had completed my observations in the evening I walked down and joined the party at their encampment on the point of land formed by the junction of the rivers; found them all in good health, and much pleased at having arrived at this long wished for spot, and in order to add in some measure to the general pleasure which seemed to pervade our little community, we ordered a dram to be issued to each person; this soon produced the fiddle, and they spent the evening with much hilarity, singing & dancing, and seemed as perfectly to forget their past toils, as they appeared regardless of those to come. ...

[*Tuesday May 14th 1805.*]   one of the party wounded a brown [grizzly] bear very badly, but being alone did not think proper to pursue him. In the evening the men in two of the rear canoes discovered a large brown bear lying in the open grounds about 300 paces from the river, and six of them went out to attack him, all good hunters; they took the advantage of a small eminence which concealed them and got within 40 paces of him unperceived, two of them reserved their fires as had been previously conscerted, the four others fired nearly at the same time and put each his bullet through him, two of the balls passed through the bulk of both lobes of his lungs, in an instant this monster ran at them with open mouth, the two who had reserved their fir[e]s discharged their pieces at him as he came towards them, boath of them struck him, one only slightly and the other fortunately broke his shoulder, this however only retarded his motion for a mo-

ment only,   the men unable to reload their guns took to flight,
the bear pursued and had very nearly overtaken them before
they reached the river; two of the party betook themselves to
a canoe and the others seperated an[d] concealed themselves
among the willows, reloaded their pieces, each discharged his
piece at him as they had an opportunity   they struck him
several times again but the guns served only to direct the
bear to them,   in this manner he pursued two of them seper-
ately so close that they were obliged to throw aside their guns
and pouches and throw themselves into the river altho' the
bank was nearly twenty feet perpendicular; so enraged was
this anamal that he plunged into the river only a few feet behind the second man he had compelled [to] take refuge in
the water, when one of those who still remained on shore
shot him through the head and finally killed him;   they then
took him on shore and butch[er]ed him when they found
eight balls had passed through him in different directions;   the
bear being old the flesh was indifferent, they therefore only
took the skin and fleece, the latter made us several gallons of
oil.

It was after the sun had set before these men come up with
us, where we had been halted by an occurence, which I have
now to recappitulate, and which altho' happily passed without
ruinous injury, I cannot recollect but with the utmost trepidation and horror; this is the upseting and narrow escape of the
white perogue. It happened unfortunately for us this evening
that Charbono was at the helm of this Perogue, in stead of
Drewyer, who had previously steered her; Charbono cannot
swim and is perhaps the most timid waterman in the world;
perhaps it was equally unluckey that Capt. C. and myself
were both on shore at that moment, a circumstance which
rarely happened; and tho' we were on the shore opposite to
the perogue, were too far distant to be heard or to do more
than remain spectators of her fate; in this perogue were embarked, our papers, Instruments, books medicine, a great part
of our merchandize and in short almost every article indis-
pensibly necessary to further the views, or insure the success
of the enterprize in which we are now launched to the distance of 2200 miles. surfice it to say, that the Perogue was
under sail when a sudon squawl of wind struck her obliquely,
and turned her considerably,   the steersman allarmed, in stead
of puting, her before the wind, lufted her up into it,   the

wind was so violent that it drew the brace of the squarsail out of the hand of the man who was attending it, and instantly upset the perogue and would have turned her completely topsaturva, had it not have been from the resistance mad by the oarning [awning] against the water. In this situation Capt. C. and myself both. fired our guns to attract the attention if possible of the crew and ordered the halyards to be cut and the sail hawled in, but they did not hear us; such was their confusion and consternation at this moment, that they suffered the perogue to lye on her side for half a minute before they took the sail in. The perogue then wrighted but had filled within an inch of the gunwals; Charbono still crying to his god for mercy, had not yet recollected the rudder, nor could the repeated orders of the Bowsman, Cruzat, bring him to his recollection untill he threatend to shoot him instantly if he did not take hold of the rudder and do his duty. the waves by this time were runing very high, but the fortitude resolution and good conduct of Cruzat saved her; he ordered 2 of the men to throw out the water with some kettles that fortunately were convenient, while himself and two others rowed her as[h]ore, where she arrived scarcely above the water; we now took every article out of her and lay them to drane as well as we could for the evening, baled out the canoe and secured her.

there were two other men beside Charbono on board who could not swim, and who of course must also have perished had the perogue gone to the bottom. while the perogue lay on her side, finding I could not be heard, I for a moment forgot my own situation, and involluntarily droped my gun, threw aside my shot pouch and was in the act of unbuttoning my coat, before I recollected the folly of the attempt I was about to make; which was to throw myself into the river and indevour to swim to the perogue; the perogue was three hundred yards distant the waves so high that a perogue could scarcely live in any situation, the water excessively could, and the stream rappid; had I undertaken this project therefore, there was a hundred to one but what I should have paid the forfit of my life for the madness of my project, but this had the perogue been lost, I should have valued but little. After having all matters arranged for the evening as well as the nature of the circumstances would permit, we thought it a proper occasion to console ourselves and cheer the sperits of our

men and accordingly took a drink of grog and gave each
man a gill of sperits.

[*Thursday May 16th*]   The morning was fair and the
day proved favorable to our operations; by 4 oClock in the
evening our Instruments, Medicine, merchandize provision
&c, were perfectly dryed, repacked and put on board the
perogue. the loss we sustained was not so great as we had at
first apprehended; our medicine sustained the greatest injury,
several articles of which were intirely spoiled, and many others considerably injured,   the ballance of our losses consisted
of some gardin seeds, a small quantity of gunpowder, and a
few culinary articles which fell overboard and sunk. the Indian woman to whom I ascribe equal fortitude and resolution, with any person onboard at the time of the accedent,
caught and preserved most of the light articles which were
washed overboard.

in the early part of the day two of our men fired on a panther, a little below our encampment, and wounded it; they informed us that it was very large, had just killed a deer partly
devoured it, and in the act of concealing the ballance as they
discovered him. this morning a white bear toar Labuiche's
coat which he had left in the plains. . . .

[*Monday 20th 1805*]   The hunters returned this evening and informed us that the country continued much the
same in appearance as that we saw where we were or broken,
and that about five miles ab[ov]e the mouth of shell river a
handsome river of about fifty yards in width discharged itself
into the shell river on the Stard. or upper side;   this stream
we called Sâh-câ-ger we-âh or bird woman's River, after our
interpreter the Snake woman. . . .

[*Sunday May 26th 1805*]   In the after part of the
day I also walked out and ascended the river hills which I
found sufficiently fortiegueing. on arriving to the summit
[of] one of the highest points in the neighbourhood I thought
myself well repaid for my labour; as from this point I beheld
the Rocky Mountains for the first time,   I could only discover
a few of the most elivated points above the horizon, the most
remarkable of which by my pocket compass I found bore N.
65° W. being a little to the N. of the N.W. extremity of the
range of broken mountains seen this morning by Capt. C.

these points of the Rocky Mountains were covered with snow
and the sun shone on it in such manner as to give me the
most plain and satisfactory view. while I viewed these mountains I felt a secret pleasure in finding myself so near the
head of the heretofore conceived boundless Missouri; but
when I reflected on the difficulties which this snowey barrier
would most probably throw in my way to the Pacific, and the
sufferings and hardships of myself and party in thim, it in
some measure counterballanced the joy I had felt in the first
moments in which I gazed on them; but as I have always
held it a crime to anticipate evils I will believe it a good comfortable road untill I am compelled to believe differently.

late this evening we passed a very bad rappid which
reached quite across the river;   the party had considerable difficulty in ascending it altho' they doubled their crews and
used both the rope and the pole. while they were passing this
rappid a female Elk and it's fawn swam down through the
waves which ran very high, hence the name of Elk rappids
which they instantly gave this place,   these are the most considerable rappids which we have yet seen on the missouri and
in short the only place where there has appeared to be a sud-
don decent. This is truly a desert barren country and I feel
myself still more convinced of it's being a continuation of the
black hills. we have continued every day to pass more or less
old stick lodges of the Indians in the timbered points, there
are two even in this little bottom where we lye. . . .

[*Wednesday May 29th 1805*]   Last night we were all
allarmed by a large buffaloe Bull, which swam over from the
opposite shore and coming along side of the white perogue,
climbed over it to land,   he then allarmed ran up the bank in
full speed directly towards the fires, and was within 18 inches
of the heads of some of the men who lay sleeping before the
centinel could allarm him or make him change his course,
still more alarmed, he now took his direction immediately
towards our lodge, passing between 4 fires and within a few
inches of the heads of one range of the men as they yet lay
sleeping,   when he came near the tent, my dog saved us by
causing him to change his course a second time, which he did
by turning a little to the right, and was quickly out of sight,
leaving us by this time all in an uproar with our guns in
o[u]r hands, enquiring of each other the ca[u]se of the
alarm, which after a few moments was explained by the cen-

tinel: we were happy to find no one hirt. The next morning we found that the buffaloe in passing the perogue had trodden on a rifle, which belonged to Capt. Clark's black man, who had negligently left her in the perogue, the rifle was much bent, he had also broken the spindle; pivit, and shattered the stock of one of the blunderbushes on board, with this damage I felt well content, happey indeed, that we had sustaned no further injury,

it appears that the white perogue, which contains our most valuable stores is attended by some evil gennii.

This morning we set out at an early hour and proceded as usual by the Chord. at the distance of 2½ Miles passed a handsome river which discharged itself on the Lard. side, I walked on shore and ascended this river about a mile and a half in order to examine it. the water of this River is clearer much than any we have met with great abundance of the Argalia or Bighorned animals in the high country through which this river passes. Cap. C. who assended this R. much higher than I did has thought proper to call it *Judieths* River. on the Missouri just above the entrance of the *Judith River* I counted the remains of the fires of 126 Indian lodges which appeared to be of very recent date perhaps 12 or 15 days. Capt. Clark also saw a large encamp[m]ent just above the entrance of this river on the Stard. side of reather older date, probably. they were the same Indians. The Indian woman with us ex[a]mined the mockersons which we found at these encampments and informed us that they were not of her nation the Snake Indians, but she beleived they were some of the Indians who inhabit the country on this side of [the] Rocky Mountains and North of the Missoury and I think it most probable that they were the Minetaries of Fort de Prarie.

Today we passed on the Stard. side the remains of a vast many mangled carcases of Buffalow which had been driven over a precipice of 120 feet by the Indians and perished; the water appeared to have washed away a part of this immence pile of slaughter and still their remained the fragments of at least a hundred carcases they created a most horrid stench. in this manner the Indians of the Missouri distroy vast herds of buffaloe at a stroke. . . .

[*Friday May 31st 1805*—] This morning we proceeded at an early hour with the two perogues leaving the canoes and crews to bring on the meat of the two buffaloe that were killed last evening and which had not been brought in as it was late and a little off the river. soon after we got under way it began to rain and continued untill meridian when it ceased but still remained cloudy through the ballance of the day. The obstructions of rocky points and riffles still continue as yesterday; at those places the men are compelled to be in the water even to their armpits, and the water is yet very could, and so frequent are those point that they are one fourth of their time in the water, added to this the banks and bluffs along which they are obliged to pass are so slippery and the mud so tenacious that they are unable to wear their mockersons, and in that situation draging the heavy burthen of a canoe and walking acasionally for several hundred yards over the sharp fragments of rocks which tumble from the clifts and garnish the borders of the river; in short their labour is incredibly painfull and great, yet those faithfull fellows bear it without a murmur. The toe rope of the white perogue, the only one indeed of hemp, and that on which we most depended, gave way today at a bad point, the perogue swung and but slightly touched a rock; yet was very near overseting; I fear her evil gennii will play so many pranks with her that she will go to the bottomm some of those days.

The hills and river Clifts which we passed today exhibit a most romantic appearance. The bluffs of the river rise to the hight of from 2 to 300 feet and in most places nearly perpendicular; they are formed of remarkable white sandstone which is sufficiently soft to give way readily to the impression of water; two or thre thin horizontal stratas of white freestone, on which the rains or water make no impression, lie imbeded in these clifts of soft stone near the upper part of them; the earth on the top of these Clifts is a dark rich loam, which forming a graduly ascending plain extends back from ½ a mile to a mile where the hills commence and rise abruptly to a hight of about 300 feet more. The water in the course of time in decending from those hills and plains on either side of the river has trickled down the soft sand clifts and woarn it into a thousand grotesque figures, which with the help of a little immagination and an oblique view, at a distance are made to represent eligant ranges of lofty freestone buildings, having their parapets well stocked with statuary; collumns of various sculpture both grooved and plain, are also seen supporting long galleries in front of those buildings; in other places on a much nearer approach and with the

help of less immagination we see the remains or ruins of eligant buildings; some collumns standing and almost entire
with their pedestals and capitals; others retaining their
pedestals but deprived by time or accident of their capitals,
some lying prostrate an broken othe[r]s in the form of vast
pyramids of connic structure bearing a serees of other pyramids on their tops becoming less as they ascend and finally
terminating in a sharp point. nitches and alcoves of various
forms and sizes are seen at different hights as we pass. the
thin stratas of hard freestone intermixed with the soft sandstone seems to have aided the water in forming this curious
scenery. As we passed on it seemed as if those seens of
visionary inchantment would never have and [an] end; for
here it is too that nature presents to the view of the traveler
vast ranges of walls of tolerable workmanship, so perfect
indeed are those walls that I should have thought that nature
had attempted here to rival the human art of masonry had I
not recollected that she had first began her work. These walls
rise to the hight in many places of 100 feet, are perpendicular, with two regular faces and are from one to 12 feet thick,
each wall retains the same thickness at top which it possesses
at bottom. . . .

[*Monday June 3rd 1805*]   This morning early we
passed over and formed a camp on the point formed by the
junction of the two large rivers. here in the course of the day
I continued my observations. An interesting question was
now to be determined; which of these rivers was the Missouri, or that river which the Minnetares call *Amahte Arzzha*
or Missouri, and which they had discribed to us as approaching very near to the Columbia river. to mistake the
stream at this period of the season, two months of the traveling season having now elapsed, and to ascend such stream
to the rocky Mountain or perhaps much further before we
could inform ourselves whether it did approach the Columbia
or not, and then be obliged to return and take the other
stream would not only loose us the whole of this season but
would probably so dishearten the party that it might defeat
the expedition altogether. convinced we were that the utmost
circumspection and caution was necessary in deciding on the
stream to be taken. to this end an investigation of both
streams was the first thing to be done; to learn their widths,
debths, comparative rappidity of their courants and thence

the comparitive bodies of water furnished by each; accordingly we dispatched two light canoes with three men in each up those streams; we also sent out several small parties by land with instructions to penetrate the country as far as they conveniently can permitting themselves time to return this evening and indeavour if possible to discover the distant bearing of those rivers by ascending the rising grounds.

between the time of my A. M. and meridian [observations] Capt. C. & myself stroled out to the top of the hights in the fork of these rivers from whence we had an extensive and most inchanting view; the country in every derection around us was one vast plain in which innumerable herds of Buffalow were seen attended by their shepperds the wolves; the solatary antelope which now had their young were distributed over it's face; some herds of Elk were also seen; the verdure perfectly cloathed the ground, the weather was pleasant and fair; to the South we saw a range of lofty mountains which we supposed to be a continuation of the S. Mountains, stretching themselves from S. E. to N. W. terminating abbrubtly about S. West from us; these were partially covered with snow; behind these Mountains and at a great distance, a second and more lofty range of mountains appeared to strech across the country in the same direction with the others, reaching from West, to the N of N. W., where their snowey tops lost themselves beneath the horizon. this last range was perfectly covered with snow. the direction of the rivers could be seen but little way, soon loosing the break of our channels, to our view, in the common plain. on our return to camp we boar a little to the left and discovered a handsome little river falling into the N. fork on Lard. side about 1½ Mls. above our camp. this little river has as much timber in it's bottoms as either of the larger streams.

we took the width of the two rivers, found the left hand or S. fork 372 yards and the N. fork 200. The no[r]th fork is deeper than the other but it's courant not so swift; it's waters run in the same boiling and roling manner which has uniformly characterized the Missouri throughout it's whole course so far; it's waters are of a whitish brown colour very thick and terbid, also characteristic of the Missouri; while the South fork is perfectly transparent runds very rappid but with a smoth unriffled surface it's bottom composed of round and flat smooth stones like most rivers issuing from a mountainous country. the bed of the N. fork composed of some

gravel but principally mud; in short the air & character of
this river is so precisely that of the missouri below that the
party with very few exceptions have already pronounced the
N. fork to be the Missouri; myself and Capt. C. not quite so
precipitate have not yet decided but if we were to give our
opinions I believe we should be in the minority, certain it is
that the North fork gives the colouring matter and character
which is retained from hence to the gulph of Mexico. I am
confident that this river rises in and passes a great distance
through an open plain country I expect that it has some of
it's sou[r]ces on the Eastern side of the rocky mountain
South of the Saskashawan, but that it dose not penetrate the
first range of these Mountains. and that much the greater
part of it's sources are in a northwardly direction towards the
lower and middle parts of the Saskashawan in the open
plains. convinced I am that if it penetrated the Rocky Mountains to any great distance it's waters would be clearer unless
it should run an immence distance indeed after leaving those
mountains through these level plains in order to acquire it's
turbid hue. what astonishes us a little is that the Indians who
appeared to be so well acquainted with the geography of this
country should not have mentioned this river on wright hand
if it be not the Missouri; *the river that scolds at all others,* as
they call it if there is in reality such an one, ought agreeably
to their account, to have fallen in a considerable distance below, and on the other hand if this right hand or N. fork be
the Missouri I am equally astonished at their not mentioning
the S. fork which they must have passed in order to get to
those large falls which they mention on the Missouri. thus
have our cogitating faculties been busily employed all day.

Those who have remained at camp today have been busily
engaged in dressing skins for cloathing, notwithstanding that
many of them have their feet so mangled and bruised with
the stones and rough ground over which they passed barefoot,
that they can scarcely walk or stand; at least it is with great
pain they do either. for some days past they were unable to
wear their mockersons; they have fallen off considerably, but
nothwithstanding the difficulties past, or those which seem
now to menace us, they still remain perfectly cheerful. In the
evening the parties whom we had sent out returned agreeably
to instructions. The parties who had been sent up the rivers
in canoes informed that they ascended some distance and had

then left their canoes and walked up the rivers a considerable distance further barely leaving themselves time to return; the North fork was not so rappid as the other and afforded the easiest navigation of course; six (7) feet appeared to be the shallowest water of the S. Branch and 5 feet that of the N. Their accounts were by no means satisfactory nor did the information we acquired bring us nigher to the decision of our question or determine us which stream to take.

Capt. C. and myself concluded to set out early the next morning with a small party each, and ascend these rivers untill we could perfectly satisfy ourselves of the one, which it would be most expedient for us to take on our main journey to the Pacific. accordingly it was agreed that I should ascend the right hand fork and he the left. I gave orders to Serj. Pryor Drewyer, Shields, Windsor, Cruzatte and La Page to hold themselves in readiness to accompany me in the morning. Capt. Clark also selected Reubin & Joseph Fields, Sergt. Cass, Shannon and his black man York, to accompany him. we agreed to go up those rivers one day and a halfs march or further if it should appear necessary to satisfy us more fully of the point in question. I take my Octant with me also, this I confide [to] La Page. . . .

[*Friday June 7th 1805*—]   It continued to rain almost without intermission last night and as I expected we had a most disagreable and wrestless night. Our camp possessing no allurements, we left our watery beads at an early hour and continued our rout down the river. it still continues to rain the wind hard from N.E. and could. the grownd remarkably, slipry, insomuch that we were unable to walk on the sides of the bluffs where we had passed as we ascended the river. notwithstanding the rain that has now fallen the earth of these bluffs is not wet to a greater debth than 2 inches; in it's present state it is precisely like walking over frozen grownd which is thawed to small debth and slips equally as bad. this clay not only appears to require more water to saturate it as I before observed than any earth I ever observed but when saturated it appcars on the other hand to yeald it's moisture with equal difficulty.

In passing along the face of one of these bluffs today I sliped at a narrow pass of about 30 yards in length and but for a quick and fortunate recovery by means of my espontoon I should been precipitated into the river down a craggy pricipice of about ninety feet. I had scarcely reached a place on which I could stand with tolerable safety even with the assistance of my espoontoon before I heard a voice behind me cry out god god Capt. what shall I do on turning about I found it was Windsor who had sliped and fallen abut the center of this narrow pass and was lying prostrate on his belley, with his wright hand arm and leg over the precipice while he was holding on with the left arm and foot as well as he could which appeared to be with much difficulty. I discovered his danger and the trepidation which he was in gave me still further concern for I expected every instant to see him loose his strength and slip off; altho' much allarmed at his situation I disguised my feelings and spoke very calmly to him and assured him that he was in no kind of danger, to take the knife out of his belt behind him with his wright hand and dig a hole with it in the face of the bank to receive his wright foot which he did and then raised himself to his knees; I then directed him to take off his mockersons and to come forward on his hands and knees holding the knife in one hand and the gun in the other this he happily effected and escaped. those who were some little distance bhind returned by my orders and waded the river at the foot of the bluff where the water was breast deep.

it was useless we knew to attempt the plains on this part of the river in consequence of the numerous steep ravines which intersected and which were quite as bad as the river bluffs. we therefore continued our rout down the river sometimes in the mud and water of the bottom lands, at others in the river to our breasts and when the water became so deep that we could not wade we cut footsteps in the face of the steep bluffs with our knives and proceded. we continued our disagreeable march th[r]ough the rain mud and water untill late in the evening having traveled only about 18 Miles, and encamped in an old Indian stick lodge which afforded us a dry and comfortable shelter. during the day we had killed six deer some of them in very good order altho' none of them had yet entirely discarded their winter coats. we had reserved and brought with us a good supply of the best peices; we roasted and eat a hearty supper of our venison not having taisted a mosel before during the day; I now laid myself down on some willow boughs to a comfortable nights rest, and felt indeed as if I was fully repaid for the toil and pain of the day, so much will a good shelter, a dry bed, and comfortable supper revive the sperits of the waryed, wet and hungry traveler.

George Catlin

Buffalo Country

George Catlin (1796–1872), a lawyer and largely self-taught painter, said that his life's mission crystallized for him in the early 1820s. After observing a delegation of Indians from "the wilds of the Far West" pass through Philadelphia, Catlin decided that "nothing short of the loss of my life shall prevent me from visiting their country, and of becoming their historian." In 1832, Catlin began making his notable pictorial record of the tribes of the Upper Missouri; in 1834, he accompanied mounted dragoons into the plains country of the Comanche and Pawnee; and in 1836, he became the first white man to visit the quarries in Minnesota where Indians gathered the pipestone mineral now called catlinite in honor of the artist. The result of these initial travels (he would later visit Indians on the Pacific coast and spend six years with tribes in Central and South America) is the most comprehensive pictorial record we have of Western Indians and their wilderness homelands before their destruction. Aware of the urgency of his mission, Catlin worked with great energy and speed. In one period of eighty-six days, he traveled fifteen hundred miles and painted sixty-six portraits, forty-four village and ceremonial scenes, and twenty-five wilderness scenes. Catlin carried his wilderness paintings to the eastern states, to England, and to Paris, where Charles Baudelaire found them to have "something of the mysterious that pleases me more than I can say." The same passion that makes his paintings so striking lifts his writing to moments of eloquence, as in the visionary passage from Letters and Notes on the Manners, Customs, and Conditions of North American Indians *(1841), where Catlin makes the earliest plea on record for protection of wilderness in a national park.*

The buffalo calf, during the first six months is red, and has so much the appearance of a red calf in cultivated fields, that it could easily be mingled and mistaken amongst them. In the fall, when it changes its hair it takes a brown coat for the winter, which it always retains. In pursuing a large herd of buffaloes at the season when their calves are but a few weeks old, I have often been exceedingly amused with the curious manœuvres of these shy little things. Amidst the thundering confusion of a throng of several hundreds or several thousands of these animals, there will be many of the calves that lose sight of their dams; and being left behind by the throng, and the swift passing hunters, they endeavour to secrete themselves, when they are exceedingly put to it on a level prairie, where nought can be seen but the short grass of six or eight inches in height, save an occasional bunch of wild sage, a few inches higher, to which the poor affrighted things will run, and dropping on their knees, will push their noses under it, and into the grass, where they will stand for hours, with their eyes shut, imagining themselves securely hid, whilst they are standing up quite straight upon their hind feet and can easily be seen at several miles distance. It is a familiar amusement for us accustomed to these scenes, to retreat back over the ground where we have just escorted the herd, and approach these little trembling things, which stubbornly maintain their positions, with their noses pushed under the grass, and their eyes strained upon us, as we dismount from our horses and are passing around them. From this fixed position they are sure not to move, until hands are laid upon them, and then for the skins of a novice, we can extend our sympathy; or if he can preserve the skin on his bones from the furious buttings of its head, we know how to congratulate him on his signal success and good luck. In these desperate struggles, for a moment, the little thing is conquered, and makes no further resistance. And I have often, in concurrence with a known custom of the country, held my hands over the eyes of the calf, and breathed a few strong breaths into its nostrils; after which I have, with my hunting companions, rode several miles into our encampment, with the little prisoner busily following the heels of my horse the whole

From George Catlin, *Letters and Notes on the Manners, Customs, and Conditions of the North American Indians, Written during Eight Years' Travel Amongst the Wildest Tribes of Indians in North America* [1832–1839] (New York: Wiley and Putnam, 1841).

way; as closely and as affectionately as its instinct would attach it to the company of its dam!

This is one of the most extraordinary things that I have met with in the habits of this wild country, and although I had often heard of it, and felt unable exactly to believe it, I am now willing to bear testimony to the fact, from the numerous instances which I have witnessed since I came into the country. During the time that I resided at this post, in the spring of the year, on my way up the river, I assisted (in numerous hunts of the buffalo, with the Fur Company's men,) in bringing in, in the above manner, several of these little prisoners, which sometimes followed for five or six miles close to our horses' heels, and even into the Fur Company's Fort, and into the stables where our horses were led. In this way, before I left for the head waters of the Missouri, I think we had collected about a dozen, which Mr. Laidlaw was successfully raising with the aid of a good milch cow, and which were to be committed to the care of Mr. Chouteau to be transported by the return of the steamer, to his extensive plantation in the vicinity of St. Louis.*

It is truly a melancholy contemplation for the traveller in this country, to anticipate the period which is not far distant, when the last of these noble animals, at the hands of white and red men, will fall victims to their cruel and improvident rapacity; leaving these beautiful green fields, a vast and idle waste, unstocked and unpeopled for ages to come, until the bones of the one and the traditions of the other will have vanished, and left scarce an intelligible trace behind.

That the reader should not think me visionary in these contemplations, or romancing in making such assertions, I will hand him the following item of the extravagancies which are practiced in these regions, and rapidly leading to the results which I have just named.

When I first arrived at this place, on my way up the river, which was in the month of May, in 1832, and had taken up my lodgings in the Fur Company's Fort, Mr. Laidlaw, of whom I have before spoken, and also his chief clerk, Mr.

---

* The fate of these poor little prisoners, I was informed on my return to St. Louis a year afterwards, was a very disastrous one. The steamer having a distance of 1600 miles to perform, and lying a week or two on sand bars, in a country where milk could not be procured, they all perished but one, which is now flourishing in the extensive fields of this gentleman.

Halsey, and many of their men, as well as the chiefs of the
Sioux, told me, that only a few days before I arrived, (when
an immense herd of buffaloes had showed themselves on the
opposite side of the river, almost blackening the plains for a
great distance,) a party of five or six hundred Sioux Indians on
horseback, forded the river about mid-day, and spending a few
hours amongst them, recrossed the river at sun-down and came
into the Fort with *fourteen hundred fresh buffalo tongues*,
which were thrown down in a mass, and for which they
required but a few gallons of whiskey, which was soon de-
molished, indulging them in a little, and harmless carouse.

This profligate waste of the lives of these noble and useful
animals, when, from all that I could learn, not a skin or a
pound of the meat (except the tongues), was brought in,
fully supports me in the seemingly extravagant predictions
that I have made as to their extinction, which I am certain is
near at hand. In the above extravagant instance, at a season
when their skins were without fur and not worth taking off,
and their camp was so well stocked with fresh and dried
meat, that they had no occasion for using the flesh, there is a
fair exhibition of the improvident character of the savage,
and also of his recklessness in catering for his appetite, so
long as the present inducements are held out to him in his
country, for its gratification.

In this singular country, where the poor Indians have no
laws or regulations of society, making it a vice or an impropriety to drink to excess, they think it no harm to indulge in
the delicious beverage, as long as they are able to buy
whiskey to drink. They look to white men as wiser than
themselves, and able to set them examples—they see none of
these in their country but sellers of whiskey, who are constantly tendering it to them, and most of them setting the example by using it themselves; and they easily acquire a taste,
that to be catered for, where whiskey is sold at sixteen dollars
per gallon, soon impoverishes them, and must soon strip the
skin from the last buffalo's back that lives in their country, to
"be dressed by their squaws" and vended to the Traders for a
pint of diluted alcohol.

From the above remarks it will be seen, that not only the
red men, but red men and white, have aimed destruction at
the race of these animals; and with them, *beasts* have turned
hunters of buffaloes in this country, slaying them, however, in
less numbers, and for far more laudable purpose than that of

selling their skins. The white wolves, of which I have spoken in a former epistle, follow the herds of buffaloes as I have said, from one season to another, glutting themselves on the carcasses of those that fall by the deadly shafts of their enemies, or linger with disease or old age to be dispatched by these sneaking cormorants, who are ready at all times kindly to relieve them from the pangs of a lingering death.

Whilst the herd is together, the wolves never attack them, as they instantly gather for combined resistance, which they effectually make. But when the herds are travelling, it often happens that an aged or wounded one, lingers at a distance behind, and when fairly out of sight of the herd, is set upon by these voracious hunters, which often gather to the number of fifty or more, and are sure at last to torture him to death, and use him up at a meal. The buffalo, however, is a huge and furious animal, and when his retreat is cut off, makes desperate and deadly resistance, contending to the last moment for the right of life—and oftentimes deals death by wholesale, to his canine assailants, which he is tossing into the air or stamping to death under his feet.

During my travels in these regions, I have several times come across such a gang of these animals surrounding an old or a wounded bull, where it would seem, from appearances, that they had been for several days in attendance, and at intervals desperately engaged in the effort to take his life. But a short time since, as one of my hunting companions and myself were returning to our encampment with our horses loaded with meat, we discovered at a distance, a huge bull, encircled with a gang of white wolves; we rode up as near as we could without driving them away, and being within pistol shot, we had a remarkably good view, where I sat for a few moments and made a sketch in my note-book; after which, we rode up and gave the signal for them to disperse, which they instantly did, withdrawing themselves to the distance of fifty or sixty rods, when we found, to our great surprise, that the animal had made desperate resistance, until his eyes were entirely eaten out of his head—the grizzle of his nose was mostly gone—his tongue was half eaten off, and the skin and flesh of his legs torn almost literally into strings. In this tattered and torn condition, the poor old veteran stood bracing up in the midst of his devourers, who had ceased hostilities for a few minutes, to enjoy a sort of parley, recovering strength and preparing to resume the attack in a few moments again. In this group, some were reclining, to gain breath, whilst others were sneaking about and licking their chaps in anxiety for a renewal of the attack; and others, less lucky, had been crushed to death by the feet or the horns of the bull. I rode nearer to the pitiable object as he stood bleeding and trembling before me, and said to him, "Now is your time, old fellow, and you had better be off." Though blind and nearly destroyed, there seemed evidently to be a recognition of a friend in me, as he straightened up, and, trembling with excitement, dashed off at full speed upon the prairie, in a straight line. We turned our horses and resumed our march, and when we had advanced a mile or more, we looked back, and on our left, where we saw again the ill-fated animal surrounded by his tormentors, to whose insatiable voracity he unquestionably soon fell a victim.

Thus much I wrote of the buffaloes, and of the accidents that befall them, as well as of the fate that awaits them; and before I closed my book, I strolled out one day to the shade of a plum-tree, where I laid in the grass on a favourite bluff, and wrote thus:—

"It is generally supposed, and familiarly said, that a man '*falls*' into a rêverie; but I seated myself in the shade a few minutes since, resolved to *force* myself into one; and for this purpose I laid open a small pocket-map of North America, and excluding my thoughts from every other object in the world, I soon succeeded in producing the desired illusion. This little chart, over which I bent, was seen in all its parts, as nothing but the green and vivid reality. I was lifted up upon an imaginary pair of wings, which easily raised and held me floating in the open air, from whence I could behold beneath me the Pacific and the Atlantic Oceans—the great cities of the East, and the mighty rivers. I could see the blue chain of the great lakes at the North—the Rocky Mountains, and beneath them and near their base, the vast, and almost boundless plains of grass, which were speckled with the bands of grazing buffaloes!

"The world turned gently around, and I examined its surface; continent after continent passed under my eye, and yet amidst them all, I saw not the vast and vivid green, that is spread like a carpet over the Western wilds of my own country. I saw not elsewhere in the world, the myriad herds of buffaloes—my eyes scanned in vain, for they were not. And when I turned again to the wilds of my native land, I beheld them all in motion! For the distance of several hundreds of miles from North to South, they were wheeling about in vast columns and herds—some were scattered, and ran with furious wildness—some lay dead, and others were pawing the earth for a hiding-place—some were sinking down and dying, gushing out their life's blood in deep-drawn sighs—and others were contending in furious battle for the life they possessed, and the ground that they stood upon. They had long since assembled from the thickets, and secret haunts of the deep forest, into the midst of the treeless and bushless plains, as the place for their safety. I could see in an hundred places, amid the wheeling bands, and on their skirts and flanks, the leaping wild horse darting among them. I saw not the arrows, nor heard the twang of the sinewy bows that sent them; but I saw their victims fall!—on other steeds that rushed along their sides, I saw the glistening lances, which seemed to lay across them; their blades were blazing in the sun, till dipped in blood, and then I lost them! In other parts (and there were many), the vivid flash of *fire-arms* was seen—*their* victims fell too, and over their dead bodies hung suspended in air, little clouds of whitened smoke, from under which the flying horsemen had darted forward to mingle again with, and deal death to, the trampling throng.

"So strange were men mixed (both red and white) with the countless herds that wheeled and eddyed about, that all below seemed one vast extended field of battle—whole armies, in some places, seemed to blacken the earth's surface;—in other parts, regiments, battalions, wings, platoons, rank and file, and *"Indian-file"*—all were in motion; and death and destruction seemed to be the watch-word amongst them. In their turmoil, they sent up great clouds of dust, and with them came the mingled din of groans and trampling hoofs, that seemed like the rumbling of a dreadful cataract, or the roaring of distant thunder. Alternate pity and admiration harrowed up in my bosom and my brain, many a hidden thought; and amongst them a few of the beautiful notes that were once sung, and exactly in point: *'Quadrupedante putrem sonitu quatit ungula campum.'* Even such was the din amidst the quadrupeds of these vast plains. And from the craggy cliffs of the Rocky Mountains also were seen descending into the valley, the myriad Tartars, who had not horses to ride, but before their well-drawn bows the fattest of the herds were falling. Hundreds and thousands were strewed upon the

plains—they were flayed, and their reddened carcasses left;
and about them bands of wolves, and dogs, and buzzards
were seen devouring them. Contiguous, and in sight, were the
distant and feeble smokes of wigwams and villages, where the
skins were dragged, and dressed for white man's luxury!
where they were all sold for *whiskey*, and the poor Indians
laid drunk, and were crying. I cast my eyes into the towns
and cities of the East, and there I beheld buffalo robes hanging at almost every door for traffic; and I saw also the curling
smokes of a thousand *Stills*—and I said, 'Oh insatiable man,
is thy avarice such! wouldst thou tear the skin from the back
of the last animal of this noble race, *and rob thy fellow-man
of his meat, and for it give him poison!*' "

Many are the rudenesses and wilds in Nature's works, which
are destined to fall before the deadly axe and desolating
hands of cultivating man; and so amongst her ranks of *living*,
of beast and human, we often find noble stamps, or beautiful
colours, to which our admiration clings; and even in the overwhelming march of civilized improvements and refinements
do we love to cherish their existence, and lend our efforts to
preserve them in their primitive rudeness. Such of Nature's
works are always worthy of our preservation and protection;
and the further we become separated (and the face of the
country) from that pristine wildness and beauty, the more
pleasure does the mind of enlightened man feel in recurring
to those scenes, when he can have them preserved for his
eyes and his mind to dwell upon.

Of such "rudenesses and wilds," Nature has no where
presented more beautiful and lovely scenes, than those of the
vast prairies of the West; and of *man* and *beast*, no nobler
specimens than those who inhabit them—the *Indian* and the
buffalo—joint and original tenants of the soil, and fugitives
together from the approach of civilized man; they have fled
to the great plains of the West, and there, under an equal
doom, they have taken up their *last abode*, where their race
will expire, and their bones will bleach together.

It may be that *power* is *right*, and *voracity* a *virtue*; and
that these people, and these noble animals, are *righteously*
doomed to an issue that *will* not be averted. It can be easily
proved—we have a civilized science that can easily do it, or
anything else that may be required to cover the iniquities of
civilized man in catering for his unholy appetites. It can be

proved that the weak and ignorant have no *rights*—that there can be no virtue in darkness—that God's gifts have no meaning or merit until they are appropriated by civilized man—by him brought into the light, and converted to his use and luxury. We have a mode of reasoning (I forget what it is called) by which all this can be proved, and even more. The *word* and the *system* are entirely of *civilized* origin; and latitude is admirably given to them in proportion to the increase of civilized wants, which often require a *judge* to overrule the laws of nature. I say that *we* can prove such things; but an *Indian* cannot. It is a mode of reasoning unknown to him in his nature's simplicity, but admirably adapted to subserve the interests of the enlightened world, who are always their own judges, when dealing with the savage; and who, in the present refined age, have many appetites that can only be lawfully indulged, by proving God's laws defective.

It is not enough in this polished and extravagant age, that we get from the Indian his lands, and the very clothes from his back, but the food from their mouths must be stopped, to add a new and useless article to the fashionable world's luxuries. The ranks must be thinned, and the race exterminated, of this noble animal, and the Indians of the great plains left without the means of supporting life, that white men may figure a few years longer, enveloped in buffalo robes—that they may spread them, for their pleasure and elegance, over the backs of their sleighs, and trail them ostentatiously amidst the busy throng, as things of beauty and elegance that had been made for them!

Reader! listen to the following calculations, and forget them not. The buffaloes (the quadrupeds from whose backs your beautiful robes were taken, and whose myriads were once spread over the whole country, from the Rocky Mountains to the Atlantic Ocean) have recently fled before the appalling appearance of civilized man, and taken up their abode and pasturage amid the almost boundless prairies of the West. An instinctive dread of their deadly foes, who made an easy prey of them whilst grazing in the forest, has led them to seek the midst of the vast and treeless plains of grass, as the spot where they would be least exposed to the assaults of their enemies; and it is exclusively in those desolate fields of silence (yet of beauty) that they are to be found—and over these vast steppes, or prairies, have they fled, like the Indian, towards the "setting sun;" until their bands have been crowded together, and their limits confined to a narrow strip of country on this side of the Rocky Mountains.

This strip of country, which extends from the province of Mexico to lake Winnepeg on the North, is almost one entire plain of grass, which is, and ever must be, useless to cultivating man. It is here, and here chiefly, that the buffaloes dwell; and with, and hovering about them, live and flourish the tribes of Indians, whom God made for the enjoyment of that fair land and its luxuries.

It is a melancholy contemplation for one who has travelled as I have, through these realms, and seen this noble animal in all its pride and glory, to contemplate it so rapidly wasting from the world, drawing the irresistible conclusion too, which one must do, that its species is soon to be extinguished, and with it the peace and happiness (if not the actual existence) of the tribes of Indians who are joint tenants with them, in the occupancy of these vast and idle plains.

And what a splendid contemplation too, when one (who has travelled these realms, and can duly appreciate them) imagines them as they *might* in future be seen, (by some great protecting policy of government) preserved in their pristine beauty and wildness, in a *magnificent park*, where the world could see for ages to come, the native Indian in his classic attire, galloping his wild horse, with sinewy bow, and shield and lance, amid the fleeting herds of elks and buffaloes. What a beautiful and thrilling specimen for America to preserve and hold up to the view of her refined citizens and the world, in future ages! A *nation's Park*, containing man and beast, in all the wild and freshness of their nature's beauty!

I would ask no other monument to my memory, nor any other enrolment of my name amongst the famous dead, than the reputation of having been the founder of such an institution.

Such scenes might easily have been preserved, and still could be cherished on the great plains of the West, without detriment to the country or its borders; for the tracts of country on which the buffaloes have assembled, are uniformly sterile, and of no available use to cultivating man.

It is on these plains, which are stocked with buffaloes, that the finest specimens of the Indian race are to be seen. It is here, that the savage is decorated in the richest costume. It is here, and here only, that his wants are all satisfied, and even the *luxuries* of life are afforded him in abundance. And here also is he the proud and honourable man (before he has had teachers or laws), above the imported wants, which beget meanness and vice; stimulated by ideas of honour and virtue, in which the God of Nature has certainly not curtailed him.

There are, by a fair calculation, more than 300,000 Indians, who are now subsisted on the flesh of the buffaloes, and by those animals supplied with all the luxuries of life which they desire, as they know of none others. The great variety of uses to which they convert the body and other parts of that animal, are almost incredible to the person who has not actually dwelt amongst these people, and closely studied their modes and customs. Every part of their flesh is converted into food, in one shape or another, and on it they entirely subsist. The robes of the animals are worn by the Indians instead of blankets—their skins when tanned, are used as coverings for their lodges, and for their beds; undressed, they are used for constructing canoes—for saddles, for bridles—l'arrêts, lasos, and thongs. The horns are shaped into ladles and spoons—the brains are used for dressing the skins—their bones are used for saddle trees—for war clubs, and scrapers for graining the robes—and others are broken up for the marrow-fat which is contained in them. Their sinews are used for strings and backs to their bows—for thread to string their beads and sew their dresses. The feet of the animals are boiled, with their hoofs, for the glue they contain, for fastening their arrow points, and many other uses. The hair from the head and shoulders, which is long, is twisted and braided into halters, and the tail is used for a fly brush. In this wise do these people convert and use the various parts of this useful animal, and with all these luxuries of life about them, and their numerous games, they are happy (God bless them) in the ignorance of the disastrous fate that awaits them.

Yet this interesting community, with its sports, its wildnesses, its languages, and all its manners and customs, could be perpetuated, and also the buffaloes, whose numbers would increase and supply them with food for ages and centuries to come, if a system of non-intercourse could be established and preserved. But such is not to be the case—the buffalo's doom is sealed, and with their extinction must assuredly sink into real despair and starvation, the inhabitants of these vast plains, which afford for the Indians, no other

possible means of subsistence; and they must at last fall a
prey to wolves and buzzards, who will have no other bones to
pick.

It seems hard and cruel, (does it not?) that we civilized
people with all the luxuries and comforts of the world about
us, should be drawing from the backs of these useful animals
the skins for our luxury, leaving their carcasses to be devoured by the wolves—that we should draw from that country,
some 150 or 200,000 of their robes annually, the greater part
of which are taken from animals that are killed expressly for
the robe, at a season when the meat is not cured and
preserved, and for each of which skins the Indian has received but a pint of whiskey!

Such is the fact, and that number or near it, are annually
destroyed, in addition to the number that is necessarily killed
for the subsistence of 300,000 Indians, who live entirely upon
them. It may be said, perhaps, that the Fur Trade of these
great western realms, which is now limited chiefly to the purchase of buffalo robes, is of great and national importance,
and should and must be encouraged. To such a suggestion I
would reply, by merely enquiring, (independently of the poor
Indians' disasters,) how much more advantageously would
such a capital be employed, both for the weal of the country
and for the owners, if it were invested in machines for the
manufacture of *woollen robes*, of equal and superior value
and beauty; thereby encouraging the growers of wool, and
the industrious manufacturer, rather than cultivating a taste
for the use of buffalo skins; which is just to be acquired, and
then, from necessity, to be dispensed with, when a few years
shall have destroyed the last of the animals producing them.

It may be answered, perhaps, that the necessaries of life
are given in exchange for these robes; but what, I would ask,
are the necessities in Indian life, where they have buffaloes in
abundance to live on? The Indian's necessities are entirely artificial—are all created; and when the buffaloes shall have
disappeared in his country, which will be within *eight* or *ten*
years, I would ask, who is to supply him with the necessaries
of life then? and I would ask, further, (and leave the question to be answered ten years hence), when the skin shall
have been stripped from the back of the last animal, who is
to resist the ravages of 300,000 starving savages; and in their
trains, 1,500,000 wolves, whom direst necessity will have
driven from their desolate and gameless plains, to seek for

the means of subsistence along our exposed frontier? God has everywhere supplied man in a state of Nature, with the necessaries of life, and before we destroy the game of his country, or teach him new desires, he has no wants that are not satisfied.

Amongst the tribes who have been impoverished and repeatedly removed, the necessaries of life are extended with a better grace from the hands of civilized man; 90,000 of such have already been removed, and they draw from Government some 5 or 600,000 dollars annually in cash; *which money passes immediately into the hands of white men*, and for it the necessaries of life *may be* abundantly furnished. But who, I would ask, are to furnish the Indians who have been instructed in this unnatural mode—living upon *such* necessaries, and even luxuries of life, extended to them by the hands of white men, when those annuities are at an end, and the skin is stripped from the last of the animals which God gave them for their subsistence?

Reader, I will stop here, lest you might forget to answer these important queries—these are questions which I know will puzzle the world—and, perhaps it is not right that I should ask them.

John James Audubon

Missouri River Journals

*John James Audubon (1785–1851) was nearly sixty when
he made his last trek into the wilderness in 1843 aboard a
fur-company boat bound for the country of the Upper Missouri and the Yellowstone. Born in Haiti and educated in
France, Audubon previously wandered through wilderness in
Kentucky and along the Mississippi in a search for specimens
that culminated in the 1,065 life-size figures of wild birds
found in the colored plates of his* Birds of America, *published
in four volumes between 1827 and 1838. In the five-vol-
ume* Ornithological Biography *accompanying this work (written in collaboration with William MacGillivray, who supplied
Latin nomenclature and scientific information), Audubon included sixty sketches, or "episodes," about wilderness landscapes, wildlife, and frontier characters and adventures.
Although he never reached the Rocky Mountains as he
wished, Audubon undertook his trip into the Western wilderness as part of his plan to observe and paint America's animals as he had its birds. The project,* The Viviparous
Quadrupeds of North America, *conducted in collaboration
with John Bachman, was continued after Audubon's death by
his two sons. Audubon's account of his last trip is sparked by
vivid, sometimes caustic, observations that give a rare immedi-
acy to his* Missouri River Journals, *first published in 1897;
and the prose of these private writings both criticizes and
avoids the affectations found in his earlier "episodes," written
expressly for the entertainment of the reader. In reading Audubon's remarks about Catlin, however, it must be remembered that eleven years had passed since Catlin's visit to the
same region, and in that time the Mandan Indians had been
decimated by smallpox brought to their country by a fur-
company boat in 1837.*

[*May 17, 1843, Wednesday*]   . . . We have seen
floating eight Buffaloes, one Antelope, and one Deer; how
great the destruction of these animals must be during high
freshets! The cause of their being drowned in such extraordinary numbers might not astonish one acquainted with the
habits of these animals, but to one who is not, it may be well
enough for me to describe it. Some few hundred miles above
us, the river becomes confined between high bluffs or cliffs,
many of which are nearly perpendicular, and therefore extremely difficult to ascend. When the Buffaloes have leaped or
tumbled down from either side of the stream, they swim with
ease across, but on reaching these walls, as it were, the poor
animals try in vain to climb them, and becoming exhausted
by falling back some dozens of times, give up the ghost, and
float down the turbid stream; their bodies have been known
to pass, swollen and putrid, the city of St. Louis. The most
extraordinary part of the history of these drowned Buffaloes
is, that the different tribes of Indians on the shores, are ever
on the lookout for them, and no matter how putrid their flesh
may be, provided the hump proves at all fat, they swim to
them, drag them on shore, and cut them to pieces; after
which they cook and eat this loathsome and abominable flesh,
even to the marrow found in the bones. In some instances
this has been done when the whole of the hair had fallen off,
from the rottenness of the Buffalo. Ah! Mr. Catlin, I am now
sorry to see and to read your accounts of the Indians *you*
saw—how very different they must have been from any that I
have seen! Whilst we were on the top of the high hills which
we climbed this morning, and looked towards the valley
beneath us, including the river, we were undetermined as to
whether we saw as much land dry as land overflowed; the immense flat prairie on the east side of the river looked not unlike a lake of great expanse, and immediately beneath us the
last freshet had left upwards of perhaps two or three hundred
acres covered by water, with numbers of water fowl on it,
but so difficult of access as to render our wishes to kill Ducks
quite out of the question. From the tops of the hills we saw
only a continual succession of other lakes, of the same form
and nature; and although the soil was of a fair, or even good,

From John James Audubon, *Missouri River Journals*, in *Audubon
and his Journals*, edited by Maria R. Audubon (New York: Charles
Scribner's Sons, 1897).

quality, the grass grew in tufts, separated from each other, and as it grows green in one spot, it dies and turns brown in another. We saw here no "carpeted prairies," no "velvety distant landscape;" and if these things are to be seen, why, the sooner we reach them the better. . . .

[*May 18, Thursday*]   Our good captain called us all up at a quarter before four this fair morning, to tell us that four barges had arrived from Fort Pierre, and that we might write a few letters, which Mr. Laidlow, one of the partners, would take to St. Louis for us. I was introduced to that gentleman and also to Major Dripps, the Indian agent. I wrote four short letters, which I put in an envelope addressed to the Messieurs Chouteau & Co., of St. Louis, who will post them, and we have hopes that some may reach their destination. The names of these four boats are "War Eagle," "White Cloud," "Crow-feather," and "Red-fish." We went on board one of them, and found it comfortable enough. They had ten thousand Buffalo robes on the four boats; the men live entirely on Buffalo meat and pemmican. They told us that about a hundred miles above us the Buffalo were by thousands, that the prairies were covered with dead calves, and the shores lined with dead of all sorts; that Antelopes were there also, and a great number of Wolves, etc.; therefore we shall see them after a while. . . .

[*May 20, Saturday*]   . . . Three White Wolves were seen this morning, and after a while we saw a fourth, of the brindled kind, which was trotting leisurely on, about 150 yards distant from the bank, where he had probably been feeding on some carrion or other. A shot from a rifle was quite enough to make him turn off up the river again, but farther from us, at a full gallop; after a time he stopped again, when the noise of our steam pipe started him, and we soon lost sight of him in the bushes. We saw three Deer in the flat of one of the prairies, and just before our dinner we saw, rather indistinctly, a number of Buffaloes, making their way across the hills about two miles distant; after which, however, we saw their heavy tracks in a well and deep cut line across the said hills. Therefore we are now in what is pronounced to be the "Buffalo country," and may expect to see more of these animals to-morrow. . . .

[*May 23, Tuesday*]   The wind blew from the south this morning and rather stiffly. We rose early, and walked about this famous Cedar Island, where we stopped to cut large red cedars [*Juniperus virginianus*] for one and a half hours; we started at half-past five, breakfasted rather before six, and were on the lookout for our hunters. *Hunters!* Only two of them had ever been on a Buffalo hunt before. One was lost almost in sight of the river. They only walked two or three miles, and camped. Poor Squires' first experience was a very rough one; for, although they made a good fire at first, it never was tended afterwards, and his pillow was formed of a buck's horn accidentally picked up near the place. Our Sioux Indian helped himself to another, and they all felt chilly and damp. They had forgotten to take any spirits with them, and their condition was miserable. As the orb of day rose as red as blood, the party started, each taking a different direction. But the wind was unfavorable; it blew up, not down the river, and the Buffaloes, Wolves, Antelopes, and indeed every animal possessed of the sense of smell, had scent of them in time to avoid them. There happened however to be attached to this party two good and true men, that may be called hunters. One was Michaux; the other a friend of his, whose name I do not know. It happened, by hook or by crook, that these two managed to kill four Buffaloes; but one of them was drowned, as it took to the river after being shot. Only a few pieces from a young bull, and its tongue, were brought on board, most of the men being too lazy, or too far off. to cut out even the tongues of the others; and thus it is that thousands multiplied by thousands of Buffaloes are murdered in senseless play, and their enormous carcasses are suffered to be the prey of the Wolf, the Raven and the Buzzard. . . .

[*Sunday, May 28*]   . . . Both shores were dotted by groups of Buffaloes as far as the eye could reach, and although many were near the banks they kept on feeding quietly till we nearly approached them; those at the distance of half a mile never ceased their avocations. A Gray Wolf was seen swimming across our bows, and some dozens of shots were sent at the beast, which made it open its mouth and raise its head, but it never stopped swimming away from us, as fast as possible; after a while it reached a sand-bar, and immediately afterwards first trotted, and then galloped off. Three Buffaloes also crossed ahead of us, but at some distance; they all reached the shore, and scrambled up the bank. We have run better this morning than for three or four days, and if fortunate enough may reach Fort Pierre sometime to-morrow. The prairies appear better now, the grass looks green, and probably the poor Buffaloes will soon regain their flesh. We have seen more than 2,000 this morning up to this moment—twelve o'clock. . . .

[*June 7, Wednesday*]   . . . We reached Fort Clark and the Mandan Villages at half-past seven this morning. Great guns were fired from the fort and from the "Omega," as our captain took the guns from the "Trapper" at Fort Pierre. The site of this fort appears a good one, though it is placed considerably below the Mandan Village. We saw some small spots cultivated, where corn, pumpkins, and beans are grown. The fort and village are situated on the high bank, rising somewhat to the elevation of a hill. The Mandan mud huts are very far from looking poetical, although Mr. Catlin has tried to render them so by placing them in regular rows, and all of the same size and form, which is by no means the case. But different travellers have different eyes! We saw more Indians than at any previous time since leaving St. Louis; and it is possible that there are a hundred huts, made of mud, all looking like so many potato winter-houses in the Eastern States. As soon as we were near the shore, every article that could conveniently be carried off was placed under lock and key, and our division door was made fast, as well as those of our own rooms. Even the axes and poles were put by. Our captain told us that last year they stole his cap and his shot-pouch and horn, and that it was through the interference of the first chief that he recovered his cap and horn; but that a squaw had his leather belt, and would not give it up. The appearance of these poor, miserable devils, as we approached the shore, was wretched enough. There they stood in the pelting rain and keen wind, covered with Buffalo robes, red blankets, and the like, some partially and most curiously besmeared with mud; and as they came on board, and we shook hands with each of them, I felt a clamminess that rendered the ceremony most repulsive. Their legs and naked feet were covered with mud. They looked at me with apparent curiosity, perhaps on account of my beard, which produced the same effect at Fort Pierre. They all looked very poor; and our captain says they are the *ne plus ultra* of thieves. It is said there are nearly three thousand men, women, and children that, during winter, cram themselves into these miserable hovels. . . .

[*June 9, Friday*]   . . . I went up to the top of the hills, bounding the beautiful prairie, by which we had stopped to repair something about the engine. We gathered some handsome lupines, of two different species, and many other curious plants. From this elevated spot we could see the wilderness to an immense distance; the Missouri looked as if only a brook, and our steamer a very small one indeed. At this juncture we saw two men running along the shore upwards, and I supposed they had seen an Elk or something else, of which they were in pursuit. Meantime, gazing around, we saw a large lake, where we are told that Ducks, Geese, and Swans breed in great numbers; this we intend also to visit when we come down. At this moment I heard the report of a gun from the point where the men had been seen, and when we reached the steamboat, we were told that a Buffalo had been killed. From the deck I saw a man swimming round the animal; he got on its side, and floated down the stream with it. The captain sent a parcel of men with a rope; the swimmer fastened this round the neck of the Buffalo, and with his assistance, for he now swam all the way, the poor beast was brought alongside; and as the tackle had been previously fixed, it was hauled up on the fore deck. Sprague took its measurements with me, which are as follows: length from nose to root of tail, 8 feet; height of fore shoulder to hoof, 4 ft. 9½ in.; height at the rump to hoof, 4 ft. 2 in. The head was cut off, as well as one fore and one hind foot. The head is so full of symmetry, and so beautiful, that I shall have a drawing of it to-morrow, as well as careful ones of the feet. Whilst the butchers were at work, I was highly interested to see one of our Indians cutting out the milk-bag of the cow and eating it, quite fresh and raw, in pieces somewhat larger than a hen's egg. One of the stomachs was partially washed in a bucket of water, and an Indian swallowed a large portion of this. Mr. Chardon brought the remainder on the upper deck and ate it uncleaned. I had a piece well cleaned and tasted it; to my utter astonishment, it was very good, but the idea was repulsive to me; besides which, I am not a meat-eater, as you know, except when other provisions fail. The animal was in good condition; and the whole carcass was cut up and dispersed among the men below, reserving the nicer portions for the cabin. This was accomplished with great rapidity; the blood was washed away in a trice, and half an hour afterwards no one would have known that a Buffalo had been dressed on deck. . . .

[*June 11, Sunday*]   This day has been tolerably fine, though windy. We have seen an abundance of game, a great number of Elks, common Virginian Deer, Mountain Rams in two places, and a fine flock of Sharp-tailed Grouse, that, when they flew off from the ground near us, looked very much like large Meadow Larks. They were on a prairie bordering a large patch of Artemisia, which in the distance presents the appearance of acres of cabbages. We have seen many Wolves and some Buffaloes. One young bull stood on the brink of a bluff, looking at the boat steadfastly for full five minutes; and as we neared the spot, he waved his tail, and moved off briskly. On another occasion, a young bull that had just landed at the foot of a very steep bluff was slaughtered without difficulty; two shots were fired at it, and the poor thing was killed by a rifle bullet. I was sorry, for we did not stop for it, and its happy life was needlessly ended. I saw near that spot a large Hawk, and also a very small Tamias, or Ground Squirrel. Harris saw a Spermophile, of what species none of us could tell. We have seen many Elks swimming the river, and they look almost the size of a well-grown mule. They stared at us, were fired at, at an enormous distance, it is true, and yet stood still. These animals are abundant beyond belief hereabouts. We have seen much remarkably handsome scenery, but nothing at all comparing with Catlin's descriptions; his book must, after all, be altogether a humbug. Poor devil! I pity him from the bottom of my soul; had he studied, and kept up to the old French proverb that says, "Bon renommé vaut mieux que ceinture doré," he might have become an "honest man"—the quintessence of God's works. . . .

. . . A heavy shower put off running a race; but we are to have a regular Buffalo hunt, where I must act only as a spectator; for, alas! I am now too near seventy to run and load whilst going at full gallop. . . .

[*June 16, Sunday*]   . . . All was arranged, and at half-past three this afternoon we were travelling towards Fort

Union. But hours previous to this, and before our scanty dinner, Owen had seen another bull, and Harris and Bell joined us in the hunt. The bull was shot at by McKenzie, who stopped its career, but as friend Harris pursued it with two of the hunters and finished it I was about to return, and thought sport over for the day. However, at this stage of the proceedings Owen discovered another bull making his way slowly over the prairie towards us. I was the only one who had balls, and would gladly have claimed the privilege of running him, but fearing I might make out badly on my slower steed, and so lose meat which we really needed, I handed my gun and balls to Owen McKenzie, and Bell and I went to an eminence to view the chase. Owen approached the bull, which continued to advance, and was now less than a quarter of a mile distant; either it did not see, or did not heed him, and they came directly towards each other, until they were about seventy or eighty yards apart, when the Buffalo started at a good run, and Owen's mare, which had already had two hard runs this morning, had great difficulty in preserving her distance. Owen, perceiving this, breathed her a minute, and then applying the whip was soon within shooting distance, and fired a shot which visibly checked the progress of the bull, and enabled Owen to soon be alongside of him, when the contents of the second barrel were discharged into the lungs, passing through the shoulder blade. This brought him to a stand. Bell and I now started at full speed, and as soon as we were within speaking distance, called to Owen not to shoot again. The bull did not appear to be much exhausted, but he was so stiffened by the shot on the shoulder that he could not turn quickly, and taking advantage of this we approached him; as we came near he worked himself slowly round to face us, and then made a lunge at us; we then stopped on one side and commenced discharging our pistols with little or no effect, except to increase his fury with every shot. His appearance was now one to inspire terror had we not felt satisfied of our ability to avoid him. However, even so, I came very near being overtaken by him. Through my own imprudence, I placed myself directly in front of him, and as he advanced I fired at his head, and then ran *ahead* of him, instead of veering to one side, not supposing that he was able to overtake me; but turning my head over my shoulder, I saw to my horror, Mr. Bull within three feet of me, prepared to give me a taste of his horns. The next instant I turned sharply off, and

the Buffalo being unable to turn quickly enough to follow
me, Bell took the gun from Owen and shot him directly behind the shoulder blade. He tottered for a moment, with an
increased jet of blood from the mouth and nostrils, fell forward on his horns, then rolled over on his side, and was
dead. He was a very old animal, in poor case, and only part
of him was worth taking to the fort. Provost, Squires, and
Basil were left at the camp preparing for their departure after
Otter and Beaver as decided. We left them eight or nine cat-
fish and a quantity of meat, of which they took care to secure
the best, namely the boss or hump. On our homeward way
we saw several Antelopes, some quite in the prairie, others
far away on the hills, but all of them on the alert. Owen tried
unsuccessfully to approach several of them at different times.
At one place where two were seen he dismounted, and went
round a small hill (for these animals when startled or suddenly alarmed always make to these places), and we hoped
would have had a shot; but alas! no! One of the Antelopes
ran off to the top of another hill, and the other stood looking
at him, and us perhaps, till Owen (who had been re-mount-
ed) galloped off towards us. My surprise was great when I
saw the other Antelope following him at a good pace (but
not by bounds or leaps, as I had been told by a former traveller they sometimes did), until it either smelt him, or found
out he was no friend, and turning round galloped speedily off
to join the one on the lookout. We saw seven or eight
Grouse, and Bell killed one on the ground. We saw a Sandhill Crane about two years old, looking quite majestic in a
grassy bottom, but it flew away before we were near enough
to get a shot. We passed a fine pond or small lake, but no
bird was there. We saw several parcels of Ducks in sundry
places, all of which no doubt had young near. When we
turned the corner of the great prairie we found Owen's mare
close by us. She had run away while he was after Antelopes.
We tied her to a log to be ready for him when he should
reach the spot. He had to walk about three miles before he
did this. However, to one as young and alert as Owen, such
things are nothing. Once they were not to me. . . .

[*July 21, Friday*]   We were up at sunrise, and had
our coffee, after which Lafleur a mulatto, Harris, and Bell
went off after Antelopes, for we cared no more about bulls;
where the cows are, we cannot tell. Cows run faster than

bulls, yearlings faster than cows, and calves faster than any of these. Squires felt sore, and his side was very black, so we took our guns and went after Black-breasted Lark Buntings, of which we saw many, but could not near them. I found a nest of them, however, with five eggs. The nest is planted in the ground, deep enough to sink the edges of it. It is formed of dried fine grasses and roots, without any lining of hair or wool. By and by we saw Harris sitting on a high hill about one mile off, and joined him; he said the bulls they had killed last evening were close by, and I offered to go and see the bones, for I expected that the Wolves had devoured it during the night. We travelled on, and Squires returned to the camp. After about two miles of walking against a delightful strong breeze, we reached the animals; Ravens or Buzzards had worked at the eyes, but only one Wolf, apparently, had been there. They were bloated, and smelt quite unpleasant. We returned to the camp and saw a Wolf cross our path, and an Antelope looking at us. We determined to stop and try to bring him to us; I lay on my back and threw my legs up, kicking first one and then the other foot, and sure enough the Antelope walked towards us, slowly and carefully, however. In about twenty minutes he had come two or three hundred yards; he was a superb male, and I looked at him for some minutes; when about sixty yards off I could see his eyes, and being loaded with buck-shot pulled the trigger without rising from my awkward position. Off he went; Harris fired, but he only ran the faster for some hundred yards, when he turned, looked at us again, and was off. When we reached camp we found Bell there; he had shot three times at Antelopes without killing; Lafleur had also returned, and had broken the foreleg of one, but an Antelope can run fast enough with three legs, and he saw no more of it. We now broke camp, arranged the horses and turned our heads towards the Missouri, and in four and three-quarter hours reached the landing. On entering the wood we again broke branches of service-berries, and carried a great quantity over the river. I much enjoyed the trip; we had our supper, and soon to bed in our hot room, where Sprague says the thermometer has been at 99° most of the day. I noticed it was warm when walking. I must not forget to notice some things which happened on our return. First, as we came near Fox River, we thought of the horns of our bulls, and Mr. Culbertson, who knows the country like a book, drove us first to Bell's, who

knocked the horns off, then to Harris's, which was served in
the same manner; this bull had been eaten entirely except the
head, and a good portion of mine had been devoured also; it
lay immediately under "Audubon's Bluff" (the name Mr.
Culbertson gave the ridge on which I stood to see the chase),
and we could see it when nearly a mile distant. Bell's horns
were the handsomest and largest, mine next best, and Harris's
the smallest, but we are all contented. Mr. Culbertson tells
me that Harris and Bell have done wonders, for persons who
have never shot at Buffaloes from on horseback. Harris had a
fall too, during his second chase, and was bruised in the manner of Squires, but not so badly. I have but little doubt that
Squires killed his bull, as he says he shot it three times, and
Mr. Culbertson's must have died also. What a terrible
destruction of life, as it were for nothing, or next to it, as the
tongues only were brought in, and the flesh of these fine animals were left to beasts and birds of prey, or to rot on the
spots where they fell. The prairies are literally *covered* with
the skulls of the victims, and the roads the Buffalo make in
crossing the prairies have all the appearance of heavy wagon
tracks. . . .

[*August 4, Friday*]   . . . We soon saw that the
weather was becoming cloudy, and we were anxious to reach
a camping-place; but we continued to cross ranges of hills, and
hoped to see a large herd of Buffaloes. The weather was
hot "out of mind," and we continued till, reaching a fine hill,
we saw in a beautiful valley below us seventy to eighty head,
feeding peacefully in groups and singly, as might happen.
The bulls were mixed in with the cows, and we saw one or
two calves. Many bulls were at various distances from the
main group, but as we advanced towards them they galloped
off and joined the others. When the chase began it was curious to see how much swifter the cows were than the bulls,
and how soon they divided themselves into parties of seven or
eight, exerting themselves to escape from their murderous
pursuers. All in vain, however; off went the guns and down
went the cows, or stood bleeding through the nose, mouth, or
bullet holes. Mr. C. killed three, and Harris one in about half
an hour. We had quite enough, and the slaughter was ended.
We had driven up to the nearest fallen cow, and approached
close to her, and found that she was not dead, but trying to
rise to her feet. I cannot bear to see an animal suffer unnec-

essarily, so begged one of the men to take my knife and stab her to the heart, which was done. The animals were cut up and skinned, with considerable fatigue. To skin bulls and cows and cut up their bodies is no joke, even to such as are constantly in the habit of doing it. Whilst Mr. Culbertson and the rest had gone to cut up another at some distance, I remained on guard to save the meat from the Wolves, but none came before my companions returned. We found the last cow quite dead. As we were busy about her the rain fell in torrents, and I found my blanket *capote* of great service. It was now nearly sundown, and we made up our minds to camp close by, although there was no water for our horses, neither any wood. Harris and I began collecting Buffalo-dung from all around, whilst the others attended to various other affairs. The meat was all unloaded and spread on the ground, the horses made fast, the fire burned freely, pieces of liver were soon cooked and devoured, coffee drunk in abundance, and we went to rest. . . .

[*August 5, Saturday*]   . . . Provost tells me that Buffaloes become so very poor during hard winters, when the snows cover the ground to the depth of two or three feet, that they lose their hair, become covered with scabs, on which the Magpies feed, and the poor beasts die by hundreds. One can hardly conceive how it happens, notwithstanding these many deaths and the immense numbers that are murdered almost daily on these boundless wastes called prairies, besides the hosts that are drowned in the freshets, and the hundreds of young calves who die in early spring, so many are yet to be found. Daily we see so many that we hardly notice them more than the cattle in our pastures about our homes. But this cannot last; even now there is a perceptible difference in the size of the herds, and before many years the Buffalo, like the Great Auk, will have disappeared; surely this should not be permitted. . . .

John C. Frémont

West of the Great Basin

John Charles Frémont (1813–1890) was a lieutenant in the U.S. Corps of Topographical Engineers and an amateur geologist and botanist when he led his second and most famous of five expeditions into the trans-Mississippi West in 1843. With guidance by such mountain men as Tom Fitzpatrick, Kit Carson, and Joe Walker, Frémont's government-sponsored expedition took him through South Pass to the Great Salt Lake, into Oregon territory and the Great Basin, across the Sierra Nevada, down the San Joaquin Valley, across the Mojave Desert, and up to Utah Lake. Frémont identified the volcanic character of mountains in the Cascades and Rockies, but his most significant contribution was to geography, especially his naming and descriptive identification of the Great Basin as an area of interior drainage. Frémont collected geologic and zoological specimens, and despite losses in a Kansas River flood and a Sierra Nevada accident when a mule tumbled over a precipice, he also returned with more than a thousand botanical specimens. Frémont went on to a controversial career that included his participation in the Bear Flag rebellion against Mexico, a court-martial, service in the U.S. Senate, the first Republican presidential nomination, and the governorship of Arizona Territory. His Report of the Exploring Expedition to the Rocky Mountains in the Year 1842, and to Oregon and California in the years 1843-'44, written with the help of his wife, Jessie Benton Frémont, the daughter of Missouri senator Thomas Hart Benton, ran through six printings and exposed the Western wilderness to a wide public. It projected the figure of Kit Carson into the realm of folklore, and it is also credited with inspiring many emigrants onto the Oregon Trail and informing the Mormons of a "bucholic" Salt Lake Valley. Frémont consciously presented himself as one to whom "the learning at first hand from Nature herself, the drinking first at her unknown springs, became a source of never-ending delight to me." He was always

*quick to note wilderness grandeur, even in times of suffering,
as during his midwinter crossing of the Sierra Nevada, a venture more successful than his disastrous attempt a few years
later to cross the San Juans in winter.*

[*December 31st*]   After an hour's ride this morning
our hopes were once more destroyed. The valley opened out,
and before us again lay one of the dry basins. After some
search, we discovered a high water outlet, which brought us
in a few miles, and by a descent of several hundred feet, into
another long broad basin, in which we found the bed of a
stream, and obtained sufficient water by cutting the ice. The
grass on the bottoms was salt and unpalatable.

Here we concluded the year 1843, and our New Year's
Eve was rather a gloomy one. The result of our journey began to be very uncertain; the country was singularly unfavorable to travel, the grasses being frequently of a very
unwholesome character; and the hoofs of our animals were so
worn and cut by the rocks that many of them were lame, and
could scarcely be got along. . . .

[*January 3d*]   A fog, so dense that we could not see a
hundred yards, covered the country, and the men that were
sent out after the horses were bewildered and lost; and we
were consequently detained at camp until late in the day.

Our situation had now become a serious one. We had
reached and run over the position where, according to the
best maps in my possession, we should have found Mary's
Lake, or River. We were evidently on the verge of the desert
which had been reported to us; and the appearance of the
country was so forbidding that I was afraid to enter it, and
determined to bear away to the southward, keeping close
along the mountains, in the full expectation of reaching the
Buenaventura River.

This morning I put every man in the camp on foot—myself, of course, among the rest—and in this manner lightened,

From John C. Frémont, *Report of the Exploring Expedition to the
Rocky Mountains in the Year 1842, and to Oregon and California in
the Years 1843-'44* (Washington: Gales and Seaton, 1845).

by distribution, the loads of the animals. We traveled seven
or eight miles along the ridge bordering the valley, and encamped where there were a few bunches of grass on the bed
of a hill torrent, without water. There were some large ar-
temisias but the principal plants are chenopodiaceous shrubs.
The rock composing the mountains is here changed suddenly
into white granite. The fog showed the tops of the hills at
sunset, and stars enough for observations in the early evening,
and then closed over us as before. Latitude by observation,
40° 48′ 15″. . . .

[*January 6th*]   The fog continued the same, and with
Mr. Preuss and Carson, I ascended the mountain to sketch
the leading features of the country, as some indication of our
future route, while Mr. Fitzpatrick explored the country below. In a very short distance we had ascended above the mist,
but the view obtained was not very gratifying. The fog had
partially cleared off from below when we reached the summit; and in the southwest corner of a basin communicating
with that in which we had encamped we saw a lofty column
of smoke, sixteen miles distant, indicating the presence of hot
springs. There, also, appeared to be the outlet of those drain-
ing channels of the country, and as such places afforded always more or less grass, I determined to steer in that
direction. The ridge we had ascended, appeared to be composed of fragments of white granite. We saw here traces of
sheep and antelope.

Entering the neighboring valley, and crossing the bed of
another lake, after a hard day's travel over ground of yielding
mud and sand we reached the springs, where we found an
abundance of grass, which, though only tolerably good, made
this place, with reference to the past, a refreshing and agreeable spot.

This is the most extraordinary locality of hot springs we
had met during the journey. The basin of the largest one has
a circumference of several hundred feet; but there is at one
extremity a circular space, of about fifteen feet in diameter,
entirely occupied by the boiling water. It boils up at irregular
intervals, and with much noise. The water is clear, and the
spring deep; a pole about sixteen feet long was easily immersed in the center, but we had no means of forming a
good idea of the depth. It was surrounded on the margin with
a border of green grass, and near the shore the temperature

of the water was 206°. We had no means of ascertaining that of the center, where the heat was greatest; but, by dispersing the water with a pole, the temperature at the margin was increased to 208°, and in the center it was doubtless higher. By driving the pole toward the bottom, the water was made to boil up with increased force and noise. There are several other interesting places where water and smoke or gas escape, but they would require a long description. The water is impregnated with common salt, but not so much so as to render it unfit for general cooking; and a mixture of snow made it pleasant to drink.

In the immediate neighborhood the valley bottom is covered almost exclusively with chenopodiaceous shrubs of greater luxuriance, and larger growth, than we have seen them in any preceding part of the journey. I obtained this evening some astronomical observations. . . .

[*January 10th*]   We continued our reconnaissance ahead, pursuing a south direction in the basin along the ridge, the camp following slowly after. On a large trail there is never any doubt of finding suitable places for encampments. We reached the end of the basin, where we found, in a hollow of the mountain which enclosed it, an abundance of good bunch grass. Leaving a signal for the party to encamp, we continued our way up the hollow, intending to see what lay beyond the mountain. The hollow was several miles long, forming a good pass, the snow deepening to about a foot as we neared the summit. Beyond, a defile between the mountains descended rapidly about two thousand feet; and filling up all the lower space was a sheet of green water, some twenty miles broad. It broke upon our eyes like the ocean.

The neighboring peaks rose high above us, and we ascended one of them to obtain a better view. The waves were curling in the breeze, and their dark-green color showed it to be a body of deep water. For a long time we sat enjoying the view, for we had become fatigued with mountains, and the free expanse of moving waves was very grateful. It was set like a gem in the mountains, which, from our position, seemed to enclose it almost entirely. At the western end it communicated with the line of basins we had left a few days since; and on the opposite side it swept a ridge of snowy mountains, the foot of the great Sierra. Its position at first inclined us to believe it Mary's Lake, but the rugged mountains were so entirely discordant with descriptions of its low rushy shores and open country, that we concluded it some unknown body of water, which it afterward proved to be.

On our road down, the next day, we saw herds of mountain sheep, and encamped on a little stream at the mouth of the defile, about a mile from the margin of the water, to which we hurried down immediately. The water is so slightly salt that, at first, we thought it fresh, and would be pleasant to drink when no other could be had. The shore was rocky—a handsome beach, which reminded us of the sea. On some large granite boulders that were scattered about the shore, I remarked a coating of a calcareous substance, in some places a few inches, and in others a foot in thickness. Near our camp, the hills, which were of primitive rock, were also covered with this substance, which was in too great quantity on the mountains along the shore of the lake to have been deposited by water, and has the appearance of having been spread over the rocks in mass. . . .

[*January 13th*]   . . . The next morning the snow was rapidly melting under a warm sun. Part of the morning was occupied in bringing up the gun; and, making only nine miles, we encamped on the shore, opposite a very remarkable rock in the lake, which had attracted our attention for many miles. It rose, according to our estimate, six hundred feet above the water; and, from the point we viewed it, presented a pretty exact outline of the great pyramid of Cheops. . . . Like other rocks along the shore, it seemed to be encrusted with calcareous cement. This striking feature suggested a name for the lake, and I called it Pyramid Lake; and though it may be deemed by some a fanciful resemblance, I can undertake to say that the future traveler will find a much more striking resemblance between this rock and the pyramids of Egypt than there is between them and the object from which they take their name.

The elevation of this lake above the sea is four thousand eight hundred and ninety feet, being nearly seven hundred feet higher than the Great Salt Lake, from which it lies nearly west, and distant about eight degrees of longitude. The position and elevation of this lake make it an object of geographical interest. It is the nearest lake to the western rim. as the Great Salt Lake is to the eastern rim, of the Great Basin which lies between the base of the Rocky Mountains and the

Sierra Nevada, and the extent and character of which, its whole circumference and contents, it is so desirable to know.

The last of the cattle which had been driven from the Dalles was killed here for food, and was still in good condition.

[*January 15th*] A few poor-looking Indians made their appearance this morning, and we succeeded in getting one into the camp. He was naked, with the exception of a tunic of hare skins. He told us that there was a river at the end of the lake, but that he lived in the rocks near by. From the few words our people could understand, he spoke a dialect of the Snake language; but we were not able to understand enough to know whether the river ran in or out, or what was its course; consequently, there still remained a chance that this might be Mary's Lake. . . .

We selected a strong place for our encampment, a grassy bottom nearly enclosed by the river, and furnished with abundant firewood. The village, a collection of straw huts, was a few hundred yards higher up. An Indian brought in a large fish to trade, which we had the inexpressible satisfaction to find was a salmon trout; we gathered round him eagerly. The Indians were amused with our delight, and immediately brought in numbers, so that the camp was soon stocked. Their flavor was excellent—superior, in fact, to that of any fish I have ever known. They were of extraordinary size— about as large as the Columbia River salmon—generally from two to four feet in length. From the information of Mr. Walker, who passed among some lakes lying more to the eastward, this fish is common to the streams of the inland lakes. He subsequently informed me that he had obtained them weighing six pounds when cleaned and the head taken off; which corresponds very well with the size of those obtained at this place. They doubtless formed the subsistence of these people, who hold the fishery in exclusive possession. . . .

We explained to the Indians that we were endeavoring to find a passage across the mountains into the country of the whites, whom we were going to see, and told them that we wished them to bring us a guide, to whom we would give presents of scarlet cloth and other articles, which were shown to them. They looked at the reward we offered, and conferred with each other, but pointed to snow on the mountain, and drew their hands across their necks, and raised them above their heads, to show the depth, and signified that it was impossible for us to get through. They made signs that we must go to the southward, over a pass through a lower range, which they pointed out; there, they said, at the end of one day's travel, we would find people who lived near a pass in the great mountain; and to that point they engaged to furnish us a guide. They appeared to have a confused idea, from report, of whites who lived on the other side of the mountain; and once, they told us, about two years ago, a party of twelve men, like ourselves, had ascended their river, and crossed to the other waters. They pointed out to us where they had crossed; but then, they said, it was summertime; now it would be impossible. . . .

[*January 31st*]   We took our way over a gently rising ground, the dividing ridge being tolerably low; and traveling easily along a broad trail, in twelve or fourteen miles reached the upper part of the pass, when it began to snow heavily, with very cold weather. The Indians had only the usual scanty covering, and appeared to suffer greatly from the cold. All left us except our guide. Half-hidden by the storm, the mountains looked dreary; and as night began to approach, the guide showed great reluctance to go forward. I placed him between two rifles, for the way began to be difficult. Traveling a little farther, we struck a ravine, which the Indian said would conduct us to the river; and as the poor fellow suffered greatly, shivering in the snow which fell upon his naked skin, I would not detain him any longer, and he ran off to the mountain, where, he said, there was a hut near by. He had kept the blue and scarlet cloths I had given him tightly rolled up, preferring rather to endure the cold than to get them wet.

In the course of the afternoon, one of the men had a foot frostbitten; and about dark we had the satisfaction of reaching the bottoms of a stream timbered with large trees, among which we found a sheltered camp, with an abundance of such grass as the season afforded for the animals. We saw before us, in descending from the pass, a great continuous range, along which stretched the valley of the river, the lower parts steep, and dark with pines, while, above, it was hidden in clouds of snow. This we felt instantly satisfied was the central ridge of the Sierra Nevada, the great California Moun-

tain, which only now intervened between us and the waters of
the bay. We had made a forced march of twenty-six miles,
and three mules had given out on the road. Up to this point,
with the exception of two stolen by Indians, we had lost none
of the horses which had been brought from the Columbia
River, and a number of these were still strong and in tolerably good order. We had now sixty-seven animals in the
band.

We had scarcely lighted our fires when the camp was
crowded with nearly naked [Washo] Indians; some of them
were furnished with long nets in addition to bows, and appeared to have been out on the sage hills to hunt rabbits.
These nets were, perhaps, thirty to forty feet long, kept upright in the ground by slight sticks at intervals, and were
made from a kind of wild hemp, very much resembling, in
manufacture, those common among the Indians of the
Sacramento Valley. They came among us without any fear,
and scattered themselves about the fires, mainly occupied in
gratifying their astonishment. I was struck by the singular appearance of a row of about a dozen, who were sitting on
their haunches perched on a log near one of the fires, with
their quick sharp eyes following every motion.

We gathered together a few of the most intelligent of the
Indians, and held this evening an interesting council. I explained to them my intentions. I told them that we had come
from a very far country, having been traveling now nearly a
year, and that we were desirous simply to go across the
mountain into the country of the other whites. There were
two who appeared particularly intelligent—one, a somewhat
old man. He told me that before the snows fell, it was six
sleeps to the place where the whites lived, but that now it was
impossible to cross the mountain on account of the deep
snow; and showing us, as the others had done, that it was
over our heads, he urged us strongly to follow the course of
the river, which he said would conduct us to a lake in which
there were many large fish. There, he said, were many
people; there was no snow on the ground, and we might remain there until the spring.

From their descriptions we were enabled to judge that we
had encamped on the upper water of the Salmon Trout
River. It is hardly necessary to say that our communication
was only by signs, as we understood nothing of their language; but they spoke, notwithstanding, rapidly and vehe-

mently, explaining what they considered the folly of our intentions, and urging us to go down to the lake. *Táh-ve*, a word signifying "snow," we very soon learned to know, from its frequent repetition. I told him that the men and the horses were strong, and that we would break a road through the snow; and spreading before him our bales of scarlet cloth, and trinkets, showed him what we would give for a guide. It was necessary to obtain one, if possible; for I had determined here to attempt the passage of the mountain.

Pulling a bunch of grass from the ground, after a short discussion among themselves, the old man made us comprehend that if we could break through the snow, at the end of three days we would come down upon grass, which he showed us would be about six inches high, and where the ground was entirely free. So far, he said, he had been in hunting for elk; but beyond that (and he closed his eyes) he had seen nothing; but there was one among them who had been to the whites, and, going out of the lodge, he returned with a young man of very intelligent appearance. Here, said he, is a young man who has seen the whites with his own eyes; and he swore, first by the sky, and then by the ground, that what he said was true. With a large present of goods we prevailed upon this young man to be our guide, and he acquired among us the name Mélo—a word signifying friend, which they used very frequently. He was thinly clad, and nearly barefoot, his moccasins being about worn out. We gave him skins to make a new pair, and to enable him to perform his undertaking to us. The Indians remained in the camp during the night, and we kept the guide and two others to sleep in the lodge with us—Carson lying across the door, and having made them comprehend the use of our firearms.

The snow, which had intermitted in the evening, commenced falling again in the course of the night, and it snowed steadily all day. In the morning I acquainted the men with my decision, and explained to them that necessity required us to make a great effort to clear the mountains. I reminded them of the beautiful valley of the Sacramento, with which they were familiar from the descriptions of Carson, who had been there some fifteen years ago, and who, in our late privations, had delighted us in speaking of its rich pastures and abounding game, and drew a vivid contrast between its summer climate, less than a hundred miles distant and the falling snow around us. I informed them (and long experience had given them confidence in my observations and good instruments) that almost directly west, and only about seventy miles distant, was the great farming establishment of Captain Sutter—a gentleman who had formerly lived in Missouri, and, emigrating to this country, had become the possessor of a principality. I assured them that from the heights of the mountain before us we should doubtless see the valley of the Sacramento River, and with one effort place ourselves again in the midst of plenty.

The people received this decision with the cheerful obedience which had always characterized them; and the day was immediately devoted to the preparations necessary to enable us to carry it into effect. Leggings, moccasins, clothing—all were put into the best state to resist the cold. Our guide was not neglected. Extremity of suffering might make him desert; we therefore did the best we could for him. Leggings, moccasins, some articles of clothing, and a large green blanket, in addition to the blue and scarlet cloth, were lavished upon him, and to his great and evident contentment. He arrayed himself in all his colors, and, clad in green, blue, and scarlet, he made a gay-looking Indian and, with his various presents, was probably richer and better clothed than any of his tribe had ever been before.

I have already said that our provisions were very low; we had neither tallow nor grease of any kind remaining, and the want of salt became one of our greatest privations. The poor dog which had been found in the Bear River Valley, and which had been a *compagnon de voyage* ever since, had now become fat, and the mess to which it belonged requested permission to kill it. Leave was granted. Spread out on the snow, the meat looked very good, and it made a strengthening meal for the greater part of the camp. Indians brought in two or three rabbits during the day, which were purchased from them. The river was forty to seventy feet wide, and now entirely frozen over. It was wooded with large cottonwood, willow, and *grains de bœuf*. By observation, the latitude of this encampment was 38° 37′ 18″.

[*February 2d*]   It had ceased snowing, and this morning the lower air was clear and frosty; and six or seven thousand feet above, the peaks of the Sierra now and then appeared among the rolling clouds, which were rapidly dispersing before the sun. Our Indian shook his head as he pointed to the icy pinnacles shooting high up into the sky, and seeming almost immediately above us. Crossing the river on the ice, and leaving it immediately, we commenced the ascent of the mountain along the valley of a tributary stream. The people were unusually silent; for every man knew that our enterprise was hazardous, and the issue doubtful.

The snow deepened rapidly, and it soon became necessary to break a road. For this service, a party of ten was formed, mounted on the strongest horses; each man in succession opening the road on foot, or on horseback, until himself and his horse became fatigued, when he stepped aside; and, the remaining number passing ahead, he took his station in the rear. Leaving this stream, and pursuing a very direct course, we passed over an intervening ridge to the river we had left. . . .

[*February 3d*]   Turning our faces directly toward the main chain, we ascended an open hollow along a small tributary to the river, which, according to the Indians, issues from a mountain to the south. The snow was so deep in the hollow that we were obliged to travel along the steep hillsides, and over spurs, where wind and sun had in places lessened the snow, and where the grass, which appeared to be in good quality along the sides of the mountains, was exposed.

We opened our road in the same way as yesterday, but made only seven miles; and encamped by some springs at the foot of a high and steep hill, by which the hollow ascended to another basin in the mountain. The little stream below was entirely buried in snow. The springs were shaded by the boughs of a lofty cedar, which here made its first appearance; the usual height was one hundred and twenty to one hundred and thirty feet, and one that was measured near by was six feet in diameter.

There being no grass exposed here, the horses were sent back to that which we had seen a few miles below. We occupied the remainder of the day in beating down a road to the foot of the hill, a mile or two distant; the snow, being beaten down when moist, in the warm part of the day, and then hard-frozen at night, made a foundation that would bear the weight of the animals the next morning. During the day several Indians joined us on snowshoes. These were made of a circular hoop, about a foot in diameter, the interior space being filled with an open network of bark.

[*February 4th*]   I went ahead early with two or three men, each with a led horse, to break the road. We were obliged to abandon the hollow entirely, and work along the mountainside, which was very steep, and the snow covered with an icy crust. We cut a footing as we advanced, and trampled a road through for the animals; but occasionally one plunged outside the trail, and slid along the field to the bottom, a hundred yards below. . . .

Tonight we had no shelter, but we made a large fire around the trunk of one of the huge pines; and covering the snow with small boughs, on which we spread our blankets, soon made ourselves comfortable. The night was very bright and clear, and though the thermometer was only down to 10°, a strong wind which sprang up at sundown made it intensely cold, and this was one of the bitterest nights during the journey.

Two Indians joined our party here; and one of them, an old man, immediately began to harangue us, saying that ourselves and animals would perish in the snow, and that if we would go back, he would show us another and a better way across the mountain. He spoke in a very loud voice, and there was a singular repetition of phrases and arrangement of words which rendered his speech striking and not unmusical.

We had now begun to understand some words, and, with the aid of signs, easily comprehended the old man's simple ideas. "Rock upon rock—rock upon rock—snow upon snow—snow upon snow," said he; "even if you get over the snow, you will not be able to get down from the mountains." He made us the sign of precipices, and showed us how the feet of the horses would slip, and throw them off from the narrow trails which led along their sides.

Our Chinook, who comprehended even more readily than ourselves, and believed our situation hopeless, covered his head with his blanket and began to weep and lament. "I wanted to see the whites," said he; "I came away from my own people to see the whites, and I wouldn't care to die among them; but here"—and he looked around into the cold night and gloomy forest, and, drawing his blanket over his head, began again to lament. Seated around the tree, the fire illuminating the rocks and the tall bolls of the pines round about, and the old Indian haranguing, we presented a group of very serious faces. . . .

[*February 6th*]   Accompanied by Mr. Fitzpatrick, I
set out today, with a reconnoitering party, on snowshoes. We
marched all in single file, trampling the snow as heavily as we
could. Crossing the open basin, in a march of about ten miles
we reached the top of one of the peaks, to the left of the pass
indicated by our guide.

Far below us, dimmed by the distance, was a large
snowless valley, bounded on the western side, at the distance
of about a hundred miles, by a low range of mountains,
which Carson recognized with delight as the mountains bordering the coast. "There," said he, "is the little mountain—it
is fifteen years ago since I saw it; but I am just as sure as if I
had seen it yesterday." Between us, then, and this low coast
range, was the valley of the Sacramento; and no one who had
not accompanied us through the incidents of our life for the
last few months could realize the delight with which at last
we looked down upon it. At the distance of apparently thirty
miles beyond us were distinguished spots of prairie; and a
dark line, which could be traced with the glass, was imagined
to be the course of the river; but we were evidently at a great
height above the valley, and between us and the plains extended miles of snowy fields, and broken ridges of pine-cov-
ered mountains.

It was late in the day when we turned toward the camp;
and it grew rapidly cold as it drew toward night. One of the
men, Fallon, became fatigued, and his feet began to freeze,
and building a fire in the trunk of a dry old cedar, Mr.
Fitzpatrick remained with him until his clothes could be
dried, and he was in a condition to come on. After a day's
march of twenty miles, we straggled into camp, one after another, at nightfall, the greater number excessively fatigued,
only two of the party having ever traveled on snowshoes before.

All our energies were now directed to getting our animals
across the snow; and it was supposed that, after all the baggage had been drawn with the sleighs over the trail we had
made, it would be sufficiently hard to bear our animals. At
several places between this point and the ridge we had discovered some grassy spots, where the wind and sun had dispersed the snow from the sides of the hills, and these were to
form resting places to support the animals for a night in their
passage across. On our way across we had set on fire several
broken stumps, and dried trees, to melt holes in the snow for

the camps. Its general depth was five feet; but we passed over places where it was twenty feet deep, as shown by the trees.

With one party drawing sleighs loaded with baggage, I advanced today about four miles along the trail, and encamped at the first grassy spot where we expected to bring our horses. Mr. Fitzpatrick, with another party, remained behind, to form an intermediate station between us and the animals. . . .

[*February 9th*]   During the night the weather changed, the wind rising to a gale, and commencing to snow before daylight; before morning the trail was covered. We remained quiet in camp all day, in the course of which the weather improved. Four sleighs arrived toward evening, with the bedding of the men. We suffer much from the want of salt; and all the men are becoming weak from insufficient food.

[*February 10th*]   Taplin was sent back with a few men to assist Mr. Fitzpatrick; and continuing on with three sleighs carrying a part of the baggage, we had the satisfaction to encamp within two and a half miles of the head of the hollow, and at the foot of the last mountain ridge. Here two large trees had been set on fire, and in the holes, where the snow had been melted away, we found a comfortable camp.

The wind kept the air filled with snow during the day; the sky was very dark in the southwest, though elsewhere very clear. The forest here has a noble appearance: the tall cedar is abundant; its greatest height being one hundred and thirty feet, and circumference twenty, three or four feet above the ground; and here I see for the first time the white pine, of which there are some magnificent trees. Hemlock spruce is among the timber, occasionally as large as eight feet in diameter four feet above the ground; but, in ascending, it tapers rapidly to less than one foot at the height of eighty feet. I have not seen any higher than one hundred and thirty feet, and the slight upper part is frequently broken off by the wind. The white spruce is frequent; and the red pine (*Pinus colorado* of the Mexicans), which constitutes the beautiful forest along the flanks of the Sierra Nevada to the northward, is here the principal tree, not attaining a greater height than one hundred and forty feet, though with sometimes a diameter of ten. Most of these trees appeared to differ slightly from those of the same kind on the other side of the continent.

The elevation of the camp, by the boiling-point, is eight thousand and fifty feet. We are now one thousand feet above the level of the South Pass in the Rocky Mountains; and still we are not done ascending. The top of a flat ridge near was bare of snow, and very well sprinkled with bunch grass, sufficient to pasture the animals two or three days, and this was to be their main point of support. This ridge is composed of a compact trap, or basalt, of a columnar structure; over the surface are scattered large boulders of porous trap. The hills are in many places entirely covered with small fragments of volcanic rock.

Putting on our snowshoes, we spent the afternoon in exploring a road ahead. The glare of the snow, combined with great fatigue, had rendered many of the people nearly blind; but we were fortunate in having some black silk handkerchiefs, which, worn as veils, very much relieved the eyes.

[*February 11th*]   High wind continued, and our trail this morning was nearly invisible—here and there indicated by a little ridge of snow. Our situation became tiresome and dreary, requiring a strong exercise of patience and resolution.

In the evening I received a message from Mr. Fitzpatrick, acquainting me with the utter failure of his attempt to get our mules and horses over the snow—the half-hidden trail had proved entirely too slight to support them, and they had broken through, and were plunging about or lying half-buried in snow. He was occupied in endeavoring to get them back to his camp, and in the meantime sent to me for further instructions. I wrote to him to send the animals immediately back to their old pastures; and, after having made mauls and shovels, turn in all the strength of his party to open and beat a road through the snow, strengthening it with branches and boughs of the pines. . . .

[*February 13th*]   . . . The meat train did not arrive this evening, and I gave Godey leave to kill our little dog (Klamath), which he prepared in Indian fashion—scorching off the hair, and washing the skin with soap and snow, and then cutting it up into pieces, which were laid on the snow. Shortly afterward the sleigh arrived with a supply of horse meat; and we had tonight an extraordinary dinner—pea soup, mule, and dog.

[*February 14th*]   With Mr. Preuss, I ascended today

the highest peak near us, from which we had a beautiful view
of a mountain lake at our feet, about fifteen miles in length,
and so entirely surrounded by mountains that we could not
discover an outlet. We had taken with us a glass; but though
we enjoyed an extended view, the valley was half hidden in
mist, as when we had seen it before. Snow could be distinguished on the higher parts of the coast mountains; eastward,
as far as the eye could extend, it ranged over a terrible mass
of broken snowy mountains, fading off blue in the distance.

The rock composing the summit consists of a very coarse
dark volcanic conglomerate; the lower parts appeared to be
of a slaty structure. The highest trees were a few scattering
cedars and aspens. From the immediate foot of the peak, we
were two hours in reaching the summit, and one hour and a
quarter in descending. The day had been very bright, still,
and clear, and spring seems to be advancing rapidly. While
the sun is in the sky, the snow melts rapidly, and gushing
springs cover the face of the mountain in all the exposed
places; but their surface freezes instantly with the disappearance of the sun. I obtained tonight some observations; and
the result from these, and others made during our stay, gives
for the latitude 38° 41' 57", longitude 120° 25' 57", and
rate of the chronometer 25.82". . . .

[*February 16th*]   . . . The night was clear and very
long. We heard the cries of some wild animals, which had
been attracted by our fire, and a flock of geese passed over
during the night. Even these strange sounds had something
pleasant to our senses in this region of silence and desolation.

We started again early in the morning. The creek acquired
a regular breadth of about twenty feet, and we soon began to
hear the rushing of the water below the icy surface, over
which we traveled to avoid the snow; a few miles below we
broke through where the water was several feet deep, and
halted to make a fire and dry our clothes. We continued a few
miles farther, walking being very laborious without snowshoes.

I was now perfectly satisfied that we had struck the stream
on which Mr. Sutter lived; and, turning about, made a hard
push and reached the camp at dark. Here we had the
pleasure to find all the remaining animals, fifty-seven in number, safely arrived at the grassy hill near the camp; and here,
also, we were agreeably surprised with the sight of an abundance of salt. Some of the horse guard had gone to a neigh-

boring hut for pine nuts, and discovered unexpectedly a large cake of very white, fine-grained salt, which the Indians told them they had brought from the other side of the mountain; they used it to eat with their pine nuts, and readily sold it for goods.

On the 19th, the people were occupied in making a road and bringing up the baggage; and, on the afternoon of the next day, February 20, 1844, we encamped with the animals and all the matériel of the camp, on the summit of the pass in the dividing ridge, one thousand miles by our traveled road from the Dalles of the Columbia. The people, who had not yet been to this point, climbed the neighboring peak to enjoy a look at the valley.

The temperature of boiling water gave for the elevation of the encampment nine thousand three hundred and thirty-eight feet above the sea. This was two thousand feet higher than the South Pass in the Rocky Mountains, and several peaks in view rose several thousand feet still higher. Thus, at the extremity of the continent, and near the coast, the phenomenon was seen of a range of mountains still higher than the great Rocky Mountains themselves. This extraordinary fact accounts for the Great Basin, and shows that there must be a system of small lakes and rivers here scattered over a flat country, and which the extended and lofty range of the Sierra Nevada prevents from escaping to the Pacific Ocean. Latitude 38° 44'; longitude 120° 28'. Thus this pass in the Sierra Nevada, which so well deserves its name of Snowy Mountain, is eleven degrees west, and about four degrees south, of the South Pass.

[*February 21st*]   We now considered ourselves victorious over the mountain; having only the descent before us, and the valley under our eyes, we felt strong hope that we should force our way down. But this was a case in which the descent was *not* facile. Still deep fields of snow lay between, and there was a large intervening space of rough-looking mountains, through which we had yet to wind our way.

Carson roused me this morning with an early fire, and we were all up long before day, in order to pass the snow fields before the sun should render the crust soft. We enjoyed this morning a scene at sunrise, which even here was unusually glorious and beautiful. Immediately above the eastern mountains was repeated a cloud-formed mass of purple ranges, bordered with bright yellow-gold; the peaks shot up into a narrow line of crimson cloud, above which the air was filled with a greenish orange; and over all was the singular beauty of the blue sky.

Passing along a ridge which commanded the lake on our right, of which we began to discover an outlet through a chasm on the west, we passed over alternating open ground and hard-crusted snow fields which supported the animals, and encamped on the ridge after a journey of six miles. The grass was better than we had yet seen, and we were encamped in a clump of trees twenty or thirty feet high, resembling white pine. With the exception of these small clumps, the ridges were bare; and, where the snow found the support of the trees, the wind had blown it up into banks ten or fifteen feet high. It required much care to hunt out a practicable way, as the most open places frequently led to impassable banks.

We had hard and doubtful labor yet before us, as the snow appeared to be heavier where the timber began farther down, with few open spots. Ascending a height, we traced out the best line we could discover for the next day's march, and had at least the consolation to see that the mountain descended rapidly. The day had been one of April; gusty, with a few occasional flakes of snow, which, in the afternoon, enveloped the upper mountain in clouds. We watched them anxiously, as now we dreaded a snowstorm.

Shortly afterward we heard the roll of thunder, and looking toward the valley, found it all enveloped in a thunderstorm. For us, as connected with the idea of summer, it had a singular charm; and we watched its progress with excited feelings until nearly sunset, when the sky cleared off brightly, and we saw a shining line of water directing its course toward another, a broader and larger sheet. We knew that these could be no other than the Sacramento and the Bay of San Francisco; but, after our long wandering in rugged mountains, where so frequently we had met with disappointments, and where the crossing of every ridge displayed some unknown lake or river, we were yet almost afraid to believe that we were at last to escape into the genial country of which we had heard so many glowing descriptions, and dreaded again to find some vast interior lake, whose bitter waters would bring us disappointment. On the southern shore of what appeared to be the bay could be traced the gleaming line where

entered another large stream; and again the Buenaventura
rose up in our minds.

Carson had entered the valley along the southern side of
the bay, and remembered perfectly to have crossed the mouth
of a very large stream, which they had been obliged to raft;
but the country then was so entirely covered with water from
snow and rain that he had been able to form no correct impression of watercourses.

We had the satisfaction to know that at least there were
people below. Fires were lit up in the valley just at night, appearing to be in answer to ours; and these signs of life
renewed, in some measure, the gaiety of the camp. They appeared so near that we judged them to be among the timber
of some of the neighboring ridges; but, having them constantly in view day after day, and night after night, we afterward found them to be fires that had been kindled by the
Indians among the tulares, on the shore of the bay, eighty
miles distant.

Among the very few plants that appeared here was the
common blue flax. Tonight a mule was killed for food. . . .

[*February 23d*]   This was our most difficult day: we
were forced off the ridges by the quantity of snow among the
timber, and obliged to take to the mountainsides, where, occasionally, rocks and a southern exposure afforded us a
chance to scramble along. But these were steep, and slippery
with snow and ice; and the tough evergreens of the mountain
impeded our way, tore our skins, and exhausted our patience.
Some of us had the misfortune to wear moccasins with parfleche soles, so slippery that we could not keep our feet, and
generally crawled across the snow beds.

Axes and mauls were necessary today to make a road
through the snow. Going ahead with Carson to reconnoiter
the road, we reached in the afternoon the river which made
the outlet of the lake. Carson sprang over, clear across a
place where the stream was compressed among rocks, but the
parfleche sole of my moccasin glanced from the icy rock, and
precipitated me into the river. It was some few seconds before I could recover myself in the current, and Carson, thinking me hurt, jumped in after me, and we both had an icy
bath. We tried to search awhile for my gun, which had been
lost in the fall, but the cold drove us out; and making a large
fire on the bank, after we had partially dried ourselves we

went back to meet the camp. We afterward found that the gun had been slung under the ice which lined the banks of the creek.

Using our old plan of breaking the road with alternate horses, we reached the creek in the evening, and encamped on a dry open place in the ravine. Another branch, which we had followed, here comes in on the left; and from this point the mountain wall on which we had traveled today faces to the south along the right bank of the river, where the sun appears to have melted the snow; but the opposite ridge is entirely covered. Here, among the pines, the hillside produces but little grass—barely sufficient to keep life in the animals. We had the pleasure to be rained upon this afternoon; and grass was now our greatest solicitude. Many of the men looked badly, and some this evening were giving out.

[*February 24th*]   We rose at three in the morning, for an astronomical observation, and obtained for the place a latitude of 38° 46′ 58″, longitude 120° 34′ 20″. The sky was clear and pure, with a sharp wind from the northeast, and the thermometer 2° below the freezing point.

We continued down the south face of the mountain; our road leading over dry ground, we were able to avoid the snow almost entirely. In the course of the morning we struck a footpath, which we were generally able to keep; and the ground was soft to our animals' feet, being sandy or covered with mold. Green grass began to make its appearance, and occasionally we passed a hill scatteringly covered with it.

The character of the forest continued the same, and among the trees, the pine with short leaves and very large cones was abundant, some of them being noble trees. We measured one that had ten feet diameter, though the height was not more than one hundred and thirty feet. All along the river was a roaring torrent, its fall very great; and descending with a rapidity to which we had long been strangers, to our great pleasure oak trees appeared on the ridge, and soon became very frequent; on these I remarked unusually great quantities of mistletoe. Rushes began to make their appearance; and at a small creek where they were abundant, one of the messes was left with the weakest horses, while we continued on.

The opposite mountainside was very steep and continuous—unbroken by ravines, and covered with pines and snow; while on the side we were traveling, innumerable rivulets poured down from the ridge. Continuing on, we halted a moment at one of these rivulets, to admire some beautiful evergreen trees, resembling live oak, which shaded the little stream. They were forty to fifty feet high, and two in diameter, with a uniform tufted top; and the summer green of their beautiful foliage, with the singing birds, and the sweet summer wind which was whirling about the dry oak leaves, nearly intoxicated us with delight; and we hurried on, filled with excitement, to escape entirely from the horrid region of inhospitable snow to the perpetual spring of the Sacramento.

When we had traveled about ten miles, the valley opened a little to an oak and pine bottom, through which ran rivulets closely bordered with rushes, on which our half-starved horses fell with avidity; and here we made our encampment. Here the roaring torrent has already become a river, and we had descended to an elevation of three thousand eight hundred and sixty-four feet. Along our road today the rock was a white granite, which appears to constitute the upper part of the mountains on both the eastern and western slopes, while between, the central is a volcanic rock. Another horse was killed tonight, for food.

[*February 25th*] Believing that the difficulties of the road were passed, and leaving Mr. Fitzpatrick to follow slowly, as the condition of the animals required, I started ahead this morning with a party of eight, consisting (with myself) of Mr. Preuss and Mr. Talbot, Carson, Derosier, Towns, Proue, and Jacob. We took with us some of the best animals, and my intention was to proceed as rapidly as possible to the house of Mr. Sutter, and return to meet the party with a supply of provisions and fresh animals.

Continuing down the river, which pursued a very direct westerly course through a narrow valley, with only a very slight and narrow bottom land, we made twelve miles, and encamped at some old Indian huts, apparently a fishing place on the river.

The bottom was covered with trees of deciduous foliage, and overgrown with vines and rushes. On a bench of the hill near by was a field of fresh green grass, six inches long in some of the tufts, which I had the curiosity to measure. The animals were driven here; and I spent part of the afternoon sitting on a large rock among them, enjoying the pauseless rapidity with which they luxuriated in the unaccustomed food.

Francis Parkman

Hunting Indians

Francis Parkman (1823–1893) was a respectable twenty-three-year-old son of a Boston Unitarian minister when he traveled along the Oregon Trail in 1846 with his cousin, Quincy Shaw, to gain firsthand knowledge of Indians. Parkman was the most purposeful of literary travelers. His earlier wilderness excursions into the White Mountains and Canada, his college studies, and his trip to the West were intended to serve as preparation for the lifelong work that would make him one of America's great historians. His ambitious plan, as he said, was "to include the whole course of the American conflict between France and England; or, in other words, the history of the American forest; for this was the light in which I regarded it. My theme fascinated me, and I was haunted with wilderness images day and night." Wilderness is also the concern of The Oregon Trail, *for despite the title, the book is not so much a history of the emigrant trail as it is an impressionistic account of a young Bostonian's initiation into the ways of life in the land occupied by the Sioux and the buffalo. It is the most vivid impression we have of this country, and the book has remained a classic of American literature since its publication in 1849. Parkman's artistry persuades us of the excitement, monotony, and fright experienced by a young man in this strange land, and we sense that this is the experience we might have known ourselves had we been there in the 1840s. The following selection describes Parkman's search for Indians. Accompanied by Raymond, a French-Canadian mountaineer, and Pauline, his mare, Parkman leaves his other companions with the intention of joining up with a wandering band of Oglala Sioux. The campfire Parkman discovers is that of Reynal, a French-Canadian trader who travels with the band and is married to a Sioux woman.*

Raymond and I shook hands with our friends, rode out upon the prairie, and clambering the sandy hollows channelled in the sides of the hills, gained the high plains above. If a curse had been pronounced upon the land, it could not have worn an aspect more forlorn. There were abrupt broken hills, deep hollows, and wide plains; but all alike glared with an insupportable whiteness under the burning sun. The country, as if parched by the heat, was cracked into innumerable fissures and ravines, that not a little impeded our progress. Their steep sides were white and raw, and along the bottom we several times discovered the broad tracks of the grizzly bear, nowhere more abundant than in this region. The ridges of the hills were hard as rock, and strewn with pebbles of flint and coarse red jasper; looking from them, there was nothing to relieve the desert uniformity, save here and there a pine-tree clinging to the edge of a ravine, and stretching its rough shaggy arms into the scorching air. Its resinous odors recalled the pine-clad mountains of New England, and, goaded as I was with a morbid thirst, I thought with a longing desire on the crystal treasure poured in such wasteful profusion from our thousands hills. I heard, in fancy, the plunging and gurgling of waters among the shaded rocks, and saw them gleaming dark and still far down amid the crevices, the cold drops trickling from the long green mosses.

When noon came we found a little stream, with a few trees and bushes; and here we rested for an hour. Then we travelled on, guided by the sun, until, just before sunset, we reached another stream, called Bitter Cotton-wood Creek. A thick growth of bushes and old storm-beaten trees grew at intervals along its bank. Near the foot of one of the trees we flung down our saddles, and hobbling our horses, turned them loose to feed. The little stream was clear and swift, and ran musically over its white sands. Small water-birds were splashing in the shallows, and filling the air with cries and flutterings. The sun was just sinking among gold and crimson clouds behind Mount Laramie. I lay upon a log by the margin of the water, and watched the restless motions of the little fish in a deep still nook below. Strange to say, I seemed to have gained strength since the morning, and almost felt a sense of returning health.

From Francis Parkman, *The California and Oregon Trail* (New York: George P. Putnam, 1849).

We built our fire. Night came, and the wolves began to howl. One deep voice began, answered in awful responses from hills, plains, and woods. Such sounds do not disturb one's sleep upon the prairie. We picketed the mare and the mule, and did not awake until daylight. Then we turned them loose, still hobbled, to feed for an hour before starting. We were getting ready our breakfast when Raymond saw an antelope half a mile distant and said he would go and shoot it.

"Your business," said I, "is to look after the animals. I am too weak to do much, if anything happens to them, and you must keep within sight of the camp."

Raymond promised, and set out with his rifle in his hand. The mare and the mule had crossed the stream, and were feeding among the long grass on the other side, much tormented by the attacks of large green-headed flies. As I watched them, I saw them go down into a hollow, and as several minutes elapsed without their reappearing, I waded through the stream to look after them. To my vexation and alarm I discovered them at a great distance, galloping away at full speed, Pauline in advance, with her hobbles broken, and the mule, still fettered, following with awkward leaps. I fired my rifle and shouted to recall Raymond. In a moment he came running through the stream, with a red handkerchief bound round his head. I pointed to the fugitives, and ordered him to pursue them. Muttering a "Sacré," between his teeth, he set out at full speed, still swinging his rifle in his hand. I walked up to the top of a hill, and, looking away over the prairie, could distinguish the runaways, still at full gallop. Returning to the fire, I sat down at the foot of a tree. Wearily and anxiously hour after hour passed away. The loose bark dangling from the trunk behind me flapped to and fro in the wind, and the mosquitoes kept up their drowsy hum; but other than this there was no sight nor sound of life throughout the burning landscape. The sun rose higher and higher, until I knew that it must be noon. It seemed scarcely possible that the animals could be recovered. If they were not, my situation was one of serious difficulty. Shaw, when I left him, had decided to move that morning, but whither he had not determined. To look for him would be a vain attempt. Fort Laramie was forty miles distant, and I could not walk a mile without great effort. Not then having learned the philosophy of yielding to disproportionate obstacles, I resolved, come what would, to continue the pursuit of the Indians. Only one plan occurred to me; this was, to send Raymond to the fort with an order for more horses, while I remained on the spot, awaiting his return, which might take place within three days. But to remain stationary and alone for three days, in a country full of dangerous Indians, was not the most flattering of prospects; and, protracted as my Indian hunt must be by such delay, it was not easy to foretell its result. Revolving these matters, I grew hungry; and as our stock of provisions, except four or five pounds of flour, was by this time exhausted, I left the camp to see what game I could find. Nothing could be seen except four or five large curlews wheeling over my head, and now and then alighting upon the prairie. I shot two of them, and was about returning, when a startling sight caught my eye. A small, dark object, like a human head, suddenly appeared, and vanished among the thick bushes along the stream below. In that country every stranger is a suspected enemy; and I threw forward the muzzle of my rifle. In a moment the bushes were violently shaken, two heads, but not human heads, protruded, and to my great joy I recognized the downcast, disconsolate countenance of the black mule and the yellow visage of Pauline. Raymond came upon the mule, pale and haggard, complaining of a fiery pain in his chest. I took charge of the animals while he kneeled down by the side of the stream to drink. He had kept the runaways in sight as far as the Side Fork of Laramie Creek, a distance of more than ten miles; and here with great difficulty he had succeeded in catching them. I saw that he was unarmed, and asked him what he had done with his rifle. It had encumbered him in his pursuit, and he had dropped it on the prairie, thinking that he could find it on his return; but in this he had failed. The loss might prove a very serious one. I was too much rejoiced, however, at the recovery of the animals, and at the fidelity of Raymond, who might easily have deserted with them, to think much about it; and having made some tea for him in a tin vessel which we had brought with us, I told him that I would give him two hours for resting before we set out again. He had eaten nothing that day; but having no appetite, he lay down immediately to sleep. I picketed the animals among the best grass that I could find, and made fires of green wood to protect them from the flies; then sitting down again by the tree, I watched the slow movements of the sun, grudging every moment that passed.

The time I had mentioned expired, and I awoke Raymond.

We saddled and set out again, but first we went in search of
the lost rifle, and in the course of an hour were fortunate
enough to find it. Then we turned westward, and moved over
the hills and hollows at a slow pace towards the Black Hills.
The heat no longer tormented us, for a cloud was before the
sun. The air grew fresh and cool, the distant mountains
frowned more gloomily, there was a low muttering of thunder, and dense black masses of cloud rose heavily behind the
broken peaks. At first they were fringed with silver by the afternoon sun; but soon thick blackness overspread the sky, and
the desert around us was wrapped in gloom. There was an
awful sublimity in the hoarse murmuring of the thunder, and
the sombre shadows that involved the mountains and the
plain. The storm broke with a zigzag blinding flash, a terrific
crash of thunder, and a hurricane that howled over the prairie, dashing floods of water against us. Raymond looked
about him and cursed the merciless elements. There seemed
no shelter near, but we discerned at length a deep ravine
gashed in the level prairie, and saw half-way down its side an
old pine-tree, whose rough horizontal boughs formed a sort
of pent-house against the tempest. We found a practicable
passage, led our animals down, and fastened them to large
loose stones at the bottom; then climbing up, we drew our
blankets over our heads, and crouched close beneath the old
tree. Perhaps I was no competent judge of time, but it
seemed to me that we were sitting there a full hour, while
around us poured a deluge of rain, through which the rocks
on the opposite side of the gulf were barely visible. The first
burst of the tempest soon subsided, but the rain poured in
steady torrents. At length Raymond grew impatient, and
scrambling out of the ravine, gained the level prairie above.

"What does the weather look like?" asked I, from my seat
under the tree.

"It looks bad," he answered; "dark all round"; and again
he descended and sat down by my side. Some ten minutes
elapsed.

"Go up again," said I, "and take another look"; and he
clambered up the precipice. "Well, how is it?"

"Just the same, only I see one little bright spot over the top
of the mountain."

The rain by this time had begun to abate; and going down
to the bottom of the ravine, we loosened the animals, who
were standing up to their knees in water. Leading them up

the rocky throat of the ravine, we reached the plain above.
All around us was obscurity; but the bright spot above the
mountains grew wider and ruddier, until at length the clouds
drew apart, and a flood of sunbeams poured down, streaming
along the precipices, and involving them in a thin blue haze,
as soft as that which wraps the Apennines on an evening in
spring. Rapidly the clouds were broken and scattered, like
routed legions of evil spirits. The plain lay basking in sunbeams around us; a rainbow arched the desert from north to
south, and far in front a line of woods seemed inviting us to
refreshment and repose. When we reached them, they were
glistening with prismatic dew-drops, and enlivened by the
songs and flutterings of birds. Strange winged insects, be-
numbed by the rain, were clinging to the leaves and the bark
of the trees.

Raymond kindled a fire with great difficulty. The animals
turned eagerly to feed on the soft rich grass, while I, wrapping myself in my blanket, lay down and gazed on the evening landscape. The mountains, whose stern features had
frowned upon us so gloomily, seemed lighted up with a
benignant smile, and the green waving undulations of the
plain were gladdened with warm sunshine. Wet, ill, and wearied as I was, my heart grew lighter at the view, and I drew
from it an augury of good.

When morning came, Raymond awoke, coughing violently,
though I had apparently received no injury. We mounted,
crossed the little stream, pushed through the trees, and began
our journey over the plain beyond. And now, as we rode
slowly along, we looked anxiously on every hand for traces
of the Indians, not doubting that the village had passed somewhere in that vicinity; but the scanty shrivelled grass was not
more than three or four inches high, and the ground was so
hard that a host might have marched over it and left scarcely
a trace of its passage. Up hill and down hill, and clambering
through ravines, we continued our journey. As we were passing the foot of a hill, I saw Raymond, who was some rods in
advance, suddenly jerk the reins of his mule, slide from his
seat, and run in a crouching posture up a hollow; then in an
instant I heard the sharp crack of his rifle. A wounded antelope came running on three legs over the hill. I lashed
Pauline and made after him. My fleet little mare soon
brought me by his side, and, after leaping and bounding for a
few moments in vain, he stood still, as if despairing of es-

cape. His glistening eyes turned up towards my face with so
piteous a look, that it was with feelings of infinite compunc-
tion that I shot him through the head with a pistol. Raymond
skinned and cut him up, and we hung the fore-quarters to
our saddles, much rejoiced that our exhausted stock of provisions was renewed in such good time.

Gaining the top of a hill, we could see along the cloudy
verge of the prairie before us the lines of trees and shadowy
groves, that marked the course of Laramie Creek. Before
noon we reached its banks, and began anxiously to search
them for footprints of the Indians. We followed the stream
for several miles, now on the shore and now wading in the
water, scrutinizing every sand-bar and every muddy bank. So
long was the search, that we began to fear that we had left
the trail undiscovered behind us. At length I heard Raymond
shouting, and saw him jump from his mule to examine some
object under the shelving bank. I rode up to his side. It was
the impression of an Indian moccasin. Encouraged by this,
we continued our search till at last some appearances on a
soft surface of earth not far from the shore attracted my eye;
and going to examine them I found half a dozen tracks, some
made by men and some by children. Just then Raymond observed across the stream the mouth of a brook, entering it
from the south. He forded the water, rode in at the opening,
and in a moment I heard him shouting again; so I passed
over and joined him. The brook had a broad sandy bed,
along which the water trickled in a scanty stream; and on either bank the bushes were so close that the view was completely intercepted. I found Raymond stooping over the
footprints of three or four horses. Proceeding, we found those
of a man, then those of a child, then those of more horses;
till at last the bushes on each bank were beaten down and
broken, and the sand ploughed up with a multitude of footsteps, and scored across with the furrows made by the lodge-
poles that had been dragged through. It was now certain that
we had found the trail. I pushed through the bushes, and at a
little distance on the prairie beyond found the ashes of a
hundred and fifty lodge-fires, with bones and pieces of buf-
falo-robes scattered about, and the pickets to which horses
had been tied, still standing in the ground. Elated by our
success, we selected a convenient tree, and turning the animals loose, prepared to make a meal from the haunch of the
antelope.

Hardship and exposure had thriven with me wonderfully. I had gained both health and strength since leaving La Bonté's camp. Raymond and I dined together, in high spirits; for we rashly presumed that having found one end of the trail we should have little difficulty in reaching the other. But when the animals were led in, we found that our ill-luck had not ceased to follow us. As I was saddling Pauline, I saw that her eye was dull as lead, and the hue of her yellow coat visibly darkened. I placed my foot in the stirrup to mount, when she staggered and fell flat on her side. Gaining her feet with an effort, she stood by the fire with a drooping head. Whether she had been bitten by a snake, or poisoned by some noxious plant, or attacked by a sudden disorder, it was hard to say; but at all events, her sickness was sufficiently ill-timed and unfortunate. I succeeded in a second attempt to mount her, and with a slow pace we moved forward on the trail of the Indians. It led us up a hill and over a dreary plain; and here, to our great mortification the traces almost disappeared, for the ground was hard as adamant; and if its flinty surface had ever retained the dent of a hoof, the marks had been washed away by the deluge of yesterday. An Indian village, in its disorderly march, is scattered over the prairie often to the width of half a mile; so that its trail is nowhere clearly marked, and the task of following it is made doubly wearisome and difficult. By good fortune, many large ant-hills, a yard or more in diameter, were scattered over the plain, and these were frequently broken by the footprints of men and horses, and marked by traces of the lodge-poles. The succulent leaves of the prickly-pear, bruised from the same causes, also helped to guide us; so, inch by inch, we moved along. Often we lost the trail altogether, and then found it again; but late in the afternoon we were totally at fault. We stood alone, without a clew to guide us. The broken plain expanded for league after league around us, and in front the long dark ridge of mountains stretched from north to south. Mount Laramie, a little on our right, towered high above the rest, and from a dark valley just beyond one of its lower declivities, we discerned volumes of white smoke rising slowly.

"I think," said Raymond, "some Indians must be there. Perhaps we had better go." But this plan was not lightly to be adopted, and we determined still to continue our search after the lost trail. Our good stars prompted us to this decision, for we afterward had reason to believe, from information given us by the Indians, that the smoke was raised as a decoy by a Crow war party.

Evening was coming on, and there was no wood or water nearer than the foot of the mountains. So thither we turned, directing our course towards the point where Laramie Creek issues upon the prairie. When we reached it, the bare tops of the mountains were still bright with sunshine. The little river was breaking, with an angry current, from its dark prison. There was something in the close vicinity of the mountains and the loud surging of the rapids, wonderfully cheering and exhilarating. There was a grass-plot by the river bank, surrounded by low ridges, which would effectually screen us and our fire from the sight of wandering Indians. Here, among the grass, I observed numerous circles of large stones, traces of a Dahcotah winter encampment. We lay down, and did not awake till the sun was up. A large rock projected from the shore, and behind it the deep water was slowly eddying round and round. The temptation was irresistible. I threw off my clothes, leaped in, suffered myself to be borne once round with the current, and then, seizing the strong root of a water-plant, drew myself to the shore. The effect was so refreshing, that I mistook it for returning health. But scarcely were we mounted and on our way, before the momentary glow passed. Again I hung as usual in my seat, scarcely able to hold myself erect.

"Look yonder," said Raymond; "you see that big hollow there; the Indians must have gone that way, if they went anywhere about here."

We reached the gap, which was like a deep notch cut into the mountain-ridge, and here we soon found an anthill furrowed with the mark of a lodge-pole. This was quite enough; there could be no doubt now. As we rode on, the opening growing narrower, the Indians had been compelled to march in closer order, and the traces became numerous and distinct. The gap terminated in a rocky gateway, leading into a rough and steep defile, between two precipitous mountains. Here grass and weeds were bruised to fragments by the throng that had passed through. We moved slowly over the rocks, up the passage; and in this toilsome manner advanced for an hour or two, bare precipices, hundreds of feet high, shooting up on either hand. Raymond, with his hardy mule, was a few rods before me, when we came to the foot of an ascent steeper than the rest, and which I trusted might prove the highest point of the defile. Pauline strained upward for a few yards, moaning and stumbling, and then came to a dead stop, unable to proceed further. I dismounted, and attempted to lead her; but my own exhausted strength soon gave out; so I loosened the trail-rope from her neck, and tying it round my arm, crawled up on my hands and knees. I gained the top, totally spent, the sweat-drops trickling from my forehead. Pauline stood like a statue by my side, her shadow falling upon the scorching rock; and in this shade, for there was no other, I lay for some time, scarcely able to move a limb. All around, the black crags, sharp as needles at the top, stood baking in the sun, without tree or bush or blade of grass to cover their nakedness. The whole scene seemed parched with a pitiless, insufferable heat.

After a while I could mount again, and we moved on, descending the defile on its western side. There was something ridiculous in the situation. Man and horse were helpless alike. Pauline and I could neither fight nor run.

Raymond's saddle-girth slipped; and while I proceeded he stopped to repair the mischief. I came to the top of a little declivity, where a welcome sight greeted my eye; a nook of fresh green grass nestled among the cliffs, sunny clumps of bushes on one side, and shaggy old pine-trees leaning from the rocks on the other. A shrill, familiar voice saluted me, and recalled me to days of boyhood; that of the insect called the "locust" by New England schoolboys, which was clinging among the heated boughs of the old pine-trees. Then, too, as I passed the bushes, the low sound of falling water reached my ear. Pauline turned of her own accord, and pushing through the boughs, we found a black rock, overarched by the cool green canopy. An icy stream was pouring from its side into a wide basin of white sand, whence it had no visible outlet, but filtered through into the soil below. While I filled a tin cup at the spring, Pauline was eagerly plunging her head deep in the pool. Other visitors had been there before us. All around in the soft soil were the footprints of elk, deer, and the Rocky Mountain sheep; and the grizzly bear too had left the recent prints of his broad foot, with its frightful array of claws. Among these mountains was his home.

Soon after leaving the spring we found a little grassy plain, encircled by the mountains, and marked, to our great joy, with all the traces of an Indian camp. Raymond's practised eye detected certain signs, by which he recognized the spot where Reynal's lodge had been pitched and his horses picketed. I approached, and stood looking at the place. Reynal and I had, I believe, hardly a feeling in common, and it perplexed me a good deal to understand why I should look with so much interest on the ashes of his fire, when between him and me there was no other bond of sympathy than the slender and precarious one of a kindred race.

In half an hour from this we were free of the mountains. There was a plain before us, totally barren and thickly peopled in many parts with prairie dogs, who sat at the mouths of their burrows and yelped at us as we passed. The plain, as we thought, was about six miles wide; but it cost us two hours to cross it. Then another mountain-range rose before us. From the dense bushes that clothed the steeps for a thousand feet shot up black crags, all leaning one way, and shattered by storms and thunder into grim and threatening shapes. As we entered a narrow passage on the trail of the Indians, they impended frightfully above our heads.

Our course was through thick woods, in the shade and sunlight of overhanging boughs. As we wound from side to side of the passage, to avoid its obstructions, we could see at intervals, through the foliage, the awful forms of the gigantic cliffs, that seemed to hem us in on the right and on the left, before and behind.

In an open space, fenced in by high rocks, stood two Indian forts, of a square form, rudely built of sticks and logs. They were somewhat ruinous, having probably been constructed the year before. Each might have contained about twenty men. Perhaps in this gloomy spot some party had been beset by enemies, and those scowling rocks and blasted trees might not long since have looked down on a conflict, unchronicled and unknown. Yet if any traces of bloodshed remained they were hidden by the bushes and tall rank weeds.

Gradually the mountains drew apart, and the passage expanded into a plain, where again we found the traces of an Indian encampment. There were trees and bushes just before us, and we stopped here for an hour's rest and refreshment. When we had finished our meal, Raymond struck fire, and, lighting his pipe, sat down at the foot of a tree to smoke. For some time I observed him puffing away with a face of unusual solemnity. Then slowly taking the pipe from his lips, he looked up and remarked that we had better not go any farther.

"Why not?" asked I.

He said that the country was become very dangerous, that we were entering the range of the Snakes, Arapahoes, and Gros-ventre Blackfeet, and that if any of their wandering parties should meet us, it would cost us our lives; but he added with blunt fidelity, that he would go anywhere I wished. I told him to bring up the animals, and mounting them we proceeded again. I confess that, as we moved forward, the prospect seemed but a doubtful one. I would have given the world for my ordinary elasticity of body and mind, and for a horse of such strength and spirit as the journey required.

Closer and closer the rocks gathered round us, growing taller and steeper, and pressing more and more upon our path. We entered at length a defile which, in its way, I never have seen rivalled. The mountain was cracked from top to bottom, and we were creeping along the bottom of the fissure, in dampness and gloom, with the clink of hoofs on the loose shingly rocks, and the hoarse murmuring of a petulant brook which kept us company. Sometimes the water, foaming among the stones, overspread the whole narrow passage; sometimes, withdrawing to one side, it gave us room to pass dry-shod. Looking up, we could see a narrow ribbon of bright blue sky between the dark edges of the opposing cliffs. This did not last long. The passage soon widened, and sunbeams found their way down, flashing upon the black waters. The defile would spread to many rods in width; bushes, trees, and flowers would spring by the side of the brook; the cliffs would be feathered with shrubbery, that clung in every crevice, and fringed with trees, that grew along their sunny edges. Then we would be moving again in darkness. The passage seemed about four miles long, and before we reached the end of it, the unshod hoofs of our animals were broken, and their legs cut by the sharp stones. Issuing from the mountain we found another plain. All around it stood a circle of precipices, that seemed the impersonation of Silence and Solitude. Here again the Indians had encamped, as well they might, after passing with their women, children, and horses, through the gulf behind us. In one day we had made a journey which it had cost them three to accomplish.

The only outlet to this amphitheatre lay over a hill some two hundred feet high, up which we moved with difficulty. Looking from the top, we saw that at last we were free of the mountains. The prairie spread before us, but so wild and broken that the view was everywhere obstructed. Far on our left one tall hill swelled up against the sky, on the smooth, pale-green surface of which four slowly moving black specks were discernible. They were evidently buffalo, and we hailed the sight as a good augury; for where the buffalo were, there the Indians would probably be found. We hoped on that very night to reach the village. We were anxious to do so for a double reason, wishing to bring our journey to an end, and knowing moreover that though to enter the village in broad daylight would be perfectly safe, yet to encamp in its vicinity would be dangerous. But as we rode on, the sun was sinking, and soon was within half an hour of the horizon. We ascended a hill and looked about us for a spot for our encampment. The prairie was like a turbulent ocean, suddenly congealed when its waves were at the highest, and it lay half in light and half in shadow, as the rich sunshine, yellow as gold, was pouring over it. The rough bushes of the wild sage were growing everywhere, its dull pale-green overspreading hill and hollow. Yet a little way before us, a bright verdant line of grass was winding along the plain, and here and there throughout its course glistened pools of water. We went down to it, kindled a fire, and turned our horses loose to feed. It was a little trickling brook, that for some yards on either side turned the barren prairie into fertility, and here and there it spread into deep pools, where the beavers had damned it up.

We placed our last remaining piece of antelope before a scanty fire, mournfully reflecting on our exhausted stock of provisions. Just then a large gray hare, peculiar to these prairies, came jumping along, and seated himself within fifty yards to look at us. I thoughtlessly raised my rifle to shoot him, but Raymond called out to me not to fire for fear the report should reach the ears of the Indians. That night for the first time we considered that the danger to which we were exposed was of a somewhat serious character; and to those who are unacquainted with Indians, it may seem strange that our chief apprehensions arose from the supposed proximity of the people whom we intended to visit. Had any straggling party of these faithful friends caught sight of us from the hill-top, they would probably have returned in the night to plunder us of our horses, and perhaps of our scalps. But the prairie is unfavorable to nervousness; and I presume that neither Raymond nor I thought twice of the matter that evening.

For eight hours pillowed on our saddles, we lay insensible as logs. Pauline's yellow head was stretched over me when I awoke. I rose and examined her. Her feet were bruised and swollen by the accidents of yesterday, but her eye was brighter, her motions livelier, and her mysterious malady had visibly abated. We moved on, hoping within an hour to come in sight of the Indian village; but again disappointment awaited us. The trail disappeared upon a hard and stony plain. Raymond and I rode from side to side, scrutinizing every yard of ground, until at length I found traces of the lodge-poles, by the side of a ridge of rocks. We began again to follow them.

"What is that black spot out there on the prairie?"

"It looks like a dead buffalo," answered Raymond.

We rode to it, and found it to be the huge carcass of a bull killed by the hunters as they passed. Tangled hair and scraps of hide were scattered on all sides, for the wolves had made merry over it, and hollowed out the entire carcass. It was covered with myriads of large black crickets, and from its appearance must have lain there four or five days. The sight was a disheartening one, and I observed to Raymond that the Indians might still be fifty or sixty miles off. But he shook his head, and replied that they dared not go so far for fear of their enemies, the Snakes.

Soon after this we lost the trail again, and ascended a neighboring ridge, totally at a loss. Before us lay a plain perfectly flat, spreading on the right and left, without apparent limit, and bounded in front by a long broken line of hills, ten or twelve miles distant. All was open and exposed to view, yet not a buffalo nor an Indian was visible.

"Do you see that?" said Raymond: "now we had better turn round."

But as Raymond's *bourgeois* thought otherwise, we descended the hill and began to cross the plain. We had come so far that neither Pauline's limbs, nor my own could carry me back to Fort Laramie. I considered that the lines of expediency and inclination tallied exactly, and that the most prudent course was to keep forward. The ground immediately around us was thickly strewn with the skulls and bones of buffalo, for here a year or two before the Indians had made a "surround"; yet no living game was in sight. At length an antelope sprang up and gazed at us. We fired together, and both missed, although the animal stood, a fair mark, within eighty yards. This ill-success might perhaps be charged to our own eagerness, for by this time we had no provisions left except a little flour. We could see several pools of water, glistening in the distance. As we approached, wolves and antelopes bounded away through the tall grass around them, and flocks of large white plover flew screaming over their surface. Having failed of the antelope, Raymond tried his hand at the birds, with the same ill-success. The water also disappointed us. Its margin was so mired by the crowd of buffalo that our timorous animals were afraid to approach. So we turned away and moved towards the hills. The rank grass, where it was not trampled down by the buffalo, fairly swept our horses' necks.

Again we found the same execrable barren prairie offering no clew by which to guide our way. As we drew near the hills, an opening appeared, through which the Indians must have gone if they had passed that way at all. Slowly we began to ascend it. I felt the most dreary forebodings of ill-success, when on looking round I could discover neither dent of hoof, nor footprints, nor trace of lodge-pole, though the passage was encumbered by the skulls of buffalo. We heard thunder muttering: another storm was coming on.

As we gained the top of the gap, the prospect beyond began to disclose itself. First, we saw a long dark line of ragged clouds upon the horizon, while above them rose the peaks of the Medicine-Bow range, the vanguard of the Rocky Mountains; then little by little the plain came into view, a vast green uniformity, forlorn and tenantless, though Laramie Creek glistened in a waving line over its surface, without a bush or a tree upon its banks. As yet, the round projecting shoulder of a hill intercepted a part of the view. I rode in advance, when suddenly I could distinguish a few dark spots on the prairie, along the bank of the stream.

"Buffalo!" said I.

"Horses, by God!" exclaimed Raymond, lashing his mule forward as he spoke. More and more of the plain disclosed itself, and more and more horses appeared, scattered along the river bank, or feeding in bands over the prairie. Then, standing in a circle by the stream, swarming with their savage inhabitants, we saw a mile or more off, the tall lodges of the Ogillallah. Never did the heart of a wanderer more gladden at the sight of home than did mine at the sight of that Indian camp.

Henry David Thoreau

"Ktaadn"

Henry David Thoreau (1817–1862), who was born and died in Concord, Massachusetts, learned to "live at home as a traveler." Although brief excursions took him to the Maine woods, the White Mountains, the Catskills, Cape Cod, Canada and the Upper Mississippi, his most famous trip was to Ralph Waldo Emerson's woodlot, two miles from the center of Concord, where he lived for two years and wrote the first draft of his masterpiece, Walden *(1854). Thoreau's contemporaries accepted him as a nature lover with a penchant for wild nature. He wrote about wild apples, foxes, loons, swamps, lynxes, and forest trees, but he was also an artist who wrote about his relationship to these things, and in the process he added a new genre—the nature essay—to American literary history. Thoreau was a naturalist, but "the fact is," as he said of himself, "I am a transcendentalist, a mystic, and a natural philosopher to boot." In one of his best-known essays, "Walking," he spoke out for the values he identified with wilderness, and the culminating point of his provocative defense of all things wild and free is that "in Wildness is the preservation of the World." In September of 1846, Thoreau, who advocated that "a man has not seen a thing who has not felt it," interrupted his stay at Walden Pond for a trip to the Maine woods. There he encountered something other than the harmonious relationship with nature he knew at Concord. While climbing above the timberline on Mt. Katahdin, Thoreau experienced absolute wilderness, "vast, Titanic, inhuman Nature," and he felt alien to it and to himself. Other writers from Meriwether Lewis to Francis Parkman had been similarly overwhelmed by the wilderness, but Thoreau gave the frightening experience its most effective expression. In "Ktaadn," collected posthumously in* The Maine Woods *(1864), syntax breaks down in duplication of the incomprehensible chaos it tries to describe, and in that*

123

moment, inhuman Katahdin gives point to what is most human.

In the night I dreamed of trout-fishing; and, when at length I awoke, it seemed a fable that this painted fish swam there so near my couch, and rose to our hooks the last evening, and I doubted if I had not dreamed it all. So I arose before dawn to test its truth, while my companions were still sleeping. There stood Ktaadn with distinct and cloudless outline in the moonlight; and the rippling of the rapids was the only sound to break the stillness. Standing on the shore, I once more cast my line into the stream, and I found the dream to be real and the fable true. The speckled trout and silvery roach, like flying-fish, sped swiftly through the moonlight air, describing bright arcs on the dark side of Ktaadn, until moonlight, now fading into daylight, brought satiety to my mind, and the minds of my companions, who had joined me.

By six o'clock, having mounted our packs and a good blanketful of trout, ready dressed, and swung up such baggage and provision as we wished to leave behind upon the tops of saplings, to be out of the reach of bears, we started for the summit of the mountain, distant, as Uncle George said the boatmen called it, about four miles, but as I judged, and as it proved, nearer fourteen. He had never been any nearer the mountain than this, and there was not the slightest trace of man to guide us farther in this direction. At first, pushing a few rods up the Aboljacknagesic, or "open-land stream," we fastened our batteau to a tree, and traveled up the north side, through burnt lands, now partially overgrown with young aspens and other shrubbery; but soon, recrossing this stream, where it was about fifty or sixty feet wide, upon a jam of logs and rocks,—and you could cross it by this means almost anywhere,—we struck at once for the highest peak, over a mile or more of comparatively open land, still very gradually ascending the while. Here it fell to my lot, as the oldest mountain-climber, to take the lead. So, scanning the woody side of the mountain, which lay still at an indefinite distance,

From Henry David Thoreau, "Ktaadn," in *The Maine Woods* (Boston: Ticknor and Fields, 1864).

stretched out some seven or eight miles in length before us, we determined to steer directly for the base of the highest peak, leaving a large slide, by which, as I have since learned, some of our predecessors ascended, on our left. This course would lead us parallel to a dark seam in the forest, which marked the bed of a torrent, and over a slight spur, which extended southward from the main mountain, from whose bare summit we could get an outlook over the country, and climb directly up the peak, which would then be close at hand. Seen from this point, a bare ridge at the extremity of the open land, Ktaadn presented a different aspect from any mountain I have seen, there being a greater proportion of naked rock rising abruptly from the forest; and we looked up at this blue barrier as if it were some fragment of a wall which anciently bounded the earth in that direction. Setting the compass for a northeast course, which was the bearing of the southern base of the highest peak, we were soon buried in the woods.

We soon began to meet with traces of bears and moose, and those of rabbits were everywhere visible. The tracks of moose, more or less recent, to speak literally, covered every square rod on the sides of the mountain; and these animals are probably more numerous there now than ever before, being driven into this wilderness, from all sides, by the settlements. The track of a full-grown moose is like that of a cow, or larger, and of the young, like that of a calf. Sometimes we found ourselves traveling in faint paths, which they had made, like cowpaths in the woods, only far more indistinct, being rather openings, affording imperfect vistas through the dense underwood, than trodden paths; and everywhere the twigs had been browsed by them, clipped as smoothly as if by a knife. The bark of trees was stripped up by them to the height of eight or nine feet, in long, narrow strips, an inch wide, still showing the distinct marks of their teeth. We expected nothing less than to meet a herd of them every moment, and our Nimrod held his shooting-iron in readiness; but we did not go out of our way to look for them, and, though numerous, they are so wary that the unskillful hunter might range the forest a long time before he could get sight of one. They are sometimes dangerous to encounter, and will not turn out for the hunter, but furiously rush upon him and trample him to death, unless he is lucky enough to avoid them by dodging round a tree. The largest are nearly as large as a horse, and weigh sometimes one thousand pounds; and it is said that they can step over a five-foot gate in their ordinary walk. They are described as exceedingly awkward-looking animals, with their long legs and short bodies, making a ludicrous figure when in full run, but making great headway, nevertheless. It seemed a mystery to us how they could thread these woods, which it required all our suppleness to accomplish,—climbing, stooping, and winding, alternately. They are said to drop their long and branching horns, which usually spread five or six feet, on their backs, and make their way easily by the weight of their bodies. Our boatmen said, but I know not with how much truth, that their horns are apt to be gnawed away by vermin while they sleep. Their flesh, which is more like beef than venison, is common in Bangor market.

We had proceeded on thus seven or eight miles, till about noon, with frequent pauses to refresh the weary ones, crossing a considerable mountain stream, which we conjectured to be Murch Brook, at whose mouth we had camped, all the time in woods, without having once seen the summit, and rising very gradually, when the boatmen beginning to despair a little, and fearing that we were leaving the mountain on one side of us, for they had not entire faith in the compass, McCauslin climbed a tree, from the top of which he could see the peak, when it appeared that we had not swerved from a right line, the compass down below still ranging with his arm, which pointed to the summit. By the side of a cool mountain rill, amid the woods, where the water began to partake of the purity and transparency of the air, we stopped to cook some of our fishes, which we had brought thus far in order to save our hard bread and pork, in the use of which we had put ourselves on short allowance. We soon had a fire blazing, and stood around it, under the damp and sombre forest of firs and birches, each with a sharpened stick, three or four feet in length, upon which he had spitted his trout, or roach, previously well gashed and salted, our sticks, radiating like the spokes of a wheel from one centre, and each crowding his particular fish into the most desirable exposure, not with the truest regard always to his neighbor's rights. Thus we regaled ourselves, drinking meanwhile at the spring, till one man's pack, at least, was considerably lightened, when we again took up our line of march.

At length we reached an elevation sufficiently bare to afford a view of the summit, still distant and blue, almost as if retreating from us. A torrent, which proved to be the same we had crossed, was seen tumbling down in front, literally from out of the clouds. But this glimpse at our whereabouts was soon lost, and we were buried in the woods again. The wood was chiefly yellow birch, spruce, fir, mountain-ash, or round-wood, as the Maine people call it, and moose-wood. It was the worst kind of traveling; sometimes like the densest scrub-oak patches with us. The cornel, or bunch-berries, were very abundant, as well as Solomon's seal and mooseberries. Blueberries were distributed along our whole route; and in one place the bushes were drooping with the weight of the fruit, still as fresh as ever. It was the 7th of September. Such patches afforded a grateful repast, and served to bait the third party forward. When any lagged behind, the cry of "blueberries" was most effectual to bring them up. Even at this elevation we passed through a moose-yard, formed by a large flat rock, four or five rods square, where they tread down the snow in winter. At length, fearing that if we held the direct course to the summit, we should not find any water near our camping-ground, we gradually swerved to the west, till, at four o'clock, we struck again in the torrent which I have mentioned, and here, in view of the summit, the weary party decided to camp that night.

While my companions were seeking a suitable spot for this purpose, I improved the little daylight that was left in climbing the mountain alone. We were in a deep and narrow ravine, sloping up to the clouds, at an angle of nearly forty-five degrees, and hemmed in by walls of rock, which were at first covered with low trees, then with impenetrable thickets of scraggy birches and spruce-trees, and with moss, but at last bare of all vegetation but lichens, and almost continually draped in clouds. Following at the course of the torrent which occupied this,—and I mean to lay some emphasis on this word *up*,—pulling myself up by the side of perpendicular falls of twenty or thirty feet, by the roots of firs and birches, and then, perhaps, walking a level rod or two in the thin stream, for it took up the whole road, ascending by huge steps, as it were, a giant's stairway, down which a river flowed, I had soon cleared the trees, and paused on the successive shelves, to look back over the country. The torrent was from fifteen to thirty feet wide, without a tributary, and seemingly not diminishing in breadth as I advanced; but still it came rushing and roaring down, with a copious tide, over and amidst masses of bare rock, from the very clouds, as though a waterspout had just burst over the mountain. Leaving this at last, I began to work my way, scarcely less arduous than Satan's anciently through Chaos, up the nearest, though not the highest peak, at first scrambling on all fours over the tops of ancient black spruce-trees (*Abies nigra*), old as the flood, from two to ten or twelve feet in height, their tops flat and spreading, and their foliage blue, and nipped with cold, as if for centuries they had ceased growing upward against the bleak sky, the solid cold. I walked some good rods erect upon the tops of these trees, which were overgrown with moss and mountain-cranberries. It seemed that in the course of time they had filled up the intervals between the huge rocks, and the cold wind had uniformly leveled all over. Here the principle of vegetation was hard put to it. There was apparently a belt of this kind running quite round the mountain, though, perhaps, nowhere so remarkable as here. Once slumping through, I looked down ten feet, into a dark and cavernous region, and saw the stem of a spruce, on whose top I stood, as on a mass of coarse basket-work, fully nine inches in diameter at the ground. These holes were bears' dens, and the bears were even then at home. This was the sort of garden I made my way *over*, for an eighth of a mile, at the risk, it is true, of treading on some of the plants, not seeing any path *through* it,—certainly the most treacherous and porous country I ever traveled.

> "Nigh foundered on he fares, Treading the crude
> consistence, half on foot, Half flying."

But nothing could exceed the toughness of the twigs,—not one snapped under my weight, for they had slowly grown. Having slumped, scrambled, rolled, bounced, and walked, by turns, over this scraggy country, I arrived upon a side-hill, or rather side-mountain, where rocks, gray, silent rocks, were the flocks and herds that pastured, chewing a rocky cud at sunset. They looked at me with hard gray eyes, without a bleat or a low. This brought me to the skirt of a cloud, and bounded my walk that night. But I had already seen that Maine country when I turned about, waving, flowing, rippling, down below.

When I returned to my companions, they had selected a

camping-ground on the torrent's edge, and were resting on the ground; one was on the sick list, rolled in a blanket, on a damp shelf of rock. It was a savage and dreary scenery enough; so wildly rough, that they looked long to find a level and open space for the tent. We could not well camp higher, for want of fuel; and the trees here seemed so evergreen and sappy, that we almost doubted if they would acknowledge the influence of fire; but fire prevailed at last, and blazed here, too, like a good citizen of the world. Even at this height we met with frequent traces of moose, as well as of bears. As here was no cedar, we made our bed of coarser feathered spruce; but at any rate the feathers were plucked from the live tree. It was, perhaps, even a more grand and desolate place for a night's lodging than the summit would have been, being in the neighborhood of those wild trees, and of the torrent. Some more aerial and finer-spirited winds rushed and roared through the ravine all night, from time to time arousing our fire, and dispersing the embers about. It was as if we lay in the very nest of a young whirlwind. At midnight, one of my bed-fellows, being startled in his dreams by the sudden blazing up to its top of a fir-tree, whose green boughs were dried by the heat, sprang up, with a cry, from his bed, thinking the world on fire, and drew the whole camp after him.

In the morning, after whetting our appetite on some raw pork, a wafer of hard bread, and a dipper of condensed cloud or waterspout, we all together began to make our way up the falls, which I have described; this time choosing the right hand, or highest peak, which was not the one I had approached before. But soon my companions were lost to my sight behind the mountain ridge in my rear, which still seemed ever retreating before me, and I climbed alone over huge rocks, loosely poised, a mile or more, still edging toward the clouds; for though the day was clear elsewhere, the summit was concealed by mist. The mountain seemed a vast aggregation of loose rocks, as if some time it had rained rocks, and they lay as they fell on the mountain sides, nowhere fairly at rest, but leaning on each other, all rocking-stones, with cavities between, but scarcely any soil or smoother shelf. They were the raw materials of a planet dropped from an unseen quarry, which the vast chemistry of nature would anon work up, or work down, into the smiling and verdant plains and valleys of earth. This was an undone extremity of the globe; as in lignite, we see coal in the process of formation.

At length I entered within the skirts of the cloud which seemed forever drifting over the summit, and yet would never be gone, but was generated out of that pure air as fast as it flowed away; and when, a quarter of a mile farther, I reached the summit of the ridge, which those who have seen it in clearer weather say is about five miles long, and contains a thousand acres of table-land, I was deep within the hostile ranks of clouds, and all objects were obscured by them. Now the wind would blow me out a yard of clear sunlight, wherein I stood; then a gray, dawning light was all it could accomplish, the cloud-line ever rising and falling with the wind's intensity. Sometimes it seemed as if the summit would be cleared in a few moments, and smile in sunshine; but what was gained on one side was lost on another. It was like sitting in a chimney and waiting for the smoke to blow away. It was, in fact, a cloud factory,—these were the cloud-works, and the wind turned them off done from the cool, bare rocks. Occasionally, when the windy columns broke in to me, I caught sight of a dark, damp crag to the right or left; the mist driving ceaselessly between it and me. It reminded me of the creations of the old epic and dramatic poets, of Atlas, Vulcan, the Cyclops, and Prometheus. Such was Caucasus and the rock where Prometheus was bound. Æschylus had no doubt visited such scenery as this. It was vast, Titanic, and such as man never inhabits. Some part of the beholder, even some vital part, seems to escape through the loose grating of his ribs as he ascends. He is more lone than you can imagine. There is less of substantial thought and fair understanding in him than in the plains where men inhabit. His reason is dispersed and shadowy, more thin and subtile, like the air. Vast, Titanic, inhuman Nature has got him at disadvantage, caught him alone, and pilfers him of some of his divine faculty. She does not smile on him as in the plains. She seems to say sternly, Why came ye here before your time. This ground is not prepared for you. Is it not enough that I smile in the valleys? I have never made this soil for thy feet, this air for thy breathing, these rocks for thy neighbors. I cannot pity nor fondle thee here, but forever relentlessly drive thee hence to where I *am* kind. Why seek me where I have not called thee, and then complain because you find me but a stepmother? Shouldst thou freeze or starve, or shudder thy life away, here is no shrine, nor altar, nor any access to my ear.

"Chaos and ancient Night, I come no spy
    With purpose to explore or to disturb
    The secrets of your realm, but . . .
                . . . . . as my way
    Lies through your spacious empire up to light."

The tops of mountains are among the unfinished parts of
the globe, whither it is a slight insult to the gods to climb and
pry into their secrets, and try their effect on our humanity.
Only daring and insolent men, perchance, go there. Simple
races, as savages, do not climb mountains,—their tops are
sacred and mysterious tracts never visited by them. Pomola is
always angry with those who climb to the summit of Ktaadn.

According to Jackson, who, in his capacity of geological
surveyor of the State, has accurately measured it,—the altitude of Ktaadn is 5300 feet, or a little more than one mile
above the level of the sea,—and he adds, "It is then evidently
the highest point in the State of Maine, and is the most
abrupt granite mountain in New England." The peculiarities
of that spacious table-land on which I was standing, as
well as the remarkable semi-circular precipice or basin on
the eastern side, were all concealed by the mist. I had
brought my whole pack to the top, not knowing but I should
have to make my descent to the river, and possibly to the
settled portion of the State alone, and by some other route,
and wishing to have a complete outfit with me. But at length,
fearing that my companions would be anxious to reach the
river before night, and knowing that the clouds might rest on
the mountain for days, I was compelled to descend. Occasionally, as I came down, the wind would blow me a vista open,
through which I could see the country eastward, boundless
forests, and lakes, and streams, gleaming in the sun, some of
them emptying into the East Branch. There were also new
mountains in sight in that direction. Now and then some
small bird of the sparrow family would flit away before me,
unable to command its course, like a fragment of the gray
rock blown off by the wind.

I found my companions where I had left them, on the side
of the peak, gathering the mountain-cranberries, which filled
every crevice between the rocks, together with blueberries,
which had a spicier flavor the higher up they grew, but were
not the less agreeable to our palates. When the country is
settled, and roads are made, these cranberries will perhaps

become an article of commerce. From this elevation, just on the skirts of the clouds, we could overlook the country, west and south, for a hundred miles. There it was, the State of Maine, which we had seen on the map, but not much like that,—immeasurable forest for the sun to shine on, that eastern *stuff* we hear of in Massachusetts. No clearing, no house. It did not look as if a solitary traveler had cut so much as a walking-stick there. Countless lakes,—Moosehead in the southwest, forty miles long by ten wide, like a gleaming silver platter at the end of the table; Chesuncook, eighteen long by three wide, without an island; Millinocket, on the south, with its hundred islands; and a hundred others without a name; and mountains, also, whose names, for the most part, are known only to the Indians. The forest looked like a firm grass sward, and the effect of these lakes in its midst has been well compared, by one who has since visited this same spot, to that of a "mirror broken into a thousand fragments, and wildly scattered over the grass, reflecting the full blaze of the sun." It was a large farm for somebody, when cleared. According to the Gazetteer, which was printed before the boundary question was settled, this single Penobscot County, in which we were, was larger than the whole State of Vermont, with its fourteen counties; and this was only a part of the wild lands of Maine. We are concerned now, however, about natural, not political limits. We were about eighty miles, as the bird flies, from Bangor, or one hundred and fifteen, as we had ridden, and walked, and paddled. We had to console ourselves with the reflection that this view was probably as good as that from the peak, as far as it went; and what were a mountain without its attendant clouds and mists? Like ourselves, neither Bailey nor Jackson had obtained a clear view from the summit.

Setting out on our return to the river, still at an early hour in the day, we decided to follow the course of the torrent, which we supposed to be Murch Brook, as long as it would not lead us too far out of our way. We thus traveled about four miles in the very torrent itself, continually crossing and recrossing it, leaping from rock to rock, and jumping with the stream down falls of seven or eight feet, or sometimes sliding down on our backs in a thin sheet of water. This ravine had been the scene of an extraordinary freshet in the spring, apparently accompanied by a slide from the mountain. It must have been filled with a stream of stones and water, at least twenty feet above the present level of the torrent. For a rod or two, on either side of its channel, the trees were barked and splintered up to their tops, the birches bent over, twisted, and sometimes finely split, like a stable-broom; some, a foot in diameter, snapped off, and whole clumps of trees bent over with the weight of rocks piled on them. In one place we noticed a rock, two or three feet in diameter, lodged nearly twenty feet high in the crotch of a tree. For the whole four miles, we saw but one rill emptying in, and the volumes of water did not seem to be increased from the first. We traveled thus very rapidly with a downward impetus, and grew remarkably expert at leaping from rock to rock, for leap we must, and leap we did, whether there was any rock at the right distance or not. It was a pleasant picture when the foremost turned about and looked up the winding ravine, walled in with rocks and the green forest, to see, at intervals of a rod or two, a red-shirted or green-jacketed mountaineer against the white torrent, leaping down the channel with his pack on his back, or pausing upon a convenient rock in the midst of the torrent to mend a rent in his clothes, or unstrap the dipper at his belt to take a draught of the water. At one place we were startled by seeing, on a little sandy shelf by the side of the stream, the fresh print of a man's foot, and for a moment realized how Robinson Crusoe felt in a similar case; but at last we remembered that we had struck this stream on our way up, though we could not have told where, and one had descended into the ravine for a drink. The cool air above and the continual bathing of our bodies in mountain water, alternate foot, sitz, douche, and plunge baths, made this walk exceedingly refreshing, and we had traveled only a mile or two, after leaving the torrent, before every thread of our clothes was as dry as usual, owing perhaps to a peculiar quality in the atmosphere.

After leaving the torrent, being in doubt about our course, Tom threw down his pack at the foot of the loftiest sprucetree at hand, and shinned up the bare trunk some twenty feet, and then climbed through the green tower, lost to our sight, until he held the topmost spray in his hand.[1] McCauslin, in

[1] "The spruce-tree," says Springer in '51, "is generally selected, principally for the superior facilities which its numerous limbs afford the climber. To gain the first limbs of this tree, which are from twenty to forty feet from the ground, a smaller tree is undercut and lodged against it, clambering up which the top of the spruce is reached.

his younger days, had marched through the wilderness with a body of troops, under General Somebody, and with one other man did all the scouting and spying service. The General's word was, "Throw down the top of that tree," and there was no tree in the Maine woods so high that it did not lose its top in such a case. I have heard a story of two men being lost once in these woods, nearer to the settlements than this, who climbed the loftiest pine they could find, some six feet in diameter at the ground, from whose top they discovered a solitary clearing and its smoke. When at this height, some two hundred feet from the ground, one of them became dizzy, and fainted in his companion's arms, and the latter had to accomplish the descent with him, alternately fainting and reviving, as best he could. To Tom we cried, Where away does the summit bear? where the burnt lands? The last he could only conjecture; he descried, however, a little meadow and pond, lying probably in our course, which we concluded to steer for. On reaching this secluded meadow, we found fresh tracks of moose on the shore of the pond, and the water was still unsettled as if they had fled before us. A little farther, in a dense thicket, we seemed to be still on their trail. It was a small meadow, of a few acres, on the mountain side, concealed by the forest, and perhaps never seen by a white man before, where one would think that the moose might browse and bathe, and rest in peace. Pursuing this course, we soon reached the open land, which went sloping down some miles toward the Penobscot.

Perhaps I most fully realized that this was primeval, untamed, and forever untamable *Nature*, or whatever else men call it, while coming down this part of the mountain. We were passing over "Burnt Lands," burnt by lightning, perchance, though they showed no recent marks of fire, hardly so much as a charred stump, but looked rather like a natural pasture for the moose and deer, exceedingly wild and desolate, with occasional strips of timber crossing them, and low poplars springing up, and patches of blueberries here and there. I found myself traversing them familiarly, like some pasture run to waste, or partially reclaimed by man; but

---

In some cases, when a very elevated position is desired, the spruce-tree is lodged against the trunk of some lofty pine, up which we ascend to a height twice that of the surrounding forest."

To indicate the direction of pines, one throws down a branch, and a man on the ground takes the bearing.

when I reflected what man, what brother or sister or kinsman of our race made it and claimed it, I expected the proprietor to rise up and dispute my passage. It is difficult to conceive of a region uninhabited by man. We habitually presume his presence and influence everywhere. And yet we have not seen pure Nature, unless we have seen her thus vast and drear and inhuman, though in the midst of cities. Nature was here something savage and awful, though beautiful. I looked with awe at the ground I trod on, to see what the Powers had made there, the form and fashion and material of their work. This was that Earth of which we have heard, made out of Chaos and Old Night. Here was no man's garden, but the un-handselled globe. It was not lawn, nor pasture, nor mead, nor woodland, nor lea, nor arable, nor waste land. It was the fresh and natural surface of the planet Earth, as it was made forever and ever,—to be the dwelling of man, we say,—so Nature made it, and man may use it if he can. Man was not to be associated with it. It was Matter, vast, terrific,—not his Mother Earth that we have heard of, not for him to tread on, or be buried in,—no, it were being too familiar even to let his bones lie there,—the home, this, of Necessity and Fate. There was clearly felt the presence of a force not bound to be kind to man. It was a place for heathenism and supersti-tious rites,—to be inhabited by men nearer of kin to the rocks and to wild animals than we. We walked over it with a certain awe, stopping, from time to time, to pick the blueber-ries which grew there, and had a smart and spicy taste. Per-chance where *our* wild pines stand, and leaves lie on their forest floor, in Concord, there were once reapers, and hus-bandmen planted grain; but here not even the surface had been scarred by man, but it was a specimen of what God saw fit to make this world. What is it to be admitted to a museum, to see a myriad of particular things, compared with being shown some star's surface, some hard matter in its home! I stand in awe of my body, this matter to which I am bound has become so strange to me. I fear not spirits, ghosts, of which I am one,—*that* my body might,—but I fear bodies, I tremble to meet them. What is this Titan that has possession of me? Talk of mysteries! Think of our life in nature,—daily to be shown matter, to come in contact with it,—rocks, trees, wind on our cheeks! the *solid* earth! the *ac-tual* world! the *common sense! Contact! Contact! Who* are we? *where* are we?

Clarence King

Mountaineering in the Sierra Nevada

Clarence King (1842–1901), a graduate of the Sheffield School at Yale, served as assistant geologist to Josiah Whitney's California Geological Survey from 1863 to 1866. A year later, when he was only twenty-five, King was appointed director of the Geological and Geographical Exploration of the Fortieth Parallel Survey, a job which took him from eastern Colorado through the Great Basin. King culminated his public career in 1879 as first director of the newly formed United States Geological Survey. King's main scientific writing is his eight-hundred-page Systematic Geology *(1879), but his contribution to American literature is his* Mountaineering in the Sierra Nevada *(1872). King claimed that his book was an experiment to see if natural history writing might find a popular audience, but he vehemently dissociated himself from the "army of literary travelers who have planted themselves [in Yosemite] and burst into rhetoric. Here all who make California books dismount and inflate." Though capable of his own inflations, King was a conscious craftsman who tempered his aesthetic responses, influenced by his reading of Ruskin, with geologic knowledge and experience to give his work a granitic quality appropriate to the mountains he climbed and described with such exuberance. Admired by both Henry Adams and John Hay as "the best and brightest man of his generation," King foresaw that his own successful evocation of mountaineering would reach a public who would soon sully the wilderness experience he loved. "They are already shooting our buffaloes," he wrote; "it cannot be long before they will cause themselves to be honorably dragged up and down our Sierras, with perennial yellow gaiter, and ostentation of bath-tub."*

We had now an easy slope to the summit, and hurried up over rocks and ice, reaching the crest at exactly twelve o'clock. I rang my hammer upon the topmost rock; we grasped hands and I reverently named the grand peak Mount Tyndall.

To our surprise, upon sweeping the horizon with my level, there appeared two peaks equal in height with us, and two rising even higher. That which looked highest of all was a cleanly cut helmet of granite upon the same ridge with Mount Tyndall, lying about six miles south, and fronting the desert with a bold, square bluff which rises to the crest of the peak, where a white fold of snow trims it gracefully. Mount Whitney, as we afterward called it, in honor of our chief, is probably the highest land within the United States. Its summit looked glorious, but inaccessible.

The general topography overlooked by us may be thus simply outlined. Two parallel chains, enclosing an intermediate trough, face each other. Across this deep, enclosed gulf, from wall to wall, juts the thin but lofty and craggy ridge, or "divide," before described, which forms an important watershed, sending those streams which enter the chasm north of it into King's River, those south forming the most important sources of the Kern, whose straight, rapidly deepening valley stretches south, carved profoundly in granite, while the King's, after flowing longitudinally in the opposite course for eight or ten miles, turns abruptly west round the base of Mount Brewer, cuts across the western ridge, opening a gate of its own, and carves a rock channel transversely down the Sierra to the California plain.

Fronting us stood the west chain, a great mural ridge watched over by two dominant heights, Kaweah Peak and Mount Brewer, its wonderful profile defining against the western sky a multitude of peaks and spires. Bold buttresses jut out through fields of ice, and reach down stone arms among snow and *débris*. North and south of us the higher, or eastern, summit stretched on in miles and miles of snow peaks, the farthest horizon still crowded with their white points. East the whole range fell in sharp, hurrying abruptness to the desert, where, ten thousand feet below, lay a vast expanse of arid plain intersected by low, parallel ranges,

From Clarence King, *Mountaineering in the Sierra Nevada* (Boston: James R. Osgood, 1872).

traced from north to south. Upon the one side, a thousand
sculptures of stone, hard, sharp, shattered by cold into infin-
iteness of fractures and rift, springing up, mutely severe, into
the dark, austere blue of heaven; scarred and marked, except
where snow or ice, spiked down by ragged granite bolts,
shields with its pale armor these rough mountain shoulders;
storm-tinted at summit, and dark where, swooping down
from ragged cliff, the rocks plunge over cañon-walls into
blue, silent gulfs.

Upon the other hand, reaching out to horizons faint and
remote, lay plains clouded with the ashen hues of death;
stark, wind-swept floors of white, and hill-ranges, rigidly
formal, monotonously low, and lying under an unfeeling bril-
liance of light, which, for all its strange, unclouded clearness,
has yet a vague half-darkness, a suggestion of black and
shade more truly pathetic than fading twilight. No greenness
soothes, no shadow cools the glare. Owen's Lake, an oval of
acrid water, lies dense blue upon the brown sage-plain, looking like a plate of hot metal. Traced in ancient beach-lines,
here and there upon hill and plain, relics of ancient lake-
shore outline the memory of a cooler past—a period of life
and verdure when the stony chains were green islands among
basins of wide, watery expanse.

The two halves of this view, both in sight at once, express
the highest, the most acute, aspects of desolation—inanimate
forms out of which something living has gone forever. From
the desert have been dried up and blown away its seas. Their
shores and white, salt-strewn bottoms lie there in the eloquence of death. Sharp, white light glances from all the
mountain-walls, where in marks and polishings has been written the epitaph of glaciers now melted and vanished into air.
Vacant cañons lie open to the sun, bare, treeless, half
shrouded with snow, cumbered with loads of broken *débris*,
still as graves, except when flights of rocks rush down some
chasm's throat, startling the mountains with harsh, dry rattle,
their fainter echoes from below followed too quickly by dense
silence.

The serene sky is grave with nocturnal darkness. The earth
blinds you with its light. That fair contrast we love in lower
lands, between bright heavens and dark, cool earth, here re-
verses itself with terrible energy. You look up into an infinite
vault, unveiled by clouds, empty and dark, from which no
brightness seems to ray, an expanse with no graded perspec-

tive, no tremble, no vapory mobility, only the vast yawning of hollow space.

With an aspect of endless remoteness burns the small, white sun, yet its light seems to pass invisibly through the sky, blazing out with intensity upon mountain and plain, flooding rock details with painfully bright reflections, and lighting up the burnt sand and stone of the desert with a strange, blinding glare. There is no sentiment of beauty in the whole scene; no suggestion, however far remote, of sheltered landscape; not even the air of virgin hospitality that greets us explorers in so many uninhabited spots which by their fertility and loveliness of grove or meadow seem to offer man a home, or us nomads a pleasant camp-ground. Silence and desolation are the themes which nature has wrought out under this eternally serious sky.

A faint suggestion of life clings about the middle altitudes of the eastern slope, where black companies of pine, stunted from breathing the hot desert air, group themselves just beneath the bottom of perpetual snow, or grow in patches of cloudy darkness over the moraines, those piles of wreck crowded from their pathway by glaciers long dead. Something there is pathetic in the very emptiness of these old glacier valleys, these imperishable tracks of unseen engines. One's eye ranges up their broad, open channel to the shrunken white fields surrounding hollow amphitheatres which were once crowded with deep burdens of snow,—the birthplace of rivers of ice now wholly melted; the dry, clear heavens overhead blank of any promise of ever rebuilding them. I have never seen Nature when she seemed so little "Mother Nature" as in this place of rocks and snow, echoes and emptiness. It impresses me as the ruins of some bygone geological period, and no part of the present order, like a specimen of chaos which has defied the finishing hand of Time.

Of course I see its bearings upon climate, and could read a lesson quite glibly as to its usefulness as a condenser, and tell you gravely how much California has for which she may thank these heights, and how little Nevada; but looking from this summit with all desire to see everything, the one overmastering feeling is desolation, desolation!

Next to this, and more pleasing to notice, is the interest and richness of the granite forms; for the whole region, from plain to plain, is built of this dense, solid rock, and is sculp-

tured under chisel of cold in shapes of great variety, yet all
having a common spirit, which is purely Gothic.

In the much discussed origin of this order of building I
never remember to have seen, though it can hardly have escaped mention, any suggestion of the possibility of the Gothic
having been inspired by granite forms. Yet, as I sat on
Mount Tyndall, the whole mountains shaped themselves like
the ruins of cathedrals,—sharp roof-ridges, pinnacled and
statued; buttresses more spired and ornamented than Milan's;
receding doorways with pointed arches carved into black
façades of granite, doors never to be opened, innumerable
jutting points, with here and there a single cruciform peak, its
frozen roof and granite spires so strikingly Gothic I cannot
doubt that the Alps furnished the models for early cathedrals
of that order.

I thoroughly enjoyed the silence, which, gratefully contrasting with the surrounding tumult of form, conveyed to me a
new sentiment. I have lain and listened through the heavy
calm of a tropical voyage, hour after hour, longing for a
sound; and in desert nights the dead stillness has many a time
wakened me from sleep. For moments, too, in my forest life,
the groves made absolutely no breath of movement; but there
is around these summits the soundlessness of a vacuum. The
sea stillness is that of sleep; the desert, of death—this silence
is like the waveless calm of space.

All the while I made my instrumental observations the fascination of the view so held me that I felt no surprise at
seeing water boiling over our little faggot blaze at a temperature of one hundred and ninety-two degrees F., nor in observing the barometrical column stand at 17.99 inches: and it was
not till a week or so after that I realized we had felt none of
the conventional sensations of nausea, headache, and I don't
know what all, that people are supposed to suffer at extreme
altitudes; but these things go with guides and porters, I believe, and with coming down to one's hotel at evening there
to scold one's picturesque *aubergiste* in a French which
strikes upon his ear as a foreign tongue; possibly all that will
come to us with advancing time, and what is known as "doing America." They are already shooting our buffaloes; it
cannot be long before they will cause themselves to be honorably dragged up and down our Sierras, with perennial yellow
gaiter, and ostentation of bath-tub.

Having completed our observations, we packed up the instruments, glanced once again round the whole field of view, and descended to the top of our icicle ladder. Upon looking over, I saw to my consternation that during the day the upper half had broken off. Scars traced down upon the snow-field below it indicated the manner of its fall, and far below, upon the shattered *débris*, were strewn its white relics. I saw that nothing but the sudden gift of wings could possibly take us down to the snow-ridge. We held council, and concluded to climb quite round the peak in search of the best mode of descent.

As we crept about the east face, we could look straight down upon Owen's Valley, and into the vast glacier gorges, and over piles of moraines and fluted rocks, and the frozen lakes of the eastern slope. When we reached the southwest front of the mountain we found that its general form was that of an immense horseshoe, the great eastern ridge forming one side, and the spur which descended to our camp the other, we having climbed up the outer part of the toe. Within the curve of the horseshoe was a gorge, cut almost perpendicularly down two thousand feet, its side rough-hewn walls of rocks and snow, its narrow bottom almost a continuous chain of deep blue lakes with loads of ice and *débris* piles. The stream which flowed through them joined the waters from our home grove, a couple of miles below the camp. If we could reach the level of the lakes, I believed we might easily climb round them and out of the upper end of the horseshoe, and walk upon the Kern plateau round to our bivouac.

It required a couple of hours of very painstaking, deliberate climbing to get down the first descent, which we did, however, without hurting our barometer, and fortunately without the fatiguing use of the lasso; reaching finally the uppermost lake, a granite bowlful of cobalt-blue water, transparent and unrippled. So high and enclosing were the tall walls about us, so narrow and shut in the cañon, so flattened seemed the cover of sky, we felt oppressed after the expanse and freedom of our hours on the summit.

The snow-field we followed, descending farther, was irregularly honeycombed in deep pits, circular or irregular in form, and melted to a greater or less depth, holding each a large stone embedded in the bottom. It seems they must have fallen from the overhanging heights with sufficient force to plunge into the snow.

Brilliant light and strong color met our eyes at every

glance—the rocks of a deep purple-red tint, the pure alpine
lakes of a cheerful sapphire blue, the snow glitteringly white.
The walls on either side for half their height were planed and
polished by glaciers, and from the smoothly glazed sides the
sun was reflected as from a mirror.

Mile after mile we walked cautiously over the snow and
climbed round the margins of lakes, and over piles of *débris*
which marked the ancient terminal moraines. At length we
reached the end of the horseshoe, where the walls contracted
to a gateway, rising on either side in immense, vertical pillars
a thousand feet high. Through this gateway we could look
down the valley of the Kern, and beyond to the gentler ridges
where a smooth growth of forest darkened the rolling
plateau. Passing the last snow, we walked through this gateway and turned westward round the spur toward our camp.
The three miles which closed our walk were alternately
through groves of *Pinus flexilis* and upon plains of granite.

The glacier sculpture and planing are here very beautiful,
the large crystals of orthoclase with which the granite is
studded being cut down to the common level, their rosy tint
making with the white base a beautiful, burnished porphyry.

The sun was still an hour high when we reached camp, and
with a feeling of relaxation and repose we threw ourselves
down to rest by the log, which still continued blazing. We
had accomplished our purpose.

During the last hour or two of our tramp Cotter had com-
plained of his shoes, which were rapidly going to pieces.
Upon examination we found to our dismay that there was
not over half a day's wear left in them, a calamity which
gave to our difficult homeward climb a new element of danger. The last nail had been worn from my own shoes, and the
soles were scratched to the quick, but I believed them stout
enough to hold together till we should reach the main camp.

We planned a pair of moccasins for Cotter, and then spent
a pleasant evening by the camp-fire, rehearsing our climb to
the detail, sleep finally overtaking us and holding us fast
bound until broad daylight next morning, when we woke with
a sense of having slept for a week, quite bright and perfectly
refreshed for our homeward journey.

After a frugal breakfast, in which we limited ourselves to a
few cubic inches of venison, and a couple of stingy slices of
bread, with a single meagre cup of diluted tea, we shouldered

our knapsacks, which now sat lightly upon toughened shoulders, and marched out upon the granite plateau.

We had concluded that it was impossible to retrace our former way, knowing well that the precipitous divide could not be climbed from this side; then, too, we had gained such confidence in our climbing powers, from constant victory, that we concluded to attempt the passage of the great King's Cañon, mainly because this was the only mode of reaching camp, and since the geological section of the granite it exposed would afford us an exceedingly instructive study.

The broad granite plateau which forms the upper region of the Kern Valley slopes in general inclination up to the great divide. This remarkably pinnacled ridge, where it approaches the Mount Tyndall wall, breaks down into a broad depression where the Kern Valley sweeps northward, until it suddenly breaks off in precipices three thousand feet down into the King's Cañon.

The morning was wholly consumed in walking up this gently inclined plane of granite, our way leading over the glacier-polished foldings and along graded undulations among labyrinths of alpine garden and wildernesses of erratic boulders, little lake-basins, and scattered clusters of dwarfed and sombre pine.

About noon we came suddenly upon the brink of a precipice which sank sharply from our feet into the gulf of the King's Cañon. Directly opposite us rose Mount Brewer, and up out of the depths of those vast sheets of frozen snow swept spiry buttress-ridges, dividing the upper heights into those amphitheatres over which we had struggled on our outward journey. Straight across from our point of view was the chamber of rock and ice where we had camped on the first night. The wall at our feet fell sharp and rugged, its lower two-thirds hidden from our view by the projections of a thousand feet of crags. Here and there, as we looked down, small patches of ice, held in rough hollows, rested upon the steep surface, but it was too abrupt for any great fields of snow. I dislodged a boulder upon the edge and watched it bound down the rocky precipice, dash over caves a thousand feet below us, and disappear, the crash of its fall coming up to us from the unseen depths fainter and fainter, until the air only trembled with confused echoes.

A long look at the pass to the south of Mount Brewer, where we had parted from our friends, animated us with courage to begin the descent, which we did with utmost care, for the rocks, becoming more and more glacier-smoothed, afforded us hardly any firm footholds. When down about eight hundred feet we again rolled rocks ahead of us, and saw them disappear over the eaves, and only heard the sound of their stroke after many seconds, which convinced us that directly below lay a great precipice.

At this juncture the soles came entirely off Cotter's shoes, and we stopped upon a little cliff of granite to make him moccasins of our provision bags and slips of blanket, tying them on as firmly as we could with the extra straps and buckskin thongs. Climbing with these proved so insecure that I made Cotter go behind me, knowing that under ordinary circumstances I could stop him if he fell.

Here and there in the clefts of the rocks grew stunted pine bushes, their roots twisted so firmly into the crevices that we laid hold of them with the utmost confidence whenever they came within our reach. In this way we descended to within fifty feet of the brink, having as yet no knowledge of the cliffs below, except our general memory of their aspect from the Mount Brewer wall.

The rock was so steep that we descended in a sitting posture, clinging with our hands and heels. I heard Cotter say, "I think I must take off these moccasins and try it barefooted, for I don't believe I can make it." These words were instantly followed by a startled cry, and I looked round to see him slide quickly toward me, struggling and clutching at the smooth granite. As he slid by I made a grab for him with my right hand, catching him by the shirt, and, throwing myself as far in the other direction as I could, seized with my left hand a little pine tuft, which held us. I asked Cotter to edge along a little to the left, where he could get a brace with his feet and relieve me of his weight, which he cautiously did. I then threw a couple of turns with the lasso round the roots of the pine bush, and we were safe, though hardly more than twenty feet from the brink. The pressure of curiosity to get a look over that edge was so strong within me that I lengthened out sufficient lasso to reach the end, and slid slowly to the edge, where, leaning over, I looked down, getting a full view of the wall for miles. Directly beneath, a sheer cliff of three or four hundred feet stretched down to a pile of *débris* which rose to unequal heights along its face, reaching the very crest not more than a hundred feet south of us. From that point to the bottom of the cañon, broken rocks, ridges rising through vast sweeps of *débris,* tufts of pine and frozen bodies of ice covered the further slope.

I returned to Cotter, and, having loosened ourselves from the pine bush, inch by inch we crept along the granite until we supposed ourselves to be just over the top of the *débris* pile, where I found a firm brace for my feet, and lowered Cotter to the edge. He sang out, "All right!" and climbed over on the uppermost *débris,* his head only remaining in sight of me; when I lay down upon my back, making knapsack and body do friction duty, and, letting myself move, followed Cotter and reached his side.

From that point the descent required two hours of severe, constant labor, which was monotonous of itself, and would have proved excessively tiresome but for the constant interest of glacial geology beneath us. When at last we reached the bottom and found ourselves upon a velvety green meadow, beneath the shadow of wide-armed pines, we realized the amount of muscular force we had used up, and threw ourselves down for a rest of half an hour, when we rose, not quite renewed, but fresh enough to finish the day's climb.

In a few minutes we stood upon the rocks just above King's River,—a broad, white torrent fretting its way along the bottom of an impassable gorge. Looking down the stream, we saw that our right bank was a continued precipice, affording, so far as we could see, no possible descent to the river's margin, and indeed, had we gotten down, the torrent rushed with such fury that we could not possibly have crossed it. To the south of us, a little way up stream, the river flowed out from a broad, oval lake, three quarters of a mile in length, which occupied the bottom of the granite basin. Unable to cross the torrent, we must either swim the lake or climb round its head. Upon our side the walls of the basin curved to the head of the lake in sharp, smooth precipices, or broken slopes of *débris*, while on the opposite side its margin was a beautiful shore of emerald meadow, edged with a continuous grove of coniferous trees. Once upon this other side, we should have completed the severe part of our journey, crossed the gulf, and have left all danger behind us; for the long slope of granite and ice which rose upon the west side of the cañon and the Mount Brewer wall opposed to us no trials save those of simple fatigue.

Around the head of the lake were crags and precipices in

singularly forbidding arrangement. As we turned thither we saw no possible way of overcoming them. At its head the lake lay in an angle of the vertical wall, sharp and straight like the corner of a room; about three hundred feet in height, and for two hundred and fifty feet of this a pyramidal pile of blue ice rose from the lake, rested against the corner, and reached within forty feet of the top. Looking into the deep blue water of the lake, I concluded that in our exhausted state it was madness to attempt to swim it. The only alternative was to scale that slender pyramid of ice and find some way to climb the forty feet of smooth wall above it; a plan we chose perforce, and started at once to put into execution, determined that if we were unsuccessful we would fire a dead log which lay near, warm ourselves thoroughly, and attempt the swim. At its base the ice mass overhung the lake like a roof, under which the water had melted its way for a distance of not less than a hundred feet, a thin cave overhanging the water. To the very edge of this I cautiously went, and, looking down into the lake, saw through its beryl depths the white granite blocks strewn upon the bottom at least one hundred feet below me. It was exceedingly transparent, and, under ordinary circumstances, would have been a most tempting place for a dive; but at the end of our long fatigue, and with the still unknown tasks ahead, I shrank from a swim in such a chilly temperature.

We found the ice-angle difficultly steep, but made our way successfully along its edge, clambering up the crevices melted between its body and the smooth granite to a point not far from the top, where the ice had considerably narrowed, and rocks overhanging it encroached so closely that we were obliged to change our course and make our way with cut steps out upon its front. Streams of water, dropping from the overhanging rock-eaves at many points, had worn circular shafts into the ice, three feet in diameter and twenty feet in depth. Their edges offered us our only foothold, and we climbed from one to another, equally careful of slipping upon the slope itself, or falling into the wells. Upon the top of the ice we found a narrow, level platform, upon which we stood together, resting our backs in the granite corner, and looked down the awful pathway of King's Cañon, until the rest nerved us up enough to turn our eyes upward at the forty feet of smooth granite which lay between us and safety. Here and there were small projections from its surface, little protruding knobs of feldspar, and crevices riven into its face for a few inches.

As we tied ourselves together, I told Cotter to hold himself in readiness to jump down into one of these in case I fell, and started to climb up the wall, succeeding quite well for about twenty feet. About two feet above my hands was a crack, which, if my arms had been long enough to reach, would probably have led me to the very top; but I judged it beyond my powers, and, with great care, descended to the side of Cotter, who believed that his superior length of arm would enable him to make the reach.

I planted myself against the rock, and he started cautiously up the wall. Looking down the glare front of ice, it was not pleasant to consider at what velocity a slip would send me to the bottom, or at what angle, and to what probable depth, I should be projected into the ice-water. Indeed, the idea of such a sudden bath was so annoying that I lifted my eyes toward my companion. He reached my farthest point without great difficulty, and made a bold spring for the crack, reaching it without an inch to spare, and holding on wholly by his fingers. He thus worked himself slowly along the crack toward the top, at last getting his arms over the brink, and gradually drawing his body up and out of sight. It was the most splendid piece of slow gymnastics I ever witnessed. For a moment he said nothing; but when I asked if he was all right, cheerfully repeated, "All right."

It was only a moment's work to send up the two knapsacks and barometer, and receive again my end of the lasso. As I tied it round my breast, Cotter said to me, in an easy, confident tone, "Don't be afraid to bear your weight." I made up my mind, however, to make that climb without his aid, and husbanded my strength as I climbed from crack to crack. I got up without difficulty to my former point, rested there a moment, hanging solely by my hands, gathered every pound of strength and atom of will for the reach, then jerked myself upward with a swing, just getting the tips of my fingers into the crack. In an instant I had grasped it with my right hand also. I felt the sinews of my fingers relax a little, but the picture of the slope of ice and the blue lake affected me so strongly that I redoubled my grip, and climbed slowly along the crack until I reached the angle and got one arm over the edge, as Cotter had done. As I rested my body upon the edge and looked up at Cotter, I saw that, instead of a level top, he was sitting upon a smooth, roof-like slope, where the least pull would have dragged him over the brink. He had no brace for his feet, nor hold for his hands, but had seated himself calmly, with the rope tied around his breast, knowing that my only safety lay in being able to make the climb entirely unaided; certain that the least waver in his tone would have disheartened me, and perhaps made it impossible. The shock I received on seeing this affected me for a moment, but not enough to throw me off my guard, and I climbed quickly over the edge. When we had walked back out of danger we sat down upon the granite for a rest.

In all my experience of mountaineering I have never known an act of such real, profound courage as this of Cotter's. It is one thing, in a moment of excitement, to make a gallant leap, or hold one's nerves in the iron grasp of will, but to coolly seat one's self in the door of death, and silently listen for the fatal summons, and this all for a friend,—for he might easily have cast loose the lasso and saved himself,—requires as sublime a type of courage as I know.

But a few steps back we found a thicket of pine overlooking our lake, by which there flowed a clear rill of snow-water. Here, in the bottom of the great gulf, we made our bivouac; for we were already in the deep evening shadows, although the mountaintops to the east of us still burned in the reflected light. It was the luxury of repose which kept me awake half an hour or so, in spite of my vain attempts at sleep. To listen for the pulsating sound of waterfalls and arrowy rushing of the brook by our beds was too deep a pleasure to quickly yield up.

Under the later moonlight I rose and went out upon the open rocks, allowing myself to be deeply impressed by the weird Dantesque surroundings—darkness, out of which to the sky towered stern, shaggy bodies of rock; snow, uncertainly moonlit with cold pallor; and at my feet the basin of the lake, still, black, and gemmed with reflected stars, like the void into which Dante looked through the bottomless gulf of Dis. A little way off there appeared upon the brink of a projecting granite cornice two dimly seen forms; pines I knew them to be, yet their motionless figures seemed bent forward, gazing down the cañon; and I allowed myself to name them Mantuan and Florentine, thinking at the same time how grand and spacious the scenery, how powerful their attitude, and how infinitely more profound the mystery of light and

shade, than any of those hard, theatrical conceptions with
which Doré has sought to shut in our imagination. That artist, as I believe, has reached a conspicuous failure from an
overbalancing love of solid, impenetrable darkness. There is
in all his Inferno landscape a certain sharp boundary between
the real and unreal, and never the infinite suggestiveness of
great regions of half-light, in which everything may be seen,
nothing recognized. Without waking Cotter, I crept back to
my blankets, and to sleep.

The morning of our fifth and last day's tramp must have
dawned cheerfully; at least, so I suppose from its aspect when
we first came back to consciousness, surprised to find the sun
risen from the eastern mountain-wall, and the whole gorge
flooded with its direct light. Rising as good as new from our
mattress of pine twigs, we hastened to take breakfast, and
started up the long, broken slope of the Mount Brewer wall.
To reach the pass where we had parted from our friends required seven hours of slow, laborious climbing, in which we
took advantage of every outcropping spine of granite and every level expanse of ice to hasten at the top of our speed.
Cotter's feet were severely cut; his tracks upon the snow were
marked by stains of blood, yet he kept on with undiminished
spirit, never once complaining. The perfect success of our
journey so inspired us with happiness that we forgot danger
and fatigue, and chatted in liveliest strain.

It was about two o'clock when we reached the summit, and
rested a moment to look back over our new Alps, which were
hard and distinct under direct, unpoetic light; yet with all
their dense gray and white reality, their long, sculptured
ranks, and cold, still summits, we gave them a lingering, fare-
well look, which was not without its deep fulness of emotion,
then turned our backs and hurried down the *débris* slope into
the rocky amphitheatre at the foot of Mount Brewer, and by
five o'clock had reached our old camp-ground. We found
here a note pinned to a tree, informing us that the party had
gone down into the lower cañon, five miles below, that they
might camp in better pasturage.

The wind had scattered the ashes of our old campfire, and
banished from it the last sentiment of home. We hurried on,
climbing among the rocks which reached down to the crest of
the great lateral moraine, and then on in rapid stride along
its smooth crest, riveting our eyes upon the valley below,
where we knew the party must be camped.

At last, faintly curling above the sea of green treetops, a few faint clouds of smoke wafted upward into the air. We saw them with a burst of strong emotion, and ran down the steep flank of the moraine at the top of our speed. Our shouts were instantly answered by the three voices of our friends, who welcomed us to their camp-fire with tremendous hugs.

After we had outlined for them the experience of our days, and as we lay outstretched at our ease, warm in the blaze of the glorious camp-fire, Brewer said to me: "King, you have relieved me of a dreadful task. For the last three days I have been composing a letter to your family, but somehow I did not get beyond, 'It becomes my painful duty to inform you.' "

John Wesley Powell

Exploration of the Colorado River

John Wesley Powell (1834–1902) was a self-taught scientist, a college teacher, and a Civil War veteran who had lost his right arm at Shiloh before he led four small boats of ten men down the Green and Colorado rivers on a thousand-mile journey into unknown canyon country. Powell's river-run of 1869, sponsored by the Smithsonian Institution and repeated in 1871, marked the discovery of the Escalante River and the Henry Mountains, the last unknown river and mountain range in the continental United States. Despite the expedition's attractiveness as a journey of discovery and adventure, Powell's purpose was similar to that of his innovative mode of teaching when he led Illinois college students into the Rockies on the first student geological field trips. In the years following his great voyage, Powell stuck to his purpose of gathering scientific information so that Americans might better understand the wilderness, adapt to its conditions, and use its resources sensibly. In pursuing his practical goals, Powell worked to consolidate the various government surveys into the United States Geological Survey, which he directed for thirteen years, while simultaneously serving as founding director of the Bureau of Ethnology from 1879 to his death. A social vision underlay Powell's writings about structural geology, drainage systems, base-level erosion, irrigation systems, and reservoirs, but his ideas of land reform did not become an effective part of government conservation and reclamation programs until after his death, when his prophecies of dust bowls and floods caused by misuse of the land had come true. Powell published his Exploration of the Colorado River of the West (1875) in the hope that it would gather support for his program of scientific investigation of the West, but the book's immediate effect was to introduce magnificent canyon country to a large audience and to make Powell a public hero. As a work of imagination, the book combines events

*from both the 1869 and the 1871 trips into a single narra-
tive. The three men Powell wonders about at the end of the
following selection, were later discovered to have been killed
on the plateau by Shivwit Indians.*

[*August 13*]   We are now ready to start on our way
down the Great Unknown. Our boats, tied to a common
stake, chafe each other as they are tossed by the fretful river.
They ride high and buoyant, for their loads are lighter than
we could desire. We have but a month's rations remaining.
The flour has been resifted through the mosquito-net sieve;
the spoiled bacon has been dried and the worst of it boiled;
the few pounds of dried apples have been spread in the sun
and reshrunken to their normal bulk. The sugar has all melted
and gone on its way down the river. But we have a large sack
of coffee. The lightening of the boats has this advantage: they
will ride the waves better and we shall have but little to carry
when we make a portage.

We are three quarters of a mile in the depths of the earth,
and the great river shrinks into insignificance as it dashes its
angry waves against the walls and cliffs that rise to the world
above; the waves are but puny ripples, and we but pigmies,
running up and down the sands or lost among the boulders.

We have an unknown distance yet to run, an unknown
river to explore. . . .

[*August 14*]   After breakfast we enter on the waves. At
the very introduction it inspires awe. The canyon is narrower
than we have ever before seen it; the water is swifter; there
are but a few broken rocks in the channel; but the walls are
set, on either side, with pinnacles and crags; and sharp,
angular buttresses, bristling with wind- and wave-polished
spires, extend far out into the river.

Ledges of rock jut into the stream, their tops sometimes
just below the surface, sometimes rising a few or many feet
above; and island ledges and island pinnacles and island towers break the swift course of the stream into chutes and

From John Wesley Powell, *Exploration of the Colorado River of
the West and Its Tributaries* (Washington: Government Printing
Office, 1875)

eddies and whirlpools. We soon reach a place where a creek comes in from the left, and, just below, the channel is choked with boulders, which have washed down this lateral canyon and formed a dam, over which there is a fall of 30 or 40 feet; but on the boulders foothold can be had, and we make a portage. Three more such dams are found. Over one we can make a portage; at the other two are chutes through which we can run.

As we proceed the granite rises higher, until nearly a thousand feet of the lower part of the walls are composed of this rock.

About eleven o'clock we hear a great roar ahead, and approach it very cautiously. The sound grows louder and louder as we run, and at last we find ourselves above a long, broken fall, with ledges and pinnacles of rock obstructing the river. There is a descent of perhaps 75 or 80 feet in a third of a mile, and the rushing waters break into great waves on the rocks, and lash themselves into a mad, white foam. We can land just above, but there is no foothold on either side by which we can make a portage. It is nearly a thousand feet to the top of the granite; so it will be impossible to carry our boats around, though we can climb to the summit up a side gulch and, passing along a mile or two, descend to the river. This we find on examination; but such a portage would be impracticable for us, and we must run the rapid or abandon the river. There is no hesitation. We step into our boats, push off, and away we go, first on smooth but swift water, then we strike a glassy wave and ride to its top, down again into the trough, up again on a higher wave, and down and up on waves higher and still higher until we strike one just as it curls back, and a breaker rolls over our little boat. Still on we speed, shooting past projecting rocks, till the little boat is caught in a whirlpool and spun round several times. At last we pull out again into the stream. And now the other boats have passed us. The open compartment of the "Emma Dean" is filled with water and every breaker rolls over us. Hurled back from a rock, now on this side, now on that, we are carried into an eddy, in which we struggle for a few minutes, and are then out again, the breakers still rolling over us. Our boat is unmanageable, but she cannot sink, and we drift down another hundred yards through breakers—how, we scarcely know. We find the other boats have turned into an eddy at the foot of the fall and are waiting to catch us as we come, for the men have seen that our boat is swamped. They push out as we come near and pull us in against the wall. Our boat bailed, on we go again.

The walls now are more than a mile in height—a vertical distance difficult to appreciate. Stand on the south steps of the Treasury building in Washington and look down Pennsylvania Avenue to the Capitol; measure this distance overhead, and imagine cliffs to extend to that altitude, and you will understand what is meant; or stand at Canal Street in New York and look up Broadway to Grace Church, and you have about the distance; or stand at Lake Street Bridge in Chicago and look down to the Central Depot, and you have it again.

A thousand feet of this is up through granite crags; then steep slopes and perpendicular cliffs rise one above another to the summit. The gorge is black and narrow below, red and gray and flaring above, with crags and angular projections on the walls, which, cut in many places by side canyons, seem to be a vast wilderness of rocks. Down in these grand, gloomy depths we glide, ever listening, for the mad waters keep up their roar; ever watching, ever peering ahead, for the narrow canyon is winding and the river is closed in so that we can see but a few hundred yards, and what there may be below we know not; so we listen for falls and watch for rocks, stopping now and then in the bay of a recess to admire the gigantic scenery; and ever as we go there is some new pinnacle or tower, some crag or peak, some distant view of the upper plateau, some strangely shaped rock, or some deep, narrow side canyon.

Then we come to another broken fall, which appears more difficult than the one we ran this morning. A small creek comes in on the right, and the first fall of the water is over boulders, which have been carried down by this lateral stream. We land at its mouth and stop for an hour or two to examine the fall. It seems possible to let down with lines, at least a part of the way, from point to point, along the right-hand wall. So we make a portage over the first rocks and find footing on some boulders below. Then we let down one of the boats to the end of her line, when she reaches a corner of the projecting rock, to which one of the men clings and steadies her while I examine an eddy below. I think we can pass the other boats down by us and catch them in the eddy. This is soon done, and the men in the boats in the eddy pull us to their side. On the shore of this little eddy there is about two feet of gravel beach above the water. Standing on this beach, some of the men take the line of the little boat and let it drift down against another projecting angle. Here is a little shelf, on which a man from my boat climbs, and a shorter line is passed to him, and he fastens the boat to the side of the cliff; then the second one is let down, bringing the line of the third. When the second boat is tied up, the two men standing on the beach above spring into the last boat, which is pulled up alongside of ours; then we let down the boats for 25 or 30 yards by walking along the shelf, landing them again in the mouth of a side canyon. Just below this there is another pile of boulders, over which we make another portage. From the foot of these rocks we can climb to another shelf, 40 or 50 feet above the water.

On this bench we camp for the night. It is raining hard, and we have no shelter, but find a few sticks which have lodged in the rocks, and kindle a fire and have supper. We sit on the rocks all night, wrapped in our *ponchos,* getting what sleep we can.

[*August 15*]   This morning we find we can let down for 300 or 400 yards, and it is managed in this way: we pass along the wall by climbing from projecting point to point, sometimes near the water's edge, at other places 50 or 60 feet above, and hold the boat with a line while two men remain aboard and prevent her from being dashed against the rocks and keep the line from getting caught on the wall. In two hours we have brought them all down, as far as it is possible, in this way. A few yards below, the river strikes with great violence against a projecting rock and our boats are pulled up in a little bay above. We must now manage to pull out of this and clear the point below. The little boat is held by the bow obliquely up the stream. We jump in and pull out only a few strokes, and sweep clear of the dangerous rock. The other boats follow in the same manner and the rapid is passed.

It is not easy to describe the labor of such navigation. We must prevent the waves from dashing the boats against the cliffs. Sometimes, where the river is swift, we must put a bight of rope about a rock, to prevent the boat from being snatched from us by a wave; but where the plunge is too great or the chute too swift, we must let her leap and catch her below or the undertow will drag her under the falling water and sink her. Where we wish to run her out a little way from shore through a channel between rocks, we first throw in little sticks of driftwood and watch their course, to see where we must steer so that they will pass the channel in safety. And so we hold, and let go; and pull, and lift, and ward—among rocks, around rocks, and over rocks.

And now we go on through this solemn, mysterious way. The river is very deep, the canyon very narrow, and still obstructed, so that there is no steady flow of the stream; but the waters reel and roll and boil, and we are scarcely able to determine where we can go. Now the boat is carried to the right, perhaps close to the wall; again, she is shot into the stream, and perhaps is dragged over to the other side, where, caught in a whirlpool, she spins about. We can neither land nor run as we please. The boats are entirely unmanageable; no order in their running can be preserved; now one, now another, is ahead, each crew laboring for its own preservation. In such a place we come to another rapid. Two of the boats run it perforce. One succeeds in landing, but there is no foothold by which to make a portage and she is pushed out again into the stream. The next minute a great reflex wave fills the open compartment; she is water-logged, and drifts unmanageable. Breaker after breaker rolls over her and one capsizes her. The men are thrown out; but they cling to the boat, and she drifts down some distance alongside of us and we are able to catch her. She is soon bailed out and the men are aboard once more; but the oars are lost, and so a pair from the "Emma Dean" is spared. Then for two miles we find smooth water.

Clouds are playing in the canyon today. Sometimes they roll down in great masses, filling the gorge with gloom; sometimes they hang aloft from wall to wall and cover the canyon with a roof of impending storm, and we can peer long distances up and down this canyon corridor, with its cloud-roof overhead, its walls of black granite, and its river bright with the sheen of broken waters. Then a gust of wind sweeps down a side gulch and, making a rift in the clouds, reveals the blue heavens, and a stream of sunlight pours in. Then the clouds drift away into the distance, and hang around crags and peaks and pinnacles and towers and walls, and cover them with a mantle that lifts from time to time and sets them all in sharp relief. Then baby clouds creep out of side canyons, glide around points, and creep back again into more distant gorges. Then clouds arrange in strata across the canyon, with intervening vista views to cliffs and rocks beyond. The clouds are children of the heavens, and when they play among the rocks they lift them to the region above.

It rains! Rapidly little rills are formed above, and these soon grow into brooks, and the brooks grow into creeks and tumble over the walls in innumerable cascades, adding their wild music to the roar of the river. When the rain ceases the rills, brooks, and creeks run dry. The waters that fall during a rain on these steep rocks are gathered at once into the river; they could scarcely be poured in more suddenly if some vast spout ran from the clouds to the stream itself. When a storm bursts over the canyon a side gulch is dangerous, for a sudden flood may come, and the inpouring waters will raise the river so as to hide the rocks.

Early in the afternoon we discover a stream entering from the north—a clear, beautiful creek, coming down through a gorgeous red canyon. We land and camp on a sand beach above its mouth, under a great, overspreading tree with willow shaped leaves.

[*August 16*]   We must dry our rations again to-day and make oars.

The Colorado is never a clear stream, but for the past three or four days it has been raining much of the time, and the floods poured over the walls have brought down great quantities of mud, making it exceedingly turbid now. The little affluent which we have discovered here is a clear, beautiful creek, or river, as it would be termed in this western country, where streams are not abundant. We have named one stream, away above, in honor of the great chief of the "Bad Angels," and as this is in beautiful contrast to that, we conclude to name it "Bright Angel."

Early in the morning the whole party starts up to explore the Bright Angel River, with the special purpose of seeking timber from which to make oars. A couple of miles above we find a large pine log, which has been floated down from the plateau, probably from an altitude of more than 6,000 feet, but not many miles back. On its way it must have passed over many cataracts and falls, for it bears scars in evidence of the rough usage which it has received. The men roll it on skids, and the work of sawing oars is commenced.

This stream heads away back under a line of abrupt cliffs that terminates the plateau, and tumbles down more than

4,000 feet in the first mile or two of its course; then runs through a deep, narrow canyon until it reaches the river.

Late in the afternoon I return and go up a little gulch just above this creek, about 200 yards from camp, and discover the ruins of two or three old houses, which were originally of stone laid in mortar. Only the foundations are left, but irregular blocks, of which the houses were constructed, lie scattered about. In one room I find an old mealing stone, deeply worn, as if it had been much used. A great deal of pottery is strewn around, and old trails, which in some places are deeply worn into the rocks, are seen.

It is ever a source of wonder to us why these ancient people sought such inaccessible places for their homes. They were, doubtless, an agricultural race, but there are no lands here of any considerable extent that they could have cultivated. To the west of Oraibi, one of the towns in the Province of Tusayan, in northern Arizona, the inhabitants have actually built little terraces along the face of the cliff where a spring gushes out, and thus made their sites for gardens. It is possible that the ancient inhabitants of this place made their agricultural lands in the same way. But why should they seek such spots? Surely the country was not so crowded with people as to demand the utilization of so barren a region. The only solution suggested for the problem is this: We know that for a century or two after the settlement of Mexico many expeditions were sent into the country now comprising Arizona and New Mexico, for the purpose of bringing the town-building people under the dominion of the Spanish government. Many of their villages were destroyed, and the inhabitants fled to regions at that time unknown; and there are traditions among the people who inhabit the pueblos that still remain that the canyons were these unknown lands. It may be these buildings were erected at that time; sure it is that they have a much more modern appearance than the ruins scattered over Nevada, Utah, Colorado, Arizona, and New Mexico. Those old Spanish conquerors had a monstrous greed for gold and a wonderful lust for saving souls. Treasures they must have, if not on earth, why, then, in heaven; and when they failed to find heathen temples bedecked with silver, they propitiated Heaven by seizing the heathen themselves. There is yet extant a copy of a record made by a heathen artist to express his conception of the demands of the conquerors. In one part of the picture we have a lake, and near by stands a priest pouring water on the head of a native. On the other side, a poor Indian has a cord about his throat. Lines run from these two groups to a central figure, a man with beard and full Spanish panoply. The interpretation of the picture-writing is this: "Be baptized as this saved heathen, or be hanged as that damned heathen." Doubtless, some of these people preferred another alternative, and rather than be baptized or hanged they chose to imprison themselves within these canyon walls.

[*August 17*] Our rations are still spoiling; the bacon is so badly injured that we are compelled to throw it away. By an accident, this morning, the saleratus was lost overboard. We have now only musty flour sufficient for ten days and a few dried apples, but plenty of coffee. We must make all haste possible. If we meet with difficulties such as we have encountered in the canyon above, we may be compelled to give up the expedition and try to reach the Mormon settlements to the north. Our hopes are that the worst places are passed, but our barometers are all so much injured as to be useless, and we have lost our reckoning in altitude, and know not how much descent the river has yet to make.

The stream is still wild and rapid and rolls through a narrow channel. We make but slow progress, often landing against a wall and climbing around some point to see the river below. Although very anxious to advance, we are determined to run with great caution, lest by another accident we lose our remaining supplies. How precious that little flour has become! We divide it among the boats and carefully store it away, so that it can be lost only by the loss of the boat itself.

We make ten miles and a half, and camp among the rocks on the right. We have had rain from time to time all day, and have been thoroughly drenched and chilled; but between showers the sun shines with great power and the mercury in our thermometers stands at 115°, so that we have rapid change from great extremes, which are very disagreeable. It is especially cold in the rain to-night. The little canvas we have is rotten and useless; the rubber *ponchos* with which we started from Green River City have all been lost; more than half the party are without hats, not one of us has an entire suit of clothes, and we have not a blanket apiece. So we gather driftwood and build a fire; but after supper the rain, coming down in torrents, extinguishes it, and we sit up all night on the rocks, shivering, and are more exhausted by the night's discomfort than by the day's toil.

[*August 18*]   The day is employed in making portages and we advance but two miles on our journey. Still it rains.

While the men are at work making portages I climb up the granite to its summit and go away back over the rust-colored sandstones and greenish-yellow shales to the foot of the marble wall. I climb so high that the men and boats are lost in the black depths below and the dashing river is a rippling brook, and still there is more canyon above than below. All about me are interesting geologic records. The book is open and I can read as I run. All about me are grand views, too, for the clouds are playing again in the gorges. But somehow I think of the nine days' rations and the bad river, and the lesson of the rocks and the glory of the scene are but half conceived.

I push on to an angle, where I hope to get a view of the country beyond, to see if possible what the prospect may be of our soon running through this plateau, or at least of meeting with some geologic change that will let us out of the granite; but, arriving at the point, I can see below only a labyrinth of black gorges.

[*August 19*]   Rain again this morning. We are in our granite prison still, and the time until noon is occupied in making a long, bad portage.

After dinner, in running a rapid the pioneer boat is upset by a wave. We are some distance in advance of the larger boats. The river is rough and swift and we are unable to land, but cling to the boat and are carried down stream over another rapid. The men in the boats above see our trouble, but they are caught in whirlpools and are spinning about in eddies, and it seems a long time before they come to our relief. At last they do come; our boat is turned right side up and bailed out; the oars, which fortunately have floated along in company with us, are gathered up, and on we go, without even landing. The clouds break away and we have sunshine again. . . .

[*August 21*]   We start early this morning, cheered by the prospect of a fine day and encouraged also by the good run made yesterday. A quarter of a mile below camp the river turns abruptly to the left, and between camp and that point is very swift, running down in a long, broken chute and piling up against the foot of the cliff, where it turns to the left. We try to pull across, so as to go down on the other side, but the waters are swift and it seems impossible for us to escape the rock below; but, in pulling across, the bow of the boat is turned to the farther shore, so that we are swept broadside down and are prevented by the rebounding waters from striking against the wall. We toss about for a few seconds in these billows and are then carried past the danger. Below, the river turns again to the right, the canyon is very narrow, and we see in advance but a short distance. The water, too, is very swift, and there is no landing place. From around this curve there comes a mad roar, and down we are carried with a dizzying velocity to the head of another rapid. On either side high over our heads there are overhanging granite walls, and the sharp bends cut off our view, so that a few minutes will carry us into unknown waters. Away we go on one long, winding chute. I stand on deck, supporting myself with a strap fastened on either side of the gunwale. The boat glides rapidly where the water is smooth, then, striking a wave, she leaps and bounds like a thing of life, and we have a wild, exhilarating ride for ten miles, which we make in less than an hour. The excitement is so great that we forget the danger until we hear the roar of a great fall below; then we back on our oars and are carried slowly toward its head and succeed in landing just above and find that we have to make another portage. At this we are engaged until some time after dinner.

Just here we run out of the granite. Ten miles in less than half a day, and limestone walls below. Good cheer returns; we forget the storms and the gloom and the cloud-covered canyons and the black granite and the raging river, and push our boats from shore in great glee.

Though we are out of the granite, the river is still swift, and we wheel about a point again to the right, and turn, so as to head back in the direction from which we came; this brings the granite in sight again, with its narrow gorge and black crags; but we meet with no more great falls or rapids. Still, we run cautiously and stop from time to time to examine some places which look bad. Yet we make ten miles this afternoon; twenty miles in all to-day. . . .

[*August 25*]   We make 12 miles this morning, when we come to monuments of lava standing in the river,—low rocks mostly, but some of them shafts more than a hundred feet high. Going on down three or four miles, we find them increasing in number. Great quantities of cooled lava and

many cinder cones are seen on either side; and then we come
to an abrupt cataract. Just over the fall on the right wall a
cinder cone, or extinct volcano, with a well-defined crater,
stands on the very brink of the canyon. This, doubtless, is the
one we saw two or three days ago. From this volcano vast
floods of lava have been poured down into the river, and a
stream of molten rock has run up the canyon three or four
miles and down we know not how far. Just where it poured
over the canyon wall is the fall. The whole north side as far
as we can see is lined with the black basalt, and high up on
the opposite wall are patches of the same material, resting on
the benches and filling old alcoves and caves, giving the wall
a spotted appearance.

The rocks are broken in two along a line which here
crosses the river, and the beds we have seen while coming
down the canyon for the last 30 miles have dropped 800 feet
on the lower side of the line, forming what geologists call a
"fault." The volcanic cone stands directly over the fissure
thus formed. On the left side of the river, opposite, mammoth
springs burst out of this crevice, 100 or 200 feet above
the river, pouring in a stream quite equal in volume to the
Colorado Chiquito.

This stream seems to be loaded with carbonate of lime,
and the water, evaporating, leaves an incrustation on the
rocks; and this process has been continued for a long time,
for extensive deposits are noticed in which are basins with
bubbling springs. The water is salty.

We have to make a portage here, which is completed in
about three hours; then on we go.

We have no difficulty as we float along, and I am able to
observe the wonderful phenomena connected with this flood
of lava. The canyon was doubtless filled to a height of 1,200
or 1,500 feet, perhaps by more than one flood. This would
dam the water back; and in cutting through this great lava
bed, a new channel has been formed sometimes on one side,
sometimes on the other. The cooled lava, being of firmer tex-
ture than the rocks of which the walls are composed, remains
in some places; in others a narrow channel has been cut,
leaving a line of basalt on either side. It is possible that the
lava cooled faster on the sides against the walls and that the
center ran out; but this we can only conjecture. There are
other places where almost the whole of the lava is gone, only
patches of it being seen where it has caught on the walls. As

we float down we can see that it ran out into side canyons. In some places this basalt has a fine, columnar structure, often in concentric prisms, and masses of these concentric columns have coalesced. In some places, when the flow occurred the canyon was probably about the same depth that it is now, for we can see where the basalt has rolled out on the sands, and—what seems curious to me—the sands are not melted or metamorphosed to any appreciable extent. In places the bed of the river is of sandstone or limestone, in other places of lava, showing that it has all been cut out again where the sandstones and limestones appear; but there is a little yet left where the bed is of lava.

What a conflict of water and fire there must have been here! Just imagine a river of molten rock running down into a river of melted snow. What a seething and boiling of the waters; what clouds of steam rolled into the heavens!

Thirty-five miles to-day. Hurray! . . .

[*August 27*]   This morning the river takes a more southerly direction. The dip of the rocks is to the north and we are running rapidly into lower formations. Unless our course changes we shall very soon run again into the granite. This gives some anxiety. Now and then the river turns to the west and excites hopes that are soon destroyed by another turn to the south. About nine o'clock we come to the dreaded rock. It is with no little misgiving that we see the river enter these black, hard walls. At its very entrance we have to make a portage; then let down with lines past some ugly rocks. We run a mile or two farther, and then the rapids below can be seen.

About eleven o'clock we come to a place in the river which seems much worse than any we have yet met in all its course. A little creek comes down from the left. We land first on the right and clamber up over the granite pinnacles for a mile or two, but can see no way by which to let down, and to run it would be sure destruction. After dinner we cross to examine on the left. High above the river we can walk along on the top of the granite, which is broken off at the edge and set with crags and pinnacles, so that it is very difficult to get a view of the river at all. In my eagerness to reach a point where I can see the roaring fall below, I go too far on the wall, and can neither advance nor retreat. I stand with one foot on a little projecting rock and cling with my hand fixed in a little crevice. Finding I am caught here, suspended 400 feet above the river, into which I must fall if my footing fails, I call for help. The men come and pass me a line, but I cannot let go of the rock long enough to take hold of it. Then they bring two or three of the largest oars. All this takes time which seems very precious to me; but at last they arrive. The blade of one of the oars is pushed into a little crevice in the rock beyond me in such a manner that they can hold me pressed against the wall. Then another is fixed in such a way that I can step on it; and thus I am extricated.

Still another hour is spent in examining the river from this side, but no good view of it is obtained; so now we return to the side that was first examined, and the afternoon is spent in clambering among the crags and pinnacles and carefully scanning the river again. We find that the lateral streams have washed boulders into the river, so as to form a dam, over which the water makes a broken fall of 18 or 20 feet; then there is a rapid, beset with rocks, for 200 or 300 yards, while on the other side, points of the wall project into the river. Below, there is a second fall; how great, we cannot tell. Then there is a rapid, filled with huge rocks, for 100 or 200 yards. At the bottom of it, from the right wall, a great rock projects quite halfway across the river. It has a sloping surface extending up stream, and the water, coming down with all the momentum gained in the falls and rapids above, rolls up this inclined plane many feet, and tumbles over to the left. I decide that it is possible to let down over the first fall then run near the right cliff to a point just above the second, where we can pull out into a little chute, and, having run over that in safety, if we pull with all our power across the stream, we may avoid the great rock below. On my return to the boat I announce to the men that we are to run in the morning. Then we cross the river and go into camp for the night on some rocks in the mouth of the little side canyon.

After supper Captain Howland asks to have a talk with me. We walk up the little creek a short distance, and I soon find that his object is to remonstrate against my determination to proceed. He thinks that we had better abandon the river here. Talking with him, I learn that he, his brother, and William Dunn have determined to go no farther in the boats. So we return to camp. Nothing is said to the other men.

For the last two days our course has not been plotted. I sit down and do this now, for the purpose of finding where we are by dead reckoning. It is a clear night, and I take out the sextant to make observation for latitude, and I find that the astronomic determination agrees very nearly with that of the plot—quite as closely as might be expected from a meridian observation on a planet. In a direct line, we must be about 45 miles from the mouth of the Rio Virgen. If we can reach that point, we know that there are settlements up that river about 20 miles. This 45 miles in a direct line will probably be 80 or 90 by the meandering line of the river. But then we know that there is comparatively open country for many miles above the mouth of the Virgen, which is our point of destination.

As soon as I determine all this, I spread my plot on the sand and wake Howland, who is sleeping down by the river, and show him where I suppose we are, and where several Mormon settlements are situated.

We have another short talk about the morrow, and he lies down again; but for me there is no sleep. All night long I pace up and down a little path, on a few yards of sand beach, along by the river. Is it wise to go on? I go to the boats again to look at our rations. I feel satisfied that we can get over the danger immediately before us; what there may be below I know not. From our outlook yesterday on the cliffs, the canyon seemed to make another great bend to the south, and this, from our experience heretofore, means more and higher granite walls. I am not sure that we can climb out of the canyon here, and, if at the top of the wall, I know enough of the country to be certain that it is a desert of rock and sand between this and the nearest Mormon town, which, on the most direct line, must be 75 miles away. True, the late rains have been favorable to us, should we go out, for the probabilities are that we shall find water still standing in holes; and at one time I almost conclude to leave the river. But for years I have been contemplating this trip. To leave the exploration unfinished, to say that there is a part of the canyon which I cannot explore, having already nearly accomplished it, is more than I am willing to acknowledge, and I determine to go on.

I wake my brother and tell him of Howland's determination, and he promises to stay with me; then I call up Hawkins, the cook, and he makes a like promise; then Sumner and Bradley and Hall, and they all agree to go on.

[*August 28*]   At last daylight comes and we have breakfast without a word being said about the future. The meal is as solemn as a funeral. After breakfast I ask the three men if they still think it best to leave us. The elder Howland thinks it is, and Dunn agrees with him. The younger Howland tries to persuade them to go on with the party; failing in which, he decides to go with his brother.

Then we cross the river. The small boat is very much disabled and unseaworthy. With the loss of hands, consequent on the departure of the three men, we shall not be able to run all of the boats; so I decide to leave my "Emma Dean."

Two rifles and a shotgun are given to the men who are going out. I ask them to help themselves to the rations and take what they think to be a fair share. This they refuse to do, saying they have no fear but that they can get something to eat; but Billy, the cook, has a pan of biscuits prepared for dinner, and these he leaves on a rock.

Before starting, we take from the boat our barometers, fossils, the minerals, and some ammunition and leave them on the rocks. We are going over this place as light as possible. The three men help us lift our boats over a rock 25 or 30 feet high and let them down again over the first fall, and now we are all ready to start. The last thing before leaving, I write a letter to my wife and give it to Howland. Sumner gives him his watch, directing that it be sent to his sister should he not be heard from again. The records of the expedition have been kept in duplicate. One set of these is given to Howland; and now we are ready. For the last time they entreat us not to go on, and tell us that it is madness to set out in this place; that we can never get safely through it; and, further, that the river turns again to the south into the granite, and a few miles of such rapids and falls will exhaust our entire stock of rations, and then it will be too late to climb out. Some tears are shed; it is rather a solemn parting; each party thinks the other is taking the dangerous course.

My old boat left, I go on board of the "Maid of the Canyon." The three men climb a crag that overhangs the river to watch us off. The "Maid of the Canyon" pushes out. We glide rapidly along the foot of the wall, just grazing one great rock, then pull out a little into the chute of the second fall and plunge over it. The open compartment is filled when we strike the first wave below, but we cut through it, and then the men pull with all their power toward the left wall and swing clear of the dangerous rock below all right. We are scarcely a minute in running it, and find that, although it looked bad from above, we have passed many places that were worse.

The other boat follows without more difficulty. We land at the first practicable point below, and fire our guns, as a signal to the men above that we have come over in safety. Here we remain a couple of hours, hoping that they will take the smaller boat and follow us. We are behind a curve in the canyon and cannot see up to where we left them, and so we wait until their coming seems hopeless, and then push on.

And now we have a succession of rapids and falls until noon, all of which we run in safety. Just after dinner we come to another bad place. A little stream comes in from the left, and below there is a fall, and still below another fall. Above, the river tumbles down, over and among the rocks, in whirlpools and great waves, and the waters are lashed into mad, white foam. We run along the left, above this, and soon see that we cannot get down on this side, but it seems possible to let down on the other. We pull up stream again for 200 or 300 yards and cross. Now there is a bed of basalt on this northern side of the canyon, with a bold escarpment that seems to be a hundred feet high. We can climb it and walk along its summit to a point where we are just at the head of the fall. Here the basalt is broken down again, so it seems to us, and I direct the men to take a line to the top of the cliff and let the boats down along the wall. One man remains in the boat to keep her clear of the rocks and prevent her line from being caught on the projecting angles. I climb the cliff and pass along to a point just over the fall and descend by broken rocks, and find that the break of the fall is above the break of the wall, so that we cannot land, and that still below the river is very bad, and that there is no possibility of a portage. Without waiting further to examine and determine what shall be done, I hasten back to the top of the cliff to stop the boats from coming down. When I arrive I find the men have let one of them down to the head of the fall. She is in swift water and they are not able to pull her back; nor are they able to go on with the line, as it is not long enough to reach the higher part of the cliff which is just before them; so they take a bight around a crag. I send two men back for the other line. The boat is in very swift water, and Bradley is standing in the open compartment, holding out his oar to prevent her from striking against the foot of the cliff. Now she shoots out into the stream and up as far as the line will permit, and then, wheeling, drives headlong against the rock, and then out and back again, now straining on the line, now striking against the rock. As soon as the second line is brought, we pass it down to him; but his attention is all taken up with his own situation, and he does not see that we are passing him the line. I stand on a projecting rock, waving my hat to gain his attention, for my voice is drowned by the roaring of the falls. Just at this moment I see him take his knife from its sheath and step forward to cut the line. He had evidently decided that it is better to go over with the boat as it is than to wait for her to be broken to pieces. As he leans over, the boat sheers again into the stream, the stem-post breaks away and she is loose. With perfect composure Bradley seizes the great scull oar, places it in the stern rowlock, and pulls with all his power (and he is an athlete) to turn the bow of the boat down stream, for he wishes to go bow down, rather than to drift broadside on. One, two strokes he makes, and a third just as she goes over, and the boat is fairly turned, and she goes down almost beyond our sight, though we are more than a hundred feet above the river. Then she comes up again on a great wave, and down and up, then around behind some great rocks, and is lost in the mad, white foam below. We stand frozen with fear, for we see no boat. Bradley is gone! So it seems. But now, away below, we see something coming out of the waves. It is evidently a boat. A moment more, and we see Bradley standing on deck, swinging his hat to show that he is all right. But he is in a whirlpool. We have the stem-post of his boat attached to the line. How badly she may be disabled we know not. I direct Sumner and Powell to pass along the cliff and see if they can reach him from below. Hawkins, Hall, and myself run to the other boat, jump aboard, push out, and away we go over the falls. A wave rolls over us and our boat is unmanageable. Another great wave strikes us, and the boat rolls over, and tumbles and tosses, I know not how. All I know is that Bradley is picking us up. We soon have all right again, and row to the cliff and wait until Sumner and Powell can come. After a difficult climb they reach us. We run two or three miles farther and turn again to the northwest, continuing until night, when we have run out of the granite once more.

[*August 29*]   We start very early this morning. The river still continues swift, but we have no serious difficulty, and at twelve o'clock emerge from the Grand Canyon of the Colorado. We are in a valley now, and low mountains are seen in the distance, coming to the river below. We recognize this as the Grand Wash.

A few years ago a party of Mormons set out from St. George, Utah, taking with them a boat, and came down to the Grand Wash, where they divided, a portion of the party crossing the river to explore the San Francisco Mountains. Three men—Hamblin, Miller, and Crosby—taking the boat, went on down the river to Callville, landing a few miles below the mouth of the Rio Virgen. We have their manuscript journal with us, and so the stream is comparatively well known.

To-night we camp on the left bank, in a mesquite thicket.

The relief from danger and the joy of success are great. When he who has been chained by wounds to a hospital cot until his canvas tent seems like a dungeon cell, until the groans of those who lie about tortured with probe and knife are piled up, a weight of horror in his ears that he cannot throw off, cannot forget, and until the stench of festering wounds and anaesthetic drugs has filled the air with its loathsome burthen,—when he at last goes out into the open field, what a world he sees! How beautiful the sky, how bright the sunshine, what "floods of delirious music" pour from the throats of birds, how sweet the fragrance of earth and tree and blossom! The first hour of convalescent freedom seems rich recompense for all pain and gloom and terror.

Something like these are the feelings we experience to-night. Ever before us has been an unknown danger, heavier than immediate peril. Every waking hour passed in the Grand Canyon has been one of toil. We have watched with deep solicitude the steady disappearance of our scant supply of rations, and from time to time have seen the river snatch a portion of the little left, while we were a-hungered. And danger and toil were endured in those gloomy depths, where ofttimes clouds hid the sky by day and but a narrow zone of stars could be seen at night. Only during the few hours of deep sleep, consequent on hard labor, has the roar of the waters been hushed. Now the danger is over, now the toil has ceased, now the gloom has disappeared, now the firmament is bounded only by the horizon, and what a vast expanse of constellations can be seen!

The river rolls by us in silent majesty; the quiet of the camp is sweet; our joy is almost ecstasy. We sit till long after midnight talking of the Grand Canyon, talking of home, but talking chiefly of the three men who left us. Are they wandering in those depths, unable to find a way out? Are they searching over the desert lands above for water? Or are they nearing the settlements?

Clarence Dutton

Canyon Country

*Clarence Dutton (1841–1912), a Yale graduate and U.S.
Army captain, went on detached duty from the Ordnance
Corps in 1875 to serve as field geologist for the Powell survey of the plateau region of Arizona and Utah. Until he
resumed his Army commission in 1890, Dutton pursued his
field studies of geomorphology, hydrology, and vulcanism
throughout the Southwest and as far away as Oregon and
Hawaii. Between 1880 and 1885 he published four reports
and monographs for the United States Geologic Survey, most
notably* The High Plateaus of Utah *(1880) and* Tertiary
History of the Grand Canyon District *(1882). Normal expectations of such scientific treatises cannot prepare the
reader for Dutton's reports. His monograph on the Grand
Canyon is a geologic history, but it is also an attempt to find
descriptive language for the experience of apprehending "this
great innovation in natural scenery." Many of today's architectural and mythological names of the canyon's buttes,
amphitheaters, temples, and promontories remain Dutton's.
He named and described with enthusiasm, but unlike the ef-
fusions of later worshipers, his emotional and aesthetic responses did not disregard the objective fact of the canyon
itself. His purpose was to find words for a phenomenon that
was new and otherwise incomprehensible, but he recognized
the difficulties of conveying the grandeur of the unfamiliar:
"The observer who, unfamiliar with plateau scenery, stands
for the first time on the brink of the inner gorge, is almost
sure to view his surroundings with commingled feelings of
disappointment and perplexity. . . . Forms so new to the culture of civilized races and so strongly contrasted with those
which have been the ideals of thirty generations of white men
cannot be appreciated after the study of a single hour or day.
The first conception of them may not be a pleasing one. They
may seem abnormal, curious, and even grotesque."*

Wherever we reach the Grand Cañon in the Kaibab it bursts upon the vision in a moment. Seldom is any warning given that we are near the brink. At the Toroweap it is quite otherwise. There we are notified that we are near it a day before we reach it. As the final march to that portion of the chasm is made the scene gradually develops, growing by insensible degrees more grand until at last we stand upon the brink of the inner gorge, where all is before us. In the Kaibab the forest reaches to the sharp edge of the cliff and the pine trees shed their cones into the fathomless depths below.

If the approach is made at random, with no idea of reaching any particular point by a known route, the probabilities are that it is first seen from the rim of one of the vast amphitheaters which set back from the main chasm far into the mass of the plateau. It is such a point to which the reader has been brought in the preceding chapter. Of course there are degrees in the magnitude and power of the pictures presented, but the smallest and least powerful is tremendous and too great for comprehension. The scenery of the amphitheaters far surpasses in grandeur and nobility anything else of the kind in any other region, but it is mere by-play in comparison with the panorama displayed in the heart of the cañon. The supreme views are to be obtained at the extremities of the long promontories, which jut out between these recesses far into the gulf. Towards such a point we now direct our steps. The one we have chosen is on the whole the most commanding in the Kaibab front, though there are several others which might be regarded as very nearly equal to it, or as even more imposing in some respects. We named it *Point Sublime*.

The route is of the same character as that we have already traversed—open pine forest, with smooth and gently-rolling ground. The distance from the point where we first touched the rim of the amphitheater is about 5 miles. Nothing is seen of the chasm until about a mile from the end we come once more upon the brink. Reaching the extreme verge the packs are cast off, and sitting upon the edge we contemplate the most sublime and awe-inspiring spectacle in the world.

The Grand Cañon of the Colorado is a great innovation in

From Clarence Dutton, *Tertiary History of the Grand Canyon District* (Washington: Government Printing Office, 1882). Reprinted by Peregrine Smith, Inc. 1977.

modern ideas of scenery, and in our conceptions of the grandeur, beauty, and power of nature. As with all great innovations it is not to be comprehended in a day or a week, nor even in a month. It must be dwelt upon and studied, and the study must comprise the slow acquisition of the meaning and spirit of that marvelous scenery which characterizes the Plateau Country, and of which the great chasm is the superlative manifestation. The study and slow mastery of the influences of that class of scenery and its full appreciation is a special culture, requiring time, patience, and long familiarity for its consummation. The lover of nature, whose perceptions have been trained in the Alps, in Italy, Germany, or New England, in the Appalachians or Cordilleras, in Scotland or Colorado, would enter this strange region with a shock, and dwell there for a time with a sense of oppression, and perhaps with horror. Whatsoever things he had learned to regard as beautiful and noble he would seldom or never see, and whatsoever he might see would appear to him as anything but beautiful and noble. Whatsoever might be bold and striking would at first seem only grotesque. The colors would be the very ones he had learned to shun as tawdry and bizarre. The tones and shades, modest and tender, subdued yet rich, in which his fancy had always taken special delight, would be the ones which are conspicuously absent. But time would bring a gradual change. Some day he would suddenly become conscious that outlines which at first seemed harsh and trivial have grace and meaning; that forms which seemed grotesque are full of dignity; that magnitudes which had added enormity to coarseness have become replete with strength and even majesty; that colors which had been esteemed unrefined, immodest, and glaring, are as expressive, tender, changeful, and capacious of effects as any others. Great innovations, whether in art or literature, in science or in nature, seldom take the world by storm. They must be understood before they can be estimated, and must be cultivated before they can be understood.

It is so with the Grand Cañon. The observer who visits its commanding points with the expectation of experiencing forthwith a rapturous exaltation, an ecstasy arising from the realization of a degree of grandeur and sublimity never felt before, is doomed to disappointment. Supposing him to be but little familiar with plateau scenery, he will be simply bewildered. Must he, therefore, pronounce it a failure, an over-praised thing? Must he entertain a just resentment towards those who may have raised his expectations too high? The answer is that subjects which disclose their full power, meaning, and beauty as soon as they are presented to the mind have very little of those qualities to disclose. Moreover, a visitor to the chasm or to any other famous scene must necessarily come there (for so is the human mind constituted) with a picture of it created by his own imagination. He reaches the spot, the conjured picture vanishes in an instant, and the place of it must be filled anew. Surely no imagination can construct out of its own material any picture having the remotest resemblance to the Grand Cañon. In truth, the first step in attempting a description is to beg the reader to dismiss from his mind, so far as practicable, any preconceived notion of it.

Those who have long and carefully studied the Grand Cañon of the Colorado do not hesitate for a moment to pronounce it by far the most sublime of all earthly spectacles. If its sublimity consisted only in its dimensions, it could be sufficiently set forth, in a single sentence. It is more than 200 miles long, from 5 to 12 miles wide, and from 5,000 to 6,000 feet deep. There are in the world valleys which are longer and a few which are deeper. There are valleys flanked by summits loftier than the palisades of the Kaibab. Still the Grand Cañon is the sublimest thing on earth. It is so not alone by virtue of its magnitudes, but by virtue of the whole—its *ensemble*.

The common notion of a cañon is that of a deep, narrow gash in the earth, with nearly vertical walls, like a great and neatly cut trench. There are hundreds of chasms in the Plateau Country which answer very well to this notion. Many of them are sunk to frightful depths and are fifty to a hundred miles in length. Some are exceedingly narrow, as the cañons of the forks of the Virgen, where the overhanging walls shut out the sky. Some are intricately sculptured, and illuminated with brilliant colors; others are picturesque by reason of their bold and striking sculpture. A few of them are most solemn and impressive by reason of their profundity and the majesty of their walls. But, as a rule, the common cañons are neither grand nor even attractive. Upon first acquaintance they are curious and awaken interest as a new sensation, but they soon grow tiresome for want of diversity, and become at last mere bores. The impressions they produce are very transient, because of their great simplicity, and the

limited range of ideas they present. But there are some which
are highly diversified, presenting many attractive features.
These seldom grow stale or wearisome, and their presence is
generally greeted with pleasure.

It is perhaps in some respects unfortunate that the stupendous pathway of the Colorado River through the Kaibabs
was ever called a cañon, for the name identifies it with the
baser conception. But the name presents as wide a range of
signification as the word house. The log cabin of the rancher,
the painted and vine-clad cottage of the mechanic, the home
of the millionaire, the places where parliaments assemble, and
the grandest temples of worship, are all houses. Yet the contrast between Saint Marc's and the rude dwelling of the fron-
tiersman is not greater than that between the chasm of the
Colorado and the trenches in the rocks which answer to the
ordinary conception of a cañon. And as a great cathedral is
an immense development of the rudimentary idea involved in
the four walls and roof of a cabin, so is the chasm an expansion of the simple type of drainage channels peculiar to the
Plateau Country. To the conception of its vast proportions
must be added some notion of its intricate plan, the nobility
of its architecture, its colossal buttes, its wealth of ornamenta-
tion, the splendor of its colors, and its wonderful atmosphere.
All of these attributes combine with infinite complexity to
produce a whole which at first bewilders and at length over-
powers.

From the end of Point Sublime, the distance across the
chasm to the nearest point in the summit of the opposite wall
is about 7 miles. This, however, does not fairly express the
width of the chasm, for both walls are recessed by wide amphitheaters, setting far back into the platform of the country,
and the promontories are comparatively narrow strips between them. A more correct statement of the general width
would be from 11 to 12 miles. This must dispose at once of
the idea that the chasm is a narrow gorge of immense depth
and simple form. It is somewhat unfortunate that there is a
prevalent idea that in some way an essential part of the grandeur of the Grand Cañon is the narrowness of its defiles.
Much color has been given to this notion by the first illustra-
tions of the cañon from the pencil of Egloffstein in the
celebrated report of Lieutenant Ives. Never was a great subject more artistically misrepresented or more charmingly be-
littled. Nowhere in the Kaibab section is any such extreme

narrowness observable, and even in the Uinkaret section the
width of the great inner gorge is a little greater than the
depth. In truth, a little reflection will show that such a character would be inconsistent with the highest and strongest effects. For it is obvious that some notable width is necessary
to enable the eye to see the full extent of the walls. In a
chasm one mile deep, and only a thousand feet wide, this
would be quite impossible. If we compare the Marble Cañon
or the gorge at the Toroweap with wider sections it will at
once be seen that the wider ones are much stronger. If we
compare one of the longer alcoves having a width of 3 or 4
miles with the view across the main chasm the advantage will
be overwhelmingly with the latter. It is evident that for the
display of wall surface of given dimensions a certain amount
of distance is necessary. We may be too near or too far for
the right appreciation of its magnitude and proportions. The
distance must bear some ratio to the magnitude. But at what
precise limit this distance must in the present case be fixed is
not easy to determine. It can hardly be doubted that if the
cañon were materially narrower it would suffer a loss of
grandeur and effect.

The length of cañon revealed clearly and in detail at Point
Sublime is about 25 miles in each direction. Towards the
northwest the vista terminates behind the projecting mass of
Powell's Plateau. But again to the westward may be seen the
crests of the upper walls reaching through the Kanab and
Uinkaret Plateaus, and finally disappearing in the haze about
75 miles away.

The space under immediate view from our standpoint, 50
miles long and 10 to 12 wide, is thronged with a great multitude of objects so vast in size, so bold yet majestic in form,
so infinite in their details, that as the truth gradually reveals
itself to the perceptions it arouses the strongest emotions. Unquestionably the great, the overruling feature is the wall on
the opposite side of the gulf. Can mortal fancy create a picture of a mural front a mile in height, 7 to 10 miles distant,
and receding into space indefinitely in either direction? As the
mind strives to realize its proportions its spirit is broken and
its imagination completely crushed. If the wall were simple in
its character, if it were only blank and sheer, some rest might
be found in contemplating it; but it is full of diversity and
eloquent with grand suggestions. It is deeply recessed by alcoves and amphitheaters receding far into the plateau be-

yond, and usually disclosing only the portals by which they open into the main chasm. Between them the promontories jut out, ending in magnificent gables with sharp mitered angles. Thus the wall rambles in and out, turning numberless corners. Many of the angles are acute, and descend as sharp spurs like the forward edge of a plowshare. Only those alcoves which are directly opposite to us can be seen in their full length and depth. Yet so excessive, nay so prodigious, is the effect of foreshortening, that it is impossible to realize their full extensions. We have already noted this effect in the Vermilion Cliffs, but here it is much more exaggerated. At many points the profile of the façade is thrown into view by the change of trend, and its complex character is fully revealed. Like that of the Vermilion Cliffs, it is a series of many ledges and slopes, like a molded plinth, in which every stratum is disclosed as a line or a course of masonry. The Red Wall limestone is the most conspicuous member, presenting its vertical face eight hundred to a thousand feet high, and everywhere unbroken. The thinner beds more often appear in the slopes as a succession of ledges projecting through the scanty talus which never conceals them.

Numerous detached masses are also seen flanking the ends of the long promontories. These buttes are of gigantic proportions, and yet so overwhelming is the effect of the wall against which they are projected that they seem insignificant in mass, and the observer is often deluded by them, failing to perceive that they are really detached from the wall and perhaps separated from it by an interval of a mile or two.

At the foot of this palisade is a platform through which meanders the inner gorge, in whose dark and somber depths flows the river. Only in one place can the water surface be seen. In its windings the abyss which holds it extends for a short distance towards us and the line of vision enters the gorge lengthwise. Above and below this short reach the gorge swings its course in other directions and reveals only a dark, narrow opening, while its nearer wall hides its depths. This inner chasm is 1,000 to 1,200 feet deep. Its upper 200 feet is a vertical ledge of sandstone of a dark rich brownish color. Beneath it lies the granite of a dark iron-gray shade, verging towards black, and lending a gloomy aspect to the lowest deeps. Perhaps a half mile of the river is disclosed. A pale, dirty red, without glimmer or sheen, a motionless surface, a small featureless spot, inclosed in the dark shade of the gran-

ite, is all of it that is here visible. Yet we know it is a large
river, a hundred and fifty yards wide, with a headlong torrent
foaming and plunging over rocky rapids.

A little, and only a little, less impressive than the great
wall across the chasm are the buttes upon this side. And such
buttes! All others in the west, saving only the peerless
Temples of the Virgen, are mere trifles in comparison with
those of the Grand Cañon. In nobility of form, beauty of
decoration, and splendor of color, the Temples of the Virgen
must, on the whole, be awarded the palm; but those of the
Grand Cañon, while barely inferior to them in those respects,
surpass them in magnitude and fully equal them in majesty.
But while the Valley of the Virgen presents a few of these superlative creations, the Grand Cañon presents them by
dozens. In this relation the comparison would be analogous to
one between a fine cathedral town and a metropolis like London or Paris. In truth, there is only a very limited ground of
comparison between the two localities, for in style and effects
their respective structures differ as decidedly as the works of
any two well-developed and strongly contrasted styles of human architecture.

Whatsoever is forcible, characteristic, and picturesque in
the rock-forms of the Plateau Country is concentrated and intensified to the uttermost in the buttes. Wherever we find
them, whether fringing the long escarpments of terraces or
planted upon broad mesas, whether in cañons or upon expan-
sive plains, they are always bold and striking in outline and
ornate in architecture. Upon their flanks and entablatures the
decoration peculiar to the formation out of which they have
been carved is most strongly portrayed and the profiles are
most sharply cut. They command the attention with special
force and quicken the imagination with a singular power. The
secret of their impressiveness is doubtless obscure. Why one
form should be beautiful and another unattractive; why one
should be powerful, animated, and suggestive, while another
is meaningless, are questions for the metaphysician rather
than the geologist. Sufficient here is the fact. Yet there are
some elements of impressiveness which are too patent to escape recognition. In nearly all buttes there is a certain *definiteness* of form which is pecularily emphatic, and this is seen
in their profiles. Their ground-plans are almost always indefinite and capricious, but the profiles are rarely so. These are
usually composed of lines which have an approximate and

sometimes a sensibly perfect geometrical definition. They are usually few and simple in their ultimate analysis, though by combination they give rise to much variety. The ledges are vertical, the summits are horizontal, and the taluses are segments of hyperbolas of long curvature and concave upwards. These lines greatly preponderate in all cases, and though others sometimes intrude they seldom blemish greatly the effects produced by the normal ones. All this is in striking contrast with the ever-varying, indefinite profiles displayed in mountains and hills or on the slopes of valleys. The profiles generated by the combinations of these geometric lines persist along an indefinite extent of front. Such variations as occur arise not from changes in the nature of the lines, but in the modes of combination and proportions. These are never great in any front of moderate extent, but are just sufficient to relieve it from a certain monotony which would otherwise prevail. The same type and general form is persistent. Like the key-note of a song, the mind carries it in its consciousness wherever the harmony wanders.

The horizontal lines or courses are equally strong. These are the edges of the strata, and the deeply eroded seams where the superposed beds touch each other. Here the uniformity as we pass from place to place is conspicuous. The Carboniferous strata are quite the same in every section, showing no perceptible variation in thickness through great distances, and only a slight dip.

It is readily apparent, therefore, that the effect of these profiles and horizontal courses so persistent in their character is highly architectural. The relation is more than a mere analogy or suggestion; it is a vivid resemblance. Its failure or discordance is only in the ground plan, though it is not uncommon to find a resemblance, even in this respect, among the Permian buttes. Among the buttes of the Grand Cañon there are few striking instances of definiteness in ground plan. The finest butte of the chasm is situated near the upper end of the Kaibab division; but it is not visible from Point Sublime. It is more than 5,000 feet high, and has a surprising resemblance to an Oriental pagoda. We named it Vishnu's Temple.

On either side of the promontory on which we stand is a side gorge sinking nearly 4,000 feet below us. The two unite in front of the point, and, ever deepening, their trunk opens into the lowest abyss in the granite at the river. Across either

branch is a long rambling mass, one on the right of us, the
other on the left. We named them the Cloisters. They are excellent types of a whole class of buttes which stand in close
proximity to each other upon the north side of the chasm
throughout the entire extent of the Kaibab division. A far
better conception of their forms and features can be gained
by an examination of Mr. Holmes's panoramic picture than
by reading a whole volume of verbal description. The whole
prospect, indeed, is filled with a great throng of similar objects, which, as much by their multitude as by their colossal
size, confuse the senses; but these, on account of their proximity, may be most satisfactorily studied. The infinity of sharply defined detail is amazing. The eye is instantly caught and
the attention firmly held by its systematic character. The par-
allelism of the lines of bedding is most forcibly displayed in
all the windings of the façades, and these lines are crossed by
the vertical scorings of numberless waterways. Here, too, are
distinctly seen those details which constitute the peculiar style
of decoration prevailing throughout all the buttes and amphitheaters of the Kaibab. The course of the walls is never
for a moment straight, but extends as a series of cusps and
re-entrant curves. Elsewhere the reverse is more frequently
seen; the projections of the wall are rounded and are convex
towards the front, while the re-entrant portions are cusp-like
recesses. This latter style of decoration is common in the Permian buttes and is not rare in the Jurassic. It produces the effect of a thickly set row of pilasters. In the Grand Cañon the
reversal of this mode produces the effect of panels and
niches. In the western Cloister may be seen a succession of
these niches, and though they are mere details among myriads, they are really vast in dimensions. Those seen in the Red
Wall limestone are over 600 feet high, and are overhung by
arched lintels with spandrels.

As we contemplate these objects we find it quite impossible
to realize their magnitude. Not only are we deceived, but we
are conscious that we are deceived, and yet we cannot conquer the deception. We cannot long study our surroundings
without becoming aware of an enormous disparity in the effects produced upon the senses by objects which are immediate and equivalent ones which are more remote. The depth of
the gulf which separates us from the Cloisters cannot be realized. We crane over the brink, and about 700 feet below is a
talus, which ends at the summit of the cross-bedded sand-

stone. We may see the bottom of the gorge, which is about 3,800 feet beneath us, and yet the talus seems at least half-way down. Looking across the side gorge the cross-bedded sandstone is seen as a mere band at the summit of the Cloister, forming but a very small portion of its vertical extent, and, whatever the reason may conclude, it is useless to attempt to persuade the imagination that the two edges of the sandstone lie in the same horizontal plane. The eastern Cloister is nearer than the western, its distance being about a mile and a half. It seems incredible that it can be so much as one-third that distance. Its altitude is from 3,500 to 4,000 feet, but any attempt to estimate the altitude by means of visual impressions is felt at once to be hopeless. There is no stadium. Dimensions mean nothing to the senses, and all that we are conscious of in this respect is a troubled sense of immensity.

Beyond the eastern Cloister, five or six miles distant, rises a gigantic mass which we named Shiva's Temple. It is the grandest of all the buttes, and the most majestic in aspect, though not the most ornate. Its mass is as great as the mountainous part of Mount Washington. That summit looks down 6,000 feet into the dark depths of the inner abyss, over a succession of ledges as impracticable as the face of Bunker Hill Monument. All around it are side gorges sunk to a depth nearly as profound as that of the main channel. It stands in the midst of a great throng of cloister-like buttes, with the same noble profiles and strong lineaments as those immediately before us, with a plexus of awful chasms between them. In such a stupendous scene of wreck it seemed as if the fabled "Destroyer" might find an abode not wholly uncongenial.

In all the vast space beneath and around us there is very little upon which the mind can linger restfully. It is completely filled with objects of gigantic size and amazing form, and as the mind wanders over them it is hopelessly bewildered and lost. It is useless to select special points of contemplation. The instant the attention lays hold of them it is drawn to something else, and if it seeks to recur to them it cannot find them. Everything is superlative, transcending the power of the intelligence to comprehend it. There is no central point or object around which the other elements are grouped and to which they are tributary. The grandest objects are merged in a congregation of others equally grand. Hundreds of these mighty structures, miles in length, and thousands of feet in height, rear their majestic heads out of the abyss, displaying their richly-molded plinths and friezes, thrusting out their gables, wing-halls, buttresses, and pilasters, and recessed with alcoves and panels. If any one of these stupendous creations had been planted upon the plains of central Europe it would have influenced modern art as profoundly as Fusiyama has influenced the decorative art of Japan. Yet here they are all swallowed up in the confusion of multitude. It is not alone the magnitude of the individual objects that makes this spectacle so portentous, but it is still more the extravagant profusion with which they are arrayed along the whole visible extent of the broad chasm.

The color effects are rich and wonderful. They are due to the inherent colors of the rocks, modified by the atmosphere. Like any other great series of strata in the Plateau Province, the Carboniferous has its own range of characteristic colors, which might serve to distinguish it even if we had no other criterion. The summit strata are pale grey, with a faint yellowish cast. Beneath them the cross-bedded sandstone appears, showing a mottled surface of pale pinkish hue. Underneath this member are nearly 1,000 feet of the lower Aubrey sandstones, displaying an intensely brilliant red, which is somewhat masked by the talus shot down from the grey, cherty limestones at the summit. Beneath the Lower Aubrey is the face of the Red Wall limestone, from 2,000 to 3,000 feet high. It has a strong red tone, but a very peculiar one. Most of the red strata of the west have the brownish or vermilion tones, but these are rather purplish-red, as if the pigment had been treated to a dash of blue. It is not quite certain that this may not arise in part from the intervention of the blue haze, and probably it is rendered more conspicuous by this cause; but, on the whole, the purplish cast seems to be inherent. This is the dominant color-mass of the cañon, for the expanse of rock surface displayed is more than half in the Red Wall group. It is less brilliant than the fiery red of the Aubrey sandstones, but is still quite strong and rich. Beneath are the deep browns of the lower Carboniferous. The dark iron-black of the hornblendic schists revealed in the lower gorge makes but little impression upon the boundless expanse of bright colors above.

The total effect of the entire color-mass is bright and glowing. There is nothing gloomy or dark in the picture, except the opening of the inner gorge, which is too small a feature to influence materially the prevailing tone. Although the colors are bright when contrasted with normal landscapes, they are decidedly less intense than the flaming hues of the Trias or the dense cloying colors of the Permian; nor have they the refinement of those revealed in the Eocene. The intense luster which gleams from the rocks of the Plateau Country is by no means lost here, but is merely subdued and kept under some restraint. It is toned down and softened without being deprived of its character. Enough of it is left to produce color effects not far below those that are yielded by the Jura-Trias.

But though the inherent colors are less intense than some others, yet under the quickening influence of the atmosphere they produce effects to which all others are far inferior. And here language fails and description becomes impossible. Not only are their qualities exceedingly subtle, but they have little counterpart in common experience. If such are presented elsewhere they are presented so feebly and obscurely that only the most discriminating and closest observers of nature ever seize them, and they so imperfectly that their ideas of them are vague and but half real. There are no concrete notions founded in experience upon which a conception of these color effects and optical delusions can be constructed and made intelligible. A perpetual glamour envelops the landscape. Things are not what they seem, and the perceptions cannot tell us what they are. It is not probable that these effects are different in kind in the Grand Cañon from what they are in other portions of the Plateau Country. But the difference in degree is immense, and being greatly magnified and intensified many characteristics become palpable which elsewhere elude the closest observation.

In truth, the tone and temper of the landscape are constantly varying, and the changes in its aspect are very great. It is never the same, even from day to day, or even from hour to hour. In the early morning its mood and subjective influences are usually calmer and more full of repose than at other times, but as the sun rises higher the whole scene is so changed that we cannot recall our first impressions. Every passing cloud, every change in the position of the sun, recasts the whole. At sunset the pageant closes amid splendors that seem more than earthly. The direction of the full sunlight, the massing of the shadows, the manner in which the side lights are thrown in from the clouds determine these modulations, and the sensitiveness of the picture to the slightest variations in these conditions is very wonderful.

The shadows thrown by the bold abrupt forms are exceedingly dark. It is almost impossible at the distance of a very few miles to distinguish even broad details in these shadows. They are like remnants of midnight unconquered by the blaze of noonday. The want of half tones and gradations in the light and shade, which has already been noted in the Vermilion Cliffs, is apparent here, and is far more conspicuous. Our thoughts in this connection may suggest to us a still more extreme case of a similar phenomenon presented by the half-illuminated moon when viewed through a large telescope. The portions which catch the sunlight shine with great luster, but the shadows of mountains and cliffs are black and impenetrable. But there is one feature in the cañon which is certainly extraordinary. It is the appearance of the atmosphere against the background of shadow. It has a metallic luster which must be seen to be appreciated. The great wall across the chasm presents at noonday, under a cloudless sky, a singularly weird and unearthly aspect. The color is for the most part gone. In place of it comes this metallic glare of the haze. The southern wall is never so poorly lighted as at noon. Since its face consists of a series of promontories projecting towards the north, these projections catch the sunlight on their eastern sides in the forenoon, and upon their western sides in the afternoon; but near meridian the rays fall upon a few points only, and even upon these with very great obliquity. Thus at the hours of greatest illumination the wall is most obscure and the abnormal effects are then presented most forcibly. They give rise to strange delusions. The rocks then look nearly black, or very dark grey, and covered with feebly shining spots. The haze is strongly luminous, and so dense as to obscure the details already enfeebled by shade as if a leaden or mercurial vapor intervened. The shadows antagonize the perspective, and everything seems awry. The lines of stratification, dimly seen in one place and wholly effaced in another, are strangely belied, and the strata are given apparent attitudes which are sometimes grotesque and sometimes impossible.

Those who are familiar with western scenery have, no doubt, been impressed with the peculiar character of its haze—or atmosphere, in the artistic sense of the word—and have noted its more prominent qualities. When the air is free

from common smoke it has a pale blue color which is quite
unlike the neutral gray of the east. It is always apparently
more dense when we look towards the sun than when we
look away from it, and this difference in the two directions,
respectively, is a maximum near sunrise and sunset. This
property is universal, but its peculiarities in the Plateau Province become conspicuous when the strong rich colors of the
rocks are seen through it. The very air is then visible. We see
it, palpably, as a tenuous fluid, and the rocks beyond it do
not appear to be colored blue as they do in other regions, but
reveal themselves clothed in colors of their own. The Grand
Cañon is very full of this haze. It fills it to the brim. Its apparent density, as elsewhere, is varied according to the direction in which it is viewed and the position of the sun; but it
seems also to be denser and more concentrated than elsewhere. This is really a delusion arising from the fact that the
enormous magnitude of the chasm and of its component
masses dwarfs the distances; we are really looking through
miles of atmosphere under the impression that they are only
so many furlongs. This apparent concentration of haze, however, greatly intensifies all the beautiful or mysterious optical
defects which are dependent upon the intervention of the atmosphere.

Whenever the brink of the chasm is reached the chances
are that the sun is high and these abnormal effects in full
force. The cañon is asleep. Or is it under a spell of enchant-
ment which gives its bewildering mazes an aspect still more
bewildering. Throughout the long summer forenoon the
charm which binds it grows in potency. At midday the clouds
begin to gather, first in fleecy flecks, then in cumuli, and
throw their shadows into the gulf. At once the scene changes.
The slumber of the chasm is disturbed. The temples and
cloisters seem to raise themselves half awake to greet the
passing shadow. Their wilted, drooping, flattened faces expand into relief. The long promontories reach out from the
distant wall as if to catch a moment's refreshment from the
shade. The colors begin to glow; the haze loses its opaque
density and becomes more tenuous. The shadows pass, and
the chasm relapses into its dull sleep again. Thus through the
midday hours it lies in fitful slumber, overcome by the blinding glare and withering heat, yet responsive to every fluctua-
tion of light and shadow like a delicate organism.

As the sun moves far into the west the scene again

changes, slowly and imperceptibly at first, but afterwards more rapidly. In the hot summer afternoons the sky is full of cloud-play and the deep flushes with ready answers. The banks of snowy clouds pour a flood of light sidewise into the shadows and light up the gloom of the amphitheaters and alcoves, weakening the glow of the haze and rendering visible the details of the wall faces. At length, as the sun draws near the horizon, the great drama of the day begins.

Throughout the afternoon the prospect has been gradually growing clearer. The haze has relaxed its steely glare and has changed to a veil of transparent blue. Slowly the myriads of details have come out and the walls are flecked with lines of minute tracery, forming a diaper of light and shade. Stronger and sharper becomes the relief of each projection. The promontories come forth from the opposite wall. The sinuous lines of stratification which once seemed meaningless, distorted, and even chaotic, now range themselves into a true perspective of graceful curves, threading the scallop edges of the strata. The colossal buttes expand in every dimension. Their long, narrow wings, which once were folded together and flattened against each other, open out, disclosing between them vast alcoves illumined with Rembrandt lights tinged with the pale refined blue of the ever-present haze. A thousand forms, hitherto unseen or obscure, start up within the abyss, and stand forth in strength and animation. All things seem to grow in beauty, power, and dimensions. What was grand before has become majestic, the majestic becomes sublime, and, ever expanding and developing, the sublime passes beyond the reach of our faculties and becomes transcendent. The colors have come back. Inherently rich and strong, though not superlative under ordinary lights, they now begin to display an adventitious brilliancy. The western sky is all aflame. The scattered banks of cloud and wavy cirrhus have caught the waning splendor, and shine with orange and crimson. Broad slant beams of yellow light, shot through the glory-rifts, fall on turret and tower, on pinnacled crest and winding ledge, suffusing them with a radiance less fulsome, but akin to that which flames in the western clouds. The summit band is brilliant yellow; the next below is pale rose. But the grand expanse within is a deep, luminous, resplendent red. The climax has now come. The blaze of sunlight poured over an illimitable surface of glowing red is flung back into the gulf, and, commingling with the blue haze, turns it into a sea of purple of most imperial hue—so rich, so strong, so pure that it makes the heart ache and the throat tighten. However vast the magnitudes, however majestic the forms, or sumptuous the decoration, it is in these kingly colors that the highest glory of the Grand Cañon is revealed.

At length the sun sinks and the colors cease to burn. The abyss lapses back into repose. But its glory mounts upward and diffuses itself in the sky above. Long streamers of rosy light, rayed out from the west, cross the firmament and converge again in the east, ending in a pale rosy arch, which rises like a low aurora just above the eastern horizon. Below it is the dead gray shadow of the world. Higher and higher climbs the arch, followed by the darkening pall of gray, and as it ascends it fades and disappears, leaving no color except the afterglow of the western clouds and the lusterless red of the chasm below. Within the abyss the darkness gathers. Gradually the shades deepen and ascend, hiding the opposite wall and enveloping the great temples. For a few moments the summits of these majestic piles seem to float upon a sea of blackness, then vanish in the darkness, and, wrapped in the impenetrable mantle of the night, they await the glory of the coming dawn.

Verplanck Colvin

Adirondack Wilderness

Verplanck Colvin (1847–1920) dedicated thirty-five years to a boyhood passion for climbing, surveying, and mapping the Adirondack Mountains in upstate New York, and as early as 1868 he was publicly calling for the "creation of an Adirondack Park or Timber Preserve." The son of a prominent Albany lawyer, Colvin abandoned his own brief law practice to devote himself fully to his task. In his vehement speeches and writings, Colvin appealed to all interests to protect the wilderness for posterity; his arguments were like scattershot aimed at recreational, sporting, and commercial interests, but the argument that found its political mark was the importance of preserving the Adirondacks as a watershed. In 1872, Colvin became the state-appointed superintendent of the topographical survey of the region, and he immediately initiated the survey at his own expense. During the first year he discovered the true high-water source of the Hudson River and named it Lake Tear in the Clouds. There is a sense of adventure in Colvin's writings, and there is also a sense of urgency as he often refers to pressing time while driving his men up and down peaks with small consideration to hardship. Defections were common, and Colvin comments on one group of men who could not "be persuaded to proceed further, exhibiting their torn clothes and soleless gaping boots as evidence of their inability." Colvin served as state surveyor for twenty-eight years and wrote eight Reports. *The early* Reports *became his means of gathering further support for his Adirondack dream; they became popular reading and helped many people discover a place of strangeness and beauty, not in some distant country, but in New York City's backyard. In 1885, the state legislature made the Adirondacks a forest preserve, and in 1892, it created Adirondack Park, encircling over two thousand mountain lakes and six thousand miles of rivers and streams in an area larger than Yellow-stone and Yosemite combined.*

Few fully understand what the Adirondack wilderness really is. It is a mystery even to those who have crossed and re-crossed it by boats along its avenues, the lakes; and on foot through its vast and silent recesses, by following the long ghastly lines of blazed or axe-marked trees, which the daring searcher for the fur of the sable or the mink, has chopped in order that he may find his way again in that deep and often desolate forest. In these remote sections, filled with the most rugged mountains, where unnamed waterfalls pour in snowy tresses from the dark overhanging cliffs, the horse can find no footing; and the adventurous trapper or explorer must carry upon his back his blankets and a heavy stock of food. His rifle, which affords protection against wild beasts, at times replenishes his well husbanded provisions, and his axe aids him in constructing from bark or bough some temporary shelter from storm, or hews into logs and the huge trees which form the fierce, roaring, comfortable fire of the camp. Yet, though the woodsman may pass his life-time in some section of the wilderness it is still a mystery to him. Following the line of axe-marks upon the trees; venturing along the cliff walls of the streams which rush leap on leap downward to form haughty rivers; climbing on the steep wooded slopes of lakes which never knew form or name on maps, he clings to his trapping line, and shrouded and shut in by the deep, wonderful forest, emerges at length from its darkness to the daylight of the clearings, like a man who has passed under a great river or arm of the sea through a tunnel, knowing little of the wonders that had surrounded him.

It is a peculiar region; for though the geographical center of the wilderness may be readily and easily reached in the light canoe-like boats of the guides, by lakes and rivers, which form a labyrinth of passages for boats; the core, or

From Verplanck Colvin, *Report of the Topographical Survey of the Adirondack Wilderness of New York for the Year 1873* (Albany: Weed, Parsons, 1874).

rather cores, of this wilderness extend on either hand from
these broad avenues of water, and in their interior remain
to-day spots as untrodden by man, and as unknown and wild,
as when the Indian alone paddled his birchen boat upon
those streams and lakes. Amid these mountain solitudes are
places at this moment where, in all probability, the foot of
man never trod; and here the panther has his den among the
rocks, and rears his savage kittens undisturbed save by the
growl of bear or screech of lynx, or the hoarse croak of
raven taking its share of the carcass of slain deer. Of this
region, for a hundred years or more, civilized man has held
the most diverse opinions. Since the first settlement of New
York there have been constant endeavors to clear and culti-
vate it, and crumbling buildings upon its margin, here and
there, are records of wasted effort, squandered capital, and
ruin. These unfortunate attempts at settlement originated in
wild and false statements made by land speculators as to the
richness and fertility of the region, supported by the specious
argument that it must be fertile and valuable because lands
on the St. Lawrence river, further north, even in Canada,
were fruitful and productive. All this trouble, all this wasted
labor, and confusion, can be directly traced to the low state
of knowledge of the physical sciences in those days, and
the absolute ignorance which then existed, and has existed up
to a recent period, of the *science of the atmosphere* and of
climatology. The people of those days did not know that,
practically, in agriculture, every thousand feet of elevation
was equivalent in climate to one or two degrees of north latitude; or, more plainly, that if the lands of a market gardener
near New York city were suddenly raised 5,000 feet he
would find himself in a climate like that of Montreal,
Canada, the spring perhaps a month or more later in coming,
and winter like that of Labrador. When we now come to consider that this great wilderness extends from two hundred to
three hundred miles north of New York, and that of its area
two or three thousand square miles, are so elevated that the
lake and river levels have an altitude of 1,500 or 1,800 or 2,-
000 feet above the sea, and that some of the smaller lakelets,
rising to 4,000 feet, are hemmed in by mountains exceeding
5,000 feet in altitude, we readily perceive that this whole
region must have a peculiar climate and more severe than
that of the lowlands of the same latitude which are nearer to
the level of the sea. In such a region, therefore, the height of

lands above tide level becomes a measure of their climate, and consequently of their value for agricultural purposes, and thus the hypsometrical work of this survey—every height, indeed, above sea level that is determined—becomes of practical value to the farmer or cultivator, the purchaser of lands for agricultural purposes, or the political economist who desires to estimate the capacity of the state, or a portion of it for the production of food. . . .

[*August 13*]   Leaving to others the gathering of supplies for the commissariat; the day opening clear, I drew together the survey party, with two of our guides and two volunteers, and drove from our head-quarters to the foot of Hopkins' Peak, which, together with the famous mountain, Giant-of-the-Valley, I proposed that day to climb and measure. At the settlement, midway in the valley (Dibble's), one assistant was dispatched with barometer for observations at lower station synchronous with ours upon the peak. The day proving very warm, we reached the summit of Hopkins' Peak at half past 12 P.M. Gazing out upon a wealth of mountains and valleys spread before us, we regretted that there was not more time. However, seizing our opportunity, the theodolite box was taken from the knapsack of the guide carrying it, and adjusted upon its tripod on the summit of the peak. The dark evergreen forest crowding itself for standing room upon the precipitous sides of the well-named Giant Mountain behind us—the view of silent crowded crags, across the deep valley of Keene Flats—the peaceful snowy clouds and azure sky above, afforded contrasts which made the view from this point extremely beautiful. As a point determined by triangulation, it was valuable, as it gave us a commanding view of the whole Keene Flats valley, and enabled us to direct the instruments upon every point of interest within it. The labor was so important that I did not join the party who, under shelter of a ledge, beside a glowing fire, seemed to enjoy their dinner all unaware of the picturesque addition which they made to the scene. At 3:30 P.M., I concluded my measurements. The station is distinguished by a copper bolt in the rock (No. 9). Four full pages in the theodolite book represented the measurements, and in addition three valuable reconnaissance maps were made. The height of Hopkins' Peak above the sea, by our measurement, which is believed to be the first ever made, is 3,136 feet. From the observations taken during the whole day at the lower station in the deep

valley, the height of that (lower) station is computed at 963
feet above tide, and on comparison and calculation, from observations taken at the same instant of time at that lower station (Dibble's), and on the summit of the peak the height of
the mountain above the lower station is computed at 2,168
feet.

Immediately assembling the party the instruments were
packed and we descended from this summit on our way to
the Giant, which we thought, despite the lateness of the hour,
might yet be ascended and measured by a rapid march. This
second mountain ascent of the day took more time than we
had anticipated; windfalls of timber, dense thickets, descents
and ascents along a broken ridge, rendered progress slow, especially that of the guide carrying the theodolite, packed in
its box, upon his back. It was quarter to 7 P.M. when we
reached the summit of the Giant-of-the-Valley. Before us was
spread a vast and grand but gloomy depth of scenery. At our
feet, cliffs a thousand feet in height fell away to a gray map-
like picture, as chill and silent as a world deserted and left
vacant. The sun had left some crimson streaks upon the
western clouds—only sufficient to make more mournful the
sombreness of the rest—: the multitude of peaks seemed a
myriad of gray domes and ridges, sunk together in one common slumber, to last forever.

No chirp of insect, no cry of bird or beast, broke in upon
the awful silence of the scene, and as we beheld mountain on
mountain stretching into infinitude, the knowledge, that
through and over them, beyond the reach of sight, our labors
led, and would lead us, chilled all hearts and made us silent
also.

By the time that we had completed the barometrical observations—which indicate for the Giant a height of 4,530
feet—*little more than 800 feet below the height of Mt.
Marcy*—the sun had set. A division of opinion as to the
proper course to pursue now arose; for the guides asserted
that it was now too late to descend. We had not a particle of
water, the work had been exhaustive and our thirst was becoming unendurable. This decided the question, and we
resolved to descend till we found water. . . . Off the trail—in
darkness—descending cliffs—across holes and chasms—on
dead fallen timber—feeling, not seeing, we made our way
down to water, a narrow swift rill shooting down over the
rocks and precipices. Refreshed and invigorated by water—

cold and pure—the only drink which the Creator, in his wisdom, has provided for man and beast—we resolved to continue the descent; and hideous hours passed away as we crept down amid dangers which we often suddenly felt when it was almost too late to recoil. Our pocket lanterns—when the ground became such that one hand was at liberty—were of great assistance. It was one o'clock in the morning when the moon came to our aid, and we emerged from the forest, having successfully effected our descent. Marching quickly to quarters by moonlight, we satisfied our hunger by a breakfast-supper and retired for a short rest to fit us for the labors of the next day.

Daylight on the 14th showed lowering clouds that threatened storm. One of the guides, alarmed at the experiences of the previous night, withdrew, and another whom we had expected this morning did not come. As the heavy packs, deserted, could not be moved I gave the third guide leave of absence for the day, the weather settling to a heavy storm. The guide reported again at evening. He had been unable to secure any additional men.

[*August 15*]   The storm still continued and it grew cold. Proceeding to institute comparative readings of the barometers, I was shocked to find that the mountain barometer, which we had used in the measurement of the Giant, was broken and utterly useless. Only a part of the quicksilver remained, and some of this entering the crevices of the brass portion of the instrument had amalgamated with that metal and defaced and injured it. We could ill afford to part with this instrument for a day, but its immediate repair was the only resource, and it became necessary for one of the assistants to return with it to New York. Two additional guides were secured to-day, and everything being completed, orders were issued at evening for march into the wilderness the next morning.

The plan of work for the week ensuing was as follows: One assistant having in charge the broken barometer would return to New York via Albany: secure the repair of the instrument, and bringing the extra tubes and iron bottle of quicksilver, with other matters, would rejoin us at Keene Flats precisely on the sixth day. The survey party in the meanwhile would march into and explore and map the unknown region south of Keene near the Hunter's Pass; thence ascend Mt. Dix, then effect the passage of the defile which lies north of Mud or—as it is now called—Elk lake; thence climb Nipple Top mountain and descend into the Elk Pass, the defile next westward, whence we would in turn ascend the next mountain, which forms the eastern mountain wall above the Ausable lakes, thence returning exactly on the sixth day to our Keene Station.

On the morning of the 16th this plan was put into operation; the assistant set out early by team to Westport, with three guides carrying, besides their axes, six days' rations of bread and meat in packs, and the theodolite; leaving behind us trails and marked trees, we struck into the forest. Climbing into the Round mountain notch, the summit of which our measurements shows to be 2,546 feet above tide, we left the rills which run to the Ausable and descended to the head waters of the Boquet river. From a cliff which made an opening in the timber, we obtained a glimpse of Mt. Dix, bearing south 21° 45' west; making note of this bearing, we left the cliff, and, again enshrouded in the dense woods, made our way southward through this upland valley. At noon we halted for rest and dinner, and three hours afterward reached the Bouquet river, here a considerable stream. From the barometical observations the height of our bench mark at this point on the river, is found to be 2,425 feet above tide. The mountains towering on all sides and shutting it darkly in, made it seem little like an upland valley, more than three hundred feet higher than the summit of Bald Peak. Following the river through this pathless forest, which was, however, everywhere tracked by the foot-prints of wild beasts; now fording the stream to escape precipitous climbing, now clambering up over the huge rocks in its bed, over and amid which the clear water fell foaming; we pushed forward, noting at one time the entrance of a stream from the right, and at another the inrush of some miniature cataract on the left, till the steepness of the climbing and the slenderness of the stream, showed that we were approaching the sources of the Boquet river in the Hunter's Pass, which is also called the Dial Gorge. At 5:30 P.M., we unslung knapsacks and joined in constructing a camp. Ground was cleared of underwood, etc., on a small level space near the fork of a stream that shot down through a rocky flume, leap on leap a hundred feet into the river. Huge sheets of bark were peeled from the spruce trees and laid upon the frame-work of our shanty; wood for the camp fire was cut in logs and heaped, and after supper we fell easily asleep, the great fire crackling and flaming before our hut.

The morning of August 17th opened brilliantly. The golden sunshine glimmered around the mountain crests; and anxious to avail myself of so favorable a day, after breakfast the heavy baggage was left in charge of one who remained at the camp, and we immediately commenced to climb the slopes of Mount Dix, which was to be the next trigonometrical station. This was an entirely different route from that by which I ascended this mountain in 1870 where we marked a line and cut a path through the timber. Here there was no sign, but instead, paths stamped by the footprints of deer, panther and bear showed us where these creatures had found spots amid the cliffs which they could climb, and availing ourselves of these runways, we slowly toiled upward. By 9:30 A.M. we had reached a height as great as that of Camel's Hump Mountain, and carefully finding its level, we took its height by barometer, which when computed and corrected for curvature and refraction, gives for its altitude above tide 3,-548 feet. It was after 11 A.M. when we reached the level of Nipple Top, and looking across the depths of the Hunter's Pass, we could search the opposite rugged mountain for some path by which to climb it. The exact level of Nipple Top was carefully determined, and the station being favorable, a base was measured with steel tape along the mountain side, and the angular distance of that mountain from this station found by measurement with sextant from each end of the base. This would admit of an exact application of my method of leveling with barometer and hand-level, and a careful computation, based upon this work, showed Nipple Top to have a height of 4,656 feet above the sea. After struggling through dense thickets of spruce and balsam, at half-past one in the afternoon we reached the summit of Mount Dix. It was wonderfully clear, not a cloud to be seen, and the atmosphere comfortably warm. No signal was at first visible upon Bald Peak, which from this height appeared as a rocky mound, yet the unaided eye could distinguish near the shore of Lake Champlain the glimmer of the automatic stanhelio-signal upon Crown Point. Setting one man to helio-signal Bald Peak, in order, if possible, to obtain a response from the assistants stationed there, we set up theodolite and barometer, and entered on our work. Northward Mount Hurricane was seen, and the theodolite telescope was hardly directed upon it before the flash of the automatic signal I had placed there was visible, and proved the wonderful success of the invention. The angular measurements were rapidly progressed, and with the aid of the telescope the Bald Peak stanhelio automatic signal was seen, and its angular place found with precision. At a quarter to four in the afternoon our signal was answered by a flash from Bald Peak; the first intimation that we had of the presence of the assistants at their station. It was needless, for the stanhelio signal had served all our purposes. As the afternoon shadows lengthened we pushed our work without rest or conversation, and Crown Point lighthouse being visible, formed a third zero and established point, with which the other measurements were joined. Clear Pond, Mud or Elk lake, the Boreas range, Haystack, Marcy, and a multitude of other points, were reached, twelve pages in the large theodolite book being occupied with the records of measurement. Four reconnaissance maps of topography were made, and forty-six barometrical observations upon the summit gave a mean that enabled us to determine the height of the mountain with greater accuracy than ever before attainable; my computation showing Mount Dix to be 4,916 feet above tide level. The height of this mountain, according to Prof. Emmons in 1837, was 5,200 feet. It is unfortunate that without climbing or measuring it by barometer, he should have been led to record such an erroneous approximation.

Absorbed in our work we were startled by sunset to the consciousness that night had already settled in the chasm valleys below. It would be impossible to descend in the dark, amid the cliffs and ledges, where only the footprints of the catamount had guided us by daylight to places which could be scaled; and our camp and camp-guard and provisions were miles away. There was no time for discussion and I ordered a descent into the Hunter's Pass, so far down, as it would be necessary to find water and a resting place. Water, unfortunately, was not to be readily found, and soon we became entangled amid ledges, slides and cavernous rocks that rendered the previous night-descent of the Giant inferior in danger. In the darkness, clinging by roots, aiding each other from ledge to ledge, and guiding, with special care, the footsteps of those carrying the theodolite, etc., we finally found ourselves slipping on the edge of rocks draped in cold, wet, sphagnous moss, and a little lower we found water! A moment's rest and we descended further only to find that we were in a cul-de-

sac—with walls of air—turn which way we would, save
toward the mountain top; and we reached the verge of an
overhanging cliff, so high that even the tree-tops below were
not distinguishable. The slender stream leapt the edge and
was lost in the depths. Here we were compelled to halt, and
reclining at the edge of the precipice, passed the night; the
feeble fire, by its suggestions of supper—which we had no
means of gratifying—only giving edge to our hunger.

Daylight, August 18th, showed us the wildness of our situation, and the means of extrication; and, breakfastless, after
dangers unnecessary to relate, we descended to the south portal of the Hunter's Pass upon a stream which flowing southward, out of the pass, formed one of the sources of the
Hudson river. Turning northward we entered the portals of
the Hunter's Pass (the Gorge of the Dial), which so many
have longed to explore and endeavored in vain to reach, and
ascended betwixt its walls of rock to its summit. Here barometrical observations were taken. They indicate the height of the
pass above tide to be 3,247 feet. The inclosing mountains rise
over a thousand feet above, on either side, and the spectacle
is grand and imposing. Descending northward we were once
more on the St. Lawrence river side of the mountain range.
We had left camp for the ascent of Mount Dix, with the intention of returning that night, and now, fearing lest our
friend left there should become alarmed at this continued absence, we marched as rapidly toward where we thought the
camp might be as our exhaustion permitted, firing occasionally revolver shot signals to acquaint him with our approach,
but more, perhaps, with the hope that he might prepare us a
breakfast. We at length found camp and man all right. A
heavy storm in the afternoon tried the value of our bark roof,
and gave us opportunity for rest. Barometrical observations
this day give the height of this station at 2,788 feet above
tide.

[*August 19th*] Raining slightly and very threatening.
Determined, nevertheless, to set out upon the ascent of Nipple
Top mountain, on the eastern slopes of which we were encamped; followed up a stream till its course diverged from
what (so far as we could judge in the fog and storm surrounding us), would be our way; climbed steadily, and at 1 P.M.
thought we were upon the summit, but having chopped down
trees, and the clouds rolling away, we saw another summit
further south which we reached at 2 P.M., which proved to be

the true crest. Dense white cloud enveloped us, but it was in
rapid motion, and at intervals opened and showed glimpses of
chasms and mountains. Suddenly it was swept away at the
east and Mount Dix, scarred and savage rocks, rose before
us; beyond it the rolling country near Lake Champlain, with
our Bald Peak, like a little hillock, beside the distant gleaming lake. The gorgeous sunshine streaming on the distant
cirro-cumulus clouds below, produced a rare effect. Suddenly,
starting with surprise, our mingled shouts arose, for on the
breast of the cloud each saw his own form, the head surrounded by a rich *anthelia,* a circular glory of prismatic colors,
the renowned "Ulloa's rings," which that philosopher beheld
from the summit of the Pambamarca. Not one of the mountain guides had ever seen or heard of such sight before. It
was gone all too quickly, yet it seemed as though nature today were reveling in splendors, for the clouds vanishing in
the west, a sierra of mountain crags was uncurtained, torn
rugged and wild, above all which rose Ta-ha-wus, "Cleaver of
the clouds." Topographical maps were executed and in our
barometrical work we had the first record of measurement
made on this summit. From these *direct* observations the
height of Nipple Top has been computed at 4,684 feet above
tide level. It will be remembered that the height of this mountain had been taken two days before by combined barometer
and spirit level from Mount Dix, and computed at 4,656 feet.
The difference is twenty-seven feet, far within the limit given
by Humboldt for mountain measurement.

Not designing another night climb (as we carried now all
our camp equipage), we left the summit at 5:30 P.M., and
descending rapidly, reached the bottom of Elk Pass in time to
erect a shanty of boughs.

The camp was in an open grove fronting an unknown
waterfall, which from its silvery spray and step-like form I
named the *Fairy Ladder Falls*, the height of the foot of
which I found to be 3,111 feet above tide.

Rousing the men early on the 20th the last ration of flour
baked, and breakfast over, leaving at this camp all our impediments, we commenced our climb to the summit of the
next mountain eastward, which the guides had named Mount
Colvin. The knowledge that it was a mountain heretofore
unascended, unmeasured and—prominent as it was—unknown to any map, made the ascent the more interesting.
The indications of game were naturally abundant: the rocks

and ledges geologically interesting, and, judging by the outlook from inferior summits, the view from the top could not fail to be superior. A trap or *sienite* dyke was discovered, but there was no time for its examination, and reaching at length the height, its last approach a cliff almost impregnable, we drew ourselves up over the verge to find a seat upon a throne that seemed the central seat of the mountain amphitheatre. Deep in the chasm at our feet was the lower Ansable lake, each indentation of its shore sharply marked as on a map; beyond it the Gothic mountains rose, carved with wild and fantastic forms on the white rock, swept clear by avalanches and decked with scanty patches of stunted evergreens. Everywhere below were lakes and mountains so different from all maps, yet so immovably true. There was too little time to satisfy us. Here was golden sunshine, a balmy air and a wealth of work before us, but an empty larder. It was the sixth day, the evening of which I had before set as the termination of this branch expedition. Topographical reconnaissance was therefore pushed forward, and a careful measurement made, from which the height of Mount Colvin is found to be 4,142 feet above tide level.

It was after 4 P.M. when we left the summit and hurried down into the Elk Pass again, and reaching a point further south than our camp, on the Hudson river waters, we came upon a beautiful meadow, and further, on a shallow pond which we called "Lycopodium," from the occurrence of that plant near its shores. The height of the summit of Elk Pass was found to be 3,302 feet. The sun sinking fast, we hastened on, reached our camp, slung on the knapsacks we had left there, and on a run struck northward down the rugged unknown pass; yet hardly hoping to accomplish that night the miles of wilderness between us and the first settlement of Keene. Still, we strained every nerve, pressing onward without resting, seldom glancing at the compass, guided better by the sun upon the peaks, of which now and then some opening in the thick foliage of the trees would give us view.

Twilight, and still marching, despite the wish of wearied men to camp. Dark, and still marching. Night marching; and our goal gained. We were partaking of a late supper at Keene Flats, when the team drove to the door with the assistant returning from New York, barometer, etc., repaired, and every duty well discharged. In all things we had met with uninterrupted success, and every mountain and pass which we in-

tended to visit had been reached and measured, and the work
accomplished exactly within the six days set. In accordance
with directions, a quantity of bread had been prepared during
our absence, sufficient for our present needs, and every thing
was in readiness for the further prosecution of the survey. . . .

[*August 27*]   The day being clear—leaving the remainder
of the survey party at work in Panther Gorge—I took with
me two guides and reascended Mount Haystack, answering
across the deep chasm the faint, distant shouts of the assistant
now climbing Mount Marcy on his way to Long Lake. A day
of brilliant sunshine on Haystack enabled me to accomplish a
great amount of valuable work. The telescope of the instrument at one time showing the automatic signal on Mount
Hurricane, and at another, at a sharp vertical angle, making
visible the yellowish, lily-leaved surface of the water in the
Au Sable lake, feeding ground of the wild deer by night, and
again sweeping southward and bringing into view mountains
beyond the hills of Schroon.

Copper bolt No. 11 was set in the rock beneath the theodolite, and distinguishes the station. The barometrical work,
most important, was the measurements, with aid of level, of
Basin and Gothic mountains. The height of Basin mountain,
never before measured, is 4,905 feet, Gothic mountain, *also
never previously measured,* is 4,744 feet in height. These stupendous mountains—majestic landmarks of the State—had
until this time remained unknown to surveys, though all three
are superior in altitude to the famous Mt. Seward. The angular measurements from the summit of Mount Haystack on
this day afforded also the final basis for the geodesical
measurement of numerous other lofty peaks, prominent
among which is a peak known to the guides as Saddle Mountain. I have computed the height of this mountain trigono-
metrically, by the logarithms of its distance (as determined
by my triangulation), and of the vertical angles measured,
and find it to have an altitude of 4,536 feet above the sea.

Busily engaged with the angular measurements, the
sketching of reconnaissance maps, etc., we worked till late,
and descending the sharp crag reached camp.

[*August 28th*]   I had devoted to the climbing of MOUNT
SKYLGHT, which had never before been ascended, even by
the hunters or guides, though the fourth mountain in height
in the State, as I have proved. Its slopes have been deemed

almost impregnable, owing to the denseness of dwarfed trees crowding like a thicket of bayonets and fishhooks upon the steep rim and top of the mountain. Without trail or mark to guide us, we set out, and climbing to the rim, fought our way through all impediments to the summit. The mountain was measured barometrically, and the height corrected by synchronous observations at lower station in Panther Gorge, is by the *direct* measurement 4,967 feet. Numerous angles were measured and the reconnaissance sketches of topography made, have aided in completing the topographical map, showing the contour of Mount Marcy and the neighboring peaks inclosing the Summit-Water lakelets, the highest pond sources of the Hudson.

A little before 4 P.M. we put up the instruments and set out westward to explore the plateau south of Mount Marcy, where we had last season found the little lake Tear-of-the-clouds to be the loftiest water in the State, as well as the lake-head of our great river.

As we descended Skylight, we reached the level of the peak which I have named Mount Redfield, in honor of the discoverer of Mount Marcy. My measurement makes it 4,688 feet above tide. Moving rapidly toward a marsh which lies on the high plateau at the foot of this mountain, we were the first to reach, as we have been the first to map the second little pond, shown on the topographical reconnaissance map. The barometrical measurement indicates its height above tide to be 4,312 feet. The little pool is margined and embanked with luxuriant and deep sphagnous moss, and we named it Moss Lake. It was found to flow to the Hudson. As we stopped to drink from this pellucid and cold spring, offspring of this high mountain atmosphere, my eyes were startled by the sight of some very small and beautiful white bivalve shells upon the bottom. They were about three-sixteenths of an inch in diameter, and were the first of such shells I have ever met with at such an altitude. Beautifully minute and white, representatives of a race of lake dwellers, it seemed to me that this circumstance alone gave this spring-like pool the right to the title of lake. In what manner this little bivalve shell ever reached this lonely water, elevated so near 5,000 feet from sea level, it is impossible to determine. Carefully I secured specimens in a phial with water of the lake, and hastening as night approached, crossed the plateau northward to the little summit lake "Tear-of-the-clouds." The measurement which I now took, affirmed my previous result, showing this water to be 4,326 feet above the sea, leaving it superior to its companion spring, the Moss pool, which I had thought might prove to be higher than the first one reached.

We here selected the route for a new trail over the mountains which would avoid the necessity of climbing Mount Marcy. We explored the low pass between the head of the inlet of Lake Tear-of-the-clouds and the Ausable water, and found it an easy and perfectly feasible route. We descended rapidly along a rill that hurried, leap on leap, swiftly down to Marcy brook, and were in camp before dark, notwithstanding prophecies that we would have to make a night march of it.

All the work contemplated at this station was now accomplished successfully. We had even exceeded our anticipations, and in the first measurement of Mounts Haystack and Skylight, and in the verification of my discovery of the lake sources of the Hudson, had truly gratifying results. On the morning of August 29th the baggage and camp equipage were packed, and guides and surveyors alike shouldering the heavy packs and knapsacks, we set out for the summit of Mount Marcy, where, after another day's work, we intended to descend to the range westward, and march to Lake Colden the same night. . . .

On the morning of the 10th [of October], we set out for the summit of Ampersand Mountain. Taking boat and descending the Saranac river into Round Lake, we landed on the east shore, where a marked line or trail leads to the summit. The transit instrument and provisions were carried by the guides; myself and assistant carrying the barometers. In the forest the snow, which had fallen some time before, lay cold and crisp, having thawed and frozen. The air was cold even at the foot of the mountain, and gave us assurance that our encampment on the summit would be cheerless. The mountain was easy of ascent, but the heavy baggage compelled us to move slowly. Here a slip against a rock broke in pieces a choice pocket thermometer which had been carefully bestowed in an inner pocket of my coat. We had now, therefore, only the two standard detached thermometers to depend upon in our hypsometrical work. We took dinner at a spring on the trail some distance from the summit, and establishing a bench mark, found the height to be by barometer 2,960 feet from tide. Making our camp in a bark shanty on the crest, we commenced our labors. A small opening in the timber which had already been made on this summit, enabled us to determine how much of the forest on the ridge would have to be cleared before we could proceed with the work. This determined, the men immediately commenced chopping, and as tree after tree fell, and the view enlarged, the prospect became enchanting. By evening, excellent progress had been made, a sufficient horizon having been cleared, to enable me to commence the work of measurement on the morrow, there not being now even a branch to obstruct the field of the theodolite telescope when stationed on the exact peak for upward of 120° of the horizon. The view over the lake-land below, at night, was strangely beautiful. The silent lakes and sombre forests stretched away at the mountain foot, into the obscurity of night, or were lost under the shadow of some towering mountain. It being very still and the stars brightly visible, I was able with the transit to determine the magnetic variation (declination) by observations of the upper culmination of the star *a ursa minoris*. The scene, while this work was being executed, would have well suited the brush of Salvator Rosa. Upon the verge of the precipitous summit, was the glowing camp fire redly illuminating the open front of the bark camp, where the guides, in their hunters' costume, with shapeless felt hats, picturesquely reclining, looked out upon the fire or the depths.

Beside the shanty the transit instrument, carefully removed from the influence of iron or steel (pistols, knives or axes), with its standards and limbs of brilliantly polished brass and silver shining in the light of the lantern held by the assistant: the dark depths below, and the starry dome above, together formed a strange unusual spectacle. Thus we waited till the time of culmination of the star drew near—narrowly watching it through the telescope—reflected lantern light thrown within the tube, enabling us to bring it sharply on the cross hairs—then vertically downward—to find that it is not yet time by *Alioth*.—At length they are vertical—time-piece in hand, a few moments pass, then the cross hairs delicately center on the star, and the work is done. . . .

The morning of the 20th found the fire drowned out and the bark roof of the camp leaking streams of water. It was with difficulty that any thing was procured sufficiently dry with which to kindle a fire. All day rain continued to fall, and also the barometer—the pressure extremely low, being

some 8/10 below the mean; at 8 P.M. standing 27.450. The
storm was so heavy that we were compelled to keep under
shelter. From the hunters to-day I learned that a trapper
from the western side of the woods had penetrated a few
days before to Mud lake, and had evidently come by way of
some lakes or streams known only to himself. He was
thought now to be somewhere two or three miles westward
beyond the head of Mud lake, for they had heard the distant
report of a rifle in that direction. This was the very region
which I had designed to explore. On a very old chart in my
possession I had noticed a lake placed at the corner of certain
old survey lines, which lake had never since appeared on any
map. My inquiries of the guides as to the location of such a
lake had for years been met either with incredulity or pro-
fessions of ignorance as to that most remote section; but feeling
assured of its existence, I had come to call it the Lost Lake,
for obvious reasons. Three years before my efforts to reach it
when alone in the wilderness had been foiled by the failure of
my provisions. I now decided to strike out into that unknown
region on the morrow, and making a circuit through the forest
of as many miles as we could in one day, endeavor to find the
track or trail of that trapper, and, at any rate, gather topographical notes of that dubious region.

[*October 21*]   The sky is still overcast, and the storm has
raised the water in the lake a foot or more, but it has stopped
raining. Taking our boats and carrying a light lunch, we set
out. The assistant was posted on the shore of Mud Lake with
barometer, with orders to take continuous observations during
the day. One boat also was left with him. Proceeding with the
men to the upper end of the lake—a broad, soft, peat marsh,
now partially overflowed—the boat was left, and with a
glance at the compass, we struck into the forest. Paths of
deer traversed the wood everywhere, and in the wet places we
saw numerous tracks of wolves.

Pushing on into the forest, occasionally meeting doe and
buck, so unacquainted with man that they scarcely deigned to
fly, we kept a sharp look out for trail or sign of man, and
from any slight eminence peered out through the leafless trees
to see if we could discover any lake. At length we struck
some rills or brooks, which flowing westward were evidently
some of the head waters of the Oswegatchie river. Below
some low hills shut in a valley, and suspecting water, I hurried down, and in another instant a new lake was shining be-

fore me! Here we discovered signs of the trapper, and one of
the guides making search along the shore for foot-prints,
found his canoe! Embarking, we crossed the lake, a small but
handsome sheet of water. I surmised that this might be the
lost lake, but deferred for the time the search for the survey
corner. While drawing the boat ashore on an opposite sand
beach, guns were heard in the forest a mile or two south-
westward, and we started directly toward them, making a
running march. Heard no more guns, and after traveling, as
near as we could judge, to the spot where they originated, we
became involved in a dense swamp but found no one; nothing but silent woods. Marching as rapidly as we could we
came at 3 P.M. to a descent where the country westward lay
lower. The guides climbed trees, but could see neither lake
nor smoke nor even recognize hills toward Mud Lake which
we had left in the morning. Here we stopped a few moments
to eat the mere handful of food we had with us, and of
which our rapid march had before prevented our partaking.
The sun was sinking. We had neither blankets nor provisions,
and were ill prepared for a winter's night. Our march had
been so rapid that there had been no time to keep an eye on
the compass, we, therefore, took our return course by guess,
and moved as rapidly as though acquainted with the country.
Thus we ran suddenly upon another lake which we had evidently left far to the north in our outward march. Not far
from it we found a wolf-trap set in one of the paths made by
these animals, and we quickly found an obscure but sufficient
trail, following which with all possible speed we reached
again the first lake of the day. Here we had the fortune to
find the wolf trapper and his companion and accepted the hospitality of their shanty for the night. We learned from them
that the lake where we were now encamped was a good deer
pond, and that the old survey corner was exactly where I had
expected to find it.

On the following morning, October 22nd, we found the corner, and I was satisfied that this was indeed the lake so long
lost. But more than this, I learned from the trapper that there
were many ponds and lakes known to himself and one or two
other hunters which had never appeared upon any map, and
of which he spoke reluctantly, as one revealing his hidden
treasures of fur and game. The second little lake near which
we had found the wolf-trap, was called Nick's Lake after one
who had trapped there. The reconnaissance had been success-

ful, and my mind was made up as to the further course of
the survey. I determined at all hazards to locate all these new
lakes this winter, and with my party push through and explore all the unmapped region from our present station to the
Beaver river settlements far south-westward, as, indeed, I had
originally contemplated. But I could not abandon the work
commenced at Grave's mountain and its vicinity, whence I
had planned to extend the triangulation to Great Cranberry
Lake the same season. After a short mental computation of
time for work, and chances of foul weather, I engaged the
trapper then and there to meet me at the exact expiration of
ten days to act as our guide, as far as his knowledge went in
this district. Fearing that the men at Mud Lake would become alarmed at our absence, knowing that we had marched
without provisions or blankets or even an axe, we set out
early this day on our return, one of the guides preceding in
advance, the sooner to assure them of our safety. At the
shore of our lost lake I had taken barometrical observations
on the previous day, which when compared with the synchronous observations at Mud Lake showed the lost lake,
now refound, to be 16 feet higher than Mud Lake. The com-
putations afford the following altitudes:

Mud lake .... 1,745 $\frac{33}{100}$ feet above tide.
Lost lake .... 1,761 $\frac{33}{100}$ feet above tide.

Reaching the shore of Mud lake we found that the advance guide had taken the boat and proceeded to camp as directed, but had not yet returned. On the opposite shore we
could make out that the assistant was engaged at his work.
Five rapid revolver shots—the signal, "boat instantly"—
brought him to us swiftly, and embarking we proceeded to
our camp. In the afternoon the assistant returned to the
leveling station on the shore of Mud lake, while I took one
guide and marched to Grass pond, of which, with the neighboring mountains, I secured a reconnaissance map, the angles
by azimuth compass. The synchronous barometrical readings
showed Grass pond to be only five feet higher than Mud lake,
and 1,750 feet above tide level.

[*October 23*]   The morning was bright, and I ordered an
immediate return to Second pond, for the resumption of work
at Grave's mountain. The boats passed rapidly down Bog
river and we disembarked at our old camp. On examining

our stock of provisions there was found only a scant day's rations for the party remaining. One guide was, therefore, detached to return to the settlements for flour, etc., having before him a journey by boat, with portages, of ninety or one hundred miles before we should again see him. He promised to return to our relief in two days. Leaving the river, we proceeded by land and by boat to the foot of Grave's mountain, where we unslung our knapsacks and stacked the baggage at the foot of a tree on the side-hill at the lake shore. Directing the guide to carry his boat through the forest some miles northward to a lake which I designed visiting on the morrow should it happen to be stormy, I set out with the assistant for the summit of Grave's mountain. Clambering amidst the fallen timber, we reached the signal station, and opened the stone *cairn* to find the theodolite, etc., all right, though a muddy spot near showed the tracks of wild beasts. It was a cold, but clear and brilliant day, and looking eastward over the lesser ranges of mountains, we saw the distant great Adirondack peaks—Marcy, MacIntyre, and the rest—now, alas, frostily white with snow, portentous of the drear winter which would soon envelop us. Southward a thousand minor summits, of an average height of 2,000 feet above tide, extended in tumultuous ridges—all unknown to maps. Among them glimmered lakes, ran streams and rivers, which we were to locate or explore. Northward, a brilliant sight, lay the broad expanse of Great Cranberry or Oswegatchie lake, with its sharp rocky points, bays and islands spread before us, nothing intervening to hide the view or to prevent the angular measurements connecting that water with our Lake Champlain base, which lay far eastward beyond the distant serrate crests of Mounts Seward, Marcy and MacIntyre and their kindred mountains. The transit theodolite was carefully adjusted, holes being drilled in the rock for the tripod legs, copper bolt No. 15 being sunk beneath the plumb. In the course of measurement the angle for Blue mountain was reached, and while the clearing we had made on that peak could be noticed even at this distance by the naked eye, our pleasure was great when the theodolite telescope made visible the gleaming, star-like automatic signal we had placed there. On Owl's Head mountain, also, we could distinctly see the automatic stanhelio signal, and from such zeros we now at one sweep of the telescope passed to Cranberry lake, and then measured angle after angle to sharp and unmistakable points upon its shores. A small solitary tree at the center of an island, a pointed rock further west, and other spots, were in turn measured on, and then sketches of their form and place were entered under the head of "remarks" in the geodetic field-book. Thus one of the last works which I had hoped to accomplish that season, and which I had long feared might not be possible, had been brought nearly to its completion; for a few more measurements from another mountain would *determine* the position of the points in Cranberry lake, and enable me to plot the lake upon my final map, with direct reference to the distant Champlain base lines. Late in the afternoon the guide sent to make the carry with his boat, came up the western side of the mountain, shouting as he came that he had found two new lakes. It appeared that after leaving his boat at the appointed pond he had struck across toward our mountain, and while finding his way had come directly upon these waters. One was small and shallow. The second, which was deep and clear, having rocky shores and surrounded by hills clothed with dark evergreen forests, he had taken the discoverer's privilege of naming Lake Colvin. These ponds being unknown to any map, were therefore another addition to this year's list of discoveries. Clouds appearing at the horizon warned us to complete our work if possible this same day, but despite our utmost efforts night descended while more remained to be done. Again boxing up the theodolite, we made a hurried descent of the mountain, and stumbling against trees and rocks in the darkness, reached the shore of Graves' pond and our baggage, which we had left there. We had not even a bark hut, and, exhausted, lay down and slept on the mossy rocks, while the guide proceeded to gather wood and build a fire. With the light afforded by the blaze we set up poles, and throwing two rubber ponchos over them, commenced housekeeping. After a slender supper we wrapped our blankets round us, and lulled by the warmth of the fire crackling at our feet, and by the solemn hooting of an owl, who had stationed himself in a tree overhead, fell asleep.

Isabella Bird

A Lady's Life in the Rocky Mountains

Isabella Bird (1831–1904) climbed to the summit of Long's Peak in Colorado just five years after John Wesley Powell led the first ascent in 1868. Born in Yorkshire, England, the daughter of an Anglican clergyman, Isabella Bird first left for Canada and the United States in her early twenties on a sailing voyage recommended for the depression, neuralgia and chronic spinal complaint she had suffered from since childhood. For the rest of her life, she was a tireless and healthy traveler who avoided the normal routes and haunts of tourists. Before her death she had spent seven months in Japan and five months in the Malay Peninsula; she spent fifteen months and covered eight thousand miles during a second trip through China; she traveled through India, Persia, Kurdistan, and Tibet, and established hospitals in Kashmir and Punjab as well as in China and Korea. Precise geographical and botanical knowledge informed her numerous books, and although she claimed to travel "for recreation and interest solely," she was the first woman elected a Fellow of the Royal Geographical Society. In 1873, she traveled from the Hawaiian Islands to the Rocky Mountains, a place she described as "no region for tourists and women." Rejecting the sidesaddle, Bird said she "felt like a centaur" while riding astride for up to ten hours a day during the autumn and early winter in Estes Park. She expressed passionate distaste for the constraints imposed by what she called highly civilized society, and in her letters to her sister, "written without the remotest idea of publication," she showed her ability to appreciate new places and people on their own terms. In A Lady's Life in the Rocky Mountains (1879), composed from her earlier letters to her sister, she records the moment she left behind all civilization and scaled to where "peace rested for that one bright day on the Peak."

As this account of the ascent of Long's Peak could not be written at the time, I am much disinclined to write it, especially as no sort of description within my powers could enable another to realize the glorious sublimity, the majestic solitude, and the unspeakable awfulness and fascination of the scenes in which I spent Monday, Tuesday, and Wednesday.

Long's Peak, 14,700 feet high, blocks up one end of Estes Park, and dwarfs all the surrounding mountains. From it on this side rise, snow-born, the bright St. Vrain, and the Big and Little Thompson. By sunlight or moonlight its splintered grey crest is the one object which, in spite of wapiti and bighorn, skunk and grizzly, unfailingly arrests the eyes. From it come all storms of snow and wind, and the forked lightnings play round its head like a glory. It is one of the noblest of mountains, but in one's imagination it grows to be much more than a mountain. It becomes invested with a personality. In its caverns and abysses one comes to fancy that it generates and chains the strong winds, to let them loose in its fury. The thunder becomes its voice, and the lightnings do it homage. Other summits blush under the morning kiss of the sun, and turn pale the next moment; but it detains the first sunlight and holds it round its head for an hour at least, till it pleases to change from rosy red to deep blue; and the sunset, as if spell-bound, lingers latest on its crest. The soft winds which hardly rustle the pine needles down here are raging rudely up there round its motionless summit. The mark of fire is upon it; and though it has passed into a grim repose, it tells of fire and upheaval as truly, though not as eloquently, as the living volcanoes of Hawaii. Here under its shadow one learns how naturally nature worship, and the propitiation of the forces of nature, arose in minds which had no better light.

Long's Peak, "the American Matterhorn," as some call it, was ascended five years ago for the first time. I thought I should like to attempt it, but up to Monday, when Evans left for Denver, cold water was thrown upon the project. It was too late in the season, the winds were likely to be strong, etc.; but just before leaving, Evans said that the weather was looking more settled, and if I did not get farther than the timber

From Isabella Bird, *A Lady's Life in the Rocky Mountains* (London: John Murray, 1879).

line it would be worth going. Soon after he left, "Mountain Jim" came in, and he would go up as guide, and the two youths who rode here with me from Longmount and I caught at the proposal. Mrs. Edwards at once baked bread for three days, steaks were cut from the steer which hangs up conveniently, and tea, sugar, and butter were benevolently added. Our picnic was not to be a luxurious or "well-found" one, for, in order to avoid the expense of a pack mule, we limited our luggage to what our saddle horses could carry. Behind my saddle I carried three pair of camping blankets and a quilt, which reached to my shoulders. My own boots were so much worn that it was painful to walk, even about the park, in them, so Evans had lent me a pair of his hunting boots, which hung to the horn of my saddle. The horses of the two young men were equally loaded, for we had to prepare for many degrees of frost. "Jim" was a shocking figure; he had on an old pair of high boots, with a baggy pair of old trousers made of deer hide, held on by an old scarf tucked into them; a leather shirt, with three or four ragged unbuttoned waistcoats over it; an old smashed wideawake, from under which his tawny, neglected ringlets hung; and with his one eye, his one long spur, his knife in his belt, his revolver in his waistcoat pocket, his saddle covered with an old beaver skin, from which the paws hung down; his camping blankets behind him, his rifle laid across the saddle in front of him, and his axe, canteen, and other gear hanging to the horn, he was as awful-looking a ruffian as one could see. By way of contrast he rode a small Arab mare, of exquisite beauty, skittish, high spirited, gentle, but altogether too light for him, and he fretted her incessantly to make her display herself.

Heavily loaded as all our horses were, "Jim" started over the half-mile of level grass at a hard gallop, and then throwing his mare on her haunches, pulled up alongside of me, and with a grace of manner which soon made me forget his appearance, entered into a conversation which lasted for more than three hours, in spite of the manifold checks of fording streams, single file, abrupt ascents and descents, and other incidents of mountain travel. The ride was one series of glories and surprises, of "park" and glade, of lake and stream, of mountains on mountains, culminating in the rent pinnacles of Long's Peak, which looked yet grander and ghastlier as we crossed an attendant mountain 11,000 feet high. The slanting sun added fresh beauty every hour. There were dark pines against a lemon sky, grey peaks reddening and etherealizing, gorges of deep and infinite blue, floods of golden glory pouring through canyons of enormous depth, an atmosphere of absolute purity, an occasional foreground of cotton-wood and aspen flaunting in red and gold to intensify the blue gloom of the pines, the trickle and murmur of streams fringed with icicles, the strange *sough* of gusts moving among the pine tops—sights and sounds not of the lower earth, but of the solitary, beast-haunted, frozen upper altitudes. From the dry, buff grass of Estes Park we turned off up a trail on the side of a pine-hung gorge, up a steep pine-clothed hill, down to a small valley, rich in fine, sun-cured hay about eighteen inches high, and enclosed by high mountains whose deepest hollow contains a lily-covered lake, fitly named "The Lake of the Lilies." Ah, how magical its beauty was, as it slept in silence, while *there* the dark pines were mirrored motionless in its pale gold, and *here* the great white lily cups and dark green leaves rested on amethyst-colored water!

From this we ascended into the purple gloom of great pine forests which clothe the skirts of the mountains up to a height of about 11,000 feet, and from their chill and solitary depths we had glimpses of golden atmosphere and rose-lit summits, not of "the land very far off," but of the land nearer now in all its grandeur, gaining in sublimity by nearness—glimpses, too, through a broken vista of purple gorges, of the illimitable Plains lying idealized in the late sunlight, their baked, brown expanse transfigured into the likeness of a sunset sea rolling infinitely in waves of misty gold.

We rode upwards through the gloom on a steep trail blazed through the forest, all my intellect concentrated on avoiding being dragged off my horse by impending branches, or having the blankets badly torn, as those of my companions were, by sharp dead limbs, between which there was hardly room to pass—the horses breathless, and requiring to stop every few yards, though their riders, except myself, were afoot. The gloom of the dense, ancient, silent forest is to me awe inspiring. On such an evening it is soundless, except for the branches creaking in the soft wind, the frequent snap of decayed timber, and a murmur in the pine tops as of a not distant waterfall, all tending to produce *eeriness* and a sadness "hardly akin to pain." There no lumberer's axe has ever rung. The trees die when they have attained their prime, and stand there, dead and bare, till the fierce mountain winds lay them prostrate. The pines grew smaller and more sparse as we ascended, and the last stragglers wore a tortured, warring look. The timber line was passed, but yet a little higher a slope of mountain meadow dipped to the south-west towards a bright stream trickling under ice and icicles, and there a grove of the beautiful silver spruce marked our camping ground. The trees were in miniature, but so exquisitely arranged that one might well ask what artist's hand had planted them, scattering them here, clumping them there, and training their slim spires towards heaven. Hereafter, when I call up memories of the glorious, the view from this camping ground will come up. Looking east, gorges opened to the distant Plains, then fading into purple grey. Mountains with pine-clothed skirts rose in ranges, or, solitary, uplifted their grey summits, while close behind, but nearly 3,000 feet above us, towered the bald white crest of Long's Peak, its huge precipices red with the light of a sun long lost to our eyes. Close to us, in the caverned side of the Peak, was snow that, owing to its position, is eternal. Soon the afterglow came on, and before it faded a big half-moon hung out of the heavens, shining through the silver blue foliage of the pines on the frigid background of snow, and turning the whole into fairyland. The "photo" which accompanies this letter is by a courageous Denver artist who attempted the ascent just before I arrived, but, after camping out at the timber line for a week, was foiled by the perpetual storms, and was driven down again, leaving some very valuable apparatus about 3,000 feet from the summit.

Unsaddling and picketing the horses securely, making the beds of pine shoots, and dragging up logs for fuel, warmed us all. "Jim" built up a great fire, and before long we were all sitting around at it at supper. It didn't matter much that we had to drink our tea out of the battered meat tins in which it was boiled, and eat strips of beef reeking with pine smoke without plates or forks.

"Treat Jim as a gentleman and you'll find him one," I had been told; and though his manner was certainly bolder and freer than that of gentlemen generally, no imaginary fault could be found. He was very agreeable as a man of culture

as well as a child of nature; the desperado was altogether out
of sight. He was very courteous and even kind to me, which
was fortunate, as the young men had little idea of showing
even ordinary civilities. That night I made the acquaintance
of his dog "Ring," said to be the best hunting dog in Colorado, with the body and legs of a collie, but a head approaching that of a mastiff, a noble face with a wistful
human expression, and the most truthful eyes I ever saw in
an animal. His master loves him if he loves anything, but in
his savage moods ill-treats him. "Ring's" devotion never
swerves, and his truthful eyes are rarely taken off his master's
face. He is almost human in his intelligence, and, unless he is
told to do so, he never takes notice of any one but "Jim." In
a tone as if speaking to a human being, his master, pointing
to me, said, "Ring, go to that lady, and don't leave her again
to-night." "Ring" at once came to me, looked into my face, laid
his head on my shoulder, and then lay down beside me with
his head on my lap, but never taking his eyes from "Jim's"
face.

The long shadows of the pines lay upon the frosted grass,
an aurora leaped fitfully, and the moonlight, though intensely
bright, was pale beside the red, leaping flames of our pine
logs and their red glow on our gear, ourselves, and Ring's
truthful face. One of the young men sang a Latin student's
song and two Negro melodies; the other "Sweet Spirit, hear
my Prayer." "Jim" sang one of Moore's melodies in a singular falsetto, and all together sang, "The Star-spangled Ban-
ner" and "The Red, White, and Blue." Then "Jim" recited a
very clever poem of his own composition, and told some fearful Indian stories. A group of small silver spruces away from
the fire was my sleeping place. The artist who had been up
there had so woven and interlaced their lower branches as to
form a bower, affording at once shelter from the wind and a
most agreeable privacy. It was thickly strewn with young pine
shoots, and these, when covered with a blanket, with an in-
verted saddle for a pillow, made a luxurious bed. The mercury at 9 P.M. was 12° below the freezing point. "Jim," after
a last look at the horses, made a huge fire, and stretched himself out beside it, but "Ring" lay at my back to keep me
warm. I could not sleep, but the night passed rapidly. I was
anxious about the ascent, for gusts of ominous sound swept
through the pines at intervals. Then wild animals howled, and

"Ring" was perturbed in spirit about them. Then it was strange to see the notorious desperado, a red-handed man, sleeping as quietly as innocence sleeps. But, above all, it was exciting to lie there, with no better shelter than a bower of pines, on a mountain 11,000 feet high, in the very heart of the Rocky Range, under twelve degrees of frost, hearing sounds of wolves, with shivering stars looking through the fragrant canopy, with arrowy pines for bed-posts, and for a night lamp the red flames of a camp-fire.

Day dawned long before the sun rose, pure and lemon colored. The rest were looking after the horses, when one of the students came running to tell me that I must come farther down the slope, for "Jim" said he had never seen such a sunrise. From the chill, grey Peak above, from the everlasting snows, from the silvered pines, down through mountain ranges with their depths of Tyrian purple, we looked to where the Plains lay cold, in blue-grey, like a morning sea against a far horizon. Suddenly, as a dazzling streak at first, but enlarging rapidly into a dazzling sphere, the sun wheeled above the grey line, a light and glory as when it was first created. "Jim" involuntarily and reverently uncovered his head, and exclaimed, "I believe there is a God!" I felt as if, Parsee-like, I must worship. The grey of the Plains changed to purple, the sky was all one rose-red flush, on which vermilion cloud-streaks rested; the ghastly peaks gleamed like rubies, the earth and heavens were new created. Surely "the Most High dwelleth not in temples made with hands!" For a full hour those Plains simulated the ocean, down to whose limitless expanse of purple, cliff, rocks, and promontories swept down.

By seven we had finished breakfast, and passed into the ghastlier solitudes above, I riding as far as what, rightly or wrongly, are called the "Lava Beds," an expanse of large and small boulders, with snow in their crevices. It was very cold; some water which we crossed was frozen hard enough to bear the horse. "Jim" had advised me against taking any wraps, and my thin Hawaiian riding dress, only fit for the tropics, was penetrated by the keen air. The rarefied atmosphere soon began to oppress our breathing, and I found that Evans's boots were so large that I had no foothold. Fortunately, before the real difficulty of the ascent began, we found, under a rock, a pair of small overshoes, probably left by the Hayden exploring expedition, which just lasted for the day. As we were leaping from rock to rock, "Jim" said, "I was thinking in the night about your traveling alone, and wondering where you carried your Derringer, for I could see no signs of it." On my telling him that I traveled unarmed, he could hardly believe it, and adjured me to get a revolver at once.

On arriving at the "Notch" (a literal gate of rock), we found ourselves absolutely on the knifelike ridge or backbone of Long's Peak, only a few feet wide, covered with colossal boulders and fragments, and on the other side shelving in one precipitous, snow-patched sweep of 3,000 feet to a picturesque hollow, containing a lake of pure green water. Other lakes, hidden among dense pine woods, were farther off, while close above us rose the Peak, which, for about 500 feet, is a smooth, gaunt, inaccessible-looking pile of granite. Passing through the "Notch," we looked along the nearly inaccessible side of the Peak, composed of boulders and *débris* of all shapes and sizes, through which appeared broad, smooth ribs of reddish-colored granite, looking as if they upheld the towering rock mass above. I usually dislike bird's-eye and panoramic views, but, though from a mountain, this was not one. Serrated ridges, not much lower than that on which we stood, rose, one beyond another, far as that pure atmosphere could carry the vision, broken into awful chasms deep with ice and snow, rising into pinnacles piercing the heavenly blue with their cold, barren grey, on, on for ever, till the most distant range upbore unsullied snow alone. There were fair lakes mirroring the dark pine woods, canyons dark and blue-black with unbroken expanses of pines, snow-slashed pinnacles, wintry heights frowning upon lovely parks, watered and wooded, lying in the lap of summer; North Park floating off into the blue distance, Middle Park closed till another season, the sunny slopes of Estes Park, and winding down among the mountains the snowy ridge of the Divide, whose bright waters seek both the Atlantic and Pacific Ocans. There, far below, links of diamonds showed where the Grand River takes its rise to seek the mysterious Colorado, with its still unsolved enigma, and lose itself in the waters of the Pacific; and nearer the snow-born Thompson bursts forth from the ice to begin its journey to the Gulf of Mexico. Nature, rioting in her grandest mood, exclaimed with voices of grandeur, solitude, sublimity, beauty, and infinity, "Lord, what is man, that Thou art mindful of him? or the son of man, that Thou vis-

itest him?" Never-to-be-forgotten glories they were, burnt in
upon my memory by six succeeding hours of terror.

You know I have no head and no ankles, and never ought
to dream of mountaineering; and had I known that the ascent
was a real mountaineering feat I should not have felt the
slightest ambition to perform it. As it is, I am only humiliated
by my success, for "Jim" dragged me up, like a bale of
goods, by sheer force of muscle. At the "Notch" the real
business of the ascent began. Two thousand feet of solid rock
towered above us, four thousand feet of broken rock shelved
precipitously below; smooth granite ribs, with barely foothold, stood out here and there; melted snow refrozen several
times, presented a more serious obstacle; many of the rocks
were loose, and tumbled down when touched. To me it
was a time of extreme terror. I was roped to "Jim," but it
was of no use; my feet were paralyzed and slipped on the
bare rock, and he said it was useless to try to go that way,
and we retraced our steps. I wanted to return to the "Notch,"
knowing that my incompetence would detain the party, and
one of the young men said almost plainly that a woman was
a dangerous encumbrance, but the trapper replied shortly that
if it were not to take a lady up he would not go up at all. He
went on the explore, and reported that further progress on
the correct line of ascent was blocked by ice; and then for
two hours we descended, lowering ourselves by our hands
from rock to rock along a boulder-strewn sweep of 4,000 feet,
patched with ice and snow, and perilous from rolling stones.
My fatigue, giddiness, and pain from bruised ankles, and arms
half pulled out of their sockets, were so great that I should
never have gone half-way had not "Jim," *nolens volens*,
dragged me along with a patience and skill, and withal a determination that I should ascend the Peak, which never
failed. After descending about 2,000 feet to avoid the ice, we
got into a deep ravine with inaccessible sides, partly filled
with ice and snow and partly with large and small fragments
of rock, which were constantly giving away, rendering the
footing very insecure. That part to me was two hours of
painful and unwilling submission to the inevitable; of trembling, slipping, straining, of smooth ice appearing when it was
least expected, and of weak entreaties to be left behind while
the others went on. "Jim" always said that there was no danger, that there was only a short bad bit ahead, and that I
should go up even if he carried me!

Slipping, faltering, gasping from the exhausting toil in the
rarefied air, with throbbing hearts and panting lungs, we
reached the top of the gorge and squeezed ourselves between
two gigantic fragments of rock by a passage called the "Dog's
Lift," when I climbed on the shoulders of one man and then
was hauled up. This introduced us by an abrupt turn round
the south-west angle of the Peak to a narrow shelf of considerable length, rugged, uneven, and so overhung by the cliff
in some places that it is necessary to crouch to pass at all.
Above, the Peak looks nearly vertical for 400 feet; and below, the most tremendous precipice I have ever seen descends
in one unbroken fall. This is usually considered the most dangerous part of the ascent, but it does not seem so to me, for
such foothold as there is is secure, and one fancies that it is
possible to hold on with the hands. But there, and on the final, and, to my thinking, the worst part of the climb, one
slip, and a breathing, thinking, human being would lie 3,000
feet below, a shapeless, bloody heap! "Ring" refused to traverse the Ledge, and remained at the "Lift" howling piteously.
    From thence the view is more magnificent even than that
from the "Notch." At the foot of the precipice below us lay a
lovely lake, wood embosomed, from or near which the bright
St. Vrain and other streams take their rise. I thought how
their clear cold waters, growing turbid in the affluent flats,
would heat under the tropic sun, and eventually form part of
that great ocean river which renders our far-off islands habit-
able by impinging on their shores. Snowy ranges, one behind
the other, extended to the distant horizon, folding in their
wintry embrace the beauties of Middle Park. Pike's Peak,
more than one hundred miles off, lifted that vast but
shapeless summit which is the landmark of southern Colorado. There were snow patches, snow slashes, snow abysses,
snow forlorn and soiled looking, snow pure and dazzling,
snow glistening above the purple robe of pine worn by all the
mountains; while away to the east, in limitless breadth,
stretched the green-grey of the endless Plains. Giants everywhere reared their splintered crests. From thence, with a
single sweep, the eye takes in a distance of 300 miles—that
distance to the west, north, and south being made up of
mountains ten, eleven, twelve, and thirteen thousand feet in
height, dominated by Long's Peak, Gray's Peak, and Pike's
Peak, all nearly the height of Mont Blanc! On the Plains we
traced the rivers by their fringe of cottonwoods to the distant

Platte, and between us and them lay glories of mountain, canyon, and lake, sleeping in depths of blue and purple most ravishing to the eye.

As we crept from the ledge round a horn of rock I beheld what made me perfectly sick and dizzy to look at—the terminal Peak itself—a smooth, cracked face or wall of pink granite, as nearly perpendicular as anything could well be up which it was possible to climb, well deserving the name of the "American Matterhorn."[1]

Scaling, not climbing, is the correct term for this last ascent. It took one hour to accomplish 500 feet, pausing for breath every minute or two. The only foothold was in narrow cracks or on minute projections on the granite. To get a toe in these cracks, or here and there on a scarcely obvious projection, while crawling on hands and knees, all the while tortured with thirst and gasping and struggling for breath, this was the climb; but at last the Peak was won. A grand, well-defined mountain top it is, a nearly level acre of boulders, with precipitous sides all round, the one we came up being the only accessible one.

It was not possible to remain long. One of the young men was seriously alarmed by bleeding from the lungs, and the intense dryness of the day and the rarefication of the air, at a height of nearly 15,000 feet, made respiration very painful. There is always water on the Peak, but it was frozen hard as a rock, and the sucking of ice and snow increases thirst. We all suffered severely from the want of water, and the gasping for breath made our mouths and tongues so dry that articulation was difficult, and the speech of all unnatural.

From the summit were seen in unrivalled combination all the views which had rejoiced our eyes during the ascent. It was something at last to stand upon the storm-rent crown of this lonely sentinel of the Rocky Range, on one of the mightiest of the vertebrae of the backbone of the North American continent, and to see the waters start for both oceans. Uplifted above love and hate and storms of passion, calm amidst the eternal silences, fanned by zephyrs and bathed in living blue, peace rested for that one bright day on the Peak, as if it were some region

[1]Let no practical mountaineer be allured by my description into the ascent of Long's Peak. Truly terrible as it was to me, to a member of the Alpine Club it would not be a feat worth performing.

Where falls not rain, or hail, or any snow,
Or ever wind blows loudly.

We placed our names, with the date of ascent, in a tin within
a crevice, and descended to the Ledge, sitting on the smooth
granite, getting our feet into cracks and against projections,
and letting ourselves down by our hands, "Jim" going before
me, so that I might steady my feet against his powerful shoulders. I was no longer giddy, and faced the precipice of 3,500
feet without a shiver. Repassing the Ledge and Lift, we accomplished the descent through 1,500 feet of ice and snow,
with many falls and bruises, but no worse mishap, and there
separated, the young men taking the steepest but most direct
way to the "Notch," with the intention of getting ready for
the march home, and "Jim" and I taking what he thought the
safer route for me—a descent over boulders for 2,000 feet,
and then a tremendous ascent to the "Notch." I had various
falls, and once hung by my frock, which caught on a rock,
and "Jim" severed it with his hunting knife, upon which I fell
into a crevice full of soft snow. We were driven lower down
the mountains than he had intended by impassable tracts of
ice, and the ascent was tremendous. For the last 200 feet the
boulders were of enormous size, and the steepness fearful.
Sometimes I drew myself up on hands and knees, sometimes
crawled; sometimes "Jim" pulled me up by my arms or a
lariat, and sometimes I stood on his shoulders, or he made
steps for me of his feet and hands, but at six we stood on the
"Notch" in the splendor of the sinking sun, all color deepening, all peaks glorifying, all shadows purpling, all peril past.

"Jim" had parted with his *brusquerie* when we parted from
the students, and was gentle and considerate beyond anything, though I knew that he must be grievously disappointed,
both in my courage and strength. Water was an object of ear-
nest desire. My tongue rattled in my mouth, and I could
hardly articulate. It is good for one's sympathies to have for
once a severe experience of thirst. Truly, there was

Water, water, everywhere,
But not a drop to drink.

Three times its apparent gleam deceived even the mountaineer's practised eye, but we found only a foot of "glare
ice." At last, in a deep hole, he succeeded in breaking the ice,

and by putting one's arm far down one could scoop up a little water in one's hand, but it was tormentingly insufficient. With great difficulty and much assistance I recrossed the "Lava Beds," was carried to the horse and lifted upon him, and when we reached the camping ground I was lifted off him, and laid on the ground wrapped up in blankets, a humiliating termination of a great exploit. The horses were saddled, and the young men were all ready to start, but "Jim" quietly said, "Now, gentlemen, I want a good night's rest, and we shan't stir from here to-night." I believe they were really glad to have it so, as one of them was quite "finished." I retired to my arbor, wrapped myself in a roll of blankets, and was soon asleep.

When I woke, the moon was high shining through the silvery branches, whitening the bald Peak above, and glittering on the great abyss of snow behind, and pine logs were blazing like a bonfire in the cold still air. My feet were so icy cold that I could not sleep again, and getting some blankets to sit in, and making a roll of them for my back, I sat for two hours by the camp-fire. It was weird and gloriously beautiful. The students were asleep not far off in their blankets with their feet towards the fire. "Ring" lay on one side of me with his fine head on my arm, and his master sat smoking, with the fire lighting up the handsome side of his face, and except for the tones of our voices, and an occasional crackle and splutter as a pine knot blazed up, there was no sound on the mountain side. The beloved stars of my far-off home were overhead, the Plough and Pole Star, with their steady light; the glittering Pleiades, looking larger than I ever saw them, and "Orion's studded belt" shining gloriously. Once only some wild animals prowled near the camp, when "Ring," with one bound, disappeared from my side; and the horses, which were picketed by the stream, broke their lariats, stampeded, and came rushing wildly towards the fire, and it was fully half an hour before they were caught and quiet was restored. "Jim," or Mr. Nugent, as I always scrupulously called him, told stories of his early youth, and of a great sorrow which had led him to embark on a lawless and desperate life. His voice trembled, and tears rolled down his cheek. Was it semi-conscious acting, I wondered, or was his dark soul really stirred to its depths by the silence, the beauty, and the memories of youth?

We reached Estes Park at noon of the following day. A

more successful ascent of the Peak was never made, and I would not now exchange my memories of its perfect beauty and extraordinary sublimity for any other experience of mountaineering in any part of the world. Yesterday snow fell on the summit, and it will be inaccessible for eight months to come.

Plenty Coups

Vision in the
Crazy Mountains

*Plenty Coups (1848–1932), tribal chief of the Mountain
Crow people, was born in southern Montana near the Crazy
Mountains. After distinguishing himself in battle over eighty
times, he was honored with the name Aleekchea'ahoosh,
translated Many Achievements, or Plenty Coups. To "count
coup," an Indian must be the first to touch a slain enemy or,
more honorably, to strike a live warrior during battle with the
hand or "coup-stick" and escape unharmed. Plenty Coups
was a chief by the time he was twenty-five. Among many
Plains tribes, it was considered important for a young man in
his teens to go alone into the wilderness in quest of a vision
or medicine dream. In the dream he would be given a personal guardian and discover what sacred objects, or "medicine," would be a source of power to him throughout his life.
Plenty Coup's vision reveals an early Indian attitude toward
animal-persons as spiritually equal to humans. Man is not
above nature, but a part of it, and even the chickadee, who
became Plenty Coup's guardian and whom he would try to
emulate, has special powers that man does not possess. Although Indians were not conservationists in the contemporary
sense, they held that man must not just conquer animals or
learn about them, but he must respect them and learn from
them. Plenty Coups's medicine dream was considered a great
vision by the Crows. It foretold the ultimate destruction of
the buffalo and the need for the Crow people to remain
friendly with whites, not because they loved whites, but because that was the only way they might safely remain on
their homelands. Plenty Coups worked all his life for harmony between the whites and his people. In 1921, as the
representative of all Indians at the dedication of the Tomb of
the Unknown Soldier, the seventy-three-year-old chief again
pleaded "that war might end, that peace be purchased by the
blood of the Red Man and White." He left forty acres, now a*

state park, "to be used in perpetuity for the Crow people and used as a public park by them and others irrespective of race and color." Plenty Coups was the last principal chief of the Mountain Crows, for after his death, the tribe resolved in his honor that no other leader be called Tribal Chief of the Crow people. What follows is Frank Linderman's account of Plenty Coups's medicine dream as it was told to him by the eighty-year-old chief. "A dream," Emerson reminds us, "may let us deeper into the secret of nature than a hundred concerted experiments."

"I decided to go afoot to the Crazy Mountains, two long days' journey from the village. The traveling without food or drink was good for me, and as soon as I reached the Crazies I took a sweat-bath and climbed the highest peak. There is a lake at its base, and the winds are always stirring about it. But even though I fasted two more days and nights, walking over the mountain top, no Person came to me, nothing was offered. I saw several grizzly bears that were nearly white in the moonlight, and one of them came very near to me, but he did not speak. Even when I slept on that peak in the Crazies, no bird or animal or Person spoke a word to me, and I grew discouraged. I could not dream.

"Back in the village I told my closest friends about the high peaks I had seen, about the white grizzly bears, and the lake. They were interested and said they would go back with me and that we would all try to dream.

"There were three besides myself who set out, with extra moccasins and a robe to cover our sweat-lodge. We camped on good water just below the peak where I had tried to dream, quickly took our sweat-baths, and started up the mountains. It was already dark when we separated, but I found no difficulty in reaching my old bed on the tall peak that looked down on the little lake, or in making a new bed with ground-cedar and sweet-sage. Owls were hooting under

From Frank B. Linderman, *American: The Life Story of a Great Indian, Plenty-Coups, Chief of the Crows* (New York: John Day, 1930).

the stars while I rubbed my body with the sweet-smelling herbs before starting out to walk myself weak.

"When I could scarcely stand, I made my way back to my bed and slept with my feet toward the east. But no Person came to me, nothing was offered; and when the day came I got up to walk again over the mountain top, calling for Helpers as I had done the night before.

"All day the sun was hot, and my tongue was swollen for want of water; but I saw nothing, heard nothing, even when night came again to cool the mountain. No sound had reached my ears, except my own voice and the howling of wolves down on the plains.

"I knew that our great Crow warriors of other days sacrificed their flesh and blood to dream, and just when the night was leaving to let the morning come I stopped at a fallen tree, and, laying the first finger of my left hand upon the log, I cut part of it off with my knife. [The end of the left index finger on the Chief's hand is missing.] But no blood came. The stump of my finger was white as the finger of a dead man, and to make it bleed I struck it against the log until blood flowed freely. Then I began to walk and call for Helpers, hoping that some Person would smell my blood and come to aid me.

"Near the middle of that day my head grew dizzy, and I sat down. I had eaten nothing, taken no water, for nearly four days and nights, and my mind must have left me while I sat there under the hot sun on the mountain top. It must have traveled far away, because the sun was nearly down when it returned and found me lying on my face. As soon as it came back to me I sat up and looked about, at first not knowing where I was. Four war-eagles were sitting in a row along a trail of my blood just above me. But they did not speak to me, offered nothing at all.

"I thought I would try to reach my bed, and when I stood up I saw my three friends. They had seen the eagles flying over my peak and had become frightened, believing me dead. They carried me to my bed and stayed long enough to smoke with me before going back to their own places. While we smoked, the four war-eagles did not fly away. They sat there by my blood on the rocks, even after the night came on and chilled everything living on the mountain."

Again the Chief whispered aside to the Little-people, asking them if he might go on. When he finally resumed, I felt that somehow he had been reassured. His voice was very low, yet strained, as though he were tiring.

"I dreamed. I heard a voice at midnight and saw a Person standing at my feet, in the east. He said, 'Plenty-coups, the Person down there wants you now.'

"He pointed, and from the peak in the Crazy Mountains I saw a Buffalo-bull standing *where we are sitting now*. I got up and started to go to the Bull, because I knew he was the Person who wanted me. The other Person was gone. Where he had stood when he spoke to me there was nothing at all.

"The way is very long from the Crazies to this place where we are sitting today, but I came here quickly in my dream. On that hill over yonder was where I stopped to look at the Bull. He had changed into a Man-person wearing a buffalo robe with the hair outside. Later I picked up the buffalo skull that you see over there, on this very spot where the Person had stood. I have kept that skull for more than seventy years.

"The Man-person beckoned me from the hill over yonder where I had stopped, and I walked to where he stood. When I reached his side he began to sink slowly into the ground, right over there [pointing]. Just as the Man-person was disappearing he spoke. 'Follow me,' he said.

"But I was afraid. 'Come,' he said from the darkness. And I got down into the hole in the ground to follow him, walking bent-over for ten steps. Then I stood straight and saw a small light far off. It was like a window in a white man's house of today, and I knew the hole was leading us toward the Arrow Creek Mountains [the Pryors].

"In the way of the light, between it and me, I could see countless buffalo, see their sharp horns thick as the grass grows. I could smell their bodies and hear them snorting, ahead and on both sides of me. Their eyes, without number, were like little fires in the darkness of the hole in the ground, and I felt afraid among so many big bulls. The Man-person must have known this, because he said, 'Be not afraid, Plenty-coups. It was these Persons who sent for you. They will not do you harm.'

"My body was naked. I feared walking among them in such a narrow place. The burrs that are always in their hair would scratch my skin, even if their hoofs and horns did not wound me more deeply. I did not like the way the Man-person went among them. 'Fear nothing! Follow me, Plenty-coups,' he said.

"I felt their warm bodies against my own, but went on after the Man-person, edging around them or going between them all that night and all the next day, with my eyes always looking ahead at the hole of light. But none harmed me, none even spoke to me, and at last we came out of the hole in the ground and saw the Square White Butte at the mouth of Arrow Creek Canyon. It was on our right. White men call it Castle Rock, but our name for it is The-fasting-place.

"Now, out in the light of the sun, I saw that the Man-person who had led me had a rattle in his hand. It was large and painted red. [The rattle is used in ceremonials. It is sometimes made of the bladder of an animal, dried, with small pebbles inside, so that when shaken it gives a rattling sound.] When he reached the top of a knoll he turned and said to me, 'Sit here!'

"Then he shook his red rattle and sang a queer song four times. 'Look!' he pointed.

"Out of the hole in the ground came the buffalo, bulls and cows and calves without number. They spread wide and blackened the plains. Everywhere I looked great herds of buffalo were going in every direction, and still others without number were pouring out of the hole in the ground to travel on the wide plains. When at last they ceased coming out of the hole in the ground, all were gone, *all!* There was not one in sight anywhere, even out on the plains. I saw a few antelope on a hillside, but no buffalo—not a bull, not a cow, not one calf, was anywhere on the plains.

"I turned to look at the Man-person beside me. He shook his red rattle again. 'Look!' he pointed.

"Out of the hole in the ground came bulls and cows and calves past counting. These, like the others, scattered and spread on the plains. But they stopped in small bands and began to eat the grass. Many lay down, not as a buffalo does but differently, and many were spotted. Hardly any two were alike in color or size. And the bulls bellowed differently too, not deep and far-sounding like the bulls of the buffalo but sharper and yet weaker in my ears. Their tails were different, longer, and nearly brushed the ground. They were not buffalo. These were strange animals from another world.

"I was frightened and turned to the Man-person, who only shook his red rattle but did not sing. He did not even tell me to look, but I did look and saw all the Spotted-buffalo go back into the hole in the ground, until there was nothing except a few antelope anywhere in sight.

"'Do you understand this which I have shown you, Plenty-coups?' he asked me.

"'No!' I answered. How could he expect me to understand such a thing when I was not yet ten years old?

"During all the time the Spotted-buffalo were going back into the hole in the ground the Man-person had not once looked at me. He stood facing the south as though the Spotted-buffalo belonged there. 'Come, Plenty-coups,' he said finally, when the last had disappeared.

"I followed him back through the hole in the ground without seeing anything until we came out *right over there* [pointing] where we had first entered the hole in the ground. Then I saw the spring down by those trees, this very house just as it is, these trees which comfort us today, and a very old man sitting in the shade, alone. I felt pity for him because he was so old and feeble.

"'Look well upon this old man,' said the Man-person. 'Do you know him, Plenty-coups?' he asked me.

"'No,' I said, looking closely at the old man's face in the shade of *this* tree.

"'This old man is yourself, Plenty-coups,' he told me. And then I could see the Man-person no more. He was gone, and so too was the old man.

"Instead I saw only a dark forest. A fierce storm was coming fast. The sky was black with streaks of mad color through it. I saw the Four Winds gathering to strike the forest, and held my breath. Pity was hot in my heart for the beautiful trees. I felt pity for all things that lived in that forest, but was powerless to stand with them against the Four Winds that together were making war. I shielded my own face with my arm when they charged! I heard the Thunders calling out in the storm, saw beautiful trees twist like blades of grass and fall in tangled piles where the forest had been. Bending low, I heard the Four Winds rush past me as though they were not yet satisfied, and then I looked at the destruction they had left behind them.

"Only one tree, tall and straight, was left standing where the great forest had stood. The Four Winds that always make war alone had this time struck together, riding down every tree in the forest but *one*. Standing there alone among its dead tribesmen, I thought it looked sad. 'What does this mean?' I whispered in my dream.

" 'Listen, Plenty-coups,' said a voice. 'In that tree is the lodge of the Chickadee. He is least in strength but strongest of mind among his kind. He is willing to work for wisdom. The Chickadee-person is a good listener. Nothing escapes his ears, which he has sharpened by constant use. Whenever others are talking together of their successes or failures, there you will find the Chickadee-person listening to their words. But in all his listening he tends to his own business. He never intrudes, never speaks in strange company, and yet never misses a chance to learn from others. He gains success and avoids failure by learning how others succeeded or failed, and without great trouble to himself. There is scarcely a lodge he does not visit, hardly a Person he does not know, and yet everybody likes him, because he minds his own business, or pretends to.

" 'The lodges of countless Bird-people were in that forest when the Four Winds charged it. Only one is left unharmed, the lodge of the Chickadee-person. Develop your body, but do not neglect your mind, Plenty-coups. It is the mind that leads a man to power, not strength of body.'"

Theodore Roosevelt

Hunting in the Badlands

Theodore Roosevelt (1858–1919) was an undergraduate member of the Harvard Natural History Society and the Nuttall Ornithological Club of Cambridge when he published a pamphlet about the summer birds of the Adirondacks. Later in his life, Roosevelt's wilderness expedition into Brazil was responsible for adding 1,375 specimens of birds and 450 mammals to the American Museum of Natural History. A letter to William Beebe about the naturalist's taxonomy of pheasants was the last Roosevelt wrote before his death. As president, Roosevelt made conservation an issue of national importance. To Roosevelt's Chief of the Forestry Service, Gifford Pinchot, conservation meant efficient use of the wilderness for utilitarian purposes, a notion opposed by preservationists such as Roosevelt's friend John Muir. Roosevelt, who was the first president to work for both government development of natural resources and for wilderness preservation, sometimes found his loyalties divided, but during his presidency he established the Bureau of Reclamation, made the Grand Canyon one of sixteen national monuments, convened two important conservation congresses, doubled the number of national parks, created over fifty wildlife refuges, and added 148 million acres to the country's forest preserves. Roosevelt's first book, Hunting Trips of a Ranchman *(1885), recorded his experiences during the two years he spent on his ranches in Dakota Territory early in his career. Although Roosevelt criticized the slaughter of wildlife by commercial hunters, he defended hunting for sport, a wilderness activity that draws the most vehement defenders and detractors. In the following selection, he presents the wilderness from the point of view of the hunter who stalks the only hoofed mammal indigenous to North America, the pronghorn.*

I never but once took a trip of any length with antelope
hunting for its chief object. This was one June, when all the
men were away on the round-up. As is usual during the busy
half of the ranchman's year, the spring and summer, when men
have no time to hunt and game is out of condition, we had
been living on salt pork, beans, potatoes, and bread; and I
had hardly had a rifle in my hand for months; so, finding I
had a few days to spare, I thought I should take a short trip
to the prairie, in the beautiful June weather, and get a little
sport and a little fresh meat out of the bands of prong-horn
bucks, which I was sure to encounter. Intending to be gone
but a couple of days, it was not necessary to take many articles. Behind my saddle I carried a blanket for bedding, and
an oil-skin coat to ward off the wet; a large metal cup with
the handle riveted, not soldered on, so that water could be
boiled in it; a little tea and salt, and some biscuits; and a
small waterproof bag containing my half-dozen personal
necessaries—not forgetting a book. The whole formed a
small, light pack, very little encumbrance to stout old Manitou. In June, fair weather can generally be counted on in the
dry plains country.

I started in the very earliest morning, when the intense
brilliancy of the stars had just begun to pale before the first
streak of dawn. By the time I left the river bottom and
struck off up the valley of a winding creek, which led through
the Bad Lands, the eastern sky was growing rosy; and soon
the buttes and cliffs were lighted up by the level rays of the
cloudless summer sun. The air was fresh and sweet, and
odorous with the sweet scents of the springtime that was but
barely past; the dew lay heavy, in glittering drops, on the
leaves and the blades of grass, whose vivid green, at this season, for a short time brightens the desolate and sterile-looking
wastes of the lonely Western plains. The rose-bushes were all
in bloom, and their pink blossoms clustered in every point
and bend of the stream; and the sweet, sad songs of the her-
mit thrushes rose from the thickets, while the meadow larks
perched boldly in sight as they uttered their louder and more
cheerful music. The round-up had passed by our ranch, and
all the cattle with our brands, the Maltese cross and cut dew-
lap, or the elkhorn and triangle, had been turned loose; they

From Theodore Roosevelt, *Hunting Trips of a Ranchman* (New
York: Putnam, 1885).

had not yet worked away from the river, and I rode by long strings of them, walking in single file off to the hills, or standing in groups to look at me as I passed.

Leaving the creek I struck off among a region of scoria buttes, the ground rising into rounded hills through whose grassy covering the red volcanic rock showed in places, while bowlder-like fragments of it were scattered all through the valleys between. There were a few clumps of bushes here and there, and near one of them were two magpies, who lighted on an old buffalo skull, bleached white by sun and snow. Magpies are birds that catch the eye at once from their bold black and white plumage and long tails; and they are very saucy and at the same time very cunning and shy. In spring we do not often see them; but in the late fall and winter they will come close round the huts and outbuildings on the lookout for anything to eat. If a deer is hung up and they can get at it they will pick it to pieces with their sharp bills; and their carnivorous tastes and their habit of coming round hunters' camps after the game that is left out call to mind their kinsman, the whiskey-jack or moose-bird of the Northern forests.

After passing the last line of low, rounded scoria buttes, the horse stepped out on the border of the great, seemingly endless stretches of rolling or nearly level prairie, over which I had planned to travel and hunt for the next two or three days. At intervals of ten or a dozen miles this prairie was crossed by dry creeks, with, in places in their beds, pools or springs of water, and alongside a spindling growth of trees and bushes; and my intention was to hunt across these creeks, and camp by some waterhole in one of them at night.

I rode over the land in a general southerly course, bending to the right or left according to the nature of the ground and the likelihood of finding game. Most of the time the horse kept on a steady single-foot, but this was varied by a sharp lope every now and then, to ease the muscles of both steed and rider. The sun was well up, and its beams beat fiercely down on our heads from out of the cloudless sky; for at this season, though the nights and the early morning and late evening are cool and pleasant, the hours around noon are very hot. My glass was slung alongside the saddle, and from every one of the scattered hillocks the country was scanned carefully far and near; and the greatest caution was used in riding up over any divide, to be sure that no game on the opposite side was scared by the sudden appearance of my horse or myself.

Nowhere, not even at sea, does a man feel more lonely than when riding over the far-reaching, seemingly never-ending plains; and after a man has lived a little while on or near them, their very vastness and loneliness and their melancholy monotony have a strong fascination for him. The landscape seems always the same, and after the traveler has plodded on for miles and miles he gets to feel as if the distance was indeed boundless. As far as the eye can see there is no break; either the prairie stretches out into perfectly level flats, or else there are gentle, rolling slopes, whose crests mark the divides between the drainage systems of the different creeks; and when one of these is ascended, immediately another precisely like it takes its place in the distance, and so roll succeeds roll in a succession as interminable as that of the waves of the ocean. Nowhere else does one seem so far off from all mankind; the plains stretch out in deathlike and measureless expanse, and as he journeys over them they will for many miles be lacking in all signs of life. Although he can see so far, yet all objects on the outermost verge of the horizon, even though within the ken of his vision, look unreal and strange; for there is no shade to take away from the bright glare, and at a little distance things seem to shimmer and dance in the hot rays of the sun. The ground is scorched to a dull brown, and against its monotonous expanse any objects stand out with a prominence that makes it difficult to judge of the distance at which they are. A mile off one can see, through the strange shimmering haze, the shadowy white outlines of something which looms vaguely up till it looks as large as the canvas-top of a prairie wagon; but as the horseman comes nearer it shrinks and dwindles and takes clearer form, until at last it changes into the ghastly staring skull of some mighty buffalo, long dead and gone to join the rest of his vanished race.

When the grassy prairies are left and the traveler enters a region of alkali desert and sage-brush, the look of the country becomes even more grim and forbidding. In places the alkali forms a white frost on the ground that glances in the sunlight like the surface of a frozen lake; the dusty little sage-brush, stunted and dried up, sprawls over the parched ground, from which it can hardly extract the small amount of nourishment necessary for even its weazened life; the spiny cactus alone seems to be really in its true home. Yet even in such places antelope will be found, as alert and as abounding with vivacious life as elsewhere. Owing to the magnifying and distorting power of the clear, dry plains air, every object, no matter what its shape or color or apparent distance, needs the closest examination. A magpie sitting on a white skull, or a couple of ravens, will look, a quarter of a mile off, like some curious beast; and time and again a raw hunter will try to stalk a lump of clay or a burned stick; and after being once or twice disappointed he is apt to rush to the other extreme, and conclude too hastily that a given object is not an antelope, when it very possibly is.

During the morning I came in sight of several small bands or pairs of antelope. Most of them saw me as soon as or before I saw them, and, after watching me with intense curiosity as long as I was in sight and at a distance, made off at once as soon as I went into a hollow or appeared to be approaching too near. Twice, in scanning the country narrowly with the glasses, from behind a sheltering divide, bands of prong-horn were seen that had not discovered me. In each case the horse was at once left to graze, while I started off after the game, nearly a mile distant. For the first half mile I could walk upright or go along half stooping; then, as the distance grew closer, I had to crawl on all fours and keep behind any little broken bank, or take advantage of a small, dry watercourse; and toward the end work my way flat on my face, wriggling like a serpent, using every stunted sage-brush or patch of cactus as a cover, bareheaded under the blazing sun. In each case, after nearly an hour's irksome, thirsty work, the stalk failed. One band simply ran off without a second's warning, alarmed at some awkward movement on my part, and without giving a chance for a shot. In the other instance, while still at very long and uncertain range, I heard the sharp barking alarm-note of one of the prong-horn; the whole band instantly raising their heads and gazing intently at their would-be destroyer. They were a very long way off; but, seeing it was hopeless to try to get nearer I rested my rifle over a little mound of earth and fired. The dust came up in a puff to one side of the nearest antelope; the whole band took a few jumps and turned again; the second shot struck at their feet, and they went off like so many racehorses, being missed again as they ran. I sat up by a sage-brush thinking they would of course not come back, when to my surprise I saw them wheel round with the precision of a cavalry squadron, all in line and fronting me, the white and brown markings on their heads and throats showing like the facings on soldiers' uniforms; and then back they came charging up till again within long range, when they wheeled their line as if on a pivot and once more made off, this time for good, not heeding an ineffectual fusillade from the Winchester. Antelope often go through a series of regular revolutions, like so many trained horsemen, wheeling, turning, halting, and running as if under command; and their coming back to again run the (as it proved very harmless) gantlet of my fire was due either to curiosity or to one of those panicky freaks which occasionally seize those ordinarily wary animals, and cause them to run into danger easily avoided by creatures commonly much more readily approached than they are. I had fired half a dozen shots without effect; but while no one ever gets over his feeling of self-indignation at missing an easy shot at close quarters, any one who hunts antelope and is not of a disposition so timid as never to take chances, soon learns that he has to expect to expend a good deal of powder and lead before bagging his game.

By midday we reached a dry creek and followed up its course for a mile or so, till a small spot of green in the side of a bank showed the presence of water, a little pool of which lay underneath. The ground was so rotten that it was with difficulty I could get Manitou down where he could drink; but at last both of us satisfied our thirst, and he was turned loose to graze, with his saddle off, so as to cool his back, and I, after eating a biscuit, lay on my face on the ground—there was no shade of any sort near—and dozed until a couple of hours' rest and feed had put the horse in good trim for the afternoon ride. When it came to crossing over the dry creek on whose bank we had rested, we almost went down in a quicksand, and it was only by frantic struggles and flounderings that we managed to get over.

On account of these quicksands and mud-holes, crossing the creeks on the prairie is often very disagreeable work. Even when apparently perfectly dry the bottom may have merely a thin crust of hard mud and underneath a fathomless bed of slime. If the grass appears wet and with here and there a few tussocks of taller blades in it, it is well to avoid it. Often a man may have to go along a creek nearly a mile before he can find a safe crossing, or else run the risk of seeing his horse mired hard and fast. When a horse is once in a mud-hole it will perhaps so exhaust itself by its first desperate and fruitless struggle that it is almost impossible to get it out. Its bridle and saddle have to be taken off; if another horse is along the lariat is drawn from the pommel of the latter's saddle to the neck of the one that is in, and it is hauled out by main force. Otherwise a man may have to work half a day, fixing the horse's legs in the right position and then taking it by the forelock and endeavoring to get it to make a plunge; each plunge bringing it perhaps a few inches nearer the firm ground. Quicksands are even more dangerous than these mud-holes, as, if at all deep, a creature that can not get out immediately is sure to be speedily engulfed. Many parts of the Little Missouri are impassable on account of these quicksands. Always in crossing unknown ground that looks dangerous it is best to feel your way very cautiously along and, if possible, to find out some cattle trail or even game trail which can be followed.

For some time after leaving the creek nothing was seen; until, on coming over the crest of the next great divide, I came in sight of a band of six or eight prong-horn about a quarter of a mile off to my right hand. There was a slight breeze from the southeast, which blew diagonally across my path toward the antelopes. The latter, after staring at me a minute, as I rode slowly on, suddenly started at full speed to run directly up wind, and therefore in a direction that would cut the line of my course less than half a mile ahead of where I was. Knowing that when antelope begin running in a straight line they are very hard to turn, and seeing that they would have to run a longer distance than my horse would to intercept them, I clapped spurs into Manitou, and the game old fellow, a very fleet runner, stretched himself down to the ground and seemed to go almost as fast as the quarry. As I had expected, the latter, when they saw me running, merely straightened themselves out and went on, possibly faster than before, without changing the line of their flight, keeping right up wind. Both horse and antelope fairly flew over the ground, their courses being at an angle that would certainly bring them together. Two of the antelope led, by some fifty yards or so, the others, who were all bunched together.

Nearer and nearer we came, Manitou in spite of carrying myself and the pack behind the saddle, gamely holding his own, while the antelope, with outstretched necks, went at an even, regular gait that offered a strong contrast to the spring-ing bounds with which a deer runs. At last the two leading animals crossed the line of my flight ahead of me; when I pulled short up, leaped from Manitou's back, and blazed into the band as they went by not forty yards off, aiming well ahead of a fine buck who was on the side nearest me. An an-telope's gait is so even that it offers a good running mark; and as the smoke blew off I saw the buck roll over like a rab-bit, with both shoulders broken. I then emptied the Winches-ter at the rest of the band, breaking one hind leg of a young buck. Hastily cutting the throat of, and opening, the dead buck, I again mounted and started off after the wounded one. But, though only on three legs, it went astonishingly fast, having had a good start; and after following it over a mile I gave up the pursuit, though I had gained a good deal; for the heat was very great, and I did not deem it well to tire the horse at the beginning of the trip. Returning to the carcass, I cut off the hams and strung them beside the saddle; an ante-lope is so spare that there is very little more meat on the body.

This trick of running in a straight line is another of the an-telope's peculiar characteristics which frequently lead it into danger. Although with so much sharper eyes than a deer, an-telope are in many ways far stupider animals, more like sheep, and they especially resemble the latter in their habit of following a leader, and in their foolish obstinacy in keeping to a course they have once adopted. If a horseman starts to head off a deer the latter will always turn long before he has come within range, but quite often an antelope will merely increase his speed and try to pass ahead of his foe. Almost al-ways, however, one if alone will keep out of gunshot, owing to the speed at which he goes, but if there are several in a band which is well strung out, the leader only cares for his own safety and passes well ahead himself. The others follow like sheep, without turning in the least from the line the first followed, and thus may pass within close range. If the leader bounds into the air, those following will often go through ex-actly the same motions; and if he turns, the others are very apt to each in succession run up and turn in the same place, unless the whole band are manœuvring together, like a squad-ron of cavalry under orders, as has already been spoken of.

After securing the buck's hams and head (the latter for the sake of the horns, which were unusually long and fine), I pushed rapidly on without stopping to hunt, to reach some large creek which should contain both wood and water, for even in summer a fire adds greatly to the comfort and cosiness of a night camp. When the sun had nearly set we went over a divide and came in sight of a creek fulfilling the required conditions. It wound its way through a valley of rich bottom land, cottonwood trees of no great height or size growing in thick groves along its banks, while its bed contained many deep pools of water, some of it fresh and good. I rode into a great bend, with a grove of trees on its right and containing excellent feed. Manitou was loosed, with the lariat round his neck, to feed where he wished until I went to bed, when he was to be taken to a place where the grass was thick and succulent, and tethered out for the night. There was any amount of wood with which a fire was started for cheerfulness, and some of the coals were soon raked off apart to cook over. The horse blanket was spread on the ground, with the oil-skin over it as a bed, underneath a spreading cottonwood tree, while the regular blanket served as covering. The metal cup was soon filled with water and simmering over the coals to make tea, while an antelope steak was roasting on a forked stick. It is wonderful how cosy a camp, in clear weather, becomes if there is a good fire and enough to eat, and how sound the sleep is afterward in the cool air, with the brilliant stars glimmering through the branches overhead.

John Burroughs

Birch Browsings

John Burroughs (1837–1921), the preeminent naturalist of the Mid-Hudson River and Catskill regions of New York, was the most gifted and popular author of the nature essay in the late nineteenth and early twentieth centuries. Born and raised on a farm in the Catskills, Burroughs was a rural schoolteacher before spending nine years as a government employee in Washington, D.C. There he became a close friend of Walt Whitman, who was the subject of Burroughs's first book and who suggested the title for Burroughs's first volume of nature essays, Wake-Robin *(1871). In 1873, Burroughs moved to a fruit farm at West Park in New York's Mid-Hudson Valley. Although he camped in Yosemite with John Muir and in Yellowstone with Roosevelt, and traveled with Muir to the Grand Canyon and to Alaska, Burroughs was less interested in the sublime panoramas of wild nature than in a more intimate and personal one: "One has only to sit in the woods or fields, or by the shore of the river or lake, and nearly everything of interest will come round to him, the birds, the animals, the insects." Although Burroughs was knowledgeable in science, he preferred to call himself a "nature essayist" rather than a "scientific writer," explaining that "until science is mixed with emotion and appeals to the heart and imagination, it is like dead inorganic matter; and when it is so mixed and so transformed it is literature." Burroughs did have a scientific impulse for precise observation and accurate description, and in his essay "Real and Sham Natural History," he attacked the sentimentalizers of nature, whom Roosevelt, joining the attack, called "Nature Fakers." The twenty-seven volumes of Burroughs's work are the product of a writing career that spanned half a century. The selection that follows describes his experience when he ventured into wilder country than that along the banks of the Hudson.*

The region of which I am about to speak lies in the southern part of the State of New York, and comprises parts of three counties,—Ulster, Sullivan, and Delaware. It is drained by tributaries of both the Hudson and Delaware, and, next to the Adirondack section, contains more wild land than any other tract in the State. The mountains which traverse it, and impart to it its severe northern climate, belong properly to the Catskill range. On some maps of the State they are called the Pine Mountains, though with obvious local impropriety, as pine, so far as I have observed, is nowhere found upon them. "Birch Mountains" would be a more characteristic name, as on their summits birch is the prevailing tree . . .

In 1868 a party of three of us set out for a brief trouting excursion to a body of water called Thomas's Lake, situated in the same chain of mountains. On this excursion, more particularly than on any other I have ever undertaken, I was taught how poor an Indian I should make, and what a ridiculous figure a party of men may cut in the woods when the way is uncertain and the mountains high.

We left our team at a farmhouse near the head of the Mill Brook, one June afternoon, and with knapsacks on our shoulders struck into the woods at the base of the mountain, hoping to cross the range that intervened between us and the lake by sunset. We engaged a good-natured but rather indolent young man, who happened to be stopping at the house, and who had carried a knapsack in the Union armies, to pilot us a couple of miles into the woods so as to guard against any mistakes at the outset. It seemed the easiest thing in the world to find the lake. The lay of the land was so simple, according to accounts, that I felt sure I could go to it in the dark. "Go up this little brook to its source on the side of the mountain," they said. "The valley that contains the lake heads directly on the other side." What could be easier? But on a little further inquiry, they said we should "bear well to the left" when we reached the top of the mountain. This opened the doors again; "bearing well to the left" was an uncertain performance in strange woods. We might bear so well to the left that it would bring us ill. But why bear to the left at all, if the lake was directly opposite? Well, not quite opposite; a little to the left. There were two or three other val-

From John Burroughs, "Birch Browsings," in *Wake-Robin* (New York: Hurd and Houghton, 1871).

leys that headed in near there. We could easily find the right one. But to make assurance doubly sure, we engaged a guide, as stated, to give us a good start, and go with us beyond the bearing-to-the-left point. He had been to the lake the winter before and knew the way. Our course, the first half hour, was along an obscure wood-road which had been used for drawing ash logs off the mountain in winter. There was some hemlock, but more maple and birch. The woods were dense and free from underbrush, the ascent gradual. Most of the way we kept the voice of the creek in our ear on the right. I approached it once, and found it swarming with trout. The water was as cold as one ever need wish. After a while the ascent grew steeper, the creek became a mere rill that issued from beneath loose, moss-covered rocks and stones, and with much labor and puffing we drew ourselves up the rugged declivity. Every mountain has its steepest point, which is usually near the summit, in keeping, I suppose, with the providence that makes the darkest hour just before day. It is steep, steeper, steepest, till you emerge on the smooth level or gently rounded space at the top, which the old ice-gods polished off so long ago.

We found this mountain had a hollow in its back where the ground was soft and swampy. Some gigantic ferns, which we passed through, came nearly to our shoulders. We passed also several patches of swamp honeysuckles, red with blossoms.

Our guide at length paused on a big rock where the land began to dip down the other way, and concluded that he had gone far enough, and that we would now have no difficulty in finding the lake. "It must lie right down there," he said, pointing with his hand. But it was plain that he was not quite sure in his own mind. He had several times wavered in his course, and had shown considerable embarrassment when bearing to the left across the summit. Still we thought little of it. We were full of confidence, and, bidding him adieu, plunged down the mountain-side, following a spring run that we had no doubt led to the lake.

In these woods, which had a southeastern exposure, I first began to notice the wood thrush. In coming up the other side I had not seen a feather of any kind, or heard a note. Now the golden *trillide-de* of the wood thrush sounded through the silent woods. While looking for a fish-pole about half way down the mountain, I saw a thrush's nest in a little sapling about ten feet from the ground.

After continuing our descent till our only guide, the spring run, became quite a trout brook, and its tiny murmur a loud brawl, we began to peer anxiously through the trees for a glimpse of the lake, or for some conformation of the land that would indicate its proximity. An object which we vaguely discerned in looking under the near trees and over the more distant ones proved, on further inspection, to be a patch of plowed ground. Presently we made out a burnt fallow near it. This was a wet blanket to our enthusiasm. No lake, no sport, no trout for supper that night. The rather indolent young man had either played us a trick, or, as seemed more likely, had missed the way. . . .

When we lay down, there was apparently not a mosquito in the woods; but the "no-see-ems," as Thoreau's Indian aptly named the midges, soon found us out, and after the fire had gone down annoyed us much. My hands and wrists suddenly began to smart and itch in a most unaccountable manner. My first thought was that they had been poisoned in some way. Then the smarting extended to my neck and face, even to my scalp, when I began to suspect what was the matter. So, wrapping myself up more thoroughly, and stowing my hands away as best I could, I tried to sleep, being some time behind my companions, who appeared not to mind the "no-see-ems." I was further annoyed by some little irregularity on my side of the couch. The chambermaid had not beaten it up well. One huge lump refused to be mollified, and each attempt to adapt it to some natural hollow in my own body brought only a moment's relief. But at last I got the better of this also and slept. Late in the night I woke up, just in time to hear a golden-crowned thrush sing in a tree near by. It sang as loud and cheerily as at midday, and I thought myself after all, quite in luck. Birds occasionally sing at night, just as the cock crows. I have heard the hairbird, and the note of the kingbird; and the ruffed grouse infrequently drums at night. . . .

As soon as it was fairly light we were up and ready to resume our march. A small bit of bread-and-butter and a swallow or two of whiskey was all we had for breakfast that morning. Our supply of each was very limited, and we were anxious to save a little of both, to relieve the diet of trout to which we looked forward.

At an early hour we reached the rock where we had parted with the guide, and looked around us into the dense, trackless woods with many misgivings. To strike out now on our own hook, where the way was so blind and after the experience we had just had, was a step not to be carelessly taken. The tops of these mountains are so broad, and a short distance in the woods seems so far, that one is by no means master of the situation after reaching the summit. And then there are so many spurs and offshoots and changes of direction, added to the impossibility of making any generalization by the aid of the eye, that before one is aware of it he is very wide of his mark. . . .

After looking in vain for the line of marked trees, we moved off to the left in a doubtful, hesitating manner, keeping on the highest ground and blazing the trees as we went. We were afraid to go down hill, lest we should descend too soon; our vantage-ground was high ground. A thick fog coming on, we were more bewildered than ever. Still we pressed forward, climbing up ledges and wading through ferns for about two hours, when we paused by a spring that issued from beneath an immense wall of rock that belted the highest part of the mountain. There was quite a broad plateau here, and the birch wood was very dense, and the trees of unusual size.

After resting and exchanging opinions, we all concluded that it was best not to continue our search incumbered as we were; but we were not willing to abandon it altogether, and I proposed to my companions to leave them beside the spring with our traps, while I made one thorough and final effort to find the lake. If I succeeded and desired them to come forward, I was to fire my gun three times; if I failed and wished to return, I would fire it twice, they of course responding.

So, filling my canteen from the spring, I set out again, taking the spring run for my guide. Before I had followed it two hundred yards it sank into the ground at my feet. I had half a mind to be superstitious and to believe that we were under a spell, since our guides played us such tricks. However, I determined to put the matter to a further test, and struck out boldly to the left. This seemed to be the keyword,—to the left, to the left. The fog had now lifted, so that I could form a better idea of the lay of the land. Twice I looked down the steep sides of the mountain, sorely tempted to risk a plunge. Still I hesitated and kept along on the brink. As I stood on a rock deliberating, I heard a crackling of the brush, like the tread of some large game, on a plateau below me. Suspecting the truth of the case, I moved stealthily down, and found a herd of young cattle leisurely browsing. We had several times crossed their trail, and had seen that morning a level, grassy place on the top of the mountain, where they had passed the night. Instead of being frightened, as I had expected, they seemed greatly delighted, and gathered around me as if to inquire the tidings from the outer world,—perhaps the quotations of the cattle market. They came up to me, and eagerly licked my hand, clothes, and gun. Salt was what they were after, and they were ready to swallow anything that contained the smallest percentage of it. They were mostly yearlings and as sleek as moles. They had a very gamy look. We were afterwards told that, in the spring, the farmers round about turn into these woods their young cattle, which do not come out again till fall. They are then in good condition,—not fat, like grass-fed cattle, but trim and supple, like deer. Once a month the owner hunts them up and salts them. They have their beats, and seldom wander beyond well-defined limits. It was interesting to see them feed. They browsed on the low limbs and bushes, and on the various plants, munching at everything without any apparent discrimination.

They attempted to follow me, but I escaped them by clambering down some steep rocks. I now found myself gradually edging down the side of the mountain, keeping around it in a spiral manner, and scanning the woods and the shape of the ground for some encouraging hint or sign. Finally the woods became more open, and the descent less rapid. The trees were remarkably straight and uniform in size. Black birches, the first I had seen, were very numerous. I felt encouraged. Listening attentively, I caught, from a breeze just lifting the drooping leaves, a sound that I willingly believed was made by a bullfrog. On this hint, I tore down through the woods at my highest speed. Then I paused and listened again. This time there was no mistaking it; it was the sound of frogs. Much elated, I rushed on. By and by I could hear them as I ran. *Pthrung, pthrung,* croaked the old ones; *pug, pug,* shrilly joined in the smaller fry.

Then I caught, through the lower trees, a gleam of blue, which I first thought was distant sky. A second look and I knew it to be water, and in a moment more I stepped from the woods and stood upon the shore of the lake. I exulted

silently. There it was at last, sparkling in the morning sun,
and as beautiful as a dream. It was so good to come upon
such open space and such bright hues, after wandering in the
dim, dense woods! The eye is as delighted as an escaped bird,
and darts gleefully from point to point.

The lake was a long oval, scarcely more than a mile in circumference, with evenly wooded shores, which rose gradually
on all sides. After contemplating the scene for a moment, I
stepped back into the woods, and, loading my gun as heavily
as I dared, discharged it three times. The reports seemed to
fill all the mountains with sound. The frogs quickly hushed,
and I listened for the response. But no response came. Then I
tried again and again, but without evoking an answer. One of
my companions, however, who had climbed to the top of the
high rocks in the rear of the spring, thought he heard faintly
one report. It seemed an immense distance below him, and
far around under the mountain. I knew I had come a long
way, and hardly expected to be able to communicate with my
companions in the manner agreed upon. I therefore started
back, choosing my course without any reference to the circui-
tous route by which I had come, and loading heavily and firing at intervals. I must have aroused many long-dormant
echoes from a Rip Van Winkle sleep. As my powder got low,
I fired and halloed alternately, till I came near splitting both
my throat and gun. Finally, after I had begun to have a very
ugly feeling of alarm and disappointment, and to cast about
vaguely for some course to pursue in the emergency that
seemed near at hand,—namely, the loss of my companions
now I had found the lake,—a favoring breeze brought me the
last echo of a response. I rejoined with spirit, and hastened
with all speed in the direction whence the sound had come,
but, after repeated trials, failed to elicit another answering
sound. This filled me with apprehension again. I feared that
my friends had been misled by the reverberations, and I pictured them to myself hastening in the opposite direction. Paying little attention to my course, but paying dearly for my
carelessness afterward, I rushed forward to undeceive them.
But they had not been deceived, and in a few moments an
answering shout revealed them near at hand. I heard their
tramp, the bushes parted, and we three met again.

In answer to their eager inquiries, I assured them that I
had seen the lake, that it was at the foot of the mountain,

and that we could not miss it if we kept straight down from where we then were.

My clothes were soaked with perspiration, but I shouldered my knapsack with alacrity, and we began the descent. I noticed that the woods were much thicker, and had quite a different look from those I had passed through, but thought nothing of it, as I expected to strike the lake near its head, whereas I had before come out at its foot. We had not gone far when we crossed a line of marked trees, which my companions were disposed to follow. It intersected our course nearly at right angles, and kept along and up the side of the mountain. My impression was that it led up from the lake, and that by keeping our own course we should reach the lake sooner than if we followed this line.

About half way down the mountain, we could see through the interstices the opposite slope. I encouraged my comrades by telling them that the lake was between us and that, and not more than half a mile distant. We soon reached the bottom, where we found a small stream and quite an extensive alder swamp, evidently the ancient bed of a lake. I explained to my half-vexed and half-incredulous companions that we were probably above the lake, and that this stream must lead to it. "Follow it," they said; "we will wait here till we hear from you."

So I went on, more than ever disposed to believe that we were under a spell, and that the lake had slipped from my grasp after all. Seeing no favorable sign as I went forward, I laid down my accoutrements, and climbed a decayed beech that leaned out over the swamp and promised a good view from the top. As I stretched myself up to look around from the highest attainable branch, there was suddenly a loud crack at the root. With a celerity that would at least have done credit to a bear, I regained the ground, having caught but a momentary glimpse of the country, but enough to convince me no lake was near. Leaving all incumbrances here but my gun, I still pressed on, loath to be thus baffled. After floundering through another alder swamp for nearly half a mile, I flattered myself that I was close on to the lake. I caught sight of a low spur of the mountain sweeping around like a half-extended arm, and I fondly imagined that within its clasp was the object of my search. But I found only more alder swamp. After this region was cleared, the creek began to descend the mountain very rapidly. Its banks became high and narrow, and it went whirling away with a sound that seemed to my ears like a burst of ironical laughter. I turned back with a feeling of mingled disgust, shame, and vexation. In fact I was almost sick, and when I reached my companions, after an absence of nearly two hours, hungry, fatigued, and disheartened, I would have sold my interest in Thomas's Lake at a very low figure. For the first time, I heartily wished myself well out of the woods. Thomas might keep his lake, and the enchanters guard his possession! I doubted if he had ever found it the second time, or if any one else ever had.

My companions, who were quite fresh, and who had not felt the strain of baffled purpose as I had, assumed a more encouraging tone. After I had rested a while, and partaken sparingly of the bread and whiskey, which in such an emergency is a great improvement on bread and water, I agreed to their proposition that we should make another attempt. As if to reassure us, a robin sounded his cheery call near by, and the winter wren, the first I had heard in these woods, set his music-box going, which fairly ran over with fine, gushing, lyrical sounds. There can be no doubt but this bird is one of our finest songsters. If it would only thrive and sing well when caged, like the canary, how far it would surpass that bird! It has all the vivacity and versatility of the canary, without any of its shrillness. Its song is indeed a little cascade of melody.

We again retraced our steps, rolling the stone, as it were, back up the mountain, determined to commit ourselves to the line of marked trees. These we finally reached, and, after exploring the country to the right, saw that bearing to the left was still the order. The trail led up over a gentle rise of ground, and in less than twenty minutes we were in the woods I had passed through when I found the lake. The error I had made was then plain; we had come off the mountain a few paces too far to the right, and so had passed down on the wrong side of the ridge, into what we afterwards learned was the valley of Alder Creek.

We now made good time, and before many minutes I again saw the mimic sky glance through the trees. As we approached the lake a solitary woodchuck, the first wild animal we had seen since entering the woods, sat crouched upon the root of a tree a few feet from the water, apparently completely nonplussed by the unexpected appearance of danger on the land side. All retreat was cut off, and he looked his fate in the face without flinching. I slaughtered him just as a savage would have done, and from the same motive,—I wanted his carcass to eat. . . .

The birds were unusually plentiful and noisy about the head of this lake; robins, blue jays, and woodpeckers greeted me with their familiar notes. The blue jays found an owl or some wild animal a short distance above me, and, as is their custom on such occasions, proclaimed it at the top of their voices, and kept on till the darkness began to gather in the woods.

I also heard here, as I had at two or three other points in the course of the day, the peculiar, resonant hammering of some species of woodpecker upon the hard, dry limbs. It was unlike any sound of the kind I had ever before heard, and, repeated at intervals through the silent woods, was a very marked and characteristic feature. Its peculiarity was the ordered succession of the raps, which gave it the character of a premeditated performance. There were first three strokes following each other rapidly, then two much louder ones with longer intervals between them. I heard the drumming here, and the next day at sunset at Furlow Lake, the source of Dry Brook, and in no instance was the order varied. There was melody in it, such as a woodpecker knows how to evoke from a smooth dry branch. It suggested something quite as pleasing as the liveliest bird-song, and was if anything more woodsy and wild. As the yellow-bellied woodpecker was the most abundant species in these woods, I attributed it to him. It is the one sound that still links itself with those scenes in my mind.

At sunset the grouse began to drum in all parts of the woods about the lake. I could hear five at one time, *thump, thump, thump, thump, thr-r-r-r-r-rr*. It was a homely, welcome sound. As I returned to camp at twilight, along the shore of the lake, the frogs also were in full chorus. The older ones ripped out their responses to each other with terrific force and volume. I know of no other animal capable of giving forth so much sound, in proportion to its size, as a frog. Some of these seemed to bellow as loud as a two-year-old bull. They were of immense size, and very abundant. No frog-eater had ever been there. Near the shore we felled a tree which reached far out in the lake. Upon the trunk and branches the frogs had soon collected in large numbers, and

gamboled and splashed about the half-submerged top, like a
parcel of schoolboys, making nearly as much noise.

After dark, as I was frying the fish, a panful of the largest
trout was accidentally capsized in the fire. With rueful coun-
tenances we contemplated the irreparable loss our commissariat had sustained by this mishap; but remembering there
was virtue in ashes, we poked the half-consumed fish from
the bed of coals and ate them, and they were good.

We lodged that night on a brush-heap and slept soundly.
The green, yielding beech-twigs, covered with a buffalo robe,
were equal to a hair mattress. The heat and smoke from a
large fire kindled in the afternoon had banished every "no-
see-em" from the locality, and in the morning the sun was
above the mountain before we awoke.

I immediately started again for the inlet, and went far up
the stream toward its source. A fair string of trout for breakfast was my reward. The cattle with the bell were at the head
of the valley, where they had passed the night. Most of them
were two-year-old steers. They came up to me and begged for
salt, and scared the fish by their importunities.

We finished our bread that morning, and ate every fish we
could catch, and about ten o'clock prepared to leave the lake.
The weather had been admirable, and the lake was a gem,
and I would gladly have spent a week in the neighborhood;
but the question of supplies was a serious one, and would
brook no delay. . . .

We were now close to the settlement, and began to hear
human sounds. One rod more, and we were out of the woods.
It took us a moment to comprehend the scene. Things looked
very strange at first; but quickly they began to change and to
put on familiar features. Some magic scene-shifting seemed to
take place before my eyes, till, instead of the unknown settlement which I at first seemed to look upon, there stood the
farmhouse at which we had stopped two days before, and at
the same moment we heard the stamping of our team in the
barn. We sat down and laughed heartily over our good luck.
Our desperate venture had resulted better than we had dared
to hope, and had shamed our wisest plans. At the house our
arrival had been anticipated about this time, and dinner was
being put upon the table.

It was then five o'clock, so that we had been in the woods
just forty-eight hours; but if time is only phenomenal, as the
philosophers say, and life only in feeling, as the poets aver,

we were some months, if not years, older at that moment than we had been two days before. Yet younger, too,—though this be a paradox,—for the birches had infused into us some of their own suppleness and strength.

John Muir

The Range of Light

John Muir (1838–1914), a self-described "poetico-trampo-geologist-bot. and ornith-natural, etc!—etc!—etc!," became the turn of the century's most notable spokesman for wilderness. "When I was a boy in Scotland," he wrote, "I was fond of everything that was wild, and all my life I've been growing fonder and fonder of wild places." Before Muir found his spiritual home in Yosemite when he was thirty, he had worked eleven years on his family's frontier homestead in Wisconsin, studied geology, chemistry, and botany as a special student at the University of Wisconsin, showed remarkable talent for mechanical invention, tramped up the Mississippi and into the wilds of Canada, suffered month-long blindness after an accident in an Indianapolis factory ("this affliction has driven me into the sweet fields"), and walked a thousand miles from Indiana to the Gulf of Mexico. In Yosemite, where he worked as a sheepherder and mill hand, Muir came to national attention when he challenged the prevailing scientific theory that a sudden collapse of the earth's surface had created the spectacular Yosemite Valley. Muir later discovered sixty-five living glaciers in the Sierra to support the fact that its valleys had been sculpted by ice. But Muir is best remembered for his later role, after ten years as a successful fruit farmer in Martinez, when he devoted himself completely to conservation issues, serving for twenty-two years as the first president of the Sierra Club, battling to make Yosemite a national park, and lobbying unsuccessfully to prevent Yosemite's Hetch Hetchy Valley from being damned and flooded into a municipal reservoir. Although Muir's writings had appeared in magazines and newspapers, his first book, The Mountains of California *(1894), did not appear until he was nearly sixty. It brought a special emphasis to wilderness literature. Storms, floods, winds, and other hardships that were merely endured by earlier adventurers became delightful experiences to Muir. Sensation achieved a religious intensity, and mountaineering became not an ordeal of conquest or self-testing, but a chance to experience our "spiritual affinities" with mountains, trees, glaciers—all the "Majesty of the Inanimate" that was the preoccupation of Muir's life and work.*

Arriving on the summit of this dividing crest, one of the most exciting pieces of pure wilderness was disclosed that I ever discovered in all my mountaineering. There, immediately in front, loomed the majestic mass of Mount Ritter, with a glacier swooping down its face nearly to my feet, then curving westward and pouring its frozen flood into a dark blue lake, whose shores were bound with precipices of crystalline snow; while a deep chasm drawn between the divide and the glacier separated the massive picture from everything else. I could see only the one sublime mountain, the one glacier, the one lake; the whole veiled with one blue shadow—rock, ice, and water close together without a single leaf or sign of life. After gazing spellbound, I began instinctively to scrutinize every notch and gorge and weathered buttress of the mountain, with reference to making the ascent. The entire front above the glacier appeared as one tremendous precipice, slightly receding at the top, and bristling with spires and pinnacles set above one another in formidable array. Massive lichen-stained battlements stood forward here and there, hacked at the top with angular notches, and separated by frosty gullies and recesses that have been veiled in shadow ever since their creation; while to right and left, as far as I could see, were huge, crumbling buttresses, offering no hope to the climber. The head of the glacier sends up a few finger-like branches through narrow *couloirs;* but these seemed too steep and short to be available, especially as I had no ax with which to cut steps, and the numerous narrow-throated gullies down which stones and snow are avalanched seemed hopelessly steep, besides being interrupted by vertical cliffs; while the whole front was rendered still more terribly forbidding by the chill shadow and the gloomy blackness of the rocks.

From John Muir, *The Mountains of California* (New York: Century, 1894).

Descending the divide in a hesitating mood, I picked my way across the yawning chasm at the foot, and climbed out upon the glacier. There were no meadows now to cheer with their brave colors, nor could I hear the dun-headed sparrows, whose cheery notes so often relieve the silence of our highest mountains. The only sounds were the gurgling of small rills down in the veins and crevasses of the glacier, and now and then the rattling report of falling stones, with the echoes they shot out into the crisp air.

I could not distinctly hope to reach the summit from this side, yet I moved on across the glacier as if driven by fate. Contending with myself, the season is too far spent, I said, and even should I be successful, I might be storm-bound on the mountain; and in the cloud-darkness, with the cliffs and crevasses covered with snow, how could I escape? No; I must wait till next summer. I would only approach the mountain now, and inspect it, creep about its flanks, learn what I could of its history, holding myself ready to flee on the approach of the first storm-cloud. But we little know until tried how much of the uncontrollable there is in us, urging across glaciers and torrents, and up dangerous heights, let the judgment forbid as it may.

I succeeded in gaining the foot of the cliff on the eastern extremity of the glacier, and there discovered the mouth of a narrow avalanche gully, through which I began to climb, intending to follow it as far as possible, and at least obtain some fine wild views for my pains. Its general course is oblique to the plane of the mountain-face, and the metamorphic slates of which the mountain is built are cut by cleavage planes in such a way that they weather off in angular blocks, giving rise to irregular steps that greatly facilitate climbing on the sheer places. I thus made my way into a wilderness of crumbling spires and battlements, built together in bewildering combinations, and glazed in many places with a thin coating of ice, which I had to hammer off with stones. The situation was becoming gradually more perilous, but, having passed several dangerous spots, I dared not think of descending; for, so steep was the entire ascent, one would inevitably fall to the glacier in case a single misstep were made. Knowing, therefore, the tried danger beneath, I became all the more anxious concerning the developments to be made above, and began to be conscious of a vague foreboding of what actually befell; not that I was given to fear, but rather because my instincts,

usually so positive and true, seemed vitiated in some way,
and were leading me astray. At length, after attaining an elevation of about 12,800 feet, I found myself at the foot of a
sheer drop in the bed of the avalanche channel I was tracing,
which seemed absolutely to bar further progress. It was only
about forty-five or fifty feet high, and somewhat roughened
by fissures and projections; but these seemed so slight and insecure, as footholds, that I tried hard to avoid the precipice
altogether, by scaling the wall of the channel on either side.
But, though less steep, the walls were smoother than the obstructing rock, and repeated efforts only showed that I must
either go right ahead or turn back. The tried dangers beneath
seemed even greater than that of the cliff in front; therefore,
after scanning its face again and again, I began to scale it,
picking my holds with intense caution. After gaining a point
about halfway to the top, I was suddenly brought to a dead
stop, with arms outspread, clinging close to the face of the
rock, unable to move hand or foot either up or down. My
doom appeared fixed. I *must* fall. There would be a moment
of bewilderment, and then a lifeless rumble down the one
general precipice to the glacier below.

When this final danger flashed upon me, I became nerve-
shaken for the first time since setting foot on the mountains,
and my mind seemed to fill with a stifling smoke. But this terrible eclipse lasted only a moment, when life blazed forth
again with preternatural clearness. I seemed suddenly to become possessed of a new sense. The other self, bygone experiences, instinct, or Guardian Angel,—call it what you will,—
came forward and assumed control. Then my trembling
muscles became firm again, every rift and flaw in the rock
was seen as through a microscope, and my limbs moved with
positiveness and precision with which I seemed to have nothing
at all to do. Had I been borne aloft upon wings, my deliverance
could not have been more complete.

Above this memorable spot, the face of the mountain is
still more savagely hacked and torn. It is a maze of yawning
chasms and gullies, in the angles of which rise beetling crags
and piles of detached boulders that seemed to have been gotten ready to be launched below. But the strange influx of
strength I had received seemed inexhaustible. I found a way
without effort, and soon stood upon the topmost crag in the
blessed light.

How truly glorious the landscape circled around this noble

summit!—giant mountains, valleys innumerable, glaciers and meadows, rivers and lakes, with the wide blue sky bent tenderly over them all. But in my first hour of freedom from that terrible shadow, the sunlight in which I was laving seemed all in all.

Looking southward along the axis of the range, the eye is first caught by a row of exceedingly sharp and slender spires, which rise openly to a height of about a thousand feet, above a series of short, residual glaciers that lean back against their bases; their fantastic sculpture and the unrelieved sharpness with which they spring out of the ice rendering them peculiarly wild and striking. These are "The Minarets." Beyond them you behold a sublime wilderness of mountains, their snowy summits towering together in crowded abundance, peak beyond peak, swelling higher, higher as they sweep on southward, until the culminating point of the range is reached on Mount Whitney, near the head of the Kern River, at an elevation of nearly 14,700 feet above the level of the sea.

Westward, the general flank of the range is seen flowing sublimely away from the sharp summits, in smooth undulations; a sea of huge gray granite waves dotted with lakes and meadows, and fluted with stupendous cañons that grow steadily deeper as they recede in the distance. Below this gray region lies the dark forest zone, broken here and there by upswelling ridges and domes; and yet beyond lies a yellow, hazy belt, marking the broad plain of the San Joaquin, bounded on its farther side by the blue mountains of the coast.

Turning now to the northward, there in the immediate foreground is the glorious Sierra Crown, with Cathedral Peak, a temple of marvelous architecture, a few degrees to the left of it; the gray, massive form of Mammoth Mountain to the right; while Mounts Ord, Gibbs, Dana, Conness, Tower Peak, Castle Peak, Silver Mountain, and a host of noble companions, as yet nameless, make a sublime show along the axis of the range.

Eastward, the whole region seems a land of desolation covered with beautiful light. The torrid volcanic basin of Mono, with its one bare lake fourteen miles long; Owen's Valley and the broad lava table-land at its head, dotted with craters, and the massive Inyo Range, rivaling even the Sierra in height; these are spread, map-like, beneath you, with countless ranges beyond, passing and overlapping one another and fading on the glowing horizon.

At a distance of less than 3,000 feet below the summit of Mount Ritter you may find tributaries of the San Joaquin and Owen's rivers, bursting forth from the ice and snow of the glaciers that load its flanks; while a little to the north of here are found the highest affluents of the Tuolumne and Merced. Thus, the fountains of four of the principal rivers of California are within a radius of four or five miles.

Lakes are seen gleaming in all sorts of places, round, or oval, or square, like very mirrors; others narrow and sinuous, drawn close around the peaks like silver zones, the highest reflecting only rocks, snow, and the sky. But neither these nor the glaciers, nor the bits of brown meadow and moorland that occur here and there, are large enough to make any marked impression upon the mighty wilderness of mountains. The eye, rejoicing in its freedom, roves about the vast expanse, yet returns again and again to the fountain peaks. Perhaps some one of the multitude excites special attention, some gigantic castle with turret and battlement, or some Gothic cathedral more abundantly spired than Milan's. But, generally, when looking for the first time from an all-embracing standpoint like this, the inexperienced observer is oppressed by the incomprehensible grandeur, variety, and abundance of the mountains rising shoulder to shoulder beyond the reach of vision; and it is only after they have been studied one by one, long and lovingly, that their far-reaching harmonies become manifest. Then, penetrate the wilderness where you may, the main telling features, to which all the surrounding topography is subordinate, are quickly perceived, and the most complicated clusters of peaks stand revealed harmoniously correlated and fashioned like works of art— eloquent monuments of the ancient ice-rivers that brought them into relief from the general mass of the range. The cañons, too, some of them a mile deep, mazing wildly through the mighty host of mountains, however lawless and ungovernable at first sight they appear, are at length recognized as the necessary effects of causes which followed each other in harmonious sequence—Nature's poems carved on tables of stone—the simplest and most emphatic of her glacial compositions.

Could we have been here to observe during the glacial period, we should have overlooked a wrinkled ocean of ice as continuous as that now covering the landscapes of Greenland; filling every valley and cañon with only the tops of the fountain peaks rising darkly above the rock-encumbered ice-waves like islets in a stormy sea—those islets the only hints of the glorious landscapes now smiling in the sun. Standing here in the deep, brooding silence all the wilderness seems motionless, as if the work of creation were done. But in the midst of this outer steadfastness we know there is incessant motion and change. Ever and anon, avalanches are falling from yonder peaks. These cliff-bound glaciers, seemingly wedged and immovable, are flowing like water and grinding the rocks beneath them. The lakes are lapping their granite shores and wearing them away, and every one of these rills and young rivers is fretting the air into music, and carrying the mountains to the plains. Here are the roots of all the life of the valleys, and here more simply than elsewhere is the eternal flux of nature manifested. Ice changing to water, lakes to meadows, and mountains to plains. And while we thus contemplate Nature's methods of landscape creation, and, reading the records she has carved on the rocks, reconstruct, however imperfectly, the landscapes of the past, we also learn that as these we now behold have succeeded those of the pre-glacial age, so they in turn are withering and vanishing to be succeeded by others yet unborn.

But in the midst of these fine lessons and landscapes, I had to remember that the sun was wheeling far to the west, while a new way down the mountain had to be discovered to some point on the timber line where I could have a fire; for I had not even burdened myself with a coat. I first scanned the western spurs, hoping some way might appear through which I might reach the northern glacier, and cross its snout; or pass around the lake into which it flows, and thus strike my morning track. This route was soon sufficiently unfolded to show that, if practicable at all, it would require so much time that reaching camp that night would be out of the question. I therefore scrambled back eastward, descending the southern slopes obliquely at the same time. Here the crags seemed less formidable, and the head of a glacier that flows northeast came in sight, which I determined to follow as far as possible, hoping thus to make my way to the foot of the peak on the east side, and thence across the intervening cañons and ridges to camp.

The inclination of the glacier is quite moderate at the head, and, as the sun had softened the *névé*, I made safe and rapid progress, running and sliding, and keeping up a sharp outlook for crevasses. About half a mile from the head, there is an ice-cascade, where the glacier pours over a sharp declivity and is shattered into massive blocks separated by deep, blue fissures. To thread my way through the slippery mazes of the crevassed portion seemed impossible, and I endeavored to avoid it by climbing off to the shoulder of the mountain. But the slopes rapidly steepened and at length fell away in sheer precipices, compelling a return to the ice. Fortunately, the day had been warm enough to loosen the ice-crystals so as to admit of hollows being dug in the rotten portions of the blocks, thus enabling me to pick my way with far less difficulty than I had anticipated. Continuing down over the snout, and along the left lateral moraine, was only a confident saunter, showing that the ascent of the mountain by way of this glacier is easy, provided one is armed with an ax to cut steps here and there.

The lower end of the glacier was beautifully waved and barred by the outcropping edges of the bedded ice-layers which represent the annual snowfalls, and to some extent the irregularities of structure caused by the weathering of the walls of crevasses, and by separate snowfalls which have been followed by rain, hail, thawing and freezing, etc. Small rills were gliding and swirling over the melting surface with a smooth, oily appearance, in channels of pure ice—their quick, compliant movements contrasting most impressively with the rigid, invisible flow of the glacier itself, on whose back they all were riding.

Night drew near before I reached the eastern base of the mountain, and my camp lay many a rugged mile to the north; but ultimate success was assured. It was now only a matter of endurance and ordinary mountain-craft. The sunset was, if possible, yet more beautiful than that of the day before. The Mono landscape seemed to be fairly saturated with warm, purple light. The peaks marshaled along the summit were in shadow, but through every notch and pass streamed vivid sunfire, soothing and irradiating their rough, black angles, while companies of small, luminous clouds hovered above them like very angels of light.

Darkness came on, but I found my way by the trends of the cañons and the peaks projected against the sky. All excitement died with the light, and then I was weary. But the joyful sound of the waterfall across the lake was heard at last, and soon the stars were seen reflected in the lake itself.

Taking my bearings from these, I discovered the little pine thicket in which my nest was, and then I had a rest such as only a tired mountaineer may enjoy. After lying loose and lost for awhile, I made a sunrise fire, went down to the lake, dashed water on my head, and dipped a cupful for tea. The revival brought about by bread and tea was as complete as the exhaustion from excessive enjoyment and toil. Then I crept beneath the pine-tassels to bed. The wind was frosty and the fire burned low, but my sleep was none the less sound, and the evening constellations had swept far to the west before I awoke. . . .

One of the most beautiful and exhilarating storms I ever enjoyed in the Sierra occurred in December, 1874, when I happened to be exploring one of the tributary valleys of the Yuba River. The sky and the ground and the trees had been thoroughly rain-washed and were dry again. The day was intensely pure, one of those incomparable bits of California winter, warm and balmy and full of white sparkling sunshine, redolent of all the purest influences of the spring, and at the same time enlivened with one of the most bracing wind-storms conceivable. Instead of camping out, as I usually do, I then chanced to be stopping at the house of a friend. But when the storm began to sound, I lost no time in pushing out into the woods to enjoy it. For on such occasions Nature has always something rare to show us, and the danger to life and limb is hardly greater than one would experience crouching deprecatingly beneath a roof.

It was still early morning when I found myself fairly adrift. Delicious sunshine came pouring over the hills, lighting the tops of the pines, and setting free a steam of summery fragrance that contrasted strangely with the wild tones of the storm. The air was mottled with pine-tassels and bright green plumes, that went flashing past in the sunlight like birds pursued. But there was not the slightest dustiness, nothing less pure than leaves, and ripe pollen, and flecks of withered bracken and moss. I heard trees falling for hours at the rate of one every two or three minutes; some uprooted, partly on account of the loose, water-soaked condition of the ground; others broken straight across, where some weakness caused by fire had determined the spot. The gestures of the various trees made a delightful study. Young Sugar Pines, light and feathery as squirrel-tails, were bowing almost to the ground;

while the grand old patriarchs, whose massive boles had been tried in a hundred storms, waved solemnly above them, their long, arching branches streaming fluently on the gale, and every needle thrilling and ringing and shedding off keen lances of light like a diamond. The Douglas Spruces, with long sprays drawn out in level tresses, and needles massed in a gray, shimmering glow, presented a most striking appearance as they stood in bold relief along the hilltops. The madroños in the dells, with their red bark and large glossy leaves tilted every way, reflected the sunshine in throbbing spangles like those one so often sees on the rippled surface of a glacier lake. But the Silver Pines were now the most impressively beautiful of all. Colossal spires 200 feet in height waved like supple goldenrods chanting and bowing low as if in worship, while the whole mass of their long, tremulous foliage was kindled into one continuous blaze of white sun-fire. The force of the gale was such that the most steadfast monarch of them all rocked down to its roots with a motion plainly perceptible when one leaned against it. Nature was holding high festival, and every fiber of the most rigid giants thrilled with glad excitement.

I drifted on through the midst of this passionate music and motion, across many a glen, from ridge to ridge; often halting in the lee of a rock for shelter, or to gaze and listen. Even when the grand anthem had swelled to its highest pitch, I could distinctly hear the varying tones of individual trees,—Spruce, and Fir, and Pine, and leafless Oak,—and even the infinitely gentle rustle of the withered grasses at my feet. Each was expressing itself in its own way,—singing its own song, and making its own peculiar gestures,—manifesting a richness of variety to be found in no other forest I have yet seen. The coniferous woods of Canada, and the Carolinas, and Florida, are made up of trees that resemble one another about as nearly as blades of grass, and grow close together in much the same way. Coniferous trees, in general, seldom possess individual character, such as is manifest among Oaks and Elms. But the California forests are made up of a greater number of distinct species than any other in the world. And in them we find, not only a marked differentiation into special groups, but also a marked individuality in almost every tree, giving rise to storm effects indescribably glorious.

Toward midday, after a long, tingling scramble through copses of hazel and ceanothus, I gained the summit of the highest ridge in the neighborhood; and then it occurred to me that it would be a fine thing to climb one of the trees to obtain a wider outlook and get my ear close to the Æolian music of its topmost needles. But under the circumstances the choice of a tree was a serious matter. One whose instep was not very strong seemed in danger of being blown down, or of being struck by others in case they should fall; another was branchless to a considerable height above the ground, and at the same time too large to be grasped with arms and legs in climbing; while others were not favorably situated for clear views. After cautiously casting about, I made choice of the tallest of a group of Douglas Spruces that were growing close together like a tuft of grass, no one of which seemed likely to fall unless all the rest fell with it. Though comparatively young, they were about 100 feet high, and their lithe, brushy tops were rocking and swirling in wild ecstasy. Being accustomed to climb trees in making botanical studies, I experienced no difficulty in reaching the top of this one, and never before did I enjoy so noble an exhilaration of motion. The slender tops fairly flapped and swished in the passionate torrent, bending and swirling backward and forward, round and round, tracing indescribable combinations of vertical and horizontal curves, while I clung with muscles firm braced, like a bobolink on a reed.

In its widest sweeps my tree-top described an arc of from twenty to thirty degrees, but I felt sure of its elastic temper, having seen others of the same species still more severely tried—bent almost to the ground indeed, in heavy snows—without breaking a fiber. I was therefore safe, and free to take the wind into my pulses and enjoy the excited forest from my superb outlook. The view from here must be extremely beautiful in any weather. Now my eye roved over the piny hills and dales as over fields of waving grain, and felt the light running in ripples and broad swelling undulations across the valleys from ridge to ridge, as the shining foliage was stirred by corresponding waves of air. Oftentimes these waves of reflected light would break up suddenly into a kind of beaten foam, and again, after chasing one another in regular order, they would seem to bend forward in concentric curves, and disappear on some hillside, like sea-waves on a shelving shore. The quantity of light reflected from the bent needles was so great as to make whole groves appear as if covered with snow, while the black shadows beneath the trees greatly enhanced the effect of the silvery splendor.

Excepting only the shadows there was nothing somber in all this wild sea of pines. On the contrary, notwithstanding this was the winter season, the colors were remarkably beautiful. The shafts of the pine and libocedrus were brown and purple, and most of the foliage was well tinged with yellow; the laurel groves, with the pale undersides of their leaves turned upward, made masses of gray; and then there was many a dash of chocolate color from clumps of manzanita, and jet of vivid crimson from the bark of the madroños, while the ground on the hillsides, appearing here and there through openings between the groves, displayed masses of pale purple and brown.

The sounds of the storm corresponded gloriously with this wild exuberance of light and motion. The profound bass of the naked branches and boles booming like waterfalls; the quick, tense vibrations of the pine-needles, now rising to a shrill, whistling hiss, now falling to a silky murmur; the rustling of laurel groves in the dells, and the keen metallic click of leaf on leaf—all this was heard in easy analysis when the attention was calmly bent.

The varied gestures of the multitude were seen to fine advantage, so that one could recognize the different species at a distance of several miles by this means alone, as well as by their forms and colors, and the way they reflected the light. All seemed strong and comfortable, as if really enjoying the storm, while responding to its most enthusiastic greetings. We hear much nowadays concerning the universal struggle for existence, but no struggle in the common meaning of the word was manifest here; no recognition of danger by any tree; no deprecation; but rather an invincible gladness as remote from exultation as from fear.

I kept my lofty perch for hours, frequently closing my eyes to enjoy the music by itself or to feast quietly on the delicious fragrance that was streaming past. The fragrance of the woods was less marked than that produced during warm rain, when so many balsamic buds and leaves are steeped like tea; but, from the chafing of resiny branches against each other, and the incessant attrition of myriads of needles, the gale was spiced to a very tonic degree. And besides the fragrance from these local sources there were traces of scents brought from afar. For this wind came first from the sea, rubbing against its fresh, briny waves, then distilled through the redwoods, threading rich ferny gulches, and spreading itself in broad undulating currents over many a flower-enameled ridge of the coast mountains, then across the golden plains, up the purple foot-hills, and into these piny woods with the varied incense gathered by the way.

Winds are advertisements of all they touch, however much or little we may be able to read them; telling their wanderings even by their scents alone. Mariners detect the flowery perfume of land-winds far at sea, and sea-winds carry the fragrance of dulse and tangle far inland, where it is quickly recognized, though mingled with the scents of a thousand land-flowers. As an illustration of this, I may tell here that I breathed sea-air on the Firth of Forth, in Scotland, while a boy; then was taken to Wisconsin, where I remained nineteen years; then, without in all this time having breathed one breath of the sea, I walked quietly, alone, from the middle of the Mississippi Valley to the Gulf of Mexico, on a botanical excursion, and while in Florida, far from the coast, my attention wholly bent on the splendid tropical vegetation about me, I suddenly recognized a sea-breeze, as it came sifting through the palmettos and blooming vine-tangles, which at once awakened and set free a thousand dormant associations, and made me a boy again in Scotland, as if all the intervening years had been annihilated.

Most people like to look at mountain rivers, and bear them in mind; but few care to look at the winds, though far more beautiful and sublime, and though they become at times about as visible as flowing water. When the north winds in winter are making upward sweeps over the curving summits of the High Sierra, the fact is sometimes published with flying snow-banners a mile long. Those portions of the winds thus embodied can scarce be wholly invisible, even to the darkest imagination. And when we look around over an agitated forest, we may see something of the wind that stirs it, by its effects upon the trees. Yonder it descends in a rush of water-like ripples, and sweeps over the bending pines from hill to hill. Nearer, we see detached plumes and leaves, now speeding by on level currents, now whirling in eddies, or, escaping over the edges of the whirls, soaring aloft on grand, upswelling domes of air, or tossing on flame-like crests. Smooth, deep currents, cascades, falls, and swirling eddies, sing around every tree and leaf, and over all the varied topography of the region with telling changes of form, like mountain rivers conforming to the features of their channels.

After tracing the Sierra streams from their fountains to the plains, marking where they bloom white in falls, glide in crystal plumes, surge gray and foam-filled in boulder-choked gorges, and slip through the woods in long, tranquil reaches—after thus learning their language and forms in detail, we may at length hear them chanting all together in one grand anthem, and comprehend them all in clear inner vision, covering the range like lace. But even this spectacle is far less sublime and not a whit more substantial than what we may behold of these storm-streams of air in the mountain woods.

We all travel the milky way together, trees and men; but it never occurred to me until this storm-day, while swinging in the wind, that trees are travelers, in the ordinary sense. They make many journeys, not extensive ones, it is true; but our own little journeys, away and back again, are only little more than tree-wavings—many of them not so much.

When the storm began to abate, I dismounted and sauntered down through the calming woods. The storm-tones died away, and, turning toward the east, I beheld the countless hosts of the forests hushed and tranquil, towering above one another on the slopes of the hills like a devout audience. The setting sun filled them with amber light, and seemed to say, while they listened, "My peace I give unto you."

As I gazed on the impressive scene, all the so-called ruin of the storm was forgotten, and never before did these noble woods appear so fresh, so joyous, so immortal.

Mary Austin

Land of Little Rain

Mary Austin (1868–1934) discovered in California a country quite different from the spectacular peaks of John Muir's Range of Light. She called it the Land of Little Rain, and it stretched across the high desert country east of the Sierra toward the creosote and yuccas and sagebrush of Nevada, a region of dread to early travelers who spoke of its crossing as the jornada del muerto, *the journey of death. To Mary Austin it was a country to celebrate, for nowhere else might one better experience union with the rhythms of creation than in a country "forsaken of most things but beauty and madness and death and God." Born in Illinois, Austin moved to California with her brothers and widowed mother in 1888 to settle on a homestead in the southern San Joaquin Valley. With her husband she later moved to the Panamint region and various areas of the Owens River Valley, where she wrote about the arid land and its dwellers for* The Overland Monthly *in the 1890s. During her subsequent prolific career, while lecturing for feminist, socialist, and American Indian causes, she published over two hundred stories, essays, poems, and reviews, nine novels, three plays, and twelve other books of nonfiction. After the success of her first book, she lived in Carmel and New York, traveled to England and Italy, returned to the desert country in Arizona and New Mexico after the First World War, and settled permanently in Santa Fe for the last ten years of her life. In New Mexico she collected, translated, and interpreted American Indian songs and myths, culminating an interest that began with the Paiutes and Shoshoni in the first of her thirty-five books,* The Land of Little Rain *(1903). From the ritualistic patterns of Indian storytelling, music, and dance and their harmonious linkage to the creative rhythms of the seasons and the land, Austin had come to know, as she said, "It is not that we work on the Cosmos, but it works in us."*

East away from the Sierras, south from Panamint and Amargosa, east and south many an uncounted mile, is the Country of Lost Borders.

Ute, Paiute, Mojave, and Shoshone inhabit its frontiers, and as far into the heart of it as a man dare go. Not the law, but the land sets the limit. Desert is the name it wears upon the maps, but the Indian's is the better word. Desert is a loose term to indicate land that supports no man; whether the land can be bitted and broken to that purpose is not proven. Void of life it never is, however dry the air and villainous the soil.

This is the nature of that country. There are hills, rounded, blunt, burned, squeezed up out of chaos, chrome and vermilion painted, aspiring to the snowline. Between the hills lie high level-looking plains full of intolerable sun glare, or narrow valleys drowned in a blue haze. The hill surface is streaked with ash drift and black, unweathered lava flows. After rains water accumulates in the hollows of small closed valleys, and, evaporating, leaves hard dry levels of pure desertness that get the local name of dry lakes. Where the mountains are steep and the rains heavy, the pool is never quite dry, but dark and bitter, rimmed about with the efflorescence of alkaline deposits. A thin crust of it lies along the marsh over the vegetating area, which has neither beauty nor freshness. In the broad wastes open to the wind the sand drifts in hummocks about the stubby shrubs, and between them the soil shows saline traces. The sculpture of the hills here is more wind than water work, though the quick storms do sometimes scar them past many a year's redeeming. In all the Western desert edges there are essays in miniature at the famed, terrible Grand Cañon, to which, if you keep on long enough in this country, you will come at last.

Since this is a hill country one expects to find springs, but not to depend upon them; for when found they are often brackish and unwholesome, or maddening, slow dribbles in a thirsty soil. Here you find the hot sink of Death Valley, or high rolling districts where the air has always a tang of frost. Here are the long heavy winds and breathless calms on the tilted mesas where dust devils dance, whirling up into a wide, pale sky. Here you have no rain when all the earth cries for

From Mary Austin, *The Land of Little Rain* (Boston: Houghton Mifflin, 1903).

it, or quick downpours called cloud-bursts for violence. A land of lost rivers, with little in it to love; yet a land that once visited must be come back to inevitably. If it were not so there would be little told of it.

This is the country of three seasons. From June on to November it lies hot, still, and unbearable, sick with violent unrelieving storms; then on until April, chill, quiescent, drinking its scant rain and scanter snows; from April to the hot season again, blossoming, radiant, and seductive. These months are only approximate; later or earlier the rain-laden wind may drift up the water gate of the Colorado from the Gulf, and the land sets its seasons by the rain.

The desert floras shame us with their cheerful adaptations to the seasonal limitations. Their whole duty is to flower and fruit, and they do it hardly, or with tropical luxuriance, as the rain admits. It is recorded in the report of the Death Valley expedition that after a year of abundant rains, on the Colorado desert was found a specimen of Amaranthus ten feet high. A year later the same species in the same place matured in the drought at four inches. One hopes the land may breed like qualities in her human offspring, not tritely to "try," but to do. Seldom does the desert herb attain the full stature of the type. Extreme aridity and extreme altitude have the same dwarfing effect, so that we find in the high Sierras and in Death Valley related species in miniature that reach a comely growth in mean temperatures. Very fertile are the desert plants in expedients to prevent evaporation, turning their foliage edgewise toward the sun, growing silky hairs, exuding viscid gum. The wind, which has a long sweep, harries and helps them. It rolls up dunes and the stocky stems, encompassing and protective, and above the dunes, which may be, as with the mesquite, three times as high as a man, the blossoming twigs flourish and bear fruit.

There are many areas in the desert where drinkable water lies within a few feet of the surface, indicated by the mesquite and the bunch grass (Sporobolus airoides). It is this nearness of unimagined help that makes the tragedy of desert deaths. It is related that the final breakdown of that hapless party that gave Death Valley its forbidding name occurred in a locality where shallow wells would have saved them. But how were they to know that? Properly equipped it is possible to go safely across the ghastly sink, yet every year it takes its toll of death, and yet men find there sun-dried mummies, of whom no trace or recollection is preserved. To underestimate one's thirst, to pass a given landmark to the right or left, to find a dry spring where one looked for running water—there is no help for any of these things.

Along springs and sunken watercourses one is surprised to find such water-loving plants as grow widely in moist ground, but the true desert breeds its own kind, each in its particular habitat. The angle of the slope, the frontage of a hill, the structure of the soil determines the plant. South-looking hills are nearly bare, and the lower tree-line higher here by a thousand feet. Cañons running east and west will have one wall naked and one clothed. Around dry lakes and marshes the herbage preserves a set and orderly arrangement. Most species have well-defined areas of growth, the best index the voiceless land can give the traveler of his whereabouts.

If you have any doubt about it, know that the desert begins with the creosote. This immortal shrub spreads down into Death Valley and up to the lower timber-line, odorous and medicinal as you might guess from the name, wandlike, with shining fretted foliage. Its vivid green is grateful to the eye in a wilderness of gray and greenish white shrubs. In the spring it exudes a resinous gum which the Indians of those parts know how to use with pulverized rock for cementing arrow points to shafts. Trust Indians not to miss any virtues of the plant world!

Nothing the desert produces expresses it better than the unhappy growth of the tree yuccas. Tormented, thin forests of it stalk drearily in the high mesas, particularly in that triangular slip that fans out eastward from the meeting of the Sierras and coastwise hills where the first swings across the southern end of the San Joaquin Valley. The yucca bristles with bayonet-pointed leaves, dull green, growing shaggy with age, tipped with panicles of fetid, greenish bloom. After death, which is slow, the ghostly hollow network of its woody skeleton, with hardly power to rot, makes the moonlight fearful. Before the yucca has come to flower, while yet its bloom is a creamy cone-shaped bud of the size of a small cabbage, full of sugary sap, the Indians twist it deftly out of its fence of daggers and roast it for their own delectation. So it is that in those parts where man inhabits one sees young plants of *Yucca arborensis* infrequently. Other yuccas, cacti, low herbs, a thousand sorts, one finds journeying east from the coastwise hills. There is neither poverty of soil nor species to account for the sparseness of desert growth, but simply that each plant requires more room. So much earth must be preëmpted to extract so much moisture. The real struggle for existence, the real brain of the plant, is underground; above there is room for a rounded perfect growth. In Death Valley, reputed the very core of desolation, are nearly two hundred identified species.

Above the lower tree-line, which is also the snow-line, mapped out abruptly by the sun, one finds spreading growth of piñon, juniper, branched nearly to the ground, lilac and sage, and scattering white pines.

There is no special preponderance of self-fertilized or wind-fertilized plants, but everywhere the demand for and evidence of insect life. Now where there are seeds and insects there will be birds and small mammals and where these are, will come the slinking, sharp-toothed kind that prey on them. Go as far as you dare in the heart of a lonely land, you cannot go so far that life and death are not before you. Painted lizards slip in and out of rock crevices, and pant on the white hot sands. Birds, hummingbirds even, nest in the cactus scrub; woodpeckers befriend the demoniac yuccas; out of the stark, treeless waste rings the music of the night-singing mockingbird. If it be summer and the sun well down, there will be a burrowing owl to call. Strange, furry, tricksy things dart across the open places, or sit motionless in the conning towers of the creosote. The poet may have "named all the birds without a gun," but not the fairy-footed, ground-inhabiting, furtive, small folk of the rainless regions. They are too many and too swift; how many you would not believe without seeing the footprint tracings in the sand. They are nearly all night workers, finding the days too hot and white. In mid-desert where there are no cattle, there are no birds of carrion, but if you go far in that direction the chances are that you will find yourself shadowed by their tilted wings. Nothing so large as a man can move unspied upon in that country, and they know well how the land deals with strangers. There are hints to be had here of the way in which a land forces new habits on its dwellers. The quick increase of suns at the end of spring sometimes overtakes birds in their nesting and effects a reversal of the ordinary manner of incubation. It becomes necessary to keep eggs cool rather than warm. One hot, stifling spring in the Little Antelope I had occasion to pass and repass frequently the nest of a pair of meadowlarks, located unhappily in the shelter of a very slender weed. I never caught them sitting except near night, but at midday they stood, or drooped above it, half-fainting with pitifully parted bills, between their treasure and the sun. Sometimes both of them together with wings spread and half lifted continued a spot of shade in a temperature that constrained me at last in a fellow feeling to spare them a bit of canvas for permanent shelter. There was a fence in that country shutting in a cattle range, and along its fifteen miles of posts one could be sure of finding a bird or two in every strip of shadow; sometimes the sparrow and the hawk, with wings trailed and beaks parted, drooping in the white truce of noon.

If one is inclined to wonder at first how so many dwellers came to be in the loneliest land that ever came out of God's hands, what they do there and why stay, one does not wonder so much after having lived there. None other than this long brown land lays such a hold on the affections. The rainbow hills, the tender bluish mists, the luminous radiance of the spring, have the lotus charm. They trick the sense of time, so that once inhabiting there you always mean to go away without quite realizing that you have not done it. Men who have lived there, miners and cattle-men, will tell you this, not so fluently, but emphatically, cursing the land and going back to it. For one thing there is the divinest, cleanest air to be breathed anywhere in God's world. Some day the world will understand that, and the little oases on the windy tops of hills will harbor for healing its ailing, house-weary broods. There is promise there of great wealth in ores and earths, which is no wealth by reason of being so far removed from water and workable conditions, but men are bewitched by it and tempted to try the impossible.

You should hear Salty Williams tell how he used to drive eighteen and twenty-mule teams from the borax marsh to Mojave, ninety miles, with the trail wagon full of water barrels. Hot days the mules would go so mad for drink that the clank of the water bucket set them into an uproar of hideous, maimed noises, and a tangle of harness chains, while Salty would sit on the high seat with the sun glare heavy in his eyes, dealing out curses of pacification in a level, uninterested voice until the clamor fell off from sheer exhaustion. There was a line of shallow graves along that road; they used to count on dropping a man or two of every new gang of coolies brought out in the hot season. But when he lost his swamper, smitten without warning at the noon halt, Salty quit his job; he said it was "too durn hot." The swamper he buried by the way with stones upon him to keep the coyotes from digging him up, and seven years later I read the penciled lines on the pine headboard, still bright and unweathered.

But before that, driving up on the Mojave stage, I met Salty again crossing Indian Wells, his face from the high seat, tanned and ruddy as a harvest moon, looming through the golden dust above his eighteen mules. The land had called him.

The palpable sense of mystery in the desert air breeds fables, chiefly of lost treasure. Somewhere within its stark borders, if one believes report, is a hill strewn with nuggets; one seamed with virgin silver; an old clayey water-bed where Indians scooped up earth to make cooking pots and shaped them reeking with grains of pure gold. Old miners drifting about the desert edges, weathered into the semblance of the tawny hills, will tell you tales like these convincingly. After a little sojourn in that land you will believe them on their own account. It is a question whether it is not better to be bitten by the little horned snake of the desert that goes sidewise and strikes without coiling, than by the tradition of a lost mine.

And yet—and yet—is it not perhaps to satisfy expectation that one falls into the tragic key in writing of desertness? The more you wish of it the more you get, and in the mean time lose much of pleasantness. In that country which begins at the foot of the east slope of the Sierras and spreads out by less and less lofty hill ranges toward the Great Basin, it is possible to live with great zest, to have red blood and delicate joys, to pass and repass about one's daily performance an area that would make an Atlantic seaboard State, and that with no peril, and, according to our way of thought, no particular difficulty. At any rate, it was not people who went into the desert merely to write it up who invented the fabled Hassaympa, of whose waters, if any drink, they can no more see fact as naked fact, but all radiant with the color of romance. I, who must have drunk of it in my twice seven years' wanderings, am assured that it is worth while.

For all the toll the desert takes of a man it gives compensations, deep breaths, deep sleep, and the communion of the stars. It comes upon one with new force in the pauses of the

night that the Chaldeans were a desert-bred people. It is hard
to escape the sense of mastery as the stars move in the wide
clear heavens to rising and settings unobscured. They look
large and near and palpitant; as if they moved on some
stately service not needful to declare. Wheeling to their sta-
tions in the sky, they make the poor world-fret of no account.
Of no account you who lie out there watching, nor the lean
coyote that stands off in the scrub from you and howls and
howls.

John C. Van Dyke

The Desert

John Charles Van Dyke (1856–1932) was the first among early twentieth-century desert writers to draw public attention to the Southwestern desert as a region of beauty. Van Dyke, who described himself as both an "outdoorsman" and "indoorsman," began a lifetime interest in wilderness hiking, canoeing, and camping as a boy when his family moved from the Raritan Valley in New Jersey to a farm in Minnesota. As an indoorsman, Van Dyke became a professor of art history at Rutgers and lectured on modern art at Columbia, Harvard, and Princeton. The years of study, as Van Dyke said, were frequently "interrupted by much travel on both hemispheres, by many returns to the sea, the mountains, the prairies, and the desert." He wrote over forty books on both art and nature but "nature had proved the most lasting love of all. . . . The spell of the wild grows with the years and becomes more insistent." In 1897, he traveled for his health to the Mojave Desert, where his brother had settled. In his efforts to come to know the desert, Van Dyke spent the next few years tramping alone for months at a time across the Mojave, Colorado, and Sonoran deserts. He wrote about desert wildlife and vegetation, but his primary response was to the "tones of color, shades of light, and drifts of air" that produced "the dream landscapes of the Southwestern desert." In The Desert *(1901), exclamation marks fly like sparks from a roman candle as Van Dyke creates his light show of colors and shifting forms. But just when it seems that Van Dyke is interested in the desert as only aesthetic spectacle, the man himself appears alone in the night, and the mystery of the desert becomes a physical presence. It is then that Van Dyke can be understood as the man who criticized earlier desert travelers for reducing the desert landscapes to a human level through architectural terms and mythological names. In his opposition to those who tampered with the desert, he be-*

273

*came an uncompromising conservationist, advocating that
"the deserts should never be reclaimed. They are the breathing spaces of the West and should be preserved forever."*

How silently, even swiftly, the days glide by out in the
desert, in the waste, in the wilderness! How "the morning and
the evening make up the day" and the purple shadows slip in
between with a midnight all stars! And how day by day the
interest grows in the long overlooked commonplace things of
nature! In a few weeks we are studying bushes, bowlders,
stones, sand-drifts—things we never thought of looking at in
any other country. And after a time we begin to make mental
notes on the changes of light, air, clouds, and blue sky. At
first we are perhaps bothered about the intensity of the sky,
for we have always heard of the "deep blue" that overhangs
the desert; and we expect to see it at any and all times. But
we discover that it shows itself in its greatest depth only in
the morning before sunrise. Then it is a dark blue, bordering
upon purple; and for some time after the sun comes up it
holds a deep blue tinge. At noon it has passed through a
whole gamut of tones and is pale blue, yellowish, lilac-toned,
or rosy; in the late afternoon it has changed again to pink or
gold or orange; and after twilight and under the moon, warm
purples stretch across the whole reach of the firmament from
horizon to horizon.

But the changes in the blue during the day have no con-
stancy to a change. There is no fixed purpose about them.
The caprices of light, heat, and dust control the appearances.
Sometimes the sky at dawn is as pallid as a snowdrop with
pearly grays just emerging from the blue; and again it may
be flushed with saffron, rose, and pink. When there are clouds
and great heat the effect is often very brilliant. The colors are
intense in chrome-yellows, golds, carmines, magentas,
malachite-greens—a body of gorgeous hues upheld by enormous side wings of paler tints that encircle the horizon to the
north and south, and send waves of color far up the sky to

From John C. Van Dyke, *The Desert: Further Studies in Natural
Appearances* (New York: Charles Scribner's Sons, 1901).

the cool zenith. Such dawns are seldom seen in moist countries, nor are they usual on the desert, except during the hot
summer months.

The prevailing note of the sky, the one oftenest seen, is of
course, blue—a color we may not perhaps linger over because it is so common. And yet how seldom it is appreciated!
Our attention is called to it in art—in a hawthorn jar as large
as a sugar-bowl, made in a certain period, in a certain Oriental school. The æsthetic world is perhaps set agog by this
ceramic blue. But what are its depth and purity compared to
the ethereal blue! Yet the color is beautiful in the jar and infinitely more beautiful in the sky—that is beautiful in itself
and merely as color. It is not necessary that it should mean
anything. Line and tint do not always require significance to
be beautiful. There is no tale or text or testimony to be tortured out of the blue sky. It is a splendid body of color; no
more.

You cannot always see the wonderful quality of this sky-
blue from the desert valley, because it is disturbed by reflections, by sand-storms, by lower air-strata. The report it makes
of itself when you begin to gain altitude on a mountain's side
is quite different. At four thousand feet the blue is certainly
more positive, more intense, than at sea-level; at six thousand
feet it begins to darken and deepen, and it seems to fit in the
saddles and notches of the mountains like a block of lapis la-
zuli; at eight thousand feet it has darkened still more and has
a violet hue about it. The night sky at this altitude is almost
weird in its purples. A deep violet fits up close to the rim of
the moon, and the orb itself looks like a silver wafer pasted
upon the sky.

The darkening of the sky continues as the height increases.
If one could rise to, say, fifty thousand feet, he would probably see the sun only as a shining point of light, and the
firmament merely as a blue-black background. The diffusion
of light must decrease with the growing thinness of the atmos-
pheric envelope. At what point it would cease and the sky
become perfectly black would be difficult to say, but certainly
the limit would be reached when our atmosphere practically
ceased to exist. Space from necessity must be black except
where the straight beams of light stream from the sun and
the stars.

The bright sky-colors, the spectacular effects, are not to be
found high up in the blue of the dome. The air in the zenith

is too thin, too free from dust, to take deep colorings of red
and orange. These colors belong near the earth, along the
horizons where the aërial envelope is dense. The lower strata
of atmosphere are in fact responsible for the gorgeous sunsets, the tinted hazes, the Indian-summer skies, the hot September glows. These all appear in their splendor when the
sun is near the horizon-line and its beams are falling through
the many miles of hot, dust-laden air that lie along the surface of the earth. The air at sunset after a day of intense
heat-radiation is usually so thick that only the long and
strong waves of color can pass through it. The blues are almost lost, the neutral tints are missing, the greens are seen
but faintly. The waves of red and yellow are the only ones
that travel through the thick air with force. And these are the
colors that tell us the story of the desert sunset.

Ordinarily the sky at evening over the desert, when seen
without clouds, shows the colors of the spectrum beginning
with red at the bottom and running through the yellows,
greens, and blues up to the purple of the zenith. In cool
weather, however, this spectrum arrangement seems swept
out of existence by a broad band of yellow-green that
stretches half way around the circle. It is a pale yellow fading
into a pale green, which in turn melts into a pale blue. In hot
weather this pallor is changed to something much richer and
deeper. A band of orange takes its place. It is a flame-
colored orange, and its hue is felt in reflection upon valley,
plain, and mountain peak. This indeed is the orange light that
converts the air in the mountain canyons into golden mist,
and is measurably responsible for the yellow sunshafts that,
streaming through the pinnacles of the western mountains,
reach far across the upper sky in ever-widening bands. This
great orange belt is lacking in that variety and vividness of
coloring that comes with clouds, but it is not wanting in a
splendor of its own. It is the broadest, the simplest, and in
many respects the sublimest sunset imaginable—a golden
dream with the sky enthroned in glory and the earth at its
feet reflecting its lustre.

But the more brilliant sunsets are only seen when there are
broken translucent clouds in the west. There are cloudy days
even on the desert. After many nights of heat, long skeins of
white stratus will gather along the horizons, and out of them
will slowly be woven forms of the cumulus and the nimbus.
And it will rain in short squalls of great violence on the lo-

mas, mesas, and bordering mountains. But usually the cloud that drenches a mountain top eight thousand feet up will pass over an intervening valley, pouring down the same flood of rain, and yet not a drop of it reaching the ground. The air is always dry and the raindrop that has to fall through eight thousand feet of it before reaching the earth, never gets there. It is evaporated and carried up to its parent cloud again. During the so-called "rainy season" you may frequently see clouds all about the horizon and overhead that are "raining"—letting down long tails and sheets of rain that are plainly visible; but they never touch the earth. The sheet lightens, breaks, and dissipates two thousand feet up. It rains, true enough, but there is no water, just as there are desert rivers, but they have no visible stream. That is the desert of it both above and below.

With the rain come trooping almost all the cloud-forms known to the sky. And the thick ones like the Nimbus carry with them a chilling, deadening effect. The rolls and sheets of rain clouds that cover the heavens at times rob the desert of light, air, and color at one fell swoop. Its beauty vanishes as by magic. Instead of colored haze there is gray gloom settling along the hills and about the mesas. The sands lose their lustre and become dull and formless, the vegetation darkens to a dead gray, and the mountains turn slate-colored, mouldy, unwholesome looking. A mantle of drab envelops the scene, and the glory of the desert has departed.

All the other cloud-forms, being more or less transparent, seem to aid rather than to obscure the splendor of the sky. The most common clouds of all are the cumuli. In hot summer afternoons they gather and heap up in huge masses with turrets and domes of light that reach at times forty thousand feet above the earth. At sunset they begin to show color before any of the other clouds. If seen against the sun their edges at first gleam silver-white and then change to gold; if along the horizon to the north or south, or lying back in the eastern sky, they show dazzling white like a snowy Alp. As the sun disappears below the line they begin to warm in color, turning yellow, pink, and rose. Finally they darken into lilac and purple, then sink and disappear entirely. The smaller forms of cumulus that appear in the west at evening are always splashes of sunset color, sometimes being shot through with yellow or scarlet. They ultimately appear floating against the night sky as spots of purple and gray.

Above the cumuli and often flung across them like bands
of gauze, are the strati—clouds of the middle air region. This
veil or sheet-cloud might be called a twilight cloud, giving out
as it does its greatest splendor after the sun has disappeared
below the verge. It then takes all colors and with singular
vividness. At times it will overspread the whole west as a
sheet of brilliant magenta, but more frequently it blares with
scarlet, carmine, crimson, flushing up and then fading out,
shifting from one color to another; and finally dying out in a
beautiful ashes of roses. When these clouds and all their variations have faded into lilac and deep purples, there are still
bright spots of color in the upper sky where the cirri are receiving the last rays of the sun.

The cirrus with its many feathery and fleecy forms is the
thinnest, the highest, and the most brilliant in light of all the
clouds. Perhaps its brilliancy is due to its being an ice-cloud.
It seems odd that here in the desert with so much heat rising
and tempering the upper air there should be clouds of ice but
a few miles above it. The cirrus and also the higher forms of
the cumulo-stratus are masses of hoar-frost, spicules of ice
floating in the air, instead of tiny globules of vapor.

There is nothing remarkable about the desert clouds—that
is nothing very different from the clouds of other countries—
except in light, color, and background. They appear incom-
parably more brilliant and fiery here than elsewhere on the
globe. The colors, like everything else on the desert, are intense in their power, fierce in their glare. They vibrate, they
scintillate, they penetrate and tinge everything with their hue.
And then, as though heaping splendor upon splendor, what a
wonderful background they are woven upon! Great bands of
orange, green, and blue that all the melted and fused gems in
the world could not match for translucent beauty. Taken as a
whole, as a celestial tapestry, as a curtain of flame drawn between night and day, and what land or sky can rival it!

After the clouds have all shifted into purples and the
western sky has sunk into night, then up from the east the
moon—the misshapen orange-hued desert moon. How large it
looks! And how it warms the sky, and silvers the edges of the
mountain peaks, and spreads its wide light across the sands!
Up, up it rises, losing something of its orange and gaining
something in symmetry. In a few hours it is high in the heavens and has a great aureole of color about it. Look at the
ring for a moment and you will see all the spectrum colors

arranged in order. Pale hues they are but they are all there. Rainbows by day and rainbows by night! Radiant circles of colored light—not one but many. Arches above arches—not two or three but five solar bows in the sky at one time! What strange tales come out of the wilderness! But how much stranger, how much more weird and extraordinary the things that actually happen in this desert land.

High in the zenith rides the desert moon. What a flood of light comes from it! What pale, phosphorescent light! Under it miles and miles of cactus and grease-wood are half revealed, half hidden; and far away against the dark mountains the dunes of the desert shine white as snow-clad hills in December. The stars are forth, the constellations in their places, the planets large and luminous, yet none of them has much color or sparkle. The moon dims them somewhat, but even without the moon they have not the twinkle of the stars in higher, colder latitudes. The desert air seems to veil their lustre somewhat, and yet as points of light set in that purple dome of sky how beautiful they are!

Lying down there in the sands of the desert, alone and at night, with a saddle for your pillow, and your eyes staring upward at the stars, how incomprehensible it all seems! The immensity and the mystery are appalling; and yet how these very features attract the thought and draw the curiosity of man. In the presence of the unattainable and the insurmountable we keep sending a hope, a doubt, a query, up through the realms of air to Saturn's throne. What key have we wherewith to unlock that door? We cannot comprehend a tiny flame of our own invention called electricity, yet we grope at the meaning of the blazing splendor of Arcturus. Around us stretches the great sand-wrapped desert whose mystery no man knows, and not even the Sphinx could reveal; yet beyond it, above it, upward still upward, we seek the mysteries of Orion and the Pleiades.

What is it that draws us to the boundless and the fathomless? Why should the lovely things of earth—the grasses, the trees, the lakes, the little hills—appear trivial and insignificant when we come face to face with the sea or the desert or the vastness of the midnight sky? Is it that the one is the tale of things known and the other merely a hint, a suggestion of the unknown? Or have immensity, space, magnitude a peculiar beauty of their own? Is it not true that bulk and breadth are primary and essential qualities of the sublime in landscape?

And is it not the sublime that we feel in immensity and mystery? If so, perhaps we have a partial explanation of our love for sky and sea and desert waste. They are the great elements. We do not see, we hardly know if their boundaries are limited; we only feel their immensity, their mystery, and their beauty.

And quite as impressive as the mysteries are the silences. Was there ever such a stillness as that which rests upon the desert at night! Was there ever such a hush as that which steals from star to star across the firmament! You perhaps think to break the spell by raising your voice in a cry; but you will not do so again. The sound goes but a little way and then seems to come back to your ear with a suggestion of insanity about it.

A cry in the night! Overhead the planets in their courses make no sound, the earth is still, the very animals are mute. Why then the cry of the human? How it jars the harmonies! How it breaks in discord upon the unities of earth and air and sky! Century after century that cry has gone up, mobbing high heaven; and always insanity in the cry, insanity in the crier. What folly to protest where none shall hear! There is no appeal from the law of nature. It is made for beast and bird and creeping thing. Will the human never learn that in the eye of the law he is not different from the things that creep?

Aldo Leopold

"Thinking Like a Mountain"

Aldo Leopold (1886–1948) was a professional forester who developed an eloquent defense of wilderness protection on moral grounds. Born in Iowa, Leopold was trained at the newly formed Yale School of Forestry and began work in 1909 for the U.S. Forest Service in New Mexico and Arizona Territories, where he carried out his first work in wildlife management. Leopold was a leader in the movement to establish certain national forest lands as "wilderness areas," and his efforts led to the designation of such an area in the Gila National Forest in New Mexico in 1924. Leopold later worked for the National Forest Service in Wisconsin, and in 1933 he became the first professor of game management at the University of Wisconsin, an appointment he held until his death. Leopold's writings stress the necessity of man's changing his fundamental relationship to the wilderness from one of utilitarian interest to moral responsibility. Ethics, not economics, should govern man's relationship to the wilderness, for the natural world is not a collection of things solely for man's use, but a community of interdependent parts to which man belongs. "The Land Ethic," as Leopold develops it, changes man's role from that of conqueror of the natural world to that of a plain citizen and member of it. In relation to the wilderness and the rest of the natural world, Leopold maintains, "A thing is right when it tends to preserve the integrity, stability, and beauty of the biotic community. It is wrong when it tends otherwise." Leopold's writings are now recognized as among the most important and forceful expressions of an "ecological conscience" in the first half of this century, but it took seven years for Leopold to find a publisher for A Sand County Almanac (1949), and it finally appeared the year after Leopold died of a heart attack while fighting a grass fire near his Sand County farm in Wisconsin.

Thinking Like a Mountain

A deep chesty bawl echoes from rimrock to rimrock, rolls
down the mountain, and fades into the far blackness of the
night. It is an outburst of wild defiant sorrow, and of con-
tempt for all the adversities of the world.

Every living thing (and perhaps many a dead one as well)
pays heed to that call. To the deer it is a reminder of the way
of all flesh, to the pine a forecast of midnight scuffles and of
blood upon the snow, to the coyote a promise of gleanings to
come, to the cowman a threat of red ink at the bank, to the
hunter a challenge of fang against bullet. Yet behind these
obvious and immediate hopes and fears there lies a deeper
meaning, known only to the mountain itself. Only the mountain has lived long enough to listen objectively to the howl of
a wolf.

Those unable to decipher the hidden meaning know nevertheless that it is there, for it is felt in all wolf country, and
distinguishes that country from all other land. It tingles in the
spine of all who hear wolves by night, or who scan their
tracks by day. Even without sight or sound of wolf, it is im-
plicit in a hundred small events: the midnight whinny of a
pack horse, the rattle of rolling rocks, the bound of a fleeing
deer, the way shadows lie under the spruces. Only the inedu-
cable tyro can fail to sense the presence or absence of wolves,
or the fact that mountains have a secret opinion about them.

My own conviction on this score dates from the day I saw
a wolf die. We were eating lunch on a high rimrock, at the
foot of which a turbulent river elbowed its way. We saw what
we thought was a doe fording the torrent, her breast awash in
white water. When she climbed the bank toward us and
shook out her tail, we realized our error: it was a wolf. A
half-dozen others, evidently grown pups, sprang from the willows and all joined in a welcoming mêlée of wagging tails
and playful maulings. What was literally a pile of wolves
writhed and tumbled in the center of an open flat at the foot
of our rimrock.

In those days we had never heard of passing up a chance

From Aldo Leopold, *A Sand County Almanac and Sketches Here
and There* (New York: Oxford University Press, 1949).

to kill a wolf. In a second we were pumping lead into the pack, but with more excitement than accuracy: how to aim a steep downhill shot is always confusing. When our rifles were empty, the old wolf was down, and a pup was dragging a leg into impassable slide-rocks.

We reached the old wolf in time to watch a fierce green fire dying in her eyes. I realized then, and have known ever since, that there was something new to me in those eyes— something known only to her and to the mountain. I was young then, and full of trigger-itch; I thought that because fewer wolves meant more deer, that no wolves would mean hunters' paradise. But after seeing the green fire die, I sensed that neither the wolf nor the mountain agreed with such a view.

Since then I have lived to see state after state extirpate its wolves. I have watched the face of many a newly wolfless mountain, and seen the south-facing slopes wrinkle with a maze of new deer trails. I have seen every edible bush and seedling browsed, first to anaemic desuetude, and then to death. I have seen every edible tree defoliated to the height of a saddlehorn. Such a mountain looks as if someone had given God a new pruning shears, and forbidden Him all other exercise. In the end the starved bones of the hoped-for deer herd, dead of its own too-much, bleach with the bones of the dead sage, or molder under the high-lined junipers.

I now suspect that just as a deer herd lives in mortal fear of its wolves, so does a mountain live in mortal fear of its deer. And perhaps with better cause, for while a buck pulled down by wolves can be replaced in two or three years, a range pulled down by too many deer may fail of replacement in as many decades.

So also with cows. The cowman who cleans his range of wolves does not realize that he is taking over the wolf's job of trimming the herd to fit the range. He has not learned to think like a mountain. Hence we have dustbowls, and rivers washing the future into the sea.

We all strive for safety, prosperity, comfort, long life, and dullness. The deer strives with his supple legs, the cowman with trap and poison, the statesman with pen, the most of us with machines, votes, and dollars, but it all comes to the same thing: peace in our time. A measure of success in this is

all well enough, and perhaps is a requisite to objective thinking, but too much safety seems to yield only danger in the
long run. Perhaps this is behind Thoreau's dictum: In
wildness is the salvation of the world. Perhaps this is the hidden meaning in the howl of the wolf, long known among
mountains, but seldom perceived among men. . . .

The Green Lagoons

It is the part of wisdom never to revisit a wilderness, for
the more golden the lily, the more certain that someone has
gilded it. To return not only spoils a trip, but tarnishes a
memory. It is only in the mind that shining adventure remains forever bright. For this reason, I have never gone back
to the Delta of the Colorado since my brother and I explored
it, by canoe, in 1922.

For all we could tell, the Delta had lain forgotten since
Hernando de Alarcón landed there in 1540. When we
camped on the estuary which is said to have harbored his
ships, we had not for weeks seen a man or a cow, an axe-cut
or a fence. Once we crossed an old wagon track, its maker
unknown and its errand probably sinister. Once we found a
tin can; it was pounced upon as a valuable utensil.

Dawn on the Delta was whistled in by Gambel quail,
which roosted in the mesquites overhanging camp. When the
sun peeped over the Sierra Madre, it slanted across a hundred
miles of lovely desolation, a vast flat bowl of wilderness
rimmed by jagged peaks. On the map the Delta was bisected
by the river, but in fact the river was nowhere and everywhere, for he could not decide which of a hundred green lagoons offered the most pleasant and least speedy path to the
Gulf. So he traveled them all, and so did we. He divided and
rejoined, he twisted and turned, he meandered in awesome
jungles, he all but ran in circles, he dallied with lovely groves,
he got lost and was glad of it, and so were we. For the last
word in procrastination, go travel with a river reluctant to
lose his freedom in the sea.

'He leadeth me by still waters' was to us only a phrase in a
book until we had nosed our canoe through the green lagoons. If David had not written the psalm, we should have
felt constrained to write our own. The still waters were of a
deep emerald hue, colored by algae, I suppose, but no less

green for all that. A verdant wall of mesquite and willow separated the channel from the thorny desert beyond. At each
bend we saw egrets standing in the pools ahead, each white
statue matched by its white reflection. Fleets of cormorants
drove their black prows in quest of skittering mullets; avocets, willets, and yellow-legs dozed one-legged on the bars;
mallards, widgeons, and teal sprang skyward in alarm. As the
birds took the air, they accumulated in a small cloud ahead,
there to settle, or to break back to our rear. When a troop of
egrets settled on a far green willow, they looked like a premature snowstorm.

All this wealth of fowl and fish was not for our delectation
alone. Often we came upon a bobcat, flattened to some half-
immersed driftwood log, paw poised for mullet. Families of
raccoons waded the shallows, munching water beetles. Coyotes watched us from inland knolls, waiting to resume their
breakfast of mesquite beans, varied, I suppose, by an occasional crippled shore bird, duck, or quail. At every shallow
ford were tracks of burro deer. We always examined these
deer trails, hoping to find signs of the despot of the Delta, the
great jaguar, *el tigre*.

We saw neither hide nor hair of him, but his personality
pervaded the wilderness; no living beast forgot his potential
presence, for the price of unwariness was death. No deer
rounded a bush, or stopped to nibble pods under a mesquite
tree, without a premonitory sniff for *el tigre*. No campfire
died without talk of him. No dog curled up for the night,
save at his master's feet; he needed no telling that the king of
cats still ruled the night; that those massive paws could fell
an ox, those jaws shear off bones like a guillotine.

By this time the Delta has probably been made safe for
cows, and forever dull for adventuring hunters. Freedom
from fear has arrived, but a glory has departed from the
green lagoons.

When Kipling smelled the supper smokes of Amritsar, he
should have elaborated, for no other poet has sung, or
smelled, this green earth's firewoods. Most poets must have
subsisted on anthracite.

On the Delta one burns only mesquite, the ultimate in
fragrant fuels. Brittle with a hundred frosts and floods, baked
by a thousand suns, the gnarled imperishable bones of these
ancient trees lie ready-to-hand at every camp, ready to slant
blue smoke across the twilight, sing a song of teapots, bake a

loaf, brown a kettle of quail, and warm the shins of man and
beast. When you have ladled a shovelful of mesquite coals
under the Dutch oven, take care not to sit down in that spot
before bedtime, lest you rise with a yelp that scares the quail
roosting overhead. Mesquite coals have seven lives.

We had cooked with white-oak coals in the corn belt, we
had smudged our pots with pine in the north woods, we had
browned venison ribs over Arizona juniper, but we had not
seen perfection until we roasted a young goose with Delta
mesquite.

Those geese deserved the best of brownings, for they had
bested us for a week. Every morning we watched the cackling
phalanx head inland from the Gulf, shortly to return, replete
and silent. What rare provender in what green lagoon was the
object of their quest? Again and again we moved camp
gooseward, hoping to see them settle, to find their banquet
board. One day at about 8 a.m. we saw the phalanx circle,
break ranks, sideslip, and fall to earth like maple leaves.
Flock after flock followed. At long last we had found their
rendezvous.

Next morning at the same hour we lay in wait beside an
ordinary-looking slough, its bars covered with yesterday's
goosetracks. We were already hungry, for it had been a long
tramp from camp. My brother was eating a cold roast quail.
The quail was halfway to his mouth when a cackle from the
sky froze us to immobility. That quail hung in midair when
the flock circled at leisure, debated, hesitated, and finally
came in. That quail fell in the sand when the guns spoke, and
all the geese we could eat lay kicking on the bar.

More came, and settled. The dog lay trembling. We ate
quail at leisure, peering through the blind, listening to the
small-talk. Those geese were gobbling *gravel*. As one flock
filled up and left, another arrived, eager for their delectable
stones. Of all the millions of pebbles in the green lagoons,
those on this particular bar suited them best. The difference,
to a snow goose, was worth forty miles of flying. It was
worth a long hike to us.

Most small game on the Delta was too abundant to hunt.
At every camp we hung up, in a few minutes' shooting,
enough quail for tomorrow's use. Good gastronomy de-
manded at least one frosty night on the stringer as the necessary interlude between roosting in a mesquite and roasting
over mesquite.

All game was of incredible fatness. Every deer laid down so much tallow that the dimple along his backbone would have held a small pail of water, had he allowed us to pour it. He didn't.

The origin of all this opulence was not far to seek. Every mesquite and every tornillo was loaded with pods. The dried-up mud flats bore an annual grass, the grain-like seeds of which could be scooped up by the cupful. There were great patches of a legume resembling coffeeweed; if you walked through these, your pockets filled up with shelled beans.

I remember one patch of wild melons, or *calabasillas*, covering several acres of mudflat. The deer and coons had opened the frozen fruits, exposing the seeds. Doves and quail fluttered over this banquet like fruit-flies over a ripe banana.

We could not, or at least did not, eat what the quail and deer did, but we shared their evident delight in this milk-and-honey wilderness. Their festival mood became our mood; we all reveled in a common abundance and in each other's well-being. I cannot recall feeling, in settled country, a like sensitivity to the mood of the land.

Camp-keeping in the Delta was not all beer and skittles. The problem was water. The lagoons were saline; the river, where we could find it, was too muddy to drink. At each new camp we dug a new well. Most wells, however, yielded only brine from the Gulf. We learned, the hard way, where to dig for sweet water. When in doubt about a new well, we lowered the dog by his hind legs. If he drank freely, it was the signal for us to beach the canoe, kindle the fire, and pitch the tent. Then we sat at peace with the world while the quail sizzled in the Dutch oven, and the sun sank in glory behind the San Pedro Mártir. Later, dishes washed, we rehearsed the day, and listened to the noises of the night.

Never did we plan the morrow, for we had learned that in the wilderness some new and irresistible distraction is sure to turn up each day before breakfast. Like the river, we were free to wander.

To travel by plan in the Delta is no light matter; we were reminded of this whenever we climbed a cottonwood for a wider view. The view was so wide as to discourage prolonged scrutiny, especially toward the northwest, where a white streak at the foot of the Sierra hung in perpetual mirage. This was the great salt desert, on which, in 1829, Alexander Pattie died of thirst, exhaustion, and mosquitoes. Pattie had a plan: to cross the Delta to California.

Once we had a plan to portage from one green lagoon to a greener one. We knew it was there by the waterfowl hovering over it. The distance was 300 yards through a jungle of *cachinilla,* a tall spear-like shrub which grows in thickets of incredible density. The floods had bent down the spears, which opposed our passage in the manner of a Macedonian phalanx. We discreetly withdrew, persuaded that our lagoon was prettier anyhow.

Getting caught in a maze of *cachinilla* phalanxes was a real danger that no one had mentioned, whereas the danger we had been warned against failed to materialize. When we launched our canoe above the border, there were dire predictions of sudden death. Far huskier craft, we were told, had been overwhelmed by the tidal bore, a wall of water that rages up the river from the Gulf with certain incoming tides. We talked about the bore, we spun elaborate schemes to circumvent it, we even saw it in our dreams, with dolphins riding its crest and an aerial escort of screaming gulls. When we reached the mouth of the river, we hung our canoe in a tree and waited two days, but the bore let us down. It did not come.

The Delta having no place names, we had to devise our own as we went. One lagoon we called the Rillito, and it is here that we saw pearls in the sky. We were lying flat on our backs, soaking up November sun, staring idly at a soaring buzzard overhead. Far beyond him the sky suddenly exhibited a rotating circle of white spots, alternately visible and invisible. A faint bugle note soon told us they were cranes, inspecting their Delta and finding it good. At the time my ornithology was homemade, and I was pleased to think them whooping cranes because they were so white. Doubtless they were sandhill cranes, but it doesn't matter. What matters is that we were sharing our wilderness with the wildest of living fowl. We and they had found a common home in the remote fastnesses of space and time; we were both back in the Pleistocene. Had we been able to, we would have bugled back their greeting. Now, from the far reaches of the years, I see them wheeling still.

All this was far away and long ago. I am told the green lagoons now raise cantaloupes. If so, they should not lack flavor.

Man always kills the thing he loves, and so we the pioneers have killed our wilderness. Some say we had to. Be that as it may, I am glad I shall never be young without wild country to be young in. Of what avail are forty freedoms without a blank spot on the map?

Rachel Carson

The Edge of the Sea

Rachel Carson (1907–1964) reminds us that wilderness as an area undominated by the works of man extends in its wildest, though not unviolated, state from the edge of the sea to its depths. A graduate of Pennsylvania College for Women, Carson received a master's degree in zoology from Johns Hopkins and taught at the University of Maryland before joining the U.S. Bureau of Fisheries as a marine biologist in 1936. Her career as both writer and scientist led to the position of chief editor for the U.S. Fish and Wildlife Service until 1952, when she resigned to devote full time to her writing. Carson is credited with helping to bring an ecological awareness to contemporary America. Her first book, Under the Sea-Wind *(1941), was followed by a best seller,* The Sea Around Us *(1951), and* The Edge of the Sea *(1955), a book intended to "take the seashore out of the category of scenery and make it come alive." In 1962 she jolted the consciences of many when* Silent Spring *brought to public attention the "alarming misfortune" that a primitive form of science "has armed itself with the most modern and terrible weapons, and that in turning them against the insects it has also turned them against the earth." Although Carson is best known for pointing out man's physical dependence on the natural world, her belief in man's spiritual dependence informs her work from its beginning. She believed that whenever there occurs any destruction or substitution of a wild or natural feature of the earth by something artificial or man-made, "we have retarded some part of man's spiritual growth." Aware of this central view informing her life's work, Carson requested that the last of the following selections from* The Edge of the Sea *be read at her funeral.*

The edge of the sea is a strange and beautiful place. All through the long history of Earth it has been an area of unrest where waves have broken heavily against the land, where the tides have pressed forward over the continents, receded, and then returned. For no two successive days is the shore line precisely the same. Not only do the tides advance and retreat in their eternal rhythms, but the level of the sea itself is never at rest. It rises or falls as the glaciers melt or grow, as the floor of the deep ocean basins shifts under its increasing load of sediments, or as the earth's crust along the continental margins warps up or down in adjustment to strain and tension. Today a little more land may belong to the sea, tomorrow a little less. Always the edge of the sea remains an elusive and indefinable boundary.

The shore has a dual nature, changing with the swing of the tides, belonging now to the land, now to the sea. On the ebb tide it knows the harsh extremes of the land world, being exposed to heat and cold, to wind, to rain and drying sun. On the flood tide it is a water world, returning briefly to the relative stability of the open sea.

Only the most hardy and adaptable can survive in a region so mutable, yet the area between the tide lines is crowded with plants and animals. In this difficult world of the shore, life displays its enormous toughness and vitality by occupying almost every conceivable niche. Visibly, it carpets the intertidal rocks; or half hidden, it descends into fissures and crevices, or hides under boulders, or lurks in the wet gloom of sea caves. Invisibly, where the casual observer would say there is no life, it lies deep in the sand, in burrows and tubes and passageways. It tunnels into solid rock and bores into peat and clay. It encrusts weeds or drifting spars or the hard, chitinous shell of a lobster. It exists minutely, as the film of bacteria that spreads over a rock surface or a wharf piling; as spheres of protozoa, small as pinpricks, sparkling at the surface of the sea; and as Lilliputian beings swimming through dark pools that lie between the grains of sand.

The shore is an ancient world, for as long as there has been an earth and sea there has been this place of the meeting of land and water. Yet it is a world that keeps alive the sense of continuing creation and of the relentless drive of life.

From Rachel Carson, *The Edge of the Sea* (Boston: Houghton Mifflin, 1955).

Each time that I enter it, I gain some new awareness of its beauty and its deeper meanings, sensing that intricate fabric of life by which one creature is linked with another, and each with its surroundings.

In my thoughts of the shore, one place stands apart for its revelation of exquisite beauty. It is a pool hidden within a cave that one can visit only rarely and briefly when the lowest of the year's low tides fall below it, and perhaps from that very fact it acquires some of its special beauty. Choosing such a tide, I hoped for a glimpse of the pool. The ebb was to fall early in the morning. I knew that if the wind held from the northwest and no interfering swell ran in from a distant storm the level of the sea should drop below the entrance to the pool. There had been sudden ominous showers in the night, with rain like handfuls of gravel flung on the roof. When I looked out into the early morning the sky was full of a gray dawn light but the sun had not yet risen. Water and air were pallid. Across the bay the moon was a luminous disc in the western sky, suspended above the dim line of distant shore—the full August moon, drawing the tide to the low, low levels of the threshold of the alien sea world. As I watched, a gull flew by, above the spruces. Its breast was rosy with the light of the unrisen sun. The day was, after all, to be fair.

Later, as I stood above the tide near the entrance to the pool, the promise of that rosy light was sustained. From the base of the steep wall of rocks on which I stood, a moss-covered ledge jutted seaward into deep water. In the surge at the rim of the ledge the dark fronds of oarweeds swayed, smooth and gleaming as leather. The projecting ledge was the path to the small hidden cave and its pool. Occasionally a swell, stronger than the rest, rolled smoothly over the rim and broke in foam against the cliff. But the intervals between such swells were long enough to admit me to the ledge and long enough for a glimpse of that fairy pool, so seldom and so briefly exposed.

And so I knelt on the wet carpet of sea moss and looked back into the dark cavern that held the pool in a shallow basin. The floor of the cave was only a few inches below the roof, and a mirror had been created in which all that grew on the ceiling was reflected in the still water below.

Under water that was clear as glass the pool was carpeted with green sponge. Gray patches of sea squirts glistened on the ceiling and colonies of soft coral were a pale apricot color. In the moment when I looked into the cave a little elfin starfish hung down, suspended by the merest thread, perhaps by only a single tube foot. It reached down to touch its own reflection, so perfectly delineated that there might have been, not one starfish, but two. The beauty of the reflected images and of the limpid pool itself was the poignant beauty of things that are ephemeral, existing only until the sea should return to fill the little cave.

Whenever I go down into this magical zone of the low water of the spring tides, I look for the most delicately beautiful of all the shore's inhabitants—flowers that are not plant but animal, blooming on the threshold of the deeper sea. In that fairy cave I was not disappointed. Hanging from its roof were the pendent flowers of the hydroid Tubularia, pale pink, fringed and delicate as the wind flower. Here were creatures so exquisitely fashioned that they seemed unreal, their beauty too fragile to exist in a world of crushing force. Yet every detail was functionally useful, every stalk and hydranth and petal-like tentacle fashioned for dealing with the realities of existence. I knew that they were merely waiting, in that moment of the tide's ebbing, for the return of the sea. Then in the rush of water, in the surge of surf and the pressure of the incoming tide, the delicate flower heads would stir with life. They would sway on their slender stalks, and their long tentacles would sweep the returning water, finding in it all that they needed for life.

And so in that enchanted place on the threshold of the sea the realities that possessed my mind were far from those of the land world I had left an hour before. In a different way the same sense of remoteness and of a world apart came to me in a twilight hour on a great beach on the coast of Georgia. I had come down after sunset and walked far out over sands that lay wet and gleaming, to the very edge of the retreating sea. Looking back across that immense flat, crossed by winding, water-filled gullies and here and there holding shallow pools left by the tide, I was filled with awareness that this intertidal area, although abandoned briefly and rhythmically by the sea, is always reclaimed by the rising tide. There at the edge of the low water the beach with its reminders of the land seemed far away. The only sounds were those of the wind and the sea and the birds. There was one sound of wind moving over water, and another of water sliding over the sand and tumbling down the faces of its own wave forms. The flats were astir with birds, and the voice of the willet rang insistently. One of them stood at the edge of the water and gave its loud, urgent cry; an answer came from far up the beach and the two birds flew to join each other.

The flats took on a mysterious quality as dusk approached and the last evening light was reflected from the scattered pools and creeks. Then birds became only dark shadows, with no color discernible. Sanderlings scurried across the beach like little ghosts, and here and there the darker forms of the willets stood out. Often I could come very close to them before they would start up in alarm—the sanderlings running, the willets flying up, crying. Black skimmers flew along the ocean's edge silhouetted against the dull, metallic gleam, or they went flitting above the sand like large, dimly seen moths. Sometimes they "skimmed" the winding creeks of tidal water, where little spreading surface ripples marked the presence of small fish.

The shore at night is a different world, in which the very darkness that hides the distractions of daylight brings into sharper focus the elemental realities. Once, exploring the night beach, I surprised a small ghost crab in the searching beam of my torch. He was lying in a pit he had dug just above the surf, as though watching the sea and waiting. The blackness of the night possessed water, air, and beach. It was the darkness of an older world, before Man. There was no sound but the all-enveloping, primeval sounds of wind blowing over water and sand, and of waves crashing on the beach. There was no other visible life—just one small crab near the sea. I have seen hundreds of ghost crabs in other settings, but suddenly I was filled with the odd sensation that for the first time I knew the creature in its own world—that I understood, as never before, the essence of its being. In that moment time was suspended; the world to which I belonged did not exist and I might have been an onlooker from outer space. The little crab alone with the sea became a symbol that stood for life itself—for the delicate, destructible, yet incredibly vital force that somehow holds its place amid the harsh realities of the inorganic world.

The sense of creation comes with memories of a southern coast, where the sea and the mangroves, working together, are building a wilderness of thousands of small islands off the southwestern coast of Florida, separated from each other by a tortuous pattern of bays, lagoons, and narrow waterways. I remember a winter day when the sky was blue and drenched with sunlight; though there was no wind one was conscious of flowing air like cold clear crystal. I had landed on the surf-washed tip of one of those islands, and then worked my way around to the sheltered bay side. There I found the tide far out, exposing the broad mud flat of a cove bordered by the mangroves with their twisted branches, their glossy leaves, and their long prop roots reaching down, grasping and holding the mud, building the land out a little more, then again a little more.

The mud flats were strewn with the shells of that small, exquisitely colored mollusk, the rose tellin, looking like scattered petals of pink roses. There must have been a colony nearby, living buried just under the surface of the mud. At first the only creature visible was a small heron in gray and rusty plumage—a reddish egret that waded across the flat with the stealthy, hesitant movements of its kind. But other land creatures had been there, for a line of fresh tracks wound in and out among the mangrove roots, marking the path of a raccoon feeding on the oysters that gripped the supporting roots with projections from their shells. Soon I found the tracks of a shore bird, probably a sanderling, and followed them a little; then they turned toward the water and were lost, for the tide had erased them and made them as though they had never been.

Looking out over the cove I felt a strong sense of the interchangeability of land and sea in this marginal world of the shore, and of the links between the life of the two. There was also an awareness of the past and of the continuing flow of time, obliterating much that had gone before, as the sea had that morning washed away the tracks of the bird.

The sequence and meaning of the drift of time were quietly summarized in the existence of hundreds of small snails —the mangrove periwinkles—browsing on the branches and roots of the trees. Once their ancestors had been sea dwellers, bound to the salt waters by every tie of their life processes. Little by little over the thousands and millions of years the ties had been broken, the snails had adjusted themselves to life out of water, and now today they were living many feet above the tide to which they only occasionally returned. And perhaps, who could say how many ages hence, there would be in their descendants not even this gesture of remembrance for the sea.

The spiral shells of other snails—these quite minute—left winding tracks on the mud as they moved about in search of food. They were horn shells, and when I saw them I had a nostalgic moment when I wished I might see what Audubon saw, a century and more ago. For such little horn shells were the food of the flamingo, once so numerous on this coast, and when I half closed my eyes I could almost imagine a flock of these magnificent flame birds feeding in that cove, filling it with their color. It was a mere yesterday in the life of the earth that they were there; in nature, time and space are relative matters, perhaps most truly perceived subjectively in occasional flashes of insight, sparked by such a magical hour and place.

There is a common thread that links these scenes and memories—the spectacle of life in all its varied manifestations as it has appeared, evolved, and sometimes died out. Underlying the beauty of the spectacle there is meaning and significance. It is the elusiveness of that meaning that haunts us, that sends us again and again into the natural world where the key to the riddle is hidden. It sends us back to the edge of the sea, where the drama of life played its first scene on earth and perhaps even its prelude; where the forces of evolution are at work today, as they have been since the appearance of what we know as life; and where the spectacle of living creatures faced by the cosmic realities of their world is crystal clear . . . .

Some of the most beautiful pools of the shore are not exposed to the view of the casual passer-by. They must be searched for—perhaps in low-lying basins hidden by great rocks that seem to be heaped in disorder and confusion, perhaps in darkened recesses under a projecting ledge, perhaps behind a thick curtain of concealing weeds.

I know such a hidden pool. It lies in a sea cave, at low tide filling perhaps the lower third of its chamber. As the flooding tide returns the pool grows, swelling in volume until all the cave is water-filled and the cave and the rocks that form and contain it are drowned beneath the fullness of the tide. When the tide is low, however, the cave may be approached from the landward side. Massive rocks form its floor and walls and roof. They are penetrated by only a few openings—two near the floor on the sea side and one high on the landward wall.

Here one may lie on the rocky threshold and peer through
the low entrance into the cave and down into its pool. The
cave is not really dark; indeed on a bright day it glows with a
cool green light. The source of this soft radiance is the sunlight that enters through the openings low on the floor of the
pool, but only after its entrance into the pool does the light
itself become transformed, invested with a living color of
purest, palest green that it borrowed from the covering of
sponge on the floor of the cave.

Through the same openings that admit the light, fish come
in from the sea, explore the green hall, and depart again into
the vaster waters beyond. Through those low portals the tides
ebb and flow. Invisibly, they bring in minerals—the raw
materials for the living chemistry of the plants and animals
of the cave. They bring, invisibly again, the larvae of many
sea creatures—drifting, drifting in their search for a resting
place. Some may remain and settle here; others will go out
on the next tide.

Looking down into the small world confined within the
walls of the cave, one feels the rhythms of the greater sea
world beyond. The waters of the pool are never still. Their
level changes not only gradually with the rise and fall of the
tide, but also abruptly with the pulse of the surf. As the back-
wash of a wave draws it seaward, the water falls away rapidly; then with a sudden reversal the inrushing water foams
and surges upward almost to one's face.

On the outward movement one can look down and see
the floor, its details revealed more clearly in the shallowing
water. The green crumb-of-bread sponge covers much of the
bottom of the pool, forming a thick-piled carpet built of
tough little feltlike fibers laced together with glassy, double-
pointed needles of silica—the spicules or skeletal supports of
the sponge. The green color of the carpet is the pure color of
chlorophyll, this plant pigment being confined within the cells
of an alga that are scattered through the tissues of the animal
host. The sponge clings closely to the rock, by the very
smoothness and flatness of its growth testifying to the stream-
lining force of heavy surf. In quiet waters the same species
sends up many projecting cones; here these would give the
turbulent waters a surface to grip and tear.

Interrupting the green carpet are patches of other colors,
one a deep, mustard yellow, probably a growth of the sulphur
sponge. In the fleeting moment when most of the water has

drained away, one has glimpses of a rich orchid color in the deepest part of the cave—the color of the encrusting coralline algae.

Sponges and corallines together form a background for the larger tide-pool animals. In the quiet of ebb tide there is little or no visible movement even among the predatory starfish that cling to the walls like ornamental fixtures painted orange or rose or purple. A group of large anemones lives on the wall of the cave, their apricot color vivid against the green sponge. Today all the anemones may be attached on the north wall of the pool, seemingly immobile and immovable; on the next spring tides when I visit the pool again some of them may have shifted over to the west wall and there taken up their station, again seemingly immovable.

There is abundant promise that the anemone colony is a thriving one and will be maintained. On the walls and ceiling of the cave are scores of baby anemones—little glistening mounds of soft tissue, a pale, translucent brown. But the real nursery of the colony seems to be in a sort of antechamber opening into the central cave. There a roughly cylindrical space no more than a foot across is enclosed by high perpendicular rock walls to which hundreds of baby anemones cling.

On the roof of the cave is written a starkly simple statement of the force of the surf. Waves entering a confined space always concentrate all their tremendous force for a driving, upward leap; in this manner the roofs of caves are gradually battered away. The open portal in which I lie saves the ceiling of this cave from receiving the full force of such upward-leaping waves; nevertheless, the creatures that live there are exclusively a heavy-surf fauna. It is a simple black and white mosaic—the black of mussel shells, on which the white cones of barnacles are growing. For some reason the barnacles, skilled colonizers of surf-swept rocks though they be, seem to have been unable to get a foothold directly on the roof of the cave. Yet the mussels have done so. I do not know how this happened but I can guess. I can imagine the young mussels creeping in over the damp rock while the tide is out, spinning their silk threads that bind them securely, anchoring them against the returning waters. And then in time, perhaps, the growing colony of mussels gave the infant barnacles a foothold more tenable than the smooth rock, so that they were able to cement themselves to the mussel shells. However it came about, that is the way we find them now.

As I lie and look into the pool there are moments of relative quiet, in the intervals when one wave has receded and the next has not yet entered. Then I can hear the small sounds: the sound of water dripping from the mussels on the ceiling or of water dripping from seaweeds that line the walls—small, silver splashes losing themselves in the vastness of the pool and in the confused, murmurous whisperings that emanate from the pool itself—the pool that is never quite still.

Then as my fingers explore among the dark red thongs of the dulse and push away the fronds of the Irish moss that cover the walls beneath me, I begin to find creatures of such extreme delicacy that I wonder how they can exist in this cave when the brute force of storm surf is unleashed within its confined space.

Adhering to the rock walls are thin crusts of one of the bryozoans, a form in which hundreds of minute, flask-shaped cells of a brittle structure, fragile as glass, lie one against another in regular rows to form a continuous crust. The color is a pale apricot; the whole seems an ephemeral creation that would crumble away at a touch, as hoarfrost before the sun.

A tiny spiderlike creature with long and slender legs runs about over the crust. For some reason that may have to do with its food, it is the same apricot color as the bryozoan carpet beneath it; the sea spider, too, seems the embodiment of fragility.

Another bryozoan of coarser, upright growth, Flustrella, sends up little club-shaped projections from a basal mat. Again, the lime-impregnated clubs seem brittle and glassy. Over and among them, innumerable little roundworms crawl with serpentine motion, slender as threads. Baby mussels creep in their tentative exploration of a world so new to them they have not yet found a place to anchor themselves by slender silken lines.

Exploring with my lens, I find many very small snails in the fronds of seaweed. One of them has obviously not been long in the world, for its pure white shell has formed only the first turn of the spiral that will turn many times upon itself in growth from infancy to maturity. Another, no larger, is nevertheless older. Its shining amber shell is coiled like a French horn and, as I watch, the tiny creature within thrusts out a bovine head and seems to be regarding its surroundings with two black eyes, small as the smallest pinpoints.

But seemingly most fragile of all are the little calcareous sponges that here and there exist among the seaweeds. They form masses of minute, upthrust tubes of vase-like form, none more than half an inch high. The wall of each is a mesh of fine threads—a web of starched lace made to·fairy scale.

I could have crushed any of these fragile structures between my fingers—yet somehow they find it possible to exist here, amid the surging thunder of the surf that must fill this cave as the sea comes in. Perhaps the seaweeds are the key to the mystery, their resilient fronds a sufficient cushion for all the minute and delicate beings they contain.

But it is the sponges that give to the cave and its pool their special quality—the sense of a continuing flow of time. For each day that I visit the pool on the lowest tides of the summer they seem unchanged—the same in July, the same in August, the same in September. And they are the same this year as last, and presumably as they will be a hundred or a thousand summers hence.

Simple in structure, little different from the first sponges that spread their mats on ancient rocks and drew their food from a primordial sea, the sponges bridge the eons of time. The green sponge that carpets the floor of this cave grew in other pools before this shore was formed; it was old when the first creatures came out of the sea in those ancient eras of the Paleozoic, 300 million years ago; it existed even in the dim past before the first fossil record, for the hard little spicules—all that remains when the living tissue is gone—are found in the first fossil-bearing rocks, those of the Cambrian period.

So, in the hidden chamber of that pool, time echoes down the long ages to a present that is but a moment.

As I watched, a fish swam in, a shadow in the green light, entering the pool by one of the openings low on its seaward wall. Compared with the ancient sponges, the fish was almost a symbol of modernity, its fishlike ancestry traceable only half as far into the past. And I, in whose eyes the images of the two were beheld as though they were contemporaries, was a mere newcomer whose ancestors had inhabited the earth so briefly that my presence was almost anachronistic.

As I lay at the threshold of the cave thinking those thoughts, the surge of waters rose and flooded across the rock on which I rested. The tide was rising. . . .

Now I hear the sea sounds about me; the night high tide is rising, swirling with a confused rush of waters against the rocks below my study window. Fog has come into the bay from the open sea, and it lies over water and over the land's edge, seeping back into the spruces and stealing softly among the juniper and the bayberry. The restive waters, the cold wet breath of the fog, are of a world in which man is an uneasy trespasser; he punctuates the night with the complaining groan and grunt of a foghorn, sensing the power and menace of the sea.

Hearing the rising tide, I think how it is pressing also against other shores I know—rising on a southern beach where there is no fog, but a moon edging all the waves with silver and touching the wet sands with lambent sheen, and on a still more distant shore sending its streaming currents against the moonlit pinnacles and the dark caves of the coral rock.

Then in my thoughts these shores, so different in their nature and in the inhabitants they support, are made one by the unifying touch of the sea. For the differences I sense in this particular instant of time that is mine are but the differences of a moment, determined by our place in the stream of time and in the long rhythms of the sea. Once this rocky coast beneath me was a plain of sand; then the sea rose and found a new shore line. And again in some shadowy future the surf will have ground these rocks to sand and will have returned the coast to its earlier state. And so in my mind's eye these coastal forms merge and blend in a shifting, kaleidoscopic pattern in which there is no finality, no ultimate and fixed reality—earth becoming fluid as the sea itself.

On all these shores there are echoes of past and future: of the flow of time, obliterating yet containing all that has gone before; of the sea's eternal rhythms—the tides, the beat of surf, the pressing rivers of the currents—shaping, changing, dominating; of the stream of life, flowing as inexorably as any ocean current, from past to unknown future. For as the shore configuration changes in the flow of time, the pattern of life changes, never static, never quite the same from year to year. Whenever the sea builds a new coast, waves of living creatures surge against it, seeking a foothold, establishing their colonies. And so we come to perceive life as a force as tangible as any of the physical realities of the sea, a force

strong and purposeful, as incapable of being crushed or
diverted from its ends as the rising tide.

Contemplating the teeming life of the shore, we have an
uneasy sense of the communication of some universal truth
that lies just beyond our grasp. What is the message signaled
by the hordes of diatoms, flashing their microscopic lights in
the night sea? What truth is expressed by the legions of the
barnacles, whitening the rocks with their habitations, each
small creature within finding the necessities of its existence in
the sweep of the surf? And what is the meaning of so tiny a
being as the transparent wisp of protoplasm that is a sea lace,
existing for some reason inscrutable to us—a reason that demands its presence by the trillion amid the rocks and weeds
of the shore? The meaning haunts and ever eludes us, and in
its very pursuit we approach the ultimate mystery of Life itself.

Edwin Way Teale

Land of the Windy Rain

Edwin Way Teale was born in Joliet, Illinois, in 1899. As a boy, while exploring the dune country of Indiana and the woods and lake regions of the Midwest, he followed the naturalist's impulse to record his observations. Teale's interest in wildlife began with insects, and after receiving a master's degree from Columbia and working at a variety of teaching, writing, and editing jobs, he achieved recognition in the mid-1930s for his photographs and descriptions of insect life. As a full-time naturalist, writer, and photographer, Teale has extended his explorations to include a wide range of wildlife and the natural world in a number of books, including Dune Boy *(1943),* The Lost Woods *(1945),* Days Without Time *(1948),* North with the Spring *(1951), and* Wilderness World *(1954). He received the John Burroughs Medal for distinguished nature writing in 1937 and the Pulitzer Prize in 1966. In* Autumn Across America *(1956), Teale makes a twenty-thousand-mile journey to trace the natural history of a season from Cape Cod to California. Teale is aware that glimpses of a vanishing wilderness are available to most people today only in national parks and other protected areas. In the struggle to preserve these remnants of wilderness, Teale himself has become an admirable example of those he describes in the following selection as forming "the enduring component of the conservation movement . . . It is only those who are deeply and fundamentally interested in nature itself who, in the long haul, the all-important continuity of effort, carry on."*

A circle within a square—that roughly represents the Olympic Mountains. Their jagged peaks cluster around Mount Olympus and form the enduring heart of the peninsula that comprises the far northwestern corner of the United States. Rising from sea level to 5,000, 6,000, 7,000 and almost 8,000 feet in the space of less than fifty miles, the mountains lift in a great stone wall against which blows the prevailing wind from the sea. That wind has one of the highest average velocities for the entire country, more than fourteen miles an hour the year around. Like a rapidly moving conveyor belt it brings in moisture from the sea. The mountains drive it steeply upward, cool it suddenly, condense its moisture into precipitation. In effect they quickly wring the water from this ocean wind.

As a consequence the western side of the Olympics receives a greater amount of rainfall each year that any other place in America. The average is about 140 inches, approximately 2,000,000,000 gallons or 9,000,000 tons of falling rain for each square mile of land. By far the greater part of this precipitation comes between November 1 and May 1; the heaviest rains begin in autumn; the three wettest months are November, December and January. Yet during the November days we spent wandering in this land of the windy rain the silver cord that, according to Greek mythology, held gales and storms prisoner within a leather bag remained securely tied. The sun shone. The breeze only occasionally freshened into a wind. The showers were short and infrequent or the rains came in the night. Under favoring skies in this prolonged and unusually dry autumn we roamed through the green, mossy world of a northern rain forest.

We had come up the east side of the peninsula, past red-barked, red-berried madrone trees, over the Hama Hama River, past Lilliwaup—which reminded us how often in this rainy land place-names had a wet, squashy sound, like Satsop, Lilliwaup and Tumwater. Then, based at Port Angeles, we had explored the northern coast along the Strait of Juan de Fuca. We followed roads where a rat trap dangled from a pole in front of every farmhouse to hold the brown canvas bag set out for the country postman. We continued as far as Cape Flattery and the Indian village of Neah Bay where gulls and fish crows fed in the street like sparrows. Along this wild

From Edwin Way Teale, "Land of the Windy Rain," in *Autumn Across America: A Naturalist's Record of a 20,000 Mile Journey Through the North American Autumn* (New York: Dodd, Mead, 1956.

coast we had seen our first surf birds and our first black turn-stones. Then we had swung south down the outside of the peninsula, down to the Hoh River and the nineteen-mile dirt road that winds into the rain forest as far as the Hoh Ranger Station and the beginning of the path that climbs eventually up to the high meadows and the glaciers of Mount Olympus. During the two succeeding days we wandered along the lower miles of this rain-forest trail.

All around us the vine maples, the towering hemlocks, the firs and the spruces were draped and bearded with moss. Great trunks rose above us green and furry as far as we could see. Branches spread over us shaggy with the primitive spikemoss, *Selaginella*. Under our feet the plush of the forest carpet grew so dense and deep we sank at times above our shoetops. In the misty light we saw it roll on and on, wave after wave, over the moldering logs, across the uneven floor of the forest. Scientists believe 100 kinds of moss grow on the Olympic Peninsula. The green carpet that covers the forest floor is formed of many species, many strands; its warp and woof are made up of a multitude of mosses.

Here and there along the path streamers of sunshine probed between the giant trees. Drawn in glowing silver lines they slanted down through the humid air. And above each spot where they reached the saturated carpet of the moss, mist curled up like smoke from a fire being started with a burning glass. And all the while the long fingers of the spike-moss, hanging from the branches like gray-green stalactites forming under the roof of a cavern, dripped endlessly. As each drop fell it entered the plush of the living carpet without a sound. It was absorbed without a trace. Moss is nature's great silencer. This was a forest soundproofed by moss.

We stopped beside a tree where the trunk had split a third of the way down from the top and half had fallen to the ground. All down the divided tree the sheathing of moss had parted as though it were a thicker shell of bark. On some trunks the coating is so dense it has the appearance of a shaggy pelt. I was told that when natives were caught in the forest overnight in the dryer summer months they sometimes strip off great sections of this moss with their hunting knives and use them as soft, thick blankets. In rare periods of com-parative drought it is the tree-moss that dries out most quickly. At such times a conflagration will race ahead through the forest faster than fire-fighters can keep up with it.

An astonishing paradox in connection with the moisture of
the Olympic Peninsula is the fact that less than thirty miles
from the saturated forest through which we walked irrigation
farming is practiced. Around Sequim, in the northeastern corner of the peninsula, rainfall is sometimes only fourteen
inches a year, one-tenth that on the other side of the Olympics. There we saw troughs and ditches carrying water to dry
fields lying in the rain shadow of the mountains. Coming west
we had run through a succession of such areas of dryness.
Prevailing winds from the west vault over the Olympics, over
the Cascades, over the Rockies. Each time they leave most of
their moisture on the western side of the range and little remains to water the land lying on the lee side to the east. Oregon and Washington are lush and green west of the Cascades,
so dry they are often almost deserts east of the mountains.
But nowhere else did we see so dramatic a demonstration of
the effect of mountains on moisture as here within the narrow
confines of the Olympic Peninsula.

Along our path beside the Hoh the evidences of abundant
rainfall were everywhere. Combined with a mild climate and
a long growing season it had produced a tropical luxuriance
of growth. Immense tree trunks lifted from the moss and
ferns, soared upward, towered above us, disappearing at last
among the maze of the upper branches. In some cases the
lowest branch was 100 feet in the air. Here in the rain forest
of the Olympic Peninsula numerous trees attain their record
size.

The world's largest Cascade fir grows in the wild country
between the Hoh and the Bogachiel rivers and, near the
mouth of the Hoh, the western red cedar reaches its maximum size in a seamed and twisted giant. On the east fork of
the Quinault River the biggest known western hemlock has a
girth of twenty-seven feet, two inches. Among the Douglas
firs—that race of giants that with the single exception of the
sequoias are the hugest trees in America—the largest of them
all grows in the valley of the Queets River, south of the Hoh.
Four and a half feet from the ground its circumference is
fifty-three feet, four inches. And along the trail we followed,
some four miles in from the ranger station on the Hoh, one
of the most beautiful trees in the world, the Sitka spruce with
frosted needles and silvery bark tingled with lavender and
purple, reaches its maximum dimensions with a circumference of forty-one feet, six inches.

These are virgin trees in a virgin forest. Protected within the glorious living museum of this national park are some of the arboreal patriarchs of the world. Many times during our trip we felt that America's great national park system is one of its finest achievements, action by the people for the people on a high plane. Yet those who think of any national park as something permanent make a grave mistake. It can always be changed if not abolished. Its boundaries can be altered, permitting the finest of its timber to be cut. Its rules can be modified, allowing grazing here, mining there, dams destroying areas supposed to be inviolate. And because of the wonder of its trees the Olympic National Park, more than most, will always be in danger.

Decades ago John Muir declared that the Olympic Park would be attacked again and again. His prediction has been amply vindicated. Men who see no more in a tree than board feet, elected officials who refer to the nation's public lands as being "locked-up resources"—as they might refer to songbirds as being "locked-up light meat and dark"—these men we will have with us always and always they will pose a threat to our national parks. Only the vigilance of conservationists over the long haul, only an alertness to attack in a thousand guises, can prevent raids and invasions and destructions within these areas that the people believe have been permanently saved.

On June 17, 1853, Henry Thoreau noted in his journal: "If a man walks in the woods for love of them for half his days, he is esteemed a loafer; but if he spends his whole day as a speculator, shearing off those woods, he is esteemed industrious and enterprising—making earth bald before its time." That attitude is not one that disappeared when the Walden Woods were felled. It is current in every generation. It is ranged against every effort to save wild places. Those to whom the trees, the birds, the wildflowers represent only "locked-up dollars" have never known or really seen these things. They have never experienced an interest in nature for itself. Whoever stimulates a wider appreciation of nature, a wider understanding of nature, a wider love of nature for its own sake accomplishes no small thing. For from these is formed the enduring component of the conservation movement. Many people are attracted to a fight who drift away when the excitement dies down. It is only those who are deeply and fundamentally interested in nature itself who, in the long haul, the all-important continuity of effort, carry on.

Nellie and I talked of such matters under the great trees beside the Hoh and again that evening in a cabin overlooking a curving beach piled high with the flotsam of tremendous timbers. White surf thundered on the sand, swirling, seething, ripped by the offshore rocks. The sunset died beyond bleak Destruction Island while we dined on the only food we could find in a country store, crackers and corned beef and apples—saving for breakfast the sardines and oatmeal cookies and instant chocolate. Each time we awoke in our cabin we heard the roaring of the white surf in the moonlight and saw the spearheads of the spruces rising black against a starry sky. Thus passed out first night on the shore of the open Pacific.

When we left the sea and entered the forest again next morning the autumn mist was heavy among the trees. Fall is proverbially the season of ground fog and mists. The lengthening nights permit the earth to lose more of its heat, the waning strength of the sun slows down the process of warming up the ground in the morning, the lighter winds then prevailing disperse the accumulated mist less quickly. For these reasons autumn and mist are linked together in most parts of the country. Here in the moistness of the rain forest it was late in the morning before the temperature of ground and air became more nearly uniform and the heavier mist among the trees thinned away.

All along the trail winter wrens, like flitting winged mice, appeared and disappeared among the jumbles of the fallen trees. In these mossy woods they live the year around. Douglas squirrels, the chickarees with tufted ears and birdlike voices, darted off at our approach leaving behind on stump tops the kitchen middens of their cone scales. Ferns were everywhere, licorice ferns drooping like green feathers from the shaggy branchs of the vine maples, deer ferns with dry fronds like antlers, oak ferns, western bracken, delicate maidenhair ferns clinging to moist, dripping embankments, lady ferns believed by generations of European peasants to produce magic seed that made the possessor invisible, clumps of sword ferns like green vases filled with fallen leaves. And here and there we came upon splashes of brilliant red and orange where slime mold, that mysterious substance that dwells on the borderline between plant and animal life, spread away across decaying wood.

All through the forest life was rising from death. Along the length of every moldering, fallen tree seedlings were rooted, young trees were growing. Often we would see four or five giant spruces rising in a perfectly straight line as though—like peas in a garden plot—their seeds had been planted along a taut string. In their case the string was six feet thick, a log perhaps 200 feet long. Many seedlings sprout on these fallen "nurse trees" but only a few survive the first years of competition. We came upon roots that extended five feet or more down the sides of moldering logs and once, where a tree had begun growing at the top of a massive stub, roots dropped fully a dozen feet to reach the mold of the forest floor.

On this day we continued farther on the trail. For eleven of its eighteen miles it threads among the trees of the rain forest following the course of the Hoh. On old maps this river appears as the Hooch, the Huch, the Hook, the Holes and the Ohahlat. It is the largest stream on the Olympic Peninsula, carrying away 85 per cent of the melt-water from the glaciers of Mount Olympus. Now in the autumn its flow had lessened greatly. The stream ran shallow, glinting and sparkling among water-smoothed stones in its wide gravel bed.

We were looking across a stretch of rapids where the river tumbled with a swifter current when Nellie caught sight of a bird balancing itself on a boulder amid the flying spray. Slaty-blue, short-tailed and chunky, it was about the size of a starling. As we watched it bobbed rapidly several times. Then it slipped down the side of the rock and plunged head-first into the rushing torrent. It seemed inconceivable that it could escape being drowned or dashed to death against the rocks. Yet a few moments later it popped up as buoyant as a cork and mounted another rock a yard from the first. It was not only safe and sound, it was even dry. The bird we watched was the famed dipper of the West, the water ouzel of swift mountain streams. This relative of the wrens, without benefit of webbed feet or any of the other special adaptations of the water bird, is able to walk on the bed of the stream or, with the aid of its wings, swim in the swiftest current.

Time and again it disappeared in the foaming, tumbling water along the edge of a gravel bar. Once it dived into a tiny pool while on the wing. Another time it alighted on a little rug of moss between two stones. Here it turned around and around, facing first this way then that, shifting its direc-

tion a dozen times before it flitted with a rapid flutter, almost
a whirring, of its wings to another perch. Not infrequently
while clinging to some low stone it would thrust its head under the surface and peer about beneath the water. At last it
climbed onto a rock at the end of one of its dives clutching
in its bill the prize it had sought, the white larva of some
aquatic insect. Tilting back its head it gulped it down. Then
began one of the wonderful moments of the trip. For the
first time in our lives we heard the song of the water ouzel.

It went on and on like the music of the stream. The song
was clear and ringing; it was sweet and varied. On a perfectly
still morning it is said the voice of the ouzel can be heard a
mile away across a mountain lake. It progressed with trills
and warbles, whistled notes, long cadences and flutelike
phrases. It suggested the song of the mockingbird or the
brown thrasher or the catbird, rich with improvising and imi-
tating. Some notes were liquid like the gurgling of the stream,
others were short and harsh like the grating together of
stones. At moments we were reminded of the song of an ori-
ole, at other moments that of a warbling vireo. Yet in its en-
tirety it was unlike any of these. For fully ten minutes,
stopping and beginning again, the bird sang to itself, and to
us, as it wandered alone along the edge of the gravel bar.

The water ouzel is one of the few birds that sing the year
around. Wishing the song would go on for hours, we listened
entranced. But at last the music stopped and the singer darted
away downstream, flying low, only inches above the tumbling
water of the rapids. At Yellowstone, and again at Rainier, we
had glimpsed ouzels in the mountain streams but only here,
we felt, had we really come to know the bird. And only
here, beside this rain-forest river, had we heard its song.

Beyond Mount Tom Creek the trail became more and
more a cowpath followed by the wild cattle of the forest. Its
moist earth was imprinted with a lacework of heart-shaped
tracks left by the black-tailed deer. One time when we looked
back we saw the antlered head of a buck lifted above distant
underbrush as the animal watched us going away down the
trail. And again, at the edge of an open space, we came upon
two does nibbling on bright yellow fungus. Occasionally
among the deer tracks in our path we discovered more oval
hoof marks, suggesting the two halves of a coffee bean. These
were the tracks of the Roosevelt elk.

Only once did we catch a fleeting glimpse of one of these great animals—the dark head and huge dark ears of a female gazing at us among bushes and disappearing almost as soon as we turned that way. The hunting season had already begun. Pitched in the forest around the edges of the park were the tents of the elk hunters. One herd of sixty-nine animals, fortunately still within the park, had been sighted early that morning. But the main bulk of the elk had remained on the higher slopes of the mountains. Like the Columbian blacktails of Mount Rainier, in fall these animals migrate down to the lowlands. In the mild autumn of this year the early snowstorms that start the movement had been delayed, thus, no doubt, saving the lives of many an elk. For although the total number of these animals—native only to this northwestern peninsula—is estimated to be only about 6,000, as many as 5,000 special elk-hunting licenses are issued in one season to men who roam the fringes of the forest just outside the boundaries of the park. Without the protection of this sanctuary these noble animals would face quick and certain extinction.

There were times later on when our trail swung away from the river and the sound of its running water was inaudible. Then the stillness of the forest became intense. In such a silence we rested once beside a mossy stub starred from top to bottom with oxalis. Down the trail a falling leaf, huge and yellow, descended from the lower branch of a big-leaf or Oregon maple. It rode the air in a wide serpentine, stem-first, sliding to a stop like a landing airplane. Although it was fully 100 feet away our ears caught the faint scraping of its stem along the ground and among the already fallen leaves. In that profound silence we could even hear the lisping, sibilant whisper of the dry needles sifting down from the Sitka spruces.

In one of his books W. H. Hudson speaks of what he calls "forgotten memories"—recollections of experiences in the past, long buried in the mind, unthought of for years, perhaps, that some small thing, a sound, a scent, a turn of the road will bring to vivid life. Standing there I found myself reliving an odd adventure of the past, seeing again in suddenly sharpened focus a white-bearded man who looked like a Biblical prophet, a man I met but once under curious circumstances, long ago. And in its way this memory was linked intimately with falling leaf and sifting needle, with Oregon maple and Sitka spruce.

An editor had sent me from New York to a chicken farm on the edge of a small New Jersey village. One of the men who fed poultry there was reported to have the oddest collection of musical instruments on earth. I found him, a patriarchal old gentleman with mild blue eyes. He explained quite simply that he saw visions and that once, years before, he had watched 126 angels, each playing a different musical instrument. He had set out to reproduce on earth all the instruments he had seen. We examined a score or more he had completed: fiddles with three necks instead of one, a harp so huge it could be played from a second-story window, violins with crook necks and extra strings, harps and fiddles combined. All of his instruments had been turned out with no special training and with the use of ordinary carpenter tools. Yet one of his smaller violins, he told me, because of the sweetness of its tone had sold for $500. Afterwards I checked with the owner and found this was true. The wood that went into all these instruments came from a common lumber yard. But the instrument maker believed that he was guided to certain boards, ones that rang like a bell when he thumped them. All the resonance and beauty of tone in the finished product, he maintained, was inherent in the fibers of the wood.

Years later I talked with one of the leading manufacturers of fine violins in America. I remembered this idea and asked him if it was true—if certain boards are selected because their wood gives a finer tone or a greater resonance. He said no. But he added something that meant less to me then than it did on this day beside the mossy stump amid the silence of the rain forest. Most of the wood going into the construction of violins in America, he explained, comes from the West, from two trees, from the Oregon maple and the Sitka spruce.

On the outward trail later that afternoon we found ourselves in a small opening covered with the brown of autumn bracken. Golden-crowned kinglets darted among the surrounding trees, their wiry, lisping little calls coming from here, from there, from everywhere around us. It was while we were watching them that a small black-capped bird with a rufous back caught our attention—our first chestnut-backed chickadee.

In the depths of the forest, in the twilight of its shadows, birds are comparatively few. Here the varied thrush sings and here the sooty grouse makes its home. Most dwellers in dusky forests are, like this grouse, particularly dark in color. Once on our way out we saw a sparrow, with plumage almost black, flitting among the bushes. It was the sooty song sparrow of the rain forest. Pelts of the now extinct Olympic wolf show that it, too, was so dark it was almost black. If you know the rainfall of a region you can make a pretty accurate guess as to the density of color of its wildlife inhabitants. For evolution favors dark-hued creatures in the deep woods just as it favors light-colored creatures on the open desert.

It was after sunset that day when we rounded a turn on the endlessly winding road that leads down the west side of the peninsula and came upon another dark tenant of the rain forest. A dusky cottontail bolted from the shadowed roadside. Even in the distance its actions appeared peculiar. It hopped first this way, then that, as though unable to make up its mind. It would stop, then hurry on in aimless zigzag fashion, then pause again irresolute. As we drew close what appeared to be a squirrel came bounding from the roadside bushes a hundred feet or so behind the rabbit. It halted, seemed to break in two, the front half reared up, light beneath, flat-headed like a cobra, teeth showing in a weasel grin.

This was the bloodthirsty cause of the rabbit's distraction. So terrified was the cottontail it seemed literally out of its mind. In a matter of minutes it could have leaped away in a straight line and outdistanced its short-legged pursuer completely. But it appeared incapable of effective action, bereft of all powers of decision. Many times I have remembered that silent nightmare in the dusk. It was a terrible thing to see a living creature with nerves unstrung and wits departed, stupefied by terror and delivered by fear into the hands of its enemy. We were almost abreast of the rabbit before the spell was broken. Then the weasel whirled and darted into the bushes. The cottontail, in a sudden awakening to sanity, bolted away down the road in swift, effective flight.

During the days that followed we left the rain forest behind—in its quiet, subdued way the most beautiful woods we had ever seen. We wandered north into a land of birches and willows and aspens. We crossed the Fraser River, ran the gantlet of bone-china stores and Cheerio Motels, and entered

Vancouver, B.C. Here, at the farthest-north point of our trip, we turned back. From now on, during the remaining weeks of fall, we would be working southward down the coast, moving in the direction that autumn moved.

Wallace Stegner

Packhorse Paradise

Wallace Stegner was born in Iowa in 1909 and grew up on the Montana and Saskatchewan plains where his parents were homesteaders from 1914 to 1920, an experience he has re-counted in Wolf Willow: a History, a Story, and a Memory of the Last Plains Frontier *(1962). The history and country of Utah, where his family next lived and where Stegner later attended college at the University of Utah, provided subjects for a number of works, including* Mormon Country *(1942),* The Gathering of Zion: The Story of the Mormon Trail *(1964), and his latest novel,* Recapitulation *(1979). After re-ceiving a doctorate from the University of Iowa, Stegner taught at various colleges before becoming professor of En-glish and director of the Creative Writing Center at Stanford. Throughout several books of history and biography, two story collections, and twelve novels, Stegner touches a recurring theme in, as he says, "the importance of geography, es-pecially wilderness, to human personality." He has won the Pulitzer Prize for his novel,* Angle of Repose *(1971), and the National Book Award for* The Spectator Bird *(1976). An ac-tive conservationist, Stegner served as assistant to the Secre-tary of the Interior during the development of the National Parks Bill and as a member of the National Parks Advisory Board. The following selections are reprinted from* The Sound of Mountain Water *(1969). In "Packhorse Paradise," Stegner tells about a packtrip he took into the country of the Hava-supai while he was gathering details for* Beyond the Hun-dredth Meridian: John Wesley Powell and the Second Opening of the West *(1954). In his "Wilderness Letter," he argues for the protection of wilderness on grounds that transcend its accepted recreational, scientific, and material usefulness and considers the wilderness as "an intangible and spiritual re-source." As in his fiction, Stegner's contributions to wilderness literature draw their effectiveness from his alertness to those complexities and moral dilemmas we actually experience in the continuum of the living world.*

One of the special pleasures about a back road in the West is that it sometimes ends dead against a wonderful and relatively unvisited wilderness. The road from Grand Canyon to Topacoba Hilltop ends dead against a ramshackle shed and a gate that closes the bottom of the gulch. The whole place looks less like a hilltop than anything we can imagine, but our Indian guide is there, along with a half-dozen other Indians, cooking beans over an open fire. He waves his hands, white with flour, and says we shall be ready to go in thirty minutes.

Eating a lunch of oranges and cookies and a thermos of milk, we look out from the end of the gulch to the outer rim of a larger and much deeper canyon—possibly the Grand Canyon itself, possibly some tributary or bay. The heat is intense, and light glares from the rock faces and talus slopes. Ahead of us is a fourteen-mile ride into Havasu Canyon, the deep-sunk, cliff-walled sanctuary of the Havasupai Indians.

At twelve-thirty the white-handed Indian, a boy of about eighteen, leads up a skinny packhorse and loads on our sleeping bags, tarps, cooking gear, and the small amount of food we are taking for a three-day trip. He is handy at his diamond hitch, but uncommunicative; his hair grows down over his forehead and he wears big blunt spurs. The horses he brings up look to us like dwarfs, unable to carry our weight, but they do not sag when we climb on. My saddle is too small, and the stirrups won't lengthen to within six inches of where I want them; I console myself with the reflection that if I did put them down where they belong they would drag on the ground, the horse is so small.

For a quarter mile we circle the shoulder of a hill, and then, turning the corner, Mary looks back at me as if she can't believe what she has seen. Below us the trail drops in an endless series of switchbacks down an all but vertical cliff.

Wallace Stegner, "Packhorse Paradise" and "Coda: Wilderness Letter," in *The Sound of Mountain Water* (New York: Doubleday, 1969).

And this is no cleared path, no neat ledge trail built by the Park Service. This trail is specially created for breaking necks. It is full of loose, rolling rocks, boulders as big as water buckets, steep pitches of bare stone, broken corners where the edge has fallen away.

Our guide, whose name turns out to be Hardy Jones, starts down casually, leading the packhorse, and we follow with our seats uneasy in the saddle, ready to leap to safety when the horse slips. We have ridden trail horses and mules before, but never on a trail like this. But it takes us less than a half hour to relax, and to realize that our horses have neither stumbled nor slipped nor hesitated. They know all the time where all their feet are. At bad places, with a thousand-foot drop under them, they calmly gather themselves and jump from foothold to foothold like goats.

As we descend, we learn too how these stunted horses got this way. Far up on the canyon walls, among house-sized boulders and broken rockslides, we see wild horses grazing as contentedly as if they were up to their knees in bluegrass in a level pasture. A half dozen of them are in absolutely impossible places, places where no horse could get. But there they are. And there are signs too that surfootedness is not innate: two thirds of the way down we pass a week-old colt dead by the side of the trail at the bottom of a fifty-foot drop. I ask Hardy what happened. "He fall down," Hardy says.

Ahead of us, in the bottom of a wide sandy wash, a wriggly canyon head begins to sink into the red rock. As soon as we enter this deepening ditch, Hardy turns the packhorse loose up ahead to set the pace. He himself dismounts and lies down in the shade with his hat over his eyes. After a half hour he catches and passes us, and after another fifteen minutes we pass him again, snoozing in the shade. I suspect him of all sorts of things, including nursing a bottle on the sly, but I finally conclude I am wronging him. He is simply sleepy. On occasion his yawns can be heard a half mile.

Once or twice he rides up close and starts a conversation. We discover he is a good roper, and later in the month will ride to Flagstaff to compete in a rodeo. He has three good rope horses of his own, and he has finished the sixth grade in the Havasupai school. I ask him what he'll take for the pony he is riding, a slightly, tiny-footed, ladylike little mare, and he tells me, I am sure inaccurately, fifteen dollars. Then he asks me what I had to pay for the camera slung around my neck, and when I tell him, he looks incredulous and rides on ahead to take another sleep.

The canyon cuts deeper into rock the color of chocolate ice cream. At times the channel is scoured clean, and we ride over the bare cross-bedded stone. The *Grand Canyon Suite* inevitably suggests itself, and we are struck by the quality of the sound produced by hoofs on sandstone. It is in no sense a clashing or clicking sound, but is light, clear, musical, rather brittle, as if the rock were hollow.

The packhorse leads us deeper into the rock, going at a long careful stride down hewn rock stairs, snaking along a strip of ledge, squeezing under an overhang. It is an interminable, hot, baking cavern, but there are aromatic smells from weeds and shrubs. None of the varieties of trees we meet are known to us. One is a small tree like a willow, with trumpet-shaped lavender flowers, another a variety of locust covered with fuzzy yellow catkins. Still another, a formidable one to brush against, is gray-leafed, with dark-blue berries and thorns three inches long. I pick a berry and ask Hardy what it is. "No eat," he says.

2

For three hours we see nothing living except lizards and the occasional wild horses grazing like impossible Side-hill Ga-zinks on the walls. Then around a turn comes a wild whoop, and a young horse bursts into view, galloping up the bouldery creek bed past us. After him comes an Indian boy swinging a rope, and they vanish with a rush and a clatter up a slope that we have just picked our way down at a careful walk. In ten minutes the new Indian and Hardy come up behind us leading the colt, which has a foot-long cut across its chest as if from barbed wire, and which leaves bloody spots on the trail every time it puts its feet down.

Hardy is pleased at the neatness with which he roped the colt as it tried to burst past him. He breaks into a wild little humming chant, accented by grunts and "hah's," a jerky and exclamatory song like the chant of a Navajo squaw dance. As we ride he practices roping the hind feet of the horse ahead of him. After a while we are somewhat astonished to hear him singing with considerable feeling, "Oh, why did I give her that diamond?"

Now on a high rock we see a painted sign, "Supai." A handful of Indian kids whose horses are tied below sit on the top of the rock and wave and yell. We shift our sore haunches in the saddle and wonder how fourteen miles can be so long. At every turn the tight, enclosed canyon stirs with a breath of freshness, and we look ahead hopefully, but each time the walls close in around a new turn. A canyon comes in from the left, and a little brackish water with it, and there are cottonwoods of a cool and tender green, and willows head-high to a man on a stunted horse. There is a smell, too, sharp and tantalizing, like witch hazel, that comes with the cooler air as we make a right-hand turn between vertical walls.

Then suddenly, swift and quiet and almost stealthy, running a strange milky blue over pebbles like gray jade, Havasu Creek comes out of nowhere across the trail, a stream thirty feet wide and knee-deep. After more than four hours in the baking canyon, it is the most beautiful water we have ever seen; even without the drouthy preparation it would be beautiful. The horses, which have traveled twenty-eight miles today over the worst kind of going, wade into the stream and stand blowing and drinking, pushing the swift water with their noses. The roped colt tries to break away, and for a moment there is a marvelous picture at the ford, the white-toothed laughter of the Indian boys, the horses plunging, the sun coming like a spotlight across the rim and through the trees to light the momentary action in the gray stream between the banks of damp red earth.

That wonderful creek, colored with lime, the pebbles of its bed and even the weeds at its margins coated with gray travertine, is our introduction to Supai. After five minutes we come out above the village and look down upon the green oasis sunk among its cliffs. There are little houses scattered along a mile or so of bottom land, and at the lower end a schoolhouse under big cottonwoods. Men are irrigating fields of corn and squash as we pass, and fig trees are dark and rich at the trailside. At the edge of the village a bunch of men are gambling under a bower of cottonwood branches, and two kids, fooling away the afternoon, gallop their horses in a race down the trail ahead of us.

Both of us have from the beginning had the feeling that we shall probably be disappointed in Havasupai when we reach it. We have been deceived by the superlatives of travelers be-

fore, and we have seen how photographs can be made to lie.
But this is sure enough the Shangri-la everyone has said it is,
this is the valley of Kubla Khan, here is Alph the sacred
river, and here on the gardens bright with sinuous rills where
blossoms many are incense-bearing tree.

When we mount stiffly again and ride on after registering
with Mrs. Guthrie, the wife of the Indian sub-agent, we pass
little cabins of stone and logs, orchards of fig and cherry and
peach, hurrying little runnels of bright water, a swinging panorama of red-chocolate walls with the tan rimrock sharp and
high beyond them. Havasu Canyon is flat-floored, and
descends by a series of terraces. We camp below the first of
these, within fifty feet of where Havasu Creek pours over a
fifty-foot ledge into a pool fringed with cress and ferns.

The terrace above our campsite is full of what I take at
first to be the twisted roots of dead fig trees, but what turn
out to be rootlike lime deposits left by the stream, which used
to fall over the ledge here. Probably they were originally
grasses and water plants on which the mineral deposit formed
a sheath; now they writhe through the terrace, fantastically
interwound, some of them six inches in diameter. In the center of each is a round hole, as if a worm had lived there. In
these holes and in the rooty crevices is lizard heaven. Geckos
and long-tailed Uta lizards flash and dart underfoot by
hundreds, as harmless as butterflies.

The same kinds of deposits are being formed under the
pouring water of the falls; the whole cliff drips with them.
And all down the creek the water has formed semicircular
terraces like those at Mammoth Hot Springs in Yellowstone.
Each terrace forms a natural weir, and behind each weir the
water backs up deep and blue, making clear swimming pools
eight to ten feet deep and many yards across. No creek was
ever so perfectly formed for the pleasure of tourists. We
swim twice before we even eat.

When we crawl into our sleeping bags at dusk, the bats
and swallows fill the air above us, flying higher than I have
ever seen bats and swallows fly before. It is a moment before
I realize that they are flying at the level of the inner canyon
walls, catching insects at what seem from the valley floor to
be substratospheric heights. For a while we wonder how bats
fly so efficiently and dart and shift so sharply without any adequate rudder, but that speculation dwindles off into sleep.
Above us the sky is clouded, and in the night, when my face

is peppered by a spatter of rain, I awake to see the moon blurry above the rim. For a moment I think a real storm is coming on, until I realize that the noise I hear is Havasu Creek pouring over Navajo Falls and rushing on down through its curving terraces. It is for some reason a wonderful thought that here in paradise the water even after dark is blue—not a reflection of anything but really blue, blue in the cupped hands.

3

Below our camp a quarter of a mile, past a field half overgrown with apparently wild squash vines and the dark green datura, the Western Jimson weed, with its great white trumpet-flowers, Havasu Creek takes a second fall. Apart from its name, Bridal Veil, it is more than satisfactory, for it spreads wide along the ledge and falls in four or five streams down a hundred-foot cliff clothed in exotic hanging plants and curtains of travertine. The cliff is green and gray and orange, the pool below pure cobalt, and below the pool the creek gathers itself in terraces bordered with green cress.

A little below the fall a teetery suspension footbridge hangs over a deep green pool, dammed by a terrace so smooth that the water pours over it in a shining sheet like milky blue glass. And down another half mile, after a succession of pools each of which leaves us more incredulous, the stream leaps in an arching curve over Mooney Falls, the highest of the three. At its foot are the same tall cottonwoods with dusty red bark, the same emerald basin, the same terraced pools flowing away, and below the pools is another suspension footbridge on which we sit to eat lunch and converse with a friendly tree toad.

It is a long way to the mouth of the canyon, where Havasu Creek falls into the Colorado in the lower end of Grand Canyon. We stop at the abandoned lead and copper mine below Mooney Falls, where we ponder the strength of the compulsion that would drive men to bring heavy machinery piecemeal down into this pocket on the backs of horses, set it up under incredible difficulties, construct an elaborate water system and a cluster of houses and sheds, bore into the solid cliffs for ore, and then tote the ore back out miles to some road where trucks could get it. The very thought gives us

packhorse feet, and we make our way back to camp, yielding
to temptation at every pool on the creek until we have a
feeling that our skins are beginning to harden with a thin
sheath of lime. After a day, we are beginning to realize how
truly paradisiac the home of the Havasupai is.

There are in the West canyons as colorful and beautiful as
Havasu, with walls as steep and as high, with floors as ver-
dantly fertile. There are canyons more spectacularly narrow
and more spectacularly carved. But I know of none, except
possibly Oak Creek Canyon south of Flagstaff, which has
such bewitching water. In this country the mere presence of
water, even water impregnated with red mud, is much. But
water in such lavish shining streams, water so extravagantly
colorful, water which forms such terraces and pools, water
which all along its course nourishes plants that give off that
mysterious wonderful smell like witch hazel, water which
obliges by forming three falls, each more beautiful than the
last, is more than one has a right to expect.

4

Yet even Shangri-la has its imperfections, the snake lives even
in Eden. As we are working back from the canyon walls,
where we have been inspecting a small cliff dwelling, we hear
the barking of dogs. Below us is a field surrounded by fruit
trees, and in the middle of the field, staked out in a line, we
find four miserable starving mongrels. Each is tied by a
length of chain to a post; at the top of each post is a bundle
of branches loosely tied on to give a little shade. Around the
neck of each dog is a collar of baling wire wrapped with
rags, and near each a canful of muddied water is sunk in the
sand. Yelps and whines grow frantic as we cross the field,
and out of the bushes at the far end comes a staggering
skeleton with a drooping tail. In the brush from which she
emerged we find four squirming puppies.

The job of these dogs is obviously to serve as scarecrows,
and they are obviously completely expendable. Clearly they
have not been fed for days, and none of them can live beyond a day or two more.

The usual Indian callousness toward animals is not unknown to us, and we are willing in theory to accept that cultural difference without blaming the Indians. Perhaps this

Indian thought it a good idea to get rid of some of his excess dogs, and at the same time protect his fruit. But our passing through the field has stirred the miserable animals into hopefulness. The tottering skeleton of a mother dog, dragging her dry teats, tries to follow us to camp; the others howl and whine and bark until we feel like running.

Our own food is meager, since we underestimated our appetites when we packed the grub bag, and there is nothing to be bought in the canyon. All we have left to serve us for our last two meals is a can of grapefruit juice, two oranges, a can of lamb stew, four slices of bacon, six slices of bread, and a handful of chocolate bars. The oranges and the grapefruit juice will be of no use to the dogs. Chocolate might make their starving stomachs sicker. The bread and bacon and lamb stew are slim pickings for ourselves.

After a half hour of trying not to hear the howling, I go back and clean out all the water cans, refilling them from the irrigation ditch. None of the dogs is interested in the nice clean water. They are all howling louder than ever when Mary and I start a fire and heat the lamb stew, butter half the bread, lay out the oranges and the chocolate bars for dessert. They howl so loud we can't eat; the stew is gravel in our mouths. We end by spreading two slices of bread with all our remaining butter and taking those and half the stew over to the field. What we bring is a pitiful mouthful apiece, gone so quickly that we wince. Hope has leaped so high in the starving mongrels now that Mary gets three chocolate bars and distributes them. Aware that we are absurd, that our humanitarianism is stupid and perhaps immoral, granting that the dogs have to starve to death day after tomorrow anyway, we carefully divide the meal according to size of dog, and give the skeleton mother a double dose of chocolate.

Then we go home and swim and crawl into our bags, but the dismal howling goes on after dark. It has dwindled off to an occasional sick whimpering by the time we get to sleep, and we have wondered seriously if we should not rather have knocked all nine dogs on the head and paid their owner a suitable fee for the loss of his scarecrows. James Russell Lowell to the contrary notwithstanding, it is a wretched thing either to give or to share when you haven't enough to do any good.

To heighten our disenchantment, we are both bitten during the night by the bloodsucking beetles known locally as Hualpai Tigers, which leave an oozing inflammation about twenty times as irritating as a flea or chigger bite. Next time we come down here we will come with a supply of roach powder.

Not an absolutely idyllic paradise, despite its seclusion and peace and its shining blue water. We see other things when we mount Hardy's horses the next morning and start on our way out. Looking with less eager and more critical eyes, we see girls and women and old men lying on couches in the sun outside the little stone and log cabins. Tuberculosis. We notice among the Supai what Dickens noticed among all Americans a hundred years ago—the habit of spitting all the time and everywhere, even into the creek—and we are glad we dipped our drinking water from a spring. We learn from Mrs. Guthrie that the tribe is less numerous than it used to be, and that it barely holds its own now at about two hundred. A year ago a dysentery epidemic carried off more than half the young children in the village, and measles has been deadly among them.

We learn too that some of the young men, especially those few who served in the armed forces, are restless in the static life of the canyon, and want to get out. We see signs of change in the tractor that the Guthries have had packed in, a piece at a time, and which the Indians can rent for a small fee. We hear speculation about the possibilities of an automobile road into Havasu, and of a guest lodge to be owned by the Indians and run by them and for them, with Indian Service assistance. We hear of the need of increasing the income of the tribe, and of the benefit that increased tourist travel might bring. Out at the fence we hear Hardy Jones, sitting and swinging his big spurs far under the belly of his little mare, singing "Oh, why did I give her that diamond?" which he has laboriously and inaccurately transcribed from the radio onto a piece of cardboard.

The problem of what is best for Havasu—the place and the people—is curiously complex and difficult. If one looks at it purely from the standpoint of conserving natural scenery, the conclusion is inevitable that an automobile road and a guest lodge would spoil a spot that is almost unbelievably beautiful, clutter it with too many people, bring the regulation and regimentation that are necessary when crowds come to any scenic area. Fifty people at one time in Havasu would be all the canyon could stand. The present two hundred visitors a year leave no real mark, but five times that many

would. If the conservation of the canyon's charm is the principal end—and this is the view of the National Park Service,
which does have a voice in the matter since the Havasu reservation lies within the Grand Canyon National Park—the canyon should be left primitive, a packhorse paradise.

5

What of the people, the two hundred Havasupai? Those who
work with them and see the need for medical care and education and guidance know how difficult it is to bring the tribe
even these minimal things under present conditions. Communication is by packhorse and telephone; the mail comes in
twice a week, and supplies the same way, on the backs of
horses. Though there is a school, Mrs. Guthrie is teaching everyone in it, both primary and advanced pupils, because it is
impossible to get another teacher. It is equally impossible to
find and keep a doctor and a nurse; when dysentery swept
the canyon there was little anyone could do but bury the
dead; when the Guthries' own son fell ill last winter he had
to be taken out to a doctor by horse litter.

Though at the bare subsistence level the canyon can be
nearly self-sufficient, there are considerable and growing
needs induced by contact with civilization. There are
clothes—because the Havasupai no longer wear the garments
of beautifully dressed white deerskin that they used to wear.
They wear boots and Levis and shirts and Stetson hats. They
like sugar, candy, coffee, radios, dozens of things that take
cash; and cash they can now obtain only from two sources:
sale of horses or cattle to the outside, or charges at ten dollars a head for packing in tourists. The Guthries are inclined
to feel that if the flow of tourists could be increased, and if
accommodations could be created for them, the standard of
living and health and education of the whole tiny tribe could
be raised considerably.

There is no doubt about the truth of that opinion. The canyon could be made a commercial "good thing" with a little
promotion, and if the enterprise were carefully watched, the
Indians could get the whole benefit. But there is something to
be said against this proposal, too. We are morally troubled as
we talk about it, for how sure can we be that the loose and
indefinable thing called "well-being" will necessarily be pro-

moted by greater prosperity, better education, even better
health, when these things may bring with them the dilution or
destruction of the safe traditional cultural pattern? Is it better
to be well fed, well housed, well educated, and spiritually
(which is to say culturally) lost; or is it better to be secure in
a pattern of life where decisions and actions are guided by
many generations of tradition?

There is a threat that one feels in this paradise. The little
tribe with its static life may be at the edge of stagnation, of
fatalistic apathy, as some villages of the Hopi are reported to
be; it barely holds its own, the dynamics of its life reduced to
the simple repetition of a simple routine, its needs few and its
speculations uncomplicated. It is easy for that kind of equilibrium to be broken, for that kind of society to be utterly con-
founded and destroyed by contact with the civilization of
white America. It takes intelligence, and patience, and great
strength of character, and a long period of time, for any
people safely to cross a cultural boundary as these Indians
must. Perhaps doubling or trebling the number of tourists in
Havasu Canyon each year would not materially increase the
danger to the Havasupai. But build a road in, let the gates
down on the curious and careless thousands, and the whole
tribe would be swept away as the last big flood washed away
the orchards of peach trees, introduced by John Doyle Lee
when he was hiding from the Federal officers after the Mountain Meadows Massacre.

Yesterday I wanted to take a snapshot of an old Supai
packer with bushy hair and prickly thin whiskers. His asking
price was a dollar and a half. We finally settled for a half
dollar, but even at that price that packer was getting dangerously close to the commercialized status of the Indians who
with Sioux feathers in their Mojave or Paiute or Yuman hair
wander around in populous tourist spots being picturesque
for a fee. There is something to be said for the policy that
urges keeping the barrier canyons around this tribe un-
bridged, for according to the ethnologist Leslie Spier, the
Havasupai retain their native culture in purer form than any
other American Indians. Other Indians, losing their hold on
their native culture, have ceased to exist.

I doubt if there is a clear-cut answer to the problems the
Havasupai face. Inevitably there will be more and more in-
trusion on their isolation, and inevitably they must proceed
through the phase of falling between two cultures, of being

neither Indian nor white American. If they are lucky, they can make that transition slowly enough so that eventually they can patch up a new order of cultural acceptances taking good things from both the warring cultures of their inheritance. I should say they might' learn something from the white man about how to treat animals; they would do ill to lose their own native gentleness in dealing with children. They can borrow the white man's medicine and keep their own simple unspeculative friendliness with the earth. If they are lucky they can do this. If they are not lucky, their paradise might in fifty or a hundred years be like the retreat of old Yosemite, beaten dusty by the feet of tourists, and no trace of the Havasupai except squash vines gone wild in the red earth by a spring, or an occasional goat-wild horse on the talus slopes.

I should not like to be God in this paradise, and make the decisions that will decide its future. But I can hope, looking at Hardy Jones lolling in the saddle singing, "Oh, why did I give her that diamond?" that on the difficult cultural trail he is traveling no one will crowd him too hard. The trail between his simple civilization and the inconceivably complex world beyond the rims is difficult even for those who can go at their own pace. Hardy has gone part way without apparent demoralization; he listens to his radio and will go to Flagstaff and perhaps win a roping prize. But the smoke-colored colt lying with his neck broken below Topacoba Hilltop is warning of what can happen to the too young and the too inexperienced on that path.

WILDERNESS LETTER

Los Altos, Calif.

Dec. 3, 1960

David E. Pesonen
Wildland Research Center
Agricultural Experiment Station
243 Mulford Hall
University of California
Berkeley 4, Calif.

Dear Mr. Pesonen:

I believe that you are working on the wilderness portion of the Outdoor Recreation Resources Review Commission's report. If I may, I should like to urge some arguments for wilderness preservation that involve recreation, as it is ordinarily conceived, hardly at all. Hunting, fishing, hiking, mountain-climbing, camping, photography, and the enjoyment of natural scenery will all, surely, figure in your report. So will the wilderness as a genetic reserve, a scientific yardstick by which we may measure the world in its natural balance against the world in its man-made imbalance. What I want to speak for is not so much the wilderness uses, valuable as those are, but the wilderness *idea*, which is a resource in itself. Being an intangible and spiritual resource, it will seem mystical to the practical-minded—but then anything that cannot be moved by a bulldozer is likely to seem mystical to them.

I want to speak for the wilderness idea as something that has helped form our character and that has certainly shaped our history as a people. It has no more to do with recreation than churches have to do with recreation, or than the strenuousness and optimism and expansiveness of what historians call the "American Dream" have to do with recreation. Nevertheless, since it is only in this recreation survey that the values of wilderness are being compiled, I hope you will permit me to insert this idea between the leaves, as it were, of the recreation report.

Something will have gone out of us as a people if we ever let the remaining wilderness be destroyed; if we permit the last virgin forests to be turned into comic books and plastic cigarette cases; if we drive the few remaining members of the wild species into zoos or to extinction; if we pollute the last clear air and dirty the last clean streams and push our paved roads through the last of the silence, so that never again will Americans be free in their own country from the noise, the exhausts, the stinks of human and automotive waste. And so that never again can we have the chance to see ourselves single, separate, vertical and individual in the world, part of the environment of trees and rocks and soil, brother to the other animals, part of the natural world and competent to belong in it. Without any remaining wilderness we are committed wholly, without chance for even momentary reflection and rest, to a headlong drive into our technological termite-life, the Brave New World of a completely man-controlled environment. We need wilderness preserved—as much of it as is still left, and as many kinds—because it was the challenge against which our character as a people was formed. The reminder and the reassurance that it is still there is good for our spiritual health even if we never once in ten years set foot in it. It is good for us when we are young, because of the incomparable sanity it can bring briefly, as vacation and rest, into our insane lives. It is important to us when we are old simply because it is there—important, that is, simply as idea.

We are a wild species, as Darwin pointed out. Nobody ever tamed or domesticated or scientifically bred us. But for at least three millennia we have been engaged in a cumulative and ambitious race to modify and gain control of our environment, and in the process we have come close to domesticating ourselves. Not many people are likely, any more, to look upon what we call "progress" as an unmixed blessing. Just as surely as it has brought us increased comfort and more material goods, it has brought us spiritual losses, and it threatens now to become the Frankenstein that will destroy us. One means of sanity is to retain a hold on the natural world, to remain, insofar as we can, good animals. Americans still have that chance, more than many peoples; for while we were demonstrating ourselves the most efficient and ruthless environment-busters in history, and slashing and burning and cutting our way through a wilderness continent, the wilderness was working on us. It remains in us as surely as Indian names remain on the land. If the abstract dream of human liberty and human dignity became, in America, something more than an abstract dream, mark it down at least partially to the fact that we were in subtle ways subdued by what we conquered.

The Connecticut Yankee, sending likely candidates from King Arthur's unjust kingdom to his Man Factory for rehabilitation, was over-optimistic, as he later admitted. These things cannot be forced, they have to grow. To make such a man, such a democrat, such a believer in human individual dignity, as Mark Twain himself, the frontier was necessary. Hannibal and the Mississippi and Virginia City, and reaching out from those the wilderness; the wilderness as opportunity and as idea, the thing that has helped to make an American different from and, until we forget it in the roar of our industrial cities, more fortunate than other men. For an American, insofar as he is new and different at all, is a civilized man who has renewed himself in the wild. The American experience has been the confrontation by old peoples and cultures of a world as new as if it had just risen from the sea. That gave us our hope and our excitement, and the hope and excitement can be passed on to newer Americans, Americans who never saw any phase of the frontier. But only so long as we keep the remainder of our wild as a reserve and a promise—a sort of wilderness bank.

As a novelist, I may perhaps be forgiven for taking literature as a reflection, indirect but profoundly true, of our national consciousness. And our literature, as perhaps you are aware, is sick, embittered, losing its mind, losing its faith. Our novelists are the declared enemies of their society. There has hardly been a serious or important novel in this century that did not repudiate in part or in whole American technological culture for its commercialism, its vulgarity, and the way in which it has dirtied a clean continent and a clean dream. I do not expect that the preservation of our remaining wilderness is going to cure this condition. But the mere example that we can as a nation apply some other criteria than commercial and exploitative considerations would be heartening to many Americans, novelists or otherwise. We need to demonstrate our acceptance of the natural world, including ourselves; we need the spiritual refreshment that being natural can produce. And one of the best places for us to get that is in the wilderness where the fun houses, the bulldozers, and the pavements of our civilization are shut out.

Sherwood Anderson, in a letter to Waldo Frank in the 1920's, said it better than I can. "Is it not likely that when the country was new and men were often alone in the fields and the forest they got a sense of bigness outside themselves that has now in some way been lost . . . Mystery whispered in the grass, played in the branches of trees overhead, was caught up and blown across the American line in clouds of dust at evening on the prairies . . . I am old enough to remember tales that strengthen my belief in a deep semi-religious influence that was formerly at work among our people. The flavor of it hangs over the best work of Mark Twain . . . I can remember old fellows in my home town speaking feelingly of an evening spent on the big empty plains. It had taken the shrillness out of them. They had learned the trick of quiet . . ."

We could learn it too, even yet; even our children and grandchildren could learn it. But only if we save, for just such absolutely non-recreational, impractical, and mystical uses as this, all the wild that still remains to us.

It seems to me significant that the distinct downturn in our literature from hope to bitterness took place almost at the precise time when the frontier officially came to an end, in 1890, and when the American way of life had begun to turn strongly urban and industrial. The more urban it has become, and the more frantic with technological change, the sicker and more embittered our literature, and I believe our people have become. For myself, I grew up on the empty plains of Saskatchewan and Montana and in the mountains of Utah, and I put a very high valuation on what those places gave me. And if I had not been able periodically to renew myself in the mountains and deserts of western America I would be very nearly bughouse. Even when I can't get to the back country, the thought of the colored deserts of southern Utah, or the reassurance that there are still stretches of prairie where the world can be instantaneously perceived as disk and bowl, and where the little but intensely important human being is exposed to the five directions and the thirty-six winds, is a positive consolation. The idea alone can sustain me. But as the wilderness areas are progressively exploited or "improved," as the jeeps and bulldozers of uranium prospectors scar up the deserts and the roads are cut into the alpine timberlands, and as the remnants of the unspoiled and natural world are progressively eroded, every such loss is a little death in me. In us.

I am not moved by the argument that those wilderness areas which have already been exposed to grazing or mining are already deflowered, and so might as well be "harvested." For mining I cannot say much good except that its operations are generally short-lived. The extractable wealth is taken and the shafts, the tailings, and the ruins left, and in a dry country such as the American West the wounds men make in the earth do not quickly heal. Still, they are only wounds; they aren't absolutely mortal. Better a wounded wilderness than none at all. And as for grazing, if it is strictly controlled so that it does not destroy the ground cover, damage the ecology, or compete with the wildlife it is in itself nothing that

need conflict with the wilderness feeling or the validity of the
wilderness experience. I have known enough range cattle to
recognize them as wild animals; and the people who herd
them have, in the wilderness context, the dignity of rareness;
they belong on the frontier, moreover, and have a look of
rightness. The invasion they make on the virgin country is a
sort of invasion that is as old as Neolithic man, and they can,
in moderation, even emphasize a man's feeling of belonging
to the natural world. Under surveillance, they can belong; under control, they need not deface or mar. I do not believe
that in wilderness areas where grazing has never been permitted, it should be permitted; but I do not believe either that an
otherwise untouched wilderness should be eliminated from
the preservation plan because of limited existing uses such as
grazing which are in consonance with the frontier condition
and image.

Let me say something on the subject of the kinds of wilderness worth perserving. Most of those areas contemplated
are in the national forests and in high mountain country. For
all the usual recreational purposes, the alpine and forest wildernesses are obviously the most important, both as genetic
banks and as beauty spots. But for the spiritual renewal, the
recognition of identity, the birth of awe, other kinds will
serve every bit as well. Perhaps, because they are less friendly
to life, more abstractly non-human, they will serve even better. On our Saskatchewan prairie, the nearest neighbor was
four miles away, and at night we saw only two lights on all
the dark rounding earth. The earth was full of animals—field
mice, ground squirrels, weasels, ferrets, badgers, coyotes, burrowing owls, snakes. I knew them as my little brothers, as fellow creatures, and I have never been able to look upon
animals in any other way since. The sky in that country came
clear down to the ground on every side, and it was full of
great weathers, and clouds, and winds, and hawks. I hope I
learned something from knowing intimately the creatures of
the earth; I hope I learned something from looking a long
way, from looking up, from being much alone. A prairie like
that, one big enough to carry the eye clear to the sinking,
rounding horizon, can be as lonely and grand and simple in
its forms as the sea. It is as good a place as any for the wilderness experience to happen; the vanishing prairie is as
worth preserving for the wilderness idea as the alpine forests.

So are great reaches of our western deserts, scarred somewhat by prospectors but otherwise open, beautiful, waiting, close to whatever God you want to see in them. Just as a sample, let me suggest the Robbers' Roost country in Wayne County, Utah, near the Capitol Reef National Monument. In that desert climate the dozer and jeep tracks will not soon melt back into the earth, but the country has a way of making the scars insignificant. It is a lovely and terrible wilderness, such a wilderness as Christ and the prophets went out into; harshly and beautifully colored, broken and worn until its bones are exposed, its great sky without a smudge or taint from Technocracy, and in hidden corners and pockets under its cliffs the sudden poetry of springs. Save a piece of country like that intact, and it does not matter in the slightest that only a few people every year will go into it. That is precisely its value. Roads would be a desecration, crowds would ruin it. But those who haven't the strength or youth to go into it and live can simply sit and look. They can look two hundred miles, clear into Colorado; and looking down over the cliffs and canyons of the San Rafael Swell and the Robbers' Roost they can also look as deeply into themselves as anywhere I know. And if they can't even get to the places on the Aquarius Plateau where the present roads will carry them, they can simply contemplate the *idea*, take pleasure in the fact that such a timeless and uncontrolled part of earth is still there.

These are some of the things wilderness can do for us. That is the reason we need to put into effect, for its preservation, some other principle than the principles of exploitation or "usefulness" or even recreation. We simply need that wild country available to us, even if we never do more than drive to its edge and look in. For it can be a means of reassuring ourselves of our sanity as creatures, a part of the geography of hope.

Very sincerely yours,

Wallace Stegner

Edward Abbey

Desert Solitaire

Edward Abbey, a self-styled agrarian anarchist and ecological
terrorist, was born in Home, Pennsylvania, in 1927, the son
of a northern Appalachian logger and woodsman. He was
graduated from the University of New Mexico in 1952 and
published two novels, Jonathan Troy *(1954) and* The Brave
Cowboy *(1956), before receiving a master's degree in phi-*
losophy in 1956. Off and on between 1956 and 1971, Abbey
worked as a seasonal National Park Service ranger and fire
lookout in the Southwest, and his experience as a ranger in
Utah's Arches National Monument served as a basis for
Desert Solitaire: A Season in the Wilderness *(1968). In re-*
cent books, A Journey Home: Some Words in Defense of
the American West *(1977) and* Abbey's Road *(1979), he*
has become even more purposefully iconoclastic, irreverent,
offended, and offensive as he watches the last vestiges of
wilderness succumb to the powers of profit and progress. His
reactions range from sentimentality to bitterness, but nowhere
does he more dramatically demonstrate the value of what we
have lost in our mechanized world than in Desert Solitaire,
where he effectively dramatizes how we have "exchanged a
great and unbounded world for a small, comparatively meager
one."

The April mornings are bright, clear and calm. Not until the
afternoon does the wind begin to blow, raising dust and sand
in funnel-shaped twisters that spin across the desert briefly,
like dancers, and then collapse—whirlwinds from which issue
no voice or word except the forlorn moan of the elements un-

From Edward Abbey, *Desert Solitaire: A Season in the Wilderness*
(New York: McGraw-Hill, 1968).

der stress. After the reconnoitering dust devils comes the real the serious wind, the voice of the desert rising to a demented howl and blotting out sky and sun behind yellow clouds of dust, sand, confusion, embattled birds, last year's scrub-oak leaves, pollen, the husks of locusts, bark of juniper. . . .

Time of the red eye, the sore and bloody nostril, the sand-pitted windshield, if one is foolish enough to drive his car into such a storm. Time to sit indoors and continue that letter which is never finished—while the fine dust forms neat little windrows under the edge of the door and on the windowsills. Yet the springtime winds are as much a part of the canyon country as the silence and the glamorous distances, you learn, after a number of years, to love them also.

The mornings therefore, as I started to say and meant to say, are all the sweeter in the knowledge of what the afternoon is likely to bring. Before beginning the morning chores I like to sit on the sill of my doorway, bare feet planted on the bare ground and a mug of hot coffee in hand, facing the sunrise. The air is gelid, not far above freezing, but the butane heater inside the trailer keeps my back warm, the rising sun warms the front, and the coffee warms the interior.

Perhaps this is the loveliest hour of the day, though it's hard to choose. Much depends on the season. In midsummer the sweetest hour begins at sundown, after the awful heat of the afternoon. But now, in April, we'll take the opposite, that hour beginning with the sunrise. The birds, returning from wherever they go in winter, seem inclined to agree. The pinyon jays are whirling in garrulous, gregarious flocks from one stunted tree to the next and back again, erratic exuberant games without any apparent practical function. A few big ravens hang around and croak harsh clanking statements of smug satisfaction from the rimrock, lifting their greasy wings now and then to probe for lice. I can hear but seldom see the canyon wrens singing their distinctive song from somewhere up on the cliffs: a flutelike descent—never ascent—of the whole tone scale. Staking out new nesting claims, I understand. Also invisible but invariably present at some indefinable distance are the mourning doves whose plaintive call suggests irresistibly a kind of seeking out, the attempt by separated souls to restore a lost communion:

Hello . . . they seem to cry, *who . . . are . . . you?*

And the reply from a different quarter. *Hello . . .* (pause)
where . . . are . . . you?

No doubt this line of analogy must be rejected. It's foolish
and unfair to impute to the doves, with serious concerns of
their own, an interest in questions more appropriate to their
human kin. Yet their song, if not a mating call or a warning,
must be what it sounds like, a brooding meditation on space,
on solitude. The game.

Other birds, silent, which I have not yet learned to identify,
are also lurking in the vicinity, watching me. What the ornithologist terms l.g.b.'s—little gray birds—they flit about from
point to point on noiseless wings, their origins obscure.

As mentioned before, I share the housetrailer with a number of mice. I don't know how many but apparently only a
few, perhaps a single family. They don't disturb me and are
welcome to my crumbs and leavings. Where they came from,
how they got into the trailer, how they survived before my
arrival (for the trailer had been locked up for six months),
these are puzzling matters I am not prepared to resolve. My
only reservation concerning the mice is that they do attract
rattlesnakes.

I'm sitting on my doorstep early one morning, facing the
sun as usual, drinking coffee, when I happen to look down
and see almost between my bare feet, only a couple of inches
to the rear of my heels, the very thing I had in mind. No
mistaking that wedgelike head, that tip of horny segmented
tail peeping out of the coils. He's under the doorstep and in
the shade where the ground and air remain very cold. In his
sluggish condition he's not likely to strike unless I rouse him
by some careless move of my own.

There's a revolver inside the trailer, a huge British Webley
.45, loaded, but it's out of reach. Even if I had it in my
hands I'd hesitate to blast a fellow creature at such close
range, shooting between my own legs at a living target flat on
solid rock thirty inches away. It would be like murder; and
where would I set my coffee? My cherrywood walking stick
leans against the trailerhouse wall only a few feet away, but
I'm afraid that in leaning over for it I might stir up the rattler or spill some hot coffee on his scales.

Other considerations come to mind. Arches National
Monument is meant to be among other things a sanctuary
for wildlife—for all forms of wildlife. It is my duty as a park
ranger to protect, preserve and defend all living things within

the park boundaries, making no exceptions. Even if this were not the case I have personal convictions to uphold. Ideals, you might say. I prefer not to kill animals. I'm a humanist; I'd rather kill a *man* than a snake.

What to do. I drink some more coffee and study the dormant reptile at my heels. It is not after all the mighty diamondback, *Crotalus atrox,* I'm confronted with but a smaller species known locally as the horny rattler or more precisely as the Faded Midget. An insulting name for a rattlesnake, which may explain the Faded Midget's alleged bad temper. But the name is apt: he is small and dusty-looking, with a little knob above each eye—the horns. His bite though temporarily disabling would not likely kill a full-grown man in normal health. Even so I don't really want him around. Am I to be compelled to put on boots or shoes every time I wish to step outside? The scorpions, tarantulas, centipedes, and black widows are nuisance enough.

I finish my coffee, lean back and swing my feet up and inside the doorway of the trailer. At once there is a buzzing sound from below and the rattler lifts his head from his coils, eyes brightening, and extends his narrow black tongue to test the air.

After thawing out my boots over the gas flame I pull them on and come back to the doorway. My visitor is still waiting beneath the doorstep, basking in the sun, fully alert. The trailerhouse has two doors. I leave by the other and get a long-handled spade out of the bed of the government pickup. With this tool I scoop the snake into the open. He strikes, I can hear the click of the fangs against steel, see the stain of venom. He wants to stand and fight, but I am patient; I insist on herding him well away from the trailer. On guard, head aloft—that evil slit-eyed weaving head shaped like the ace of spades—tail whirring, the rattler slithers sideways, retreating slowly before me until he reaches the shelter of a sandstone slab. He backs under it.

You better stay there, cousin, I warn him; if I catch you around the trailer again I'll chop your head off.

A week later he comes back. If not him his twin brother. I spot him one morning under the trailer near the kitchen drain, waiting for a mouse. I have to keep my promise.

This won't do. If there are midget rattlers in the area there may be diamondbacks too—five, six or seven feet long, thick as a man's wrist, dangerous. I don't want them camping under my home. It looks as though I'll have to trap the mice.

However, before being forced to take that step I am lucky enough to capture a gopher snake. Burning garbage one morning at the park dump, I see a long slender yellow-brown snake emerge from a mound of old tin cans and plastic picnic plates and take off down the sandy bed of a gulch. There is a burlap sack in the cab of the truck which I carry when plucking Kleenex flowers from the brush and cactus along the road; I grab that and my stick, run after the snake and corner it beneath the exposed roots of a bush. Making sure it's a gopher snake and not something less useful, I open the neck of the sack and with a great deal of coaxing and prodding get the snake into it. The gopher snake, *Drymarchon corais couperi*, or bull snake, has a reputation as the enemy of rattlesnakes, destroying or driving them away whenever encountered.

Hoping to domesticate this sleek, handsome and docile reptile, I release him inside the trailerhouse and keep him there for several days. Should I attempt to feed him? I decide against it—let him eat mice. What little water he may need can also be extracted from the flesh of his prey.

The gopher snake and I get along nicely. During the day he curls up like a cat in the warm corner behind the heater and at night he goes about his business. The mice, singularly quiet for a change, make themselves scarce. The snake is passive, apparently contented, and makes no resistance when I pick him up with my hands and drape him over an arm or around my neck. When I take him outside into the wind and sunshine his favorite place seems to be inside my shirt, where he wraps himself around my waist and rests on my belt. In this position he sometimes sticks his head out between shirt buttons for a survey of the weather, astonishing and delighting any tourists who may happen to be with me at the time. The scales of a snake are dry and smooth, quite pleasant to the touch. Being a cold blooded creature, of course, he takes his temperature from that of the immediate environment—in this case my body.

We are compatible. From my point of view, friends. After a week of close association I turn him loose on the warm sandstone at my doorstep and leave for a patrol of the park. At noon when I return he is gone. I search everywhere beneath, nearby and inside the trailerhouse, but my companion has disappeared. Has he left the area entirely or is he hiding

somewhere close by? At any rate I am troubled no more by
rattlesnakes under the door.

The snake story is not yet ended.

In the middle of May, about a month after the gopher
snake's disappearance, in the evening of a very hot day, with
all the rosy desert cooling like a griddle with the fire turned
off, he reappears. This time with a mate.

I'm in the stifling heat of the trailer opening a can of beer,
barefooted, about to go outside and relax after a hard day
watching cloud formations. I happen to glance out the little
window near the refrigerator and see two gopher snakes on
my verandah engaged in what seems to be a kind of ritual
dance. Like a living caduceus they wind and unwind about
each other in undulant, graceful, perpetual motion, moving
slowly across a dome of sandstone. Invisible but tangible as
music is the passion which joins them—sexual? combative?
both? A shameless *voyeur*, I stare at the lovers, and then to
get a closer view run outside and around the trailer to the
back. There I get down on hands and knees and creep toward
the dancing snakes, not wanting to frighten or disturb them. I
crawl to within six feet of them and stop, flat on my belly,
watching from the snake's eye level. Obsessed with their bal-
let, the serpents seem unaware of my presence.

The two gopher snakes are nearly identical in length and
coloring; I cannot be certain that either is actually my
former household pet. I cannot even be sure that they are
male and female, though their performance resembles so
strongly a *pas de deux* by formal lovers. They intertwine and
separate, glide side by side in perfect congruence, turn like
mirror images of each other and glide back again, wind and
unwind again. This is the basic pattern but there is a variation: at regular intervals the snakes elevate their heads, facing
one another, as high as they can go, as if each is trying to
outreach or overawe the other. Their heads and bodies rise,
higher and higher, then topple together and the rite goes on.

I crawl after them, determined to see the whole thing. Suddenly and simultaneously they discover me, prone on my
belly a few feet away. The dance stops. After a moment's
pause the two snakes come straight toward me, still in
flawless unison, straight toward my face, the forked tongues
flickering, their intense wild yellow eyes staring directly into
my eyes. For an instant I am paralyzed by wonder; then,
stung by a fear too ancient and powerful to overcome I

scramble back, rising, to my knees. The snakes veer and turn and race away from me in parallel motion, their lean elegant bodies making a soft hissing noise as they slide over the sand and stone. I follow them for a short distance, still plagued by curiosity, before remembering my place and the requirements of common courtesy. For godsake let them go in peace, I tell myself. Wish them luck and (if lovers) innumerable offspring, a life of happily ever after. Not for their sake alone but for your own.

In the long hot days and cool evenings to come I will not see the gopher snakes again. Nevertheless I will feel their presence watching over me like totemic deities, keeping the rattlesnakes far back in the brush where I like them best, cropping off the surplus mouse population, maintaining useful connections with the primeval. Sympathy, mutual aid, symbiosis, continuity.

How can I descend to such anthropomorphism? Easily—but is it, in this case, entirely false? Perhaps not. I am not attributing human motives to my snake and bird acquaintances. I recognize that when and where they serve purposes of mine they do so for beautifully selfish reasons of their own. Which is exactly the way it should be. I suggest, however, that it's a foolish, simple-minded rationalism which denies any form of emotion to all animals but man and his dog. This is no more justified than the Moslems are in denying souls to women. It seems to me possible, even probable, that many of the nonhuman undomesticated animals experience emotions unknown to us. What do the coyotes mean when they yodel at the moon? What are the dolphins trying so patiently to tell us? Precisely what did those two enraptured gopher snakes have in mind when they came gliding toward my eyes over the naked sandstone? If I had been as capable of trust as I am susceptible to fear I might have learned something new or some truth so very old we have all forgotten it.

They do not sweat and whine about their condition.
They do not lie awake in the dark and weep for their sins. . . .

All men are brothers, we like to say, half-wishing sometimes in secret it were not true. But perhaps it is true. And is the evolutionary hue from protozoan to Spinoza any less certain? That also may be true. We are obliged, therefore, to spread the news, painful and bitter though it may be for some to hear, that all living things on hand are kindred. . . .

The ease and relative freedom of this lovely job at Arches follow from the comparative absence of the motorized tourists, who stay away by the millions. And they stay away because of the unpaved entrance road, the unflushable toilets in the campgrounds, and the fact that most of them have never even heard of Arches National Monument. (Could there be a more genuine testimonial to its beauty and integrity?) All this must change.

I'd been warned. On the very first day Merle and Floyd had mentioned something about developments, improvements, a sinister Master Plan. Thinking that *they* were the dreamers, I paid little heed and had soon forgotten the whole ridiculous business. But only a few days ago something happened which shook me out of my pleasant apathy.

I was sitting out back on my 33,000-acre terrace, shoeless and shirtless, scratching my toes in the sand and sipping on a tall iced drink, watching the flow of evening over the desert. Prime time: the sun very low in the west, the birds coming back to life, the shadows rolling for miles over rock and sand to the very base of the brilliant mountains. I had a small fire going near the table—not for heat or light but for the fragrance of the juniper and the ritual appeal of the clear flames. For symbolic reasons. For ceremony. When I heard a faint sound over my shoulder I looked and saw a file of deer watching from fifty yards away, three does and a velvet-horned buck, all dark against the sundown sky. They began to move. I whistled and they stopped again, staring at me. "Come on over," I said, "have a drink." They declined, moving off with casual, unhurried grace, quiet as phantoms, and disappeared beyond the rise. Smiling, thoroughly at peace, I turned back to my drink, the little fire, the subtle transformations of the immense landscape before me. On the program: rise of the full moon.

It was then I heard the discordant note, the snarling whine of a jeep in low range and four-wheel-drive, coming from an unexpected direction, from the vicinity of the old foot and horse trail that leads from Balanced Rock down toward Courthouse Wash and on to park headquarters near Moab. The jeep came in sight from beyond some bluffs, turned onto the dirt road, and came up the hill toward the entrance sta-

tion. Now operating a motor vehicle of any kind on the trails
of a national park is strictly forbidden, a nasty bureaucratic
regulation which I heartily support. My bosom swelled with
the righteous indignation of a cop: by God, I thought, I'm
going to write these sons of bitches a ticket. I put down the
drink and strode to the housetrailer to get my badge.

Long before I could find the shirt with the badge on it,
however, or the ticket book, or my shoes or my park ranger
hat, the jeep turned in at my driveway and came right up to
the door of the trailer. It was a gray jeep with a U.S. Government decal on the side—Bureau of Public Roads—and
covered with dust. Two empty water bags flapped at the
bumper. Inside were three sunburned men in twill britches
and engineering boots, and a pile of equipment: transit case,
tripod, survey rod, bundles of wooden stakes. (*Oh no!*) The
men got out, dripping with dust, and the driver grinned at
me, pointing to his parched open mouth and making horrible
gasping noises deep in his throat.

"Okay," I said, "come on in."

It was even hotter inside the trailer than outside but I
opened the refrigerator and left it open and took out a
pitcher filled with ice cubes and water. As they passed the
pitcher back and forth I got the full and terrible story, con-
firming the worst of my fears. They were a survey crew,
laying out a new road into the Arches.

And when would the road be built? Nobody knew for sure;
perhaps in a couple of years, depending on when the Park
Service would be able to get the money. The new road—to
be paved, of course—would cost somewhere between half a
million and one million dollars, depending on the bids, or
more than fifty thousand dollars per linear mile. At least
enough to pay the salaries of ten park rangers for ten years.
Too much money, I suggested—they'll never go for it back in
Washington.

The three men thought that was pretty funny. Don't worry,
they said, this road will be built. I'm worried, I said. Look,
the party chief explained, you *need* this road. He was a
pleasant-mannered, soft-spoken civil engineer with an unques-
tioning dedication to his work. A very dangerous man. Who
needs it? I said; we get very few tourists in this park. That's
why you need it, the engineer explained patiently; look, he
said, when this road is built you'll get ten, twenty, thirty
times as many tourists in here as you get now. His men

nodded in solemn agreement, and he stared at me intently,
waiting to see what possible answer I could have to that.

"Have some more water," I said. I had an answer all right
but I was saving it for later. I knew that I was dealing with a
madman.

As I type these words, several years after the little episode
of the gray jeep and the thirsty engineers, all that was foretold has come to pass. Arches National Monument has been
developed. The Master Plan has been fulfilled. Where once a
few adventurous people came on weekends to camp for a
night or two and enjoy a taste of the primitive and remote,
you will now find serpentine streams of baroque automobiles
pouring in and out, all through the spring and summer, in
numbers that would have seemed fantastic when I worked
there, from 3,000 to 30,000 to 300,000 per year, the "visita-
tion," as they call it, mounts ever upward. The little campgrounds where I used to putter around reading three-day-old
newspapers full of lies and watermelon seeds have now been
consolidated into one master campground that looks, during
the busy season, like a suburban village; elaborate house-
trailers of quilted aluminum crowd upon gigantic camper-
trucks of Fiberglas and molded plastic; through their windows
you will see the blue glow of television and hear the studio
laughter of Los Angeles; knobby kneed oldsters in plaid Ber-
mudas buzz up and down the quaintly curving asphalt road
on motorbikes; quarrels break out between campsite neighbors while others gather around their burning charcoal bri-
quettes (ground campfires no longer permitted—not enough
wood) to compare electric toothbrushes. The Comfort Sta-
tions are there, too, all lit up with electricity, fully equipped
inside, though the generator breaks down now and then and
the lights go out, or the sewage backs up in the plumbing
system (drain fields were laid out in sand over a solid bed of
sandstone), and the water supply sometimes fails, since the
3000-foot well can only produce about 5gpm—not always
enough to meet the demand. Down at the beginning of the
new road, at park headquarters, is the new entrance station
and visitor center where admission fees are collected and
where the rangers are going quietly nuts answering the same
three basic questions five hundred times a day: (1) Where's
the john? (2) How long's it take to see this place? (3)
Where's the Coke machine?

Progress has come at last to the Arches, after a million
years of neglect. Industrial Tourism has arrived. . . .

But for the time being, around my place at least, the air is
untroubled, and I become aware for the first time today of
the immense silence in which I am lost. Not a silence so
much as a great stillness—for there are a few sounds: the
creak of some bird in a juniper tree, an eddy of wind which
passes and fades like a sigh, the ticking of the watch on my
wrist—slight noises which break the sensation of absolute
silence but at the same time exaggerate my sense of the surrounding, overwhelming peace. A suspension of time, a continuous present. If I look at the small device strapped to my
wrist the numbers, even the sweeping second hand, seem
meaningless, almost ridiculous. No travelers, no campers, no
wanderers have come to this part of the desert today and for
a few moments I feel and realize that I am very much alone.

There is nothing to do but return to the trailer, open a can
of beer, eat my supper.

Afterwards I put on hat and coat and go outside again, sit
on the table, and watch the sky and the desert dissolve
slowly into mystery under the chemistry of twilight. We need
a fire. I range around the trailer, pick up some dead sticks
from under the junipers and build a little squaw fire, for
company.

Dark clouds sailing overhead across the fields of the stars.
Stars which are unusually bold and close, with an icy glitter
in their light—glints of blue, emerald, gold. Out there, spread
before me to the south, east, and north, the arches and cliffs
and pinnacles and balanced rocks of sandstone (now entrust-
ed to my care) have lost the rosy glow of sunset and become
soft, intangible, in unnamed unnameable shades of violet,
colors that seem to radiate from—not overlay—their sur-
faces.

A yellow planet floats on the west, brightest object in the
sky. Venus. I listen closely for the call of an owl, a dove, a
nighthawk, but can hear only the crackle of my fire, a breath
of wind.

The fire. The odor of burning juniper is the sweetest
fragrance on the face of the earth, in my honest judgment; I
doubt if all the smoking censers of Dante's paradise could
equal it. One breath of juniper smoke, like the perfume of
sagebrush after rain, evokes in magical catalysis, like certain

music, the space and light and clarity and piercing strangeness of the American West. Long may it burn.

The little fire wavers, flickers, begins to die. I break another branch of juniper over my knee and add the fragments to the heap of coals. A wisp of bluish smoke goes up and the wood, arid as the rock from which it came, blossoms out in fire.

> Go thou my incense upward from this hearth
> And ask the gods to pardon this clear flame.

I wait and watch, guarding the desert, the arches, the sand and barren rock, the isolated junipers and scattered clumps of sage surrounding me in stillness and simplicity under the starlight.

Again the fire begins to fail. Letting it die, I take my walking stick and go for a stroll down the road into the thickening darkness. I have a flashlight with me but will not use it unless I hear some sign of animal life worthy of investigation. The flashlight, or electrical torch as the English call it, is a useful instrument in certain situations but I can see the road well enough without it. Better, in fact.

There's another disadvantage to the use of the flashlight: like many other mechanical gadgets it tends to separate a man from the world around him. If I switch it on my eyes adapt to it and I can see only the small pool of light which it makes in front of me; I am isolated. Leaving the flashlight in my pocket where it belongs, I remain a part of the environment I walk through and my vision though limited has no sharp or definite boundary.

This peculiar limitation of the machine becomes doubly apparent when I return to the housetrailer. I've decided to write a letter (to myself) before going to bed, and rather than use a candle for light I'm going to crank up the old generator. The generator is a small four-cylinder gasoline engine mounted on a wooden block not far from the trailer. Much too close, I'd say. I open the switch, adjust the choke, engage the crank and heave it around. The engine sputters, gasps, catches fire, gains momentum, winds up into a roar, valves popping, rockers thumping, pistons hissing up and down inside their oiled jackets. Fine: power surges into the wiring, the light bulbs inside the trailer begin to glow, brighten, becoming incandescent. The lights are so bright I can't see a thing and have to shade my eyes as I stumble toward the open door of the trailer. Nor can I hear anything but the clatter of the generator. I am shut off from the natural world and sealed up, encapsulated, in a box of artificial light and tyrannical noise.

Once inside the trailer my senses adjust to the new situation and soon enough, writing the letter, I lose awareness of the lights and the whine of the motor. But I have cut myself off completely from the greater world which surrounds the man-made shell. The desert and the night are pushed back—I can no longer participate in them or observe; I have exchanged a great and unbounded world for a small, comparatively meager one. By choice, certainly; the exchange is temporarily convenient and can be reversed whenever I wish.

Finishing the letter I go outside and close the switch on the generator. The light bulbs dim and disappear, the furious gnashing of pistons whimpers to a halt. Standing by the inert and helpless engine, I hear its last vibrations die like ripples on a pool somewhere far out on the tranquil sea of desert, somewhere beyond Delicate Arch, beyond the Yellow Cat badlands, beyond the shadow line.

I wait. Now the night flows back, the mighty stillness embraces and includes me; I can see the stars again and the world of starlight. I am twenty miles or more from the nearest fellow human, but instead of loneliness I feel loveliness. Loveliness and a quiet exaltation.

John McPhee

Coming into the Country

John McPhee was born in 1931 in Princeton, New Jersey, where he continues to live and write. After graduation from Princeton University, he wrote freelance, became a staff writer for Time *in 1957, and has been a staff writer for* The New Yorker *since 1964. The natural environment and man's relationship to it have been a concern in several of McPhee's fourteen books, and the wilderness is a central concern in* The Pine Barrens *(1968),* The Survival of the Bark Canoe *(1975), and* Encounters with the Archdruid *(1971), a "narrative about a conservationist and three of his natural enemies." McPhee says, "I have always had a predilection for canoes on rivers and have avoided walking wherever possible" but "my work had led me up the Sierra Nevada and across the North Cascades, and in various eras I had walked parts of the Long Trail, the Appalachian Trail, trails of New Hampshire, the Adirondacks." In 1975, his work led him to Alaska, and to the writing of* Coming into the Country *(1977), a book that has informed a wide audience of the present condition of what many consider the only remaining wilderness in the United States. The following selection is from "The Encircled River," which describes a canoe and kayak trip down the Salmon and Kobuk rivers beyond the northern timberline in the Brooks range. "This is America's ultimate wilderness," one of the travelers remarks. "It goes no farther."*

We have moved completely out of the hills now, and beyond the riverine fringes of spruce and cottonwood are boggy flat-

From John McPhee, *Coming into the Country* (New York: Farrar, Straus and Giroux, 1977).

lands and thaw lakes. We see spruce that have been chewed
by porcupines and cottonwood chewed by beavers. Moose
tend to congregate down here on the tundra plain. In late
fall, some of the caribou that migrate through the Salmon
valley will stop here and make this their winter range. We see
a pair of loons, and lesser Canada geese, and chick mergansers with their mother. Mink, marten, muskrat, otter—creatures that live here inhabit the North Woods across the world
to Maine. We pass a small waterfall under a patterned
bluff—folded striations of schist. In bends of the river now
we come upon banks of flood-eroded soil—of mud. They im-
ply an earth mantle of some depth going back who knows
how far from the river. Brown and glistening, they are virtually identical with rural stream banks in the eastern half of
the country, with the difference that the water flowing past
these is clear. In the sixteenth century, the streams of eastern
America ran clear (except in flood), but after people began
taking the vegetation off the soil mantle and then leaving
their fields fallow when crops were not there, rain carried the
soil into the streams. The process continues, and when one
looks at such streams today, in their seasonal varieties of
chocolate, their distant past is—even to the imagination—
completely lost. For this Alaskan river, on the other hand, the
sixteenth century has not yet ended, nor the fifteenth, nor the
fifth. The river flows, as it has since immemorial time in balance with itself. The river and every rill that feeds it are in
an unmodified natural state—opaque in flood, ordinarily
clear, with levels that change within a closed cycle of the
year and of the years. The river cycle is only one of many
hundreds of cycles—biological, meteorological—that coincide
and blend here in the absence of intruding artifice. Past to
present, present reflecting past, the cycles compose this segment of the earth. It is not static, so it cannot be styled "pristine," except in the special sense that while human beings
have hunted, fished, and gathered wild food in this valley in
small groups for centuries, they have not yet begun to change
it. Such a description will fit many rivers in Alaska. This one,
though, with its considerable beauty and a geography that
places it partly within and partly beyond the extreme reach
of the boreal forest, has been thought of as sufficiently splendid to become a national wild river—to be set aside with its
immediate environs as unalterable wild terrain. Kauffmann,
Newman, Fedeler, and Pourchot are, in their various ways,

studying that possibility. The wild-river proposal, which Congress is scheduled to act upon before the end of 1978, is something of a box within a box, for it is entirely incorporated within a proposed national monument that would include not only the entire Salmon River drainage but also a large segment of the valley of the Kobuk River, of which the Salmon is a tributary. (In the blue haze of Interior Department terminology, "national monument" often enough describes certain large bodies of preserved land that in all respects except name are national parks.) The Kobuk Valley National Monument proposal, which includes nearly two million acres, is, in area, relatively modest among ten other pieces of Alaska that are similarly projected for confirmation by Congress as new parks and monuments. In all, these lands constitute over thirty-two million acres, which is more than all the Yosemites, all the Yellowstones, all the Grand Canyons and Sequoias put together—a total that would more than double the present size of the National Park System. For cartographic perspective, thirty-two million acres slightly exceeds the area of the state of New York.

Impressive as that may seem it is less than a tenth of Alaska, which consists of three hundred and seventy-five million acres. From the Alaska Purchase, in 1867, to the Alaska Statehood Act, of 1958, Alaskan land was almost wholly federal. It was open to homesteading and other forms of private acquisition, but—all communities included—less than half of one per cent actually passed to private hands. In the Statehood Act, the national government promised to transfer to state ownership a hundred and three million acres, or a little more than a quarter of Alaska. Such an area, size of California, was deemed sufficient for the needs of the population as it was then and as it might be throughout the guessable future. The generosity of this apportionment can be measured beside the fact that the 1958 population of Alaska—all natives included—was virtually the same as the population of Sacramento. Even now, after the influx of new people that followed statehood and has attended the building of the Trans-Alaska Pipeline and the supposed oil-based bonanza, there are fewer people in all Alaska than there are in San Jose. The central paradox of Alaska is that it is as small as it is large—an immense landscape with so few people in it that language is stretched to call it a frontier, let alone a state. There are four hundred thousand people in Alaska, roughly half of whom live in or around Anchorage. To the point of picayunity, the state's road system is limited. A sense of the contemporary appearance of Alaska virtually requires inspection, because the civilized imagination cannot cover such quantities of wild land. Imagine, anyway, going from New York to Chicago—or, more accurately, from the one position to the other—in the year 1500. Such journeys, no less wild, are possible, and then some, over mountains, through forests, down the streams of Alaska. Alaska is a fifth as large as the contiguous forty-eight states. The question now is, what is to be the fate of all this land? It is anything but a "frozen waste." It is green nearly half the year. As never before, it has caught the attention of conflicting interests (developers, preservers, others), and events of the nineteen-seventies are accelerating the arrival of the answer to that question.

For a time, in the nineteen-sixties, the natives of Alaska succeeded in paralyzing the matter altogether. Eskimos, Indians, and Aleuts, in coordination, pressed a claim that had been largely ignored when the Statehood Act was passed. Observing while a hundred and three million acres were legislatively prepared for a change of ownership, watching as exploration geologists came in and found the treasure of Arabia under the Arctic tundra, the natives proffered the point that their immemorial occupancy gave them special claim to Alaskan land. They engaged attorneys. They found sympathy in the federal courts and at the highest levels of the Department of the Interior. The result was that the government offered handsome compensations. Alaska has only about sixty thousand natives. They settled for a billion dollars and forty million acres of land.

The legislation that accomplished this (and a great deal more) was the Alaska Native Claims Settlement Act, of 1971. Among events of significance in the history of Alaska, this one probably stands even higher than the Statehood Act and the treaty of purchase, for it not only changed forever the status and much of the structure of native societies; it opened the way to the Trans-Alaska Pipeline, which is only the first of many big-scale projects envisioned by development-minded Alaskans, and, like a jewel cutter's chisel cleaving a rough diamond, it effected the wholesale division, subdivision, patenting, parcelling, and deeding out of physiographic Alaska.

Because conservationists were outraged by the prospective
pipeline, Congress attempted to restore a balance by including in the Native Claims Settlement Act extensive conservation provisions. The most notable of these was a paragraph
that instructed the Secretary of the Interior to choose land of
sufficient interest to its national owners, the people of the
United States, to be worthy of preservation not only as national parks and national wild rivers but also as national
wildlife refuges and national forests—some eighty million
acres in all. Choices would be difficult, since a high proportion of Alaska could answer the purpose. In the Department
of the Interior, an Alaska Planning Group was formed, and
various agencies began proposing the lands, lakes, and rivers
they would like to have, everywhere—from the Malaspina
Glacier to Cape Krusenstern, from the Porcupine drainage to
the Aniakchak Caldera.

Congress gave the agencies—gave the Secretary of the Interior—up to seven years to study and to present the case for
each selection among these national-interest lands. Personnel
began moving north. Pat Pourchot, for example, just out of
college, had taken the Civil Service examination and then had
wandered around the Denver Federal Center looking for
work. He had nothing much in mind and was ready for almost any kind of job that might be offered. He happened into
the Bureau of Outdoor Recreation. Before long, he was descending Alaskan rivers. He had almost no experience with
canoes or kayaks or with backpacking or camping, but he
learned swiftly. John Kauffmann (a friend of mine of many
years) had been planning new Park System components, such
as the C.&O. Canal National Historical Park and the Cape
Cod National Seashore. Transferring to Alaska, he built a
house in Anchorage, and soon cornered as his special province eight and a third million acres of the central Brooks
Range. When confirmed by Congress, the area will become
Gates of the Arctic National Park. It is a couple of hundred
miles wide, and is east of the Salmon River. For five years,
he has walked it, flown it, canoed its rivers—camped in many
weathers below its adze-like rising peaks. Before he came up
here, he was much in the wild (he has been a ranger in various places and is the author of a book on eastern American
rivers), but nonetheless he was a blue-blazer sort of man,
who could blend into the tussocks at the Metropolitan Club.
Unimaginable, looking at him now. If he were to take off his

shirt and shake it, the dismembered corpses of vintage
mosquitoes would fall to the ground. Tall and slim in the first
place, he is now spare. After staring so long at the sharp,
flinty peaks of the central Brooks Range, he has come to look
much like them. His physiognomy, in sun and wind, has become, more or less, grizzly. Any bear that took a bite of John
Kauffmann would be most unlikely to complete the meal.

Now, resting on a gravel island not far from the confluence of the Salmon and the Kobuk, he says he surely hopes
Congress will not forget its promises about the national-interest lands. Some conservationists, remaining bitter about the
pipeline, tend to see the park and refuge proposals as a sop
written into the Native Claims Settlement Act to hush the
noisome ecomorphs. Those who would develop the state for
its economic worth got something they much wanted with
their eight hundred miles of pipe. In return, the environmen-
talists were given a hundred and thirty words on paper. All
the paragraph provided, however, was that eighty million
acres could be temporarily set aside and studied. There was
no guarantee of preservation to follow. The Wilderness Society, Friends of the Earth, the Sierra Club, the National Audubon Society, and other conservation organizations have
formed the Alaska Coalition to remind Congress of its
promise, of its moral obligation, lest the proposed park and
refuge boundaries slowly fade from the map.

The temperature is in the low seventies. Lunch is spread
out on the ground. We have our usual Sailor Boy Pilot Bread
(heavy biscuits, baked in Tacoma), peanut butter, jam, and a
processed cheese that comes out of a tube—artifacts of the
greater society, trekked above the Arctic Circle. Other, larger
artifacts may be coming soon. The road that has been cut
beside the Trans-Alaska Pipeline will eventually be opened to
the public. Then, for the first time in human history, it will
be possible to drive a Winnebago—or, for that matter, a
Fleetwood Cadillac—from Miami Beach to the Arctic Ocean.
Inevitably, the new north road will develop branches. One
projected branch will run westward from the pipeline to
Kotzebue and Kivalina, on the Chukchi Sea. The road align-
ment, which Congress could deflect in the name of the national-interest lands, happens to cross the Salmon River right
here, where we are having lunch. We are two hundred and
fifty miles from the pipeline. We are three hundred and fifty
miles from the nearest highway. Yet here in the tundra plain,

and embedded in this transparent river, will stand perhaps, before long, the piers of a considerable bridge. I squeeze out the last of the cheese. It emerges from the tube like fluted icing.

There is little left of the river, and we cover it quickly— the canoe and the single kayak bobbing lightly, Snake Eyes riding low, its deck almost at water level. The meanders expand and the country begins to open. At the wide mouth of the Salmon, the gravel bottom is so shallow that we get out and drag Snake Eyes. We have come down through mountains, and we have more recently been immured between incised stream banks in the lower plain, and now we walk out onto a wide pebble beach on the edge of a tremendous river. Gulfs of space reach to horizon mountains. We can now see, far to the northeast, the higher, more central Brooks Range, blurred and blue and soft brown under white compiled flat-bottomed clouds. There are mountains south of us, mountains, of course, behind us. The river, running two full miles to the nearest upstream bend, appears to be a lake. Mergansers are cruising it. The Kobuk is, in places, wide, like the Yukon, but its current is slower and has nothing of the Yukon's impelling, sucking rush. The Yukon, like any number of Alaskan rivers, is opaque with pulverized rock, glacial powder. In a canoe in such a river, you can hear the grains of mountains like sandpaper on the hull. Glaciers are where the precipitation is sufficient to feed them. Two hundred inches will fall in parts of southern Alaska, and that is where the big Alaskan glaciers are. Up here, annual precipitation can be as low as fifteen inches. Many deserts get more water from the sky. The Arctic ground conserves its precipitation, however—holds it frozen half the year. So this is not a desert. Bob Fedeler, whose work with Alaska Fish and Game has taken him to rivers in much of the state, is surprised by the appearance of the Kobuk. "It is amazing to see so much clear water," he says. "In a system as vast as this one, there is usually a glacial tributary or two, and that mucks up the river."

Standing on the shore, Fedeler snaps his wrist and sends a big enamelled spoon lure, striped like a barber pole, flying over the water. Not long after it splashes, he becomes involved in a struggle with something more than a grayling. The fish sulks a little. For the most part, though, it moves. It makes runs upriver, downriver. It dashes suddenly in the direction of the tension on the line. His arms now oscillating, now steady, Fedeler keeps the line taut, keeps an equilibrium between himself and the fish, until eventually it flops on the dry gravel at his feet. It is a nine-pound salmon, the beginnings of dinner. Stell Newman catches another salmon, of about the same size. I catch one, a seven-pound adolescent, and let it go. Pat Pourchot, whose philosophical abstinence from fishing has until now been consistent, is suddenly aflush with temptation. Something like a hundred thousand salmon will come up the Kobuk in a summer. (They are counted by techniques of aerial survey.) The Kobuk is three hundred miles long and has at least fifty considerable tributaries—fifty branching streams to which salmon could be returning to spawn—and yet when they have come up the Kobuk to this point, to the mouth of the Salmon River, thirty thousand salmon turn left. As school after school arrives here, they pause, hover, reconnoitre—prepare for the run in the home stream. The riffles we see offshore are not rapids but salmon. Pourchot can stand it no longer. He may have phased himself out of fishing, but he is about to phase himself back in. Atavistic instincts take him over. His noble resolve collapses in the presence of this surge of fish.

He borrows Fedeler's rod and sends the lure on its way. He reels. Nothing. He casts again. He reels. Nothing. Out in the river, there may be less water than salmon, but that is no guarantee that one will strike. Salmon do not feed on the spawning run. They apparently bite only by instinctive reflex if something flashes close before them. Pourchot casts again. Nothing. He casts again. The lure this time stops in the river as if it were encased in cement. Could be a boulder. Could be a submerged log. The lure seems irretrievably snagged—until the river erupts. Pourchot is a big man with a flowing red beard. He is well over six feet. Blond hair tumbles across his shoulders. The muscles in his arms are strong from many hundreds of miles of paddling. This salmon, nonetheless, is dragging him up the beach. The fish leaps into the air, thrashes at the river surface, and makes charging runs of such thrust that Pourchot has no choice but to follow or break the line. He follows—fifty, seventy-five yards down the river with the salmon. The fish now changes plan and goes upstream. Pourchot follows. The struggle lasts thirty minutes, and the energy drawn away is almost half Pourchot's. He wins, though, because he is bigger. The fish is scarcely larger than his leg. When, finally, it moves out of the water and onto the gravel, it has no hook in its mouth. It has been snagged, inadvertently, in the dorsal fin. Alaska law forbids keeping any sport fish caught in that way. The salmon must take the lure in its mouth. Pourchot extracts the hook, gently lifts the big fish in his arms, and walks into the river. He will hold the salmon right side up in the water until he is certain that its shock has passed and that it has regained its faculties. Otherwise, it might turn bottom up and drown.

If that were my fish, I would be inclined to keep it, but such a thought would never cross Pourchot's mind. Moreover, one can hardly borrow the rod of a representative of the Alaska Department of Fish and Game, snag a salmon while he watches, and stuff it in a bag. Fedeler, for his part, says he guesses that ninety-five per cent of salmon caught that way are kept. Pourchot removes his hands. The salmon swims away.

Forest Eskimos, who live in five small villages on the Kobuk, do not tend to think in landscape terms that are large. They see a river not as an entity but as a pageant of parts, and every bend and eddy has a name. This place, for example—this junction of rivers—is Qalugruich paanga, which, tightly translated, means "salmon mouth." For thousands of years, to extents that have varied with cycles of plenty, the woodland Eskimos have fished here. The wall tent of an Eskimo fish camp—apparently, for the time being, empty—stands a mile or so downstream. We find .30-'06 cartridge cases sprinkled all over the beach, and a G.I. can opener of the type that comes with C rations. With the exception of some old stumps—of trees that were felled, we imagined, by a hunting party cutting firewood—we saw along the Salmon River no evidence whatever of the existence of the human race. Now we have crossed into the outermost band of civilization—suggested by a tent, by some cartridge cases, by a can opener. In the five Kobuk River villages—Noorvik, Kiana, Ambler, Shungnak, and Kobuk—live an aggregate of scarcely a thousand people. Kiana, the nearest village to us, is forty miles downstream. In recent years, caribou and salmon have been plentiful nearer home, and the people of Kiana have not needed to come this far to fish, else we might have found the broad gravel beach here covered with drying racks—salmon, split and splayed, hanging from the drying racks—and people seining for the fish going by.

We get back into the boat, shove off, and begin the run down the Kobuk. Paddling on a big lake is much the same. You fix your eye on a point two miles away and watch it until it puts you to sleep. The river bottom, nearly as distinct as the Salmon's, is no less absorbing. It is gravelled, and lightly covered with silt. In shallow places, salmon leave trails in the silt, like lines made by fingers in dust. Eskimos know that one school of salmon will follow the trails of another. In shallow bends of the river, fishing camps are set up beside the trails. "We must have fish to live," the people say; and they use every part of the salmon. They eat the eggs with bearberries. They roast, smoke, fry, boil, or dry the flesh. They bury the heads in leaf-lined pits and leave them for weeks. The result is a delicacy reminiscent of cheese. Fevers and colds are sometimes treated by placing fermented salmon on the skin of the neck and nose. A family might use as many as a thousand salmon a year. To feed dogs, many salmon are needed. Dogs eat whole fish, and they clean up the fins, intestines, and bones of the fish eaten by people. Dog teams have largely been replaced by snowmobiles (or snow machines, as they are almost universally called in Alaska), and, as a result, the salmon harvest at first declined. Snow machines, however—for all their breathtaking ability to go as fast as fifty miles an hour over roadless terrain—break down now and again, and are thus perilous. A stranded traveller cannot eat a snow machine. Dog teams in the region are increasing in number, and the take of salmon is growing as well.

Now, for the first time in days of river travel, we hear the sound of an engine. A boat rounds a bend from the west and comes into view—a plywood skiff, two women and a man, no doubt on their way from Kiana to Ambler. A thirty-five-horsepower Evinrude shoves them upcurrent. They wave and go by. There are a few kayaks in the villages, small ones for use in stream and lake hunting, but the only kayaks we are at all likely to see are the one-man Klepper and Snake Eyes.

Four miles from Qalugruich paanga, it is five in the day and time to quit. We are, after all, officially an extension of bureaucracy. Walking far back from the water, Kauffmann picks tent sites on beds of sedge. A big cottonwood log, half buried in sand, will be a bench by the fire. Mosquitoes swarm. They are not particularly bad. In this part of Alaska, nearer the coast, they sometimes fly in dense, whirling vertical columns, dark as the trunks of trees. But we have not seen such concentrations. Kauffmann talks of killing forty at a slap in the Gates of the Arctic, but the season is late now and their numbers are low. I slap my arm and kill seven.

The temperature of the Kobuk is fifty-seven degrees—so contrastingly warm after the river in the mountains that we peel off our clothes and run into the water with soap. However, by no possible illusion is this the Limpopo, and we shout and yell at the cold water, take short, thrashing swims, and shiver in the bright evening sun. The Kobuk, after all, has about the same temperature—at this time of year—as the coastal waters of Maine, for which the term most often heard is "freezing." Wool feels good after the river, and the fire, high with driftwood, even better, and a dose of Arctic snake-bite medicine even better than that. In a memo to all of us written many weeks ago, Pourchot listed, under "optional personal equipment," "Arctic snakebite medicine." There are no snakes in Alaska. But what if a snake should unexpectedly appear? The serum in my pack is from Lynchburg, Tennessee.

The salmon—filleted, rolled in flour, and sautéed on our pancake grill—is superb among fishes and fair among salmon. With few exceptions, the Pacific salmon that run in these Arctic rivers are of the variety known as chum. Their flesh lacks the high pink color of the silver, the sockeye, the king salmon. Given a choice among those, a person with a lure would not go for chum, and they are rarely fished for sport. After sockeyes and humpbacks, though, they are third in the commercial salmon fishery. Many millions of dollars' worth are packed each year. Athapaskan Indians, harvesting from the Yukon, put king salmon on their own tables and feed chum salmon to their dogs. Hence, they call chum "dog salmon." Eskimos up here in the Arctic Northwest, who rarely see another kind, are piqued when they hear this Indian term.

We look two hundred yards across the Kobuk to spruce that are reflected in the quiet surface. The expanded dimensions of our surroundings are still novel. Last night, in forest, we were close by the sound of rushing water. Sound now has become inverse to the space around us, for we sit in the middle of an immense and almost perfect stillness. We hear the fire and, from time to time, insects, birds. The sound of an airplane crosses the edge of hearing and goes out again. It is the first aircraft we have heard.

Kauffmann says he is worried, from the point of view of park planning, about the aircraft access that would probably be developed for the Salmon River. "It's not a big world up there. I'm not sure how much use it could take."

This reminds Fedeler of the cost of travel to wilderness, and makes him contemplate again who can pay to get there. "The Salmon is a nice enough river," he says. "But it is unavailable to ninety-nine point nine per cent of the people. I wouldn't go back to Fairbanks and tell everybody that they absolutely *have* to go and see the Salmon River."

"It's a fine experience."

"If you happen to have an extra six hundred bucks. Is the Park Service going to provide helicopter access or Super Cub access to some gravel bar near the headwaters?"

"Why does there have to be access?" Pourchot puts in.

"Why do there have to be wild and scenic rivers?" Fedeler wants to know. "And why this one—so far up here? Because of the cost of getting to it, the Salmon Wild River for most people would be just a thing on a map—an occasional trip for people from the Park Service, the Bureau of Outdoor Recreation, and the Alaska Department of Fish and Game. Meanwhile, with pressures what they are farther south, the sportsman in Alaska is in for some tough times."

"His numbers are increasing."

"And his opportunities are decreasing, while these federal proposals would set aside lands and rivers that only the rich can afford."

"The proposals, up here, are for the future," Kauffmann says, and he adds, after a moment, "As Yellowstone was. Throughout the history of this country, it's been possible to go to a place where no one has camped before, and now that kind of opportunity is running out. We must protect it, even if artificially. The day will come when people will want to visit such a wilderness—saving everything they have in order to see it, at whatever cost. We're talking fifty and more years hence, when there may be nowhere else to go to a place that is wild and unexplored."

I have a net over my head and cannot concentrate on this discussion, because something worse, and smaller, than

mosquitoes—clouds of little flying prickers that cut you up—
are in the air around us now and are coming through the
mesh of the head net. They follow us into the tents, ignoring
the netting there. They cut rashes in our faces all through the
night.

David Roberts

The Mountain of My Fear

David Roberts began his mountain-climbing career in Colorado, where he was born in 1943. As an undergraduate at Harvard, he was a mathematics major and a member of the Harvard Mountaineering Club. After receiving a doctorate in English from the University of Denver in 1970, he became a professor of English and director of the outdoors program at Hampshire College. He has also instructed in Colorado for both the Outward Bound School and the Adirondack Institute. Roberts has been on twelve Alaskan expeditions, and his mountaineering feats include the first big wall climbed in the Great Gorge of Ruth Glacier, a new route up the west face of Mt. Huntington, and an expedition to an unexplored range of granite peaks which his party named the Revelation Mountains. His wilderness treks have taken him twice to the Cathedral Spires, three times to the arctic Brooks Range, up the Wickersham Wall on Mt. McKinley, up the still-unclimbed east ridge of Mt. Deborah, and to the Tikchik Lakes in far western Alaska. Roberts's experiences have provided the basis for two books of nonfiction, The Mountain of My Fear *(1968), which the poet and devotee of mountaineering literature W.H. Auden praised as an "excellent book," and* Deborah: A Wilderness Narrative *(1970), which "in my opinion," wrote Auden, "is even finer." Today the wilderness presents itself to many as a last opportunity for physical adventure, and the following selection reveals the fears and depressions of such adventure as well as its pleasures. The accidents of mountain-climbing, which remained potential in the passages by Thoreau, King, Bird and Muir, here become real, and Roberts presents a contemporary response to dangers known to earlier adventurers. By making no sweeping claims and by remaining faithful to immediate events, he offers a final insight into his wilderness experience that bears the hard-earned authority of personal witness.*

Now all that remained was the quarter-mile across to the summit, a narrow, airy walkway with a 5,000-foot drop on the left and a 6,000-foot drop on the right. This was the first and only part of our climb that coincided with the French route. Although it was such a short distance to the top, we knew we couldn't afford to underestimate it, for it had taken the French four and a half hours to reach the summit from here a year and a month before. For 600 feet we moved continuously, a ghostly walk in the sky. The night seemed to muffle all sound, and I had the illusion for an instant that we were the only people alive in the world. Soon we faced two flutings, short walls of vertical snow carved and crusted by the incessant wind, which spared the ridge only a few days each year. Perhaps we had been lucky enough to hit one of them. Here it was imperative that the four of us spread as far apart as possible. Don started up toward the first fluting as I belayed from a not very solid ice ax. Traversing high, he stuck his foot through the cornice and quickly pulled it back. Through the hole he could see the dull blueness of the Ruth Glacier below. He returned to my belay spot near exhaustion from the tension and exertion of a whole day of leading. We traded places and I started for the fluting, approaching it lower. The light was returning; an orange wall of flame lit the tundra north of McKinley. I could see the contours of the nearby snow now, glimmering palely. As I neared the bottom of the first wall, I thought I saw something sticking out of the snow. I climbed over to it. Stretched tight in the air, a single, frail foot of thin rope emerged from the ice. I pulled on it, but it was stuck solid. The sight was strangely moving. It testified, in a way, both to the transience and to the persistence of man. That bit of French fixed rope was the only human thing not our own that we have found during the whole expedition. It even seemed to offer a little security. I clipped in to it although I knew it was probably weather-rotten.

It seemed best to attack the fluting high, probably even on top of the cornice. If it broke off, at least there would be the weight of the other three on the opposite side of the ridge to hold me. The snow was terrible, made more out of air than anything else. I used one of our longest aluminum daggers in my left hand, my ax in the right, trying to plant something in

From David Roberts, *The Mountain of My Fear* (New York: Vanguard Press, 1968).

the snow I could hold on to. At last, by hollowing a kind of trough out of the fluting, I could half climb, half chimney up. Just beyond its top the second fluting began. Don came up to belay me for the new obstacle. It was a little harder, but with a last spurt of energy I got over it. Though things seemed to be happening quickly to me, I took a long time on each fluting, and Matt and Ed grew cold waiting at the other end of the rope. Eventually all four of us were up, however. Then there were only three pitches left, easy ones, and suddenly I stood on top, belaying the others up. The summit itself was a cornice, so we had to remain a few feet below it, but our heads stood higher.

It was 3:30 a.m. We'd been going for sixteen hours without rest. Now we were too tired even to exalt. The sun had just risen in the northeast; a hundred and thirty miles away we could see Deborah, only a shadow in the sky. As Don looked at it I said, "This makes up for a lot." He nodded.

There was no one to tell about it. There was, perhaps, nothing to tell. All the world we could see lay motionless in the muted splendor of sunrise. Nothing stirred, only we lived; even the wind had forgotten us. Had we been able to hear a bird calling from some pine tree, or sheep bleating in some valley, the summit stillness would have been familiar; now it was different, perfect. It was as if the world had held its breath for us. Yet we were so tired . . . the summit meant first of all a place to rest. We sat down just beneath the top, ate a little of our lunch, and had a few sips of water. Ed had brought a couple of firecrackers all the way up; now he wanted to set one off, but we were afraid it would knock the cornices loose. There was so little to do, nothing we really had the energy for, no gesture appropriate to what we felt we had accomplished: only a numb happiness, almost a languor. We photographed each other and the views, trying even as we took the pictures to impress the sight on our memories more indelibly than the cameras could on the film. If only this moment could last, I thought, if no longer than we do. But I knew even then that we would forget, that someday all I should remember would be the memories themselves, rehearsed like an archaic dance; that I should stare at the pictures and try to get back inside them, reaching out for something that had slipped out of my hands and spilled in the darkness of the past. And that someday I might be so old that all that might pierce my senility would be the vague

heart-pang of something lost and inexplicably sacred, maybe
not even the name Huntington meaning anything to me, nor
the names of three friends, but only the precious sweetness
leaving its faint taste mingled with the bitter one of dying.
And that there were only four of us (four is not many), and
that surely within eighty years and maybe within five (for
climbing is dangerous) we would all be dead, the last of our
deaths closing a legacy not even the mountain itself could
forever attest to.

We sat near the summit, already beginning to feel the cold.
I got up and walked a little bit beyond, still roped, down the
top of the east ridge, which someday men would also climb.
From there I could see the underside of the summit cornice
and tell that we had judged right not to step exactly on top.
We had touched it with our ice axes, reaching out, but it
might not have borne our weight.

Ed, who was normally a heavy smoker, had sworn off for
the whole expedition. Now, out of his inexhaustible pockets,
he pulled three cigarettes. He had no trouble lighting them;
after smoking two, though, he felt so light-headed he had to
save the third. One of the things he must have looked forward to, I realized, was that ritual smoke on the summit,
partly because of the surprise he knew it would cause. But
that was only one of Ed's reasons for being there, a minor
one. I thought then, much as I had when Matt and I sat on
the glacier just after flying in, that I wanted to know how the
others felt and couldn't. Trying to talk about it now would
have seemed profane; if there was anything we shared, it was
the sudden sense of quiet and rest. For each of us, the high
place we had finally reached culminated ambitions and secret
desires we could scarcely have articulated had we wanted to.
And the chances are our various dreams were different. If we
had been able to know each others', perhaps we could not
have worked so well together. Perhaps we would have recognized, even in our partnership, the vague threats of ambition,
like boats through a fog: the unrealizable desires that drove
us beyond anything we could achieve, that drove us in the
face of danger; our unanswerable complaints against the universe—that we die, that we have so little power, that we are
locked apart, that we do not know. So perhaps the best
things that happened on the summit were what we could see
happening, not anything beneath. Perhaps it was important
for Don to watch me walk across the top of the east ridge;

for Matt to see Ed stand with a cigarette in his mouth,
staring at the sun; for me to notice how Matt sat, eating only
half his candy bar; for Ed to hear Don insist on changing to
black-and-white film. No one else could see these things; no
one else could even ask whether or not they were important.
Perhaps they were all that happened.

It was getting a little warmer. We knew we had to get
down before the sun weakened the snow, especially on the
summit ice field. Each of us as we left took a last glance
back at the summit, which looked no different than when we
had come, but for the faint footprints we had left near it.

We put fixed ropes in on all the difficult pitches, refusing
to let up or get careless now that we were so tired. For the
same reason we didn't take dexedrine tablets, though we carried them. When we reached the bivouac tent, we split into
pairs to continue down. Ed and I went first, while Don and
Matt packed up the little camp before following us. The sun,
high in a still perfect sky, had taken the magic out of the
mountain's shapes. Only the soft early light and the tension
of our expectancy could have left it as beautiful as it had
been. At last, after twenty-five straight hours of technical
climbing, we rappelled off the Nose and piled, all four together, into the tent.

Now we could relax at last, but the tent was far too
crowded. We felt giddy, and laughed and shouted as the edge
of our alertness wore off. We had brought up our pint of victory brandy—blackberry-flavored—and now indulged in a
few sips, toasting everything from Washburn to Kalispell.
Each of us managed to doze off at some time or other, with
someone else's foot or elbow in his face. In the afternoon it
grew unbearably hot and stuffy inside, and the Nose began to
drip (appropriately enough), pouring water through the roof
of the tent. We cooked all our favorite delicacies, robbing the
two food boxes rapaciously. By 6:00 p.m. it had started to
cool again, and we saw that, finally, the weather might be
turning bad, after six consecutive perfect days, a spell almost
unheard of in Alaska. It was as if the storms had politely
waited for us to finish our climb. We slept a little more, but
still couldn't get comfortable. Around 9:00 p.m. Ed suggested
that he and I go down in the night to the Alley Camp. We
were still tired, but it wouldn't be a difficult descent. Once he
and I got to the Camp, moreover, all four of us could rest in
luxurious comfort, a sleeping bag each, room to stretch out

full length, and plenty of food to wait out any storm. We dressed and were ready to go by 9:40 p.m.

The snow was in poorer condition than we liked; it hadn't refrozen yet, and might not that night since a warm wind was coming in. I knew the pitches below better than Ed, having been over them five times to his one, so I tried to shout instructions to him when the route was obscure. It got to be too dark to see a full rope-length. I went down the twenty-ninth pitch, our ice-filled chimney, feeling rather than seeing the holds. But the fixed ropes helped immensely, and since I came last on the two hard pitches (twenty-ninth and twenty-seventh), Ed didn't have to worry so much about not knowing the moves. Despite the conditions, we were moving efficiently.

At the top of the twenty-sixth pitch, the vertical inside corner Don had led so well in crampons, we stopped to rappel. We stood, side by side, attached to the bottom of the fixed rope we had just used on the pitch above. In the dark, we could discern only the outlines of each other's faces. Under our feet, we felt our crampons bite the ice. Just below the little ledge we stood on, the rock shrank vertically away, and empty space lurked over the chasm below. It was too dark to see very far down. Above us, the steepest part of the face, which we had just descended, loomed vaguely in the night. Up there, on another ledge, Don and Matt were probably sleeping. Beside us, in the mild darkness, icicles dripped trickles of water that splashed on the rocks. The fixed rope was wet; here and there ice, from the splashing, had begun to freeze on it.

We didn't have an extra rope, so we untied and attached ourselves to the fixed line, setting up a rappel with the climbing rope. Ed attached a carabiner to the anchor, through which he clipped the climbing rope, so that we could pull it down from the bottom. He wrapped the rope around his body and got ready to rappel. We were tired, but were getting down with reasonable speed. It was ten minutes before midnight.

"Just this tough one," I said. "Then it's practically walking to camp."

"Yeah," Ed answered.

He leaned back. Standing about five feet from him, I heard a sharp scraping sound. Suddenly Ed was flying backward through the air. I could see him fall, wordless, fifty feet free, then strike the steep ice below.

"Grab something, Ed!" But even as I shouted, he was sliding and bouncing down the steep ice, tangled in the rappel rope. He passed out of sight, but I heard his body bouncing below. From the route photos I knew where he had fallen; there wasn't a chance of his stopping for 4,000 feet.

Perhaps five seconds had passed. No warning, no sign of death—but Ed was gone. I could not understand. I became aware of the acute silence. All I could hear was the sound of water dripping near me. "Ed! Ed! Ed!" I shouted, without any hope of an answer. I looked at the anchor—what could have happened? The piton was still intact, but the carabiner and rope were gone with Ed. It made no sense.

I tried to shout for help to Matt and Don. But they were nearly 1,000 feet above, hidden by cliffs that deflected and snow that absorbed my voice. I realized they couldn't hear me. Even the echo of my shouts in the dark seemed tiny. I couldn't just stand there; either I must go up or I must go down. It was about an equal distance either way, but the pitches above were more difficult. I had no rope. There was no point going up, because there was nothing we could do for Ed. His body lay now, as far as anyone could ever know, on the lower Tokositna, inaccessible. An attempt even by the three of us to descend the 4,000 feet to look for him would be suicidally dangerous, especially since we would have only one rope for all of us. If I went up, I should eventually have to go down again. All it could do was add to the danger. I realized these things at the time. Yet the instinct, in my isolation, to try to join Matt and Don was so compelling that for a while I didn't even consider the other possibility. But it became obvious I had to go down.

At least the fixed ropes were still in. I used two carabiners to attach myself to them, then began to climb down the steep pitch we had started to rappel. I moved jerkily, making violent efforts, telling myself to go more slowly. But I had to use the adrenaline that was racing through me now; it was the only thing that could keep the crippling fear and grief temporarily from me.

I managed to get down the hard pitch. The snow on the Upper Park was in poor condition. I broke steps out beneath me, but held my balance with the fixed rope. I realized that I was going far too fast for safety, but slowing down was almost impossible. As I traversed to the Alley, I was sure the weak snow would break under my feet, but it held. At last I arrived at the tent. The seven pitches had taken eighteen minutes, dangerously fast. But I was there; now there was nothing to do but wait alone.

I crawled into the tent. It was full of water. Matt and I had left the back door open! In the dark I sponged it out, too tired to cry, in something like a state of shock. I took two sleeping pills and fell asleep.

In the morning I gradually woke out of a gray stupor. It seemed to be snowing lightly. I felt no sudden pang about the accident; even in sleep I must have remained aware of it. I forced myself to cook and eat a breakfast, for the sake of establishing a routine, of occupying myself. I kept thinking, *What could have happened?* The carabiner and rope were gone; nothing else had been disturbed. Perhaps the carabiner had flipped open and come loose; perhaps it had broken; perhaps Ed had clipped in, in such a way that he wasn't really clipped in at all. Nothing seemed likely. It didn't matter, really. All that mattered was that our perfect expedition, in one momentary mechanical whim, had turned into a trial of fear and sorrow for me, as it would for Matt and Don when they learned, and into sudden blankness for Ed. His death had come even before he could rest well enough to enjoy our triumph.

The time passed with terrible slowness. I knew Matt and Don would be taking their time now that it was snowing. I grew anxious for their arrival, afraid of being alone. I tried to relax, but I caught myself holding my breath, listening. Occasionally a ball of snow would roll up against the tent wall. I was sure each time that it was one of them kicking snow down from above. I would stick my head out the tent door, looking into the empty whiteness for a sign of them. My mind magnified even the sound of snowflakes hitting the tent into their distant footsteps.

I made myself eat, write in my diary, keep the tent dry, keep a supply of ice near the door. But I began to worry about Matt and Don, too. I knew there was no reason to expect them yet, but what if they had had an accident, too?

There were some firecrackers in the tent. We had tentatively arranged on the way up to shoot them off in an emergency. I might have done that now, but there was no emergency. It would be more dangerous to communicate with them than not to, because in their alarm they might abandon caution to get down fast.

I began to wonder what I would do if they didn't come. What if I heard them calling for help? I would have to go up, yet what could I do alone? I calculated that they had at most five days' food at the Nose Camp. I had enough for twenty days at the Alley Camp. I would wait five or six days, and if there was no sign of them, I would try to finish the descent alone. At the cave I could stamp a message for Sheldon; if he flew over, he would see it. If he didn't, I would eventually start to hike out, seventy miles down an unknown glacier, across rivers, through the tundra. . . .

But these were desperate thoughts, the logical extremes of possible action I might have to take; I forced myself to consider them so that no potential course of events could lurk unrealized among my fears.

Already I had begun to miss Ed in a way separate from the shock and loneliness. I longed for his cheeriness, that fund of warmth that Matt, Don, and I lacked. I had wanted so much to relax in the tent, talking and joking with him, reliving the long summit day. I hadn't climbed with him since July 11. Now it was the last day of the month, and he was gone.

I went outside the tent only to urinate. Each time, I tied a loop around my waist and clipped in to a piton outside, not only because I was afraid but because I couldn't be sure that the sleeping pills and the shock (if it was actually shock) were not impairing my judgment or balance. I felt always tense, aware that I was waiting, minute by minute. I could think of very little but the accident; I couldn't get the sight of Ed falling, sudden and soundless, out of my head.

The snow continued to fall lightly, but the tent got warmer as the hidden sun warmed the air. In the afternoon I began to hear a high, faint whining sound. It was like nothing human, but I couldn't place it. Could it be some kind of distress signal from Matt or Don? Impossible. . . . Could it be the wind blowing through a carabiner somewhere above? But there was almost no wind. Was it even real? I listened, holding my breath, straining with the effort to define the sound. I couldn't even tell if it was above the camp or below. I sang a note of the same pitch to convince myself the sound was real. It seemed to stop momentarily, but I couldn't be sure I hadn't merely begun to ignore it. Finally I noticed that when I went outside the tent, I couldn't hear it. Therefore the sound had to come from inside. At last I found it—vaporized gas, heated by the warmth of the day, was escaping from the stove's safety valve! I felt silly but measurably relieved.

I tried to relive every moment Ed and I had had together the last day, as if doing so could somehow salvage something from the tragedy. My recollections had stuck on a remark he had made in the Nose Camp as we rested after the summit. I had told him that it had been the best day I'd ever had climbing. Ed had said, "Mine too, but I don't know if I'd do the whole thing again."

I thought he was still upset about Matt's and my near-accident, and suggested so. Ed thought a moment, then said, "No. It's not only that."

We hadn't pursued it, but his attitude had seemed strange to me. For me, there was no question but that it would have been worth doing all over again. Nor for Don. And I thought Matt would have said so, too. But Ed had climbed less than we had; perhaps he wasn't so sure that climbing was the most important thing in his life, as we would have said it was in ours.

Now his remark haunted me. The accident, ultimately inexplicable beyond its mechanical cause, which itself we would never be sure of, seemed that much more unfair in view of what Ed had said. It would have been better, fairer, perhaps, had it happened to me. Yet not even in the depth of anguish could I wish that I had died instead. And that irreducible selfishness seemed to prove to me that beyond our feeling of "commitment" there lay the barriers of our disparate self-love. We were willing to place our lives in each other's hands, but I wouldn't have died for Ed. What a joke we played on ourselves—the whole affair of mountaineering seemed a farce then. But the numbness returned; I told myself to wait, to judge it all in better perspective, months, years from now.

By that night there had still been no sign of Matt or Don. I took another sleeping pill and finally dozed off. Sometime in the night, on the edge of sleeping and waking, I had a vision of Ed stumbling, bloody, broken, up to the tent, yelling out in the night, "Why didn't you come to look for me?" I woke with a jolt, then waited in the dark for the dream to dissolve. I hadn't considered, after the first moments, trying to look for Ed's body. For me alone, without a rope, to try to descend the 4,000 feet would certainly have been suicide. Yet because there was nothing to do, and because I hadn't seen Ed's dead body, a whisper of guilt had lodged in my subconscious, a whisper that grew to Ed's shout in my nightmare.

I took a sip of water and fell asleep again. In the morning I discovered my watch had stopped. An unimportant event, it hit me with stunning force. It was as if one more proof of reality were gone, one more contact with the others, Matt and Don first of all, everyone else alive in the world eventually. I set the watch arbitrarily and shook it to get it started.

That day, August 1, dragged by as the last one had. I was no more relaxed than I had been before. The weather was good for a few minutes in the morning, then clouded up again; but at least it had stopped snowing. I felt surer now that Matt and Don would get to me, but I began to dread their arrival, for it would open the wounds of shock in them, and I would have to be the strong one, at first.

I thought of how rarely an expedition is both successful and tragic, especially a small expedition. Something like 95 per cent of the dangers in a climb such as ours lay in the ascent. But we had worked for thirty-one days, many of them dangerous, on the route without a serious injury before finally getting to the summit. Going down should have taken only two or three days, and it is usually routine to descend pitches on which fixed ropes have been left. I was reminded of the first ascent of the Matterhorn, when only hours after its conquest the climbing rope broke, sending four of Edward Whymper's seven-man party to their deaths. Then I realized that the Matterhorn had been climbed one hundred years, almost to the day, before our ascent. I thought, also, of the ascent of Cerro Torre in Patagonia in 1959, still regarded by many as the hardest climb ever done. On its descent Toni Egger, one of the best mountaineers in the world, had fallen off a cold rappel to his death, leaving only Cesare Maestri to tell of their victory. But thinking of those climbs explained ours no better. I knew that Whymper, after the Matterhorn, had been persecuted by the public, some of whom even suggested he had cut the rope. I knew that, even in an age that understands mountaineering a little better than the Victorians did, vague suspicions still shrouded the Cerro Torre expedition. But even if we could explain Ed's death to mountaineers, how could we ever explain it to those who cared more about him than about any mountain?

Around 4:00 p.m. I heard the sound of a plane, probably Sheldon's, flying near the mountain. I couldn't see anything through the mist, but perhaps his very presence meant that it was clear up above, possibly that he could see our steps leading to the summit.

Around 10:00 p.m. I thought I heard a shout. I looked out of the tent, but saw nothing, and was starting to attribute the sound to a random noise of the mountain, ice breaking loose somewhere or a rock falling, when suddenly Matt came in sight at the top of the Alley. He let out a cheery yell when he saw me. I couldn't answer, but simply stared at him. Pretty soon Don came in sight and yelled, "How are things down there?" I pretended I couldn't hear him. Matt said later that they had seen our tracks from high on the mountain and therefore known that Ed and I hadn't completed the descent to the cave. This had disturbed them a little, and their mood had acquired gloominess during the treacherous last descent, on steps covered by new snow, using ice-coated fixed ropes, once belaying in a waterfall that had frozen their parkas stiff. But as they approached, Matt had seen my head poking out of the tent and for an instant had thrown off his worries. Yet my silence made him uneasy again; then, before he got to the tent, he saw that there was only one pack beside it. Then I said, "Matt, I'm alone."

He belayed Don all the way down before either of us said anything to him. When Matt told him, Don stood there frozen momentarily, looking only at the snow. Then, in a way I cannot forget, he seemed to draw a breath and swallow the impact of the shock. He said, "All right. Let's get inside the tent." His voice, calm as ever, was heavy with a sudden fatigue. But once they knew, once I saw that they were taking it without panic, being strong, I felt an overwhelming gratitude toward them: out of my fear, an impulse like love. . . .

At 4:00 a.m. I woke, hearing the faint hum of an airplane. I put my boots on and ran out of the cave. It was Sheldon. Don and Matt, awake now also, joined me as we tried to point at our sign in the snow. Sheldon seemed to see it, acknowledged us by circling, then dropped a note. It landed in the crevasse below camp, but we roped up and went to get it. He instructed us to proceed on the floor of the glacier. We packed rapidly, then left the cave, looking back as we descended the icefall for the last time. A few hours later

Sheldon returned, landing easily on the hard glacier. Matt
and I got in the plane first. In a second load he could pick up
Don and the rest of our equipment. Sheldon had seen our
tracks to the summit five days before, and Matt and Don in
the Nose Camp, but he had no idea that anything had gone
wrong. He couldn't quite believe Ed's death. We made
several passes near the bottom of the avalanche chute, but
could see no sign of anything human. Then we headed out
over the tundra.

Sheldon kept saying, "Boy, that's rough. What happened?"
All I could do was explain the facts of the accident. I
couldn't explain beyond that; I couldn't tell him the urgency
of our happiness before. Huntington faded behind us; I
couldn't explain. We had spent forty days alone there, only to
come back one man less, it seemed. We had found no answers to life: perhaps only the room in which to look for
them.